INSCRIPTIONS OF ORISSA

INSCRIPTIONS OF ORISSA

VOLUME I

(*CIRCA* FIFTH-EIGHTH CENTURIES A.D.)

SNIGDHA TRIPATHY

INDIAN COUNCIL OF HISTORICAL RESEARCH
NEW DELHI
and
MOTILAL BANARSIDASS PUBLISHERS
PRIVATE LIMITED ● DELHI

First Edition: Delhi, 1997

Published on behalf of
INDIAN COUNCIL OF HISTORICAL RESEARCH
35, Ferozeshah Road, New Delhi 110 001
by
MOTILAL BANARSIDASS PUBLISHERS PRIVATE LIMITED
Bungalow Road, Jawahar Nagar, Delhi 110 007

Also available at:

MOTILAL BANARSIDASS

41 U.A. Bungalow Road, Jawahar Nagar, Delhi 110 007
8 Mahalaxmi Chambers, 22 Warden Road, Mumbai 400 026
120 Royapettah High Road, Mylapore, Chennai 600 004
11-12 Sanas Plaza, 1302, Baji Road, Pune 411 002
16 St. Mark's Road, Bangalore 560 001
8 Camac Street, Calcutta 700 017
Ashok Rajpath, Patna 800 004
Chowk, Varanasi 221 001

ISBN: 81-208-1077-5 (Vol. I)
ISBN: 81-208-1463-0 (Set)

PRINTED IN INDIA

BY JAINENDRA PRAKASH JAIN AT SHRI JAINENDRA PRESS,
A-45 NARAINA INDUSTRIAL AREA, PHASE I,
NEW DELHI 110 028

INSCRIPTIONS OF ORISSA

INSCRIPTIONS OF ORISSA

VOLUME I

(*CIRCA* FIFTH-EIGHTH CENTURIES A.D.)

SNIGDHA TRIPATHY

INDIAN COUNCIL OF HISTORICAL RESEARCH
NEW DELHI
and
MOTILAL BANARSIDASS PUBLISHERS
PRIVATE LIMITED ● DELHI

First Edition: Delhi, 1997

Published on behalf of
INDIAN COUNCIL OF HISTORICAL RESEARCH
35, Ferozeshah Road, New Delhi 110 001
by
MOTILAL BANARSIDASS PUBLISHERS PRIVATE LIMITED
Bungalow Road, Jawahar Nagar, Delhi 110 007

Also available at:

MOTILAL BANARSIDASS

41 U.A. Bungalow Road, Jawahar Nagar, Delhi 110 007
8 Mahalaxmi Chambers, 22 Warden Road, Mumbai 400 026
120 Royapettah High Road, Mylapore, Chennai 600 004
11-12 Sanas Plaza, 1302, Baji Road, Pune 411 002
16 St. Mark's Road, Bangalore 560 001
8 Camac Street, Calcutta 700 017
Ashok Rajpath, Patna 800 004
Chowk, Varanasi 221 001

ISBN: 81-208-1077-5 (Vol. I)
ISBN: 81-208-1463-0 (Set)

PRINTED IN INDIA

BY JAINENDRA PRAKASH JAIN AT SHRI JAINENDRA PRESS,
A-45 NARAINA INDUSTRIAL AREA, PHASE I,
NEW DELHI 110 028

DEDICATION

Dedicated to the sacred memory of Prof. D.C. Sircar to whose writings I owe my little knowledge of Orissan inscriptions.

Snigdha Tripathy

FOREWORD

The value of inscriptions as a source of early Indian history has been widely recognised. In fact, the epigraphic records scattered all over India, Pakistan and Bangladesh form a very important source for the reconstruction of the political and cultural history of the Indian subcontinent from the third century B.C. to about the fourteenth century A.D. But for these records composed in Sanskritic and Dravidian languages and incised on a variety of materials—primarily lithic objects and copper-plates—our knowledge of the early history of India would have remained perfunctory. The number of inscriptions noticed till date far exceeds one hundred thousand, and a large majority of them offer valuable historical information, not available from any other source. The mass of scattered epigraphical wealth noticed or published in numerous Indian or foreign, mostly occidental periodicals devoted to orientology and other occasional publications, many of them either defunct or out of print, spread over nearly two centuries, is not easily accessible to the students of Indian history. Therefore, the necessity of bringing out properly edited and handy compilations of chronologically, dynastically, regionally or otherwise allied inscriptions had been felt for a long time. As early as 1877, a volume of Aśokan edicts was brought out by the Archaeological Survey of India as the inaugural volume of its prestigious *Corpus Inscriptionum Indicarum* series. It was followed by a couple of other volumes comprising post-Aśokan Kharoṣṭhī (or Kharoṣṭī) and Gupta and allied epigraphs. In the last nearly seven decades, only four more volumes including the inscriptions of the Vākāṭakas, Śilāhāras, Paramāras, Candellas and Kacchapaghātas and those dated in the Kalacuri-Cedi era have been brought out. In view of the urgency of the matter for historical studies and with a view to supplementing the *Corpus* series, the Indian Council of Historical Research has undertaken an ambitious programme of publication of epigraphs dating from *circa* sixth to fourteenth century A.D., the chronological limits being flexible in keeping with the dynastic or regional requirements. Fortunately, despite certain difficulties, the programme has recorded a steady progress and as many as five volumes, covering the epigraphic records of the Pallavas, Maukharis, later Guptas, Puṣpabhūtis, Yaśovarman of Kanauj, Western Gaṅgas, Gajapatis, Śarabhapurīyas, Pāṇḍuvaṁśins and Somavaṁśins, have either been published or are already in the pipeline. The volumes already published have received a welcome response.

The present volume by Dr. Snigdha Tripathy, Epigraphist, Orissa State Museum, Bhubaneswar, and a noted epigraphist with some important publications already to her credit, covers as many as sixty records of the ruling families of Orissa dating from the fifth to the eighth century A.D. The dynasties covered in the volume include the Māṭharas, Vāsiṣṭhas, Pitṛbhaktas,

Nalas, Śailōdbhavas and other miscellaneous ruling dynasties which shaped the destinies of Orissa for approximately four formative centuries of its chequered annals. I am confident that, like other volumes of the series already published, this volume will also be received well by students of early Indian history.

'Prachi', 23 Vidya Vihar
Rana Pratap Nagar
Nagpur 440 022
March 30, 1993

AJAY MITRA SHASTRI
Convener
Inscriptions of India Programme
Indian Council of Historical Research
New Delhi

PREFACE

The first volume of the *Inscriptions of Orissa* covers the period beginning with the rule of various royal families in different parts of Orissa after the southern invasion of Samudragupta, the second monarch of the Gupta dynasty of northern India. It presents a classified list of inscriptions, with their texts and abstracts, which are of great historical importance. As far as possible, the inscriptions have been arranged period-wise, from the fifth to the eighth century A.D., ending with the fall of the Śailōdbhavas in the south and some of the miscellaneous royal families in the northern part of Orissa, who have left their mark on the history and culture of this part of our country. This book has been broadly divided into five sections: *Section I*: Inscriptions of the Māṭharas, the Vāsiṣṭhas and the Pitṛbhaktas; *Section II*: Inscriptions of the Miscellaneous Unknown Royal Families of South and South-Eastern Orissa; *Section III*: Inscriptions of the Nalas and Other Unknown Royal Families of West and South-Western Orissa; *Section IV*: Miscellaneous Inscriptions of Northern Orissa; and *Section V*: Inscriptions of the Śailōdbhava Dynasty.

In order to make the work useful to scholars and for easy reference, the provenance and age of the epigraphs along with their linguistic, palaeographic and metrical peculiarities have been indicated. Further, references to previous publications on these records have also been given in order to assist scholars. Abstracts of the contents of each inscription have been provided at the end of the text for the convenience of scholars. Various technical expressions and other points of interest occurring in an inscription have been explained where necessary. An explanatory note in the form of a general introduction on the epigraphic records of the period has been included in order to broadly define the nature and scope of the records and their historical importance. I hope the system adopted in this work will enable scholars to study the history of Orissa in its proper perspective.

This research was assigned to me by the Indian Council of Historical Research, New Delhi, in 1984. My work entailed editing the inscriptions of Orissa in two volumes, of which this is the first one. My thanks are due to the authorities of the Council for giving me the privilege of preparing such a stupendous work. I owe a deep debt of gratitude to Professor Ajay Mitra Shastri, Head, Department of Ancient Indian History and Archaeology, Nagpur University, who first set me on this privileged task of exploring the epigraphic data. It is no exaggeration to say that but for his keen interest and sympathy, the book would have never been prepared. I am also grateful to Dr H.C. Das, Superintendent of the Orissa State Museum, Bhubaneswar, for kindly allowing me to utilize the photographs of some of the epigraphic records preserved in the State Museum.

Orissa State Museum
Bhubaneswar

Snigdha Tripathy

CONTENTS

ABBREVIATIONS

AR. EP	*Annual Report on (Indian* or *South Indian) Epigraphy*
ARSIE	*Annual Report on South Indian Epigraphy*
ASIR	*Archaeological Survey of India Report*, by Alexander Cunningham
CII	*Corpus Inscriptionum Indicarum*
EI	*Epigraphia Indica*
HCIP	*History and Culture of Indian People*
IA	*Indian Antiquary*, Bombay
IHQ	*Indian Historical Quarterly*
Ind. Ep.	*Indian Epigraphy*, by D.C. Sircar
IO	*Inscriptions of Orissa*, by S.N. Rajaguru
IO	*Inscriptions of Orissa*, Vol. VI, ed. by S. Tripathy
JAHRS	*Journal of the Andhra Historical Research Society*, Rajamundry
JASB	*Journal of the Asiatic Society of Bengal*, Calcutta
JBORS	*Journal of the Bihar and Orissa Research. Society*, Patna
JKHRS	*Journal of the Kalinga Historical Research Society*
JNSI	*Journal of the Numismatic Society of India*
JPASB	*Journal and Proceedings of the Asiatic Society of Bengal*
JRAS	*Journal of the Royal Asiatic Society of Great Britain and Ireland*
JRASB	*Journal of the Royal Asiatic Society of Bengal* (*Letters*), Calcutta
OHRJ	*Orissa Historical Research Journal*, Bhubaneswar
PHAI	*Political History of Ancient India*, by H.C. Rayachaudhuri, Calcutta
PIHC	*Proceedings of the Indian History Congress*
PRASWI	*Proceedings and Reports of the Archaeological Survey of Western India*
SGAMI	*Studies in the Geography of Ancient and Medieval India*, by D.C. Sircar
SII	*South Indian Inscriptions*
Sel. Ins.	*Select Inscriptions*, Vol. I, *Bearing on Indian History and Civilization*, by D.C. Sircar

LIST OF ILLUSTRATIONS

INTRODUCTION

INTRODUCTION

Situated between 17° 48" and 20° 34" north latitude and 81° 24" and 87° 29" east longitude, the present State of Orissa is bounded by the Bay of Bengal in the east, West Bengal and Bihar in the north, Madhya Pradesh in the west and Andhra Pradesh in the south. Like other States in the Indian subcontinent, Orissa is extremely rich in epigraphic records. These records far exceed in number than those found elsewhere, especially in the northern parts of India.

In ancient times, the province spanned a wider area comprising several geographical units bearing such names as Kaliṅga, Utkala, Kōsala and Kōṅgōda. Each of these specific territorial units has yielded a large number of epigraphic records, which have constituted the most reliable source of information for the reconstruction of the past history and culture of Orissa. Indeed, what we know today of the glorious past of Orissa has been reconstructed with the help of these inscriptions. Unfortunately, the scanty historical data and the defective system of dating in the regnal years of the rulers makes it difficult to arrange the records of the different royal families of this period (*c.* fifth-eighth centuries A.D.) in proper chronological order. On the other hand, these records have also contributed considerably towards clarifying some of the obscurities in the past history of Orissa. These records have, in fact, enabled scholars to determine the extent of the above-mentioned geographical units. Hence, by carefully dealing with these valuable sources of history, a relatively satisfactory picture of the period under review can be obtained. An attempt has been made here, therefore, to outline the history and culture of Orissa during this period on the basis of the epigraphs included in this volume.

SECTION I

Several copper-plate records, assigned to about the fifth and sixth centuries of the Christian era, have been discovered in the area lying between the southern part of Ganjam district in Orissa and East Godavari and other districts in the northern part of present Andhra Pradesh. Broadly speaking, the coastal land between this area formed the ancient kingdom of Kaliṅga. The history of this area after the invasion of *Dakṣiṇāpatha* (southern India) by Samudragupta, the second monarch of the imperial Gupta dynasty of northern India, is marked by the rise and fall of a number of independent kings claiming to be the lords of Kaliṅga. The Allahabad pillar inscription[1] of Samudragupta records the kingdoms conquered by him, including Kōṭṭūra, Piṣṭapura, Eraṇḍapalla and Devarāṣṭra, which are known to have been located in different parts of the region comprising ancient Kaliṅga. Their existence is also corroborated by the later inscriptions of the area. Information regarding the existence of several ruling families which held sway over the different parts of Kaliṅga during the fifth and sixth centuries is known from the copper-plate charters issued to the brāhmaṇas from the cities of Piṣṭapura, Devapura, Devarāṣṭra, Siṁhapura and other localities situated in this region. Of these royal families, some rulers claim to be scions of the Māṭhara dynasty of Kaliṅga, some are known to belong to the Vāsiṣṭha-*kula,* and others designate themselves as Pitṛbhaktas instead of referring to the royal family to which they belonged. The provenance of all their records as well as the internal evidences furnished by them apparently indicate that they ruled more or less contemporaneously in the region mentioned above.

The only source of our knowledge about the history of these ancient royal families of Kaliṅga are the seventeen copper-plate grants issued by different rulers that have been brought to light so far. Fortunately, all these records have been published in various journals with notes and plates. Although, there are a few stray published[2] articles on the history of these royal families and their times based on these records, scholars have not yet succeeded in reconstructing a comprehensive chronological account of them and the problem has remained unsolved so far. The earliest discovery of one of these copper-plate charters was made during 1884, when J.F. Fleet published the charter of Nandaprabhañjanavarman of the Māṭhara family found at Chicacole in Andhra Pradesh.[3]

Of the seventeen copper-plate records, four are known to have been issued by the rulers claiming to belong to the Māṭhara family, two are assigned to the rulers of the Vāsiṣṭha-*kula* and the rest of the charters are attributed to the kings claiming to be Pitṛbhaktas.

The earliest known king of the Māṭhara family seems to have been Śaktivarman. Only one copper-plate charter of his has been discovered so far. The royal seal attached to this charter bears a two-line legend reading: (i) *mahārājasya-śrī-* (ii) *śaktivarmaṇaḥ*. The place of issue of the charter is stated to have been Piṣṭapura, which is identified with the present Pithapuram situated in East Godavari district in Andhra Pradesh. The area around this locality formed a principality which was invaded by Samudragupta during his southern campaign. Śaktivarman has been described in his charter as the son of Vāsiṣṭhī (*vāsiṣṭhīputra*) and to have belonged to the Māṭhara family. He is known to have acquired the title of "Lord of Kaliṅga" (*kaliṅgādhipati*)

1. *CII*, Vol. III (1888), pp. 1-7.
2. For these papers see D.C. Sircar, *The Successors of the Sātavāhanas in the Lower Deccan*, pp. 74 ff. *HCIP, The Classical Age,* Vol. III (1954), pp. 211 ff. B.V. Krishna Rao, *Early Dynasties of Āndhradeśa*, pp. 385 ff. *OHRJ*, Vol. XII, No. 2 (1964), pp. 57 ff.
3. *IA*, Vol. XII (1884), pp. 48-50.

and to have ruled the kingdom for at least thirteen years. The area called Rākaluva, granted to the brāhmaṇas, is stated to have been situated in Kaliṅga-*viṣaya* (district). This is now identified with the present locality of Ragolu, the findspot of this charter, which is situated in Srikakulam district of Andhra Pradesh. This locality, as will be seen below, was later regranted by the rulers of the same region during the same period.

It may be noted here that a separate district named Kaliṅga (after the name of the kingdom) was in existence in the central region of the kingdom during the rule of this Māṭhara king. The charter reveals that Kaliṅga extended up to the river Godavari. Piṣṭapura seems to have been under the control of the Vāsiṣṭha family, which was probably inherited by Śaktivarman for the Māṭharas. Though he claimed to belong to the family of the Māṭharas, he retained his matrilineal appellation of *vāsiṣṭhīputra*. This would also indicate that the Māṭharas and the Vāsiṣṭhas were matrimonially related. It seems that the Vāsiṣṭhas again succeeded in capturing the throne of Piṣṭapura after Śaktivarman. This is clear because some of the copper-plate records, perhaps of the later members of the Vāsiṣṭha family, are known to have been issued from this place, and these rulers were possibly more or less contemporaries of the successors of Śaktivarman of the Māṭhara dynasty. Moreover, it is to be noted that the successors of Śaktivarman are not yet known to have issued charters from Piṣṭapura. It is, however, difficult to ascertain at present as to who were the earlier Vāsiṣṭha kings who preceded Śaktivarman to the throne of Piṣṭapura. Some scholars believe that the Māṭharas were the rulers of southern Kaliṅga with their headquarters at Piṣṭapura. But the localities granted in their charters would indicate that they also had control over central Kaliṅga, at least during Śaktivarman's rule. Arjunadatta, the writer of Śaktivarman's charter, was a minister (*amātya*) in his court and is also known to have served his successors by issuing copper-plate grants from Siṁhapura and other places in central Kaliṅga. Śaktivarman may presumably be taken to be the founder of the Māṭhara rule in southern Kaliṅga, though his successors had to shift their headquarters to the central and northern parts of the same kingdom. His matronymic *vāsiṣṭhīputra* would tend to suggest that he maintained the south Indian traditions of the earlier dynasties, like the Sātavāhanas and the Ikṣvākus.[4]

Another ruler of the Māṭhara dynasty was Prabhañjanavarman, who is known from the only extant charter (No. 2) issued by him from the locality called Siṁhapura. This place has been identified with the present locality of Singupuram, situated near Chicacole in Srikakulam district. The locality is believed to be in the region of central Kaliṅga, from where a majority of the copper-plate records of the Māṭhara kings and of those who were more or less their contemporaries were issued. The charter credits Prabhañjanavarman with the royal title of "Lord of the whole of Kaliṅga" (*sakala-kaliṅgādhipati*) and describes him as the one who increased the fame of the Māṭhara family. He was a devout worshipper of Nārāyaṇa (Viṣṇu). The charter also furnishes

4. *EI*, Vol. XX (1929-30), pp. 16 ff.

a pedigree of the Māṭhara kings, the predecessors of Prabhañjanavarman. He is stated to have been the son of Śaktivarman and the grandson of Śaṅkaravarman. The record further reveals that his father, Śaktivarman, ruled the land between the rivers Kṛṣṇavennā (Krishna) and the Mahanadi. This Śaktivarman has been identified with the king of the same name of the charter No. 1 who called himself Lord of Kaliṅga and belonged to the Māṭhara family. The kingdom of Kaliṅga during the rule of Śaktivarman and his son, as known from this record, covered an extensive area on the coast of the Bay of Bengal, between the lower courses of the two rivers mentioned above.

The claim of the Māṭhara king seems to have been exaggerated to some extent. The land between the rivers Krishna and the Godavari was never included in the kingdom of Kaliṅga. It is now a known fact that the Śālaṅkāyanas and the Viṣṇukuṇḍins ruled the region between these two rivers during the fifth and sixth centuries A.D. and the rulers of these royal families are not yet known to have claimed to be lords of Kaliṅga. It was probably the river Godavari and not the Krishna which formed the southern boundary of Kaliṅga. Scholars believe that the northern boundary of Māṭhara kingdom was extended up to the river Mahanadi in the Cuttack region of Orissa. But there is no evidence so far to corroborate this assumption. The Māṭharas are never known to have extended their kingdom beyond Ganjam district in the northern part of Orissa. The river mentioned in the charter seems to denote an altogether different one bearing the same name, which still continues to flow in Ganjam district. Though the name of this river has now been locally changed to Baḍanai (literally the big river), it was known as Mahanadi in ancient times and till the beginning of the twentieth century.[5] Moreover, the river has been shown as the Mahanadi in the present maps of Orissa. It joins the river Ṛsikulyā near Aska in Ganjam district. If this river is taken to be the same as the one indicated in the charter of Prabhañjanavarman, there is reason to believe that the northern boundary of Kaliṅga during the rule of the Māṭharas extended up to at least the southern part of Ganjam district. The inscriptions of this royal family and the localities mentioned in them are, in fact, known to have been found within this area between the Godavari and the present Baḍanai or the Mahanadi of our record. The *agrahāra* called Niṅgōṇḍi, created at the time of Prabhañjanavarman in Kaliṅga, is stated to have been situated on the seashore, though it has still remained unidentified. The officer named Jyeṣṭha and designated as *daṇḍanāyaka* (probably denoting a police or army officer) is not known from any other record of the family.

It is not known how long Prabhañjanavarman remained on the throne of Kaliṅga. Unfortunately, the regnal year of the king, which is usually found in the Māṭhara records, is omitted in his charter mainly due to the inadvertence of the scribe-engraver. The occasion of the grant is, however, given as the twelfth day of the bright fortnight of the month of Kārttika. An interesting statement is found in line 15 of the charter of Prabhañjanavarman,

5. T.J. Maltby, *Ganjam District Manual*, (1918), p. 2.

which reveals that an advance payment of two hundred *paṇas* was to be made by the donee as fixed annual rent for the gift land. The term *paṇa* here may have denoted either cowrie-shells or metallic coins, presumably of copper. As it is now well-known that the Māṭhara kings had no coins of their own, the metallic currency called *paṇa* in this inscription may have denoted coins of other regions which infiltrated into the kingdoms of Orissa and remained current for a long time. The revenue system prevalent during the rule of the Māṭharas and other Kaliṅga rulers of the period has been discussed separately below.

The third king of the Māṭhara dynasty was Anantaśaktivarman, who succeeded Prabhañjanavarman to the throne of Siṁhapura. Two copper-plate charters of this king have been published so far. His earliest known charter dated in his 14th regnal year was presumably issued from Siṁhapura. The second part of the name of the place of issue of the charter has been inadvertently omitted by the engraver and this has induced scholars to read the name of the locality as Vijayapura. But the practice of using the epithet *vijaya* (literally meaning 'victorious') prefixed to the name of the chief city is well-known from all the copper-plate records of the Māṭharas and their contemporaries, the Vāsiṣṭhas as well as the Pitṛbhaktas. The place of issue in this charter has been described as *mahā-hasty-aśva-skandhāvāra*, evidently indicating a military camp or headquarters. It seems that Siṁhapura was lost to the Māṭharas for quite some time. It was probably captured by their contemporaries, the Pitṛbhaktas, who were then preparing the ground to become the lords of Kaliṅga. Siṁhapura had then become a bone of contention between the Māṭharas and the Pitṛbhaktas. As will be seen later, Siṁhapura, which was earlier in the possession of the Māṭharas, came under the control of the Pitṛbhaktas who made it one of their chief cities.

Anantaśaktivarman was also a Vaiṣṇavite, a devotee of Nārāyaṇa (Viṣṇu), like his predecessors. One of the epithets in his copper-plate records indicates that he inherited the kingdom of Kaliṅga from his father, who was probably the same as the issuer of the Niṅgōṇḍi grant (No. 2) of the Māṭhara family. Besides being a devotee of Lord Viṣṇu, Anantaśaktivarman is also endowed with the epithet of *paramadaivata*, "devout worshipper of the gods", in both his copper-plate records. Like his predecessors, he also bore the title of *kaliṅgādhipati*. The Andhavaram charter of this king (No. 3), dated in his 14th regnal year, reveals the interesting fact that he granted a village named Āndōreppa to the brāhmaṇas which was previously donated by *āryaka* Śakti-*bhaṭṭāraka*. This Śakti-*bhaṭṭāraka* was evidently the same as the issuer of grant No. 1 and was also the father of Prabhañjanavarman of grant No. 2. The word *āryaka*, affixed to Śaktivarman's name in this grant, seems to have been used in the sense of grandfather of the issuer of the grant. The officer named Arjunadatta, designated as *deśākṣapaṭalādhikṛta* and mentioned as the writer of the Madras Museum plates of Anantaśaktivarman, is also known to have served as an *amātya* (minister) during the reign of Śaktivarman. The charter of his 14th regnal year was written by one Mātṛvara, who served as the *deśākṣapaṭalādhikṛta* as well as the *daṇḍanāyaka*. This person is also known from the contemporary records of the Pitṛbhaktas to have belonged to Siṁhapura.

The locality called Āndōreppa, the name of the *agrahāra*, granted by Anantaśaktivarman during the 14th year of his reign, has been identified as the present Andhavaram situated in Srikakulam district of Andhra Pradesh. It is also the findspot of the concerned copper-plate record. This locality has yielded a number of copper-plate records, including a charter of Indravarman of the early Eastern Gaṅga dynasty of Kaliṅga dated in the Gaṅga year 133 (*c.* A.D. 631).[6] The name of the locality has been mentioned in the Gaṅga record as Āndōraka-*agrahāra* and is stated to have been the residence of the donee of the said grant. Another village granted by Anantaśaktivarman in his 28th regnal year was Sakunaka, stated to have been situated near the locality called Varāhavarttani. Both the localities are mentioned in a number of copper-plate records of the early Eastern Gaṅgas, including the Chicacole plates of the Gaṅga king Anantavarman dated in the Gaṅga year 128 (*c.* A.D. 626).[7] Varāhavarttani formed a *viṣaya* or district, as known from the Gaṅga records in which the village Sakuna-*grāma* was situated.[8] Though both the places have not been identified satisfactorily, the district of Varāhavarttani has been presumed to have been situated in present Srikakulam district around the taluk of Tekkali, as a number of villages mentioned in the early Eastern Gaṅga records are stated to have been located in this ancient division and identified with their present namesake in this area of Andhra Pradesh.

Anantaśaktivarman, unlike his grandfather who ruled from Piṣṭapura, had dropped the matronymic appellation of *vāsiṣṭhiputra*. Instead, he adopted the patronymic appellation, adding to his present names the epithet *bappa-bhaṭṭāraka-pāda-prasād-āvapta-śarīra-rājya-vibhava* (who inherited the body, kingdom, prosperity and prowess through devotion at the feet of the lord, the father).

From the epigraphic records of the above three kings, it is now possible to reconstruct a tentative genealogy of the Māṭhara family in the following order of succession:

Śaṅkaravarman

↓

Śaktivarman (*vāsiṣṭhīputra*)

↓

Prabhañjanavarman

↓

Anantaśaktivarman

---

6. *IO*, Vol. II (1960), pp. 38, 193, 228, ff.; *EI*, Vol. XXX (1954), pp. 37-42; *EI*, Vol. XXXI (1955-56), pp. 200 ff.
7. *IA*, Vol. XIII (1884), pp. 120-23; *IO*, Vol. II (1960), pp. 43 ff.
8. Sakunaka-*grāma*, situated within Varāhavarttani, is also known from the Andhavaram plates of Gaṅga Anantavarman, Gaṅga year 216, *IO*, Vol. II (1960), pp. 228 ff.; *EI*, Vol. XXXI (1955-56), pp. 200 ff.

At present, nothing can be said with certainty about Śaṅkaravarman's rule in Kaliṅga. As yet he is not known to have issued any copper-plate charter. We have no evidence to show that he was the founder of the Māṭhara rule in this kingdom. No royal title has been used with his name in the charter of his grandson, which so far is the only source of information about him.

It is to be noted that the reference to Piṣṭapura is conspicuous by its absence in the charters of successors of Śaktivarman, who seems to be the real founder of the Māṭhara kingdom of Kaliṅga.The successors of this king are not yet known to have had any hold over the region around Piṣṭapura comprising southern Kaliṅga. It is only a reference to the officer named Arjunadatta in the record of Anantaśaktivarman, who was also the writer of his grandfather's charter, that may indicate that the southern part of Kaliṅga continued to be under the control of the Māṭharas till the end of their rule. Of the Māṭhara kings who are known from their charters, it was only Prabhañjanavarman who probably acquired the whole of Kaliṅga extending up to the river Godavari in the south and the river Mahanadi or the Baḍanai in the southern part of Ganjam district in the north. However, the epithets used for his father in his charter as well as the location of the gift villages in his father's record would also indicate that Śaktivarman had control over the entire Kaliṅga country.

The royal seals attached to the extant copper-plate records of the Māṭhara kings, though now very badly worn out, are found to be different from each other in respect of the use of legends. The seal of Śaktivarman's charter is oval in shape and bears two lines of writing, which is not properly legible. Hultzsch suggests, on the basis of the traces of a few letters reading *mahārā*, that the two lines may have the legend: (i) *mahārājasya-śrī*, (ii) *śaktivarmaṇaḥ*. The seal attached to the charter of Prabhañjanavarman is lost and it is not possible to know the type of seal he used and the legend on it in the absence of any other copper-plate charter issued by this king. The Andhavaram charter of Anantaśaktivarman (No. 3) bears an elliptical seal but the legend on it is badly worn out, though four lines of writing are traceable.

After Anantaśaktivarman, the region comprising southern Kaliṅga with its chief city at Piṣṭapura seems to have passed over for some time to the Vāsiṣṭha family who were presumably matrimonially related to the Māṭharas. Two copper-plate charters (Nos. 5 and 6) of a king named Anantavarman of this family are now known to the scholars. Both the records describe him as the son of Prabhañjanavarman and the grandson of Guṇavarman and as the moon of the Vāsiṣṭha family. The Siripuram grant of this king (No. 5) was issued from the victorious Devapura whereas the Srungavarapukota grant (No. 6) was made from Piṣṭapura. The latter charter credits his grandfather Guṇavarman as being the lord of Devapura.

Devapura was presumably the chief city of Devarāṣṭra, which was inherited by Anantavarman from his grandfather. Though his predecessors have been endowed in these grants with the royal title of *mahārāja*, it cannot be said with certainty that they ruled in Kaliṅga, which evidently included Devarāṣṭra during Anantavarman's rule. Devarāṣṭra is generally identified with the present Yellamanchili taluk in Vishakhapatnam district, then comprising the central part of the Kaliṅga region. This territorial unit, as we know from the Allahabad pillar inscription, constituted a separate and independent principality during the time of Samudragupta's southern invasion. It appears that the Vāsiṣṭhas under Guṇavarman acquired Devarāṣṭra after the decline of Gupta rule in this region and asserted independence. But no record of this king nor of his son Prabhañjanavarman is known to have been discovered so far. The copper-plate records of the Vāsiṣṭha king Anantavarman, as well as those of the Māṭharas, would tend to suggest that the small principalities comprising Piṣṭapura and Devapura were unified under one sceptre and were included in the kingdom of Kaliṅga during the fifth and sixth centuries A.D.

Unfortunately, the dates (presumably mentioned in the regnal year of the king) have been lost in both the copper-plate records of Anantavarman due to corrosion. His Siripuram grant, however, is stated to have been issued in the year of *mahāśvayuja*. The lunar month and the *tithi* are also mentioned. Although it does not, in any way, help us to know the specific date of the record nor the period of rule of the king, it, however, sheds light on the system of dating and various reckonings adopted in the ancient Kaliṅga region during the period of our discussion, which has been dealt with separately below.

Anantavarman was a Śaivite ruler and has been described in his records as *paramamāheśvara* (a devotee of Lord Śiva). On the other hand, the Māṭharas were Vaiṣṇavites. Unfortunately, the names of the officers, usually found associated with the execution of the charter and mentioned at the end of the records, are lost in both his grants due to corrosion, which could have provided some clue to determine the relationship between the Māṭharas and the Vāsiṣṭhas of Kaliṅga. Though the seal attached to the Siripuram plates is completely worn out, the Srungavarapukota grant bears a royal seal having the dynastic emblem of a conch in relief. In view of the similarity between the two charters of Anantavarman in many respects, it is possible to assume that his Siripuram plates also contained a seal with the same dynastic emblem. In respect of the royal seals, we find a marked difference between those of the Māṭharas and the Vāsiṣṭhas. While the Māṭharas had their seal engraved with only the legend giving the name of the issuer of the charter, the Vāsiṣṭhas had the dynastic emblem without any legend on their seals.

We find inscriptions of another royal family of the Kaliṅga region more or less contemporaneously with the Vāsiṣṭhas and the Māṭharas. This is evident from all the palaeography of the Vāsiṣṭha and Māṭhara epigraphs as well as the references to some of their royal officers who served in the courts of these ruling families. The kings of this new family, while issuing copper-plate records, have not mentioned the name of the family to which they belonged. They adopted the legend reading *pitṛbhaktaḥ* on the seals attached to their respective charters, instead of any dynastic emblem or the name of the issuer of the grant. Thus the kings of this family are still known to scholars as *pitṛbhaktas*. The legend has been taken as a sort of dynastic appellation. A close study of the epigraphic records of the Māṭharas and those of the Pitṛbhaktas would indicate that the latter had to struggle for supremacy in central Kaliṅga and for the possession of the city of Siṁhapura, which seems to have continued for several years. This is evidenced from the fact that a royal officer named Mātṛvara, who was a resident of Siṁhapura, served as a *deśākṣapaṭalādhikṛta* in the court of the Māṭhara king Anantaśaktivarman when he issued the Andhavaram charter (No. 3) in his 14th regnal year from Siṁhapura. The same person also served as the *deśākṣapaṭalādhikṛta* for the Pitṛbhakta king Umāvarman in the later years of his reign, when he issued grants from Siṁhapura.

Umāvarman was probably the earliest king of this line of rulers. He seems to have had a long struggle with the Māṭharas to acquire the city of Siṁhapura and the prestigious title of the Lord of Kaliṅga. Two of his earlier records were issued from Sunagara (Nos. 7 and 9). The date and the names of the royal officers in one of these two grants (No. 9) have been lost because the record is incomplete. The earliest known grant (No. 7) of Umāvarman is dated in his 6th regnal year, issued from Sunagara. The Tekkali grant of this king (No. 8), dated in his 9th regnal year, was issued from the victorious Vardhamānapura. But all these three charters, unlike his later grants, do not credit Umāvarman with the lordship of Kaliṅga. The other two extant charters of this king were issued in his 30th (No. 10) and 40th (No. 11) regnal years from Siṁhapura. In all these grants Umāvarman has been described as a devotee at the feet of his father (*bappa-bhaṭṭāraka-pāda-bhaktaḥ* or *pitṛ-pād-ānudhyātaḥ*). The earliest of his records was written by one Kumāradeva, designated as *deśākṣapaṭalādhikṛta* when Umāvarman was ruling from Sunagara. The executor of this grant has been stated to be Mahārājādhivarman, who seems to be either a subordinate chief under the reigning king or Umāvarman himself. The charter is stated to have been written by the donor, Umāvarman himself, though the name of the writer Keśavadeva is given at the end of the grant. This may mean that the king attested the original deed of the gift, since the record at the same time states that the king himself was the executor. Keśavadeva, the writer of this records, is stated to have been a resident of Piṣṭapura. The two charters issued in the later years of Umāvarman's reign (Nos. 10 and 11) mention Siṁhapura as the chief city of the kingdom of the Pitṛbhaktas. Both the records were written by Mātṛvara, who served as the *deśākṣapaṭalādhikṛta* till the end of Umāvarman's rule. He is again seen as the writer of the king's successor's grant. The latest known record of Umāvarman (No. 11), issued in his 40th regnal year, refers to his son named Vasuṣeṇarāja. The actual purpose of this grant has been stated to be the increase of religious merit for this son of Umāvarman. The rule of this prince as the Lord of Kaliṅga is not yet known from any other source. Umāvarman had a long reign of at least forty years. A new *agrahāra*, named after Kaliṅga, is stated in this grant to have been created and granted to a brāhmaṇa of the Vasiṣṭha *gōtra*.

The royal seals attached to the copper-plate grants of Umāvarman differ widely from each other with respect to size and the legend used therein. Though the seal of the Baranga charter (No. 7) is worn out, it, however, seems to have been somewhat similar to that of the Tekkali grant (No. 8). Both the seals are of the same size, though smaller than those attached to the later charters. They seem to have contained a legend in one line reading *pitṛbhaktaḥ*. The charters issued in the later part of his reign (Nos. 10 and 11) have bigger seals, with four lines of writing on them, though the legends cannot be fully deciphered as yet. Only the letters at the end reading *ōmavarmaṇaḥ* have been tentatively made out. These later seals of Umāvarman to some extent resemble those used by the Māṭhara king Anantaśaktivarman, who seems to be a contemporary and a rival of the former, as observed earlier. The bigger seals were perhaps adopted by the Pitṛbhaktas and especially by Umāvarman after he captured Siṁhapura and assumed the title of *kaliṅgādhipati*. Scholars have widely differed on the question of identifying Umāvarman of the grant Nos. 7 and 8 and the king of the same name of the records Nos. 9, 10 and 11. It is believed that Umāvarman of the earlier grants was a different king on the grounds that the title of *kaliṅgādhipati* was not borne by him. Further, the royal seals also differ in respect of the legend from the seals of the later charters. But the similarity found in the palaeography—the seal having a four-line legend in the grant No. 9 which is identical with those found in the later records—would eliminate all the above assumption of scholars. It is to be noted that the Dhavalapeta charter (No. 9) was not issued from Siṁhapura but from Sunagara and, in this record, Umāvarman has not been endowed with the royal title of *kaliṅgādhipati*.

The localities mentioned in the records of Umāvarman as well as their provenances are all known to have been situated in the present Srikakulam and Vishakhapatnam districts and in the southern part of Ganjam district of Andhra and Orissa, respectively.

The next king of the family of Pitṛbhaktas known from his copper-plate records is Nandaprabhañjanavarman. Three of his charters have been discovered so far (Nos. 12, 13 and 14), of which one (No. 12) is not dated. It was issued from a locality called Sārapallī which has been described in the record as a *vāsaka* of the reigning king, indicating presumably a temporary residence of the king. The place has been identified with the present Saripalle in Vishakhapatnam district. The second charter of Nandaprabhañjanavarman was issued in his 15th regnal year from the victorious Vardhamānapura, from where Umāvarman, perhaps a predecessor of this king, issued one of his grants in his 9th regnal year. The last known charter of this king was issued from Siṁhapura during his 24th regnal year. He has been described in all the three grants as a devotee at the feet of his father. The elliptical royal seals attached to these copper-plate grants, though greatly corroded, bear the one line legend reading *pitṛbhaktaḥ*, which can be traced in their rectangular incuse. All the three grants of this king credit him with the prestigious royal title of *sakalakaliṅgādhipati*. The only other ruler who had the same title was Prabhañjanavarman of the Māṭhara family. Scholars tend to regard both Prabhañjanavarman and Nandaprabhañjanavarman as contemporary rulers on the basis of the palaeographical similarity in their records.[9] But Prabhañjanavarman of the Māṭhara family must have ascended the throne of Siṁhapura long before the rule of this Pitṛbhakta king. His last extant charter (No. 14), dated in his 24th regnal year, is known to have been prepared by Mātṛvara, son of Haridatta, who also served as *deśākṣapaṭalādhikṛta* in the court of the Māṭhara Anantaśaktivarman, son of Prabhañjanavarman.

The records of all these rulers issued from Siṁhapura and prepared by Mātṛvara would indicate that he was a resident of this city and his family held the office of *deśākṣapaṭalādhikṛta* in a continuous hereditary succession. The earlier copper-plate grant of Nandaprabhañjanavarman, dated in his 15th regnal year and issued from Vardhamānapura, was written by one Kṛṣṇacandra by the order of the king himself. His second charter (No. 14) sheds interesting light on the chronology of the Māṭhara and Pitṛbhakta kings of Kaliṅga. It furnishes the information that the plot of gift land was situated in the village called Rāgōlaka, which was earlier made an *agrahāra*. It is already known from the grant of the Māṭhara king Śaktivarman (No. 1) that he made the same locality an *agrahāra*, which has been spelt in this record as Rākaluva. The village has already been identified with the present Ragolu in Srikakulam district and the findspot of both the charters of Śaktivarman and Nandaprabhañjanavarman. This information would evidently make the Māṭharas predecessors of the Pitṛbhaktas in the region of central Kaliṅga.

Though at present the actual relationship between the two Pitṛbhakta kings, Umāvarman and Nandaprabhañjanavarman, cannot be established, it may be presumed that the latter succeeded the former to the throne of Siṁhapura.

The third ruler of the family, whose two copper-plate charters are known to have been discovered so far (Nos. 15 and 16), is Caṇḍavarman, sometimes called Acaṇḍavarman. Though the royal seals attached to his copper-plate grants are very corroded, they appear to have contained the legend *pitṛbhaktaḥ* like those of his predecessors. The epithet of *bappa-bhaṭṭāraka-pāda-bhaktaḥ* together with the legend on the seals would confirm the assumption that he belonged to the Pitṛbhakta family of Kaliṅga. He is also styled as the "Lord of Kaliṅga" like his predecessors. He is known to have been a devout worshipper of Viṣṇu and is endowed with the epithets of *paramabhāgavata* and *paramadaivata* (worshipper of gods). It is sometimes believed that Caṇḍavarman may have been the son and successor of Umāvarman.[10] But the name of only one son of Umāvarman, Vasuṣeṇarāja, is known from his records so far. Though the exact relationship between Umāvarman and Caṇḍavarman cannot be determined at present, it can be

9. D.K. Ganguly, *Historical Geography and Dynastic History of Orissa*, pp. 219 ff.
10. *HCIP, The Classical Age*, Vol. III (1954), p. 211.

definitely said that Caṇḍavarman did not succeed Umāvarman to the throne of Siṁhapura in central Kaliṅga. An officer named Rudradatta, who was the son of Mātṛvara, has been mentioned as a *deśākṣapaṭalādhikṛta* and as the writer of the Bobbili charter of Caṇḍavarman dated in his 4th regnal year. Mātṛvara is already known to have served as the same officer till the end of Nandaprabhañjanavarman's rule. After him, his son Rudradatta seems to have inherited the said office during the reign of Caṇḍavarman. But this king seems to have had a short reign. His two charters are dated in his 4th and 6th regnal years.

It is not yet known who succeeded to the throne of Siṁhapura after Caṇḍavarman. Nor is it possible to determine the actual relationship of the above three rulers of Kaliṅga with each other, the information from their respective copper-plate grants being too meagre to throw any light on this. After the end of Caṇḍavarman's rule, the kingdom of Kaliṅga was probably overrun by several south Indian royal families, especially by the early Eastern Gaṅga dynasty which conquered the area around Srikakulam district and the Ganjam region in Orissa during the early part of the sixth century A.D.

Another king named Viśākhavarman is known from his lone charter (No. 17) to have been ruling round the Parlakhimedi region in the southern part of Ganjam district in Orissa during the last part of the fifth century A.D. The palaeography and the phraseology of this record closely resemble those used in the records of the Pitṛbhakta family of Kaliṅga. Though the family to which Viśākhavarman belonged is not known from his record nor from any other source, it may be assumed, on the basis of palaeography, that he was a contemporary of the Pitṛbhaktas or probably ruled immediately after the fall of the Pitṛbhaktas from Siṁhapura. His charter is known to have been issued during his 7th regnal year from Śrīpura which has been identified with the present Siripuram in Vishakhapatnam district.[11] But the locality is also believed to be the same as the present village of Batia-Sripura, situated not far from Koroshanda, the findspot of this copper-plate charter.[12]

This identification seems to be more probable. It also tends to suggest that Viśākhavarman's kingdom was greatly circumscribed and confined to the southern part of Ganjam district in Orissa. This would also corroborate the above observations made from his charter. He has been described as a *paramadaivata* and a devotee at the feet of his father, like the Pitṛbhakta kings of Kaliṅga. Unfortunately, the royal seal attached to his charter, which could have thrown welcome light on the dynasty to which he belonged, is lost. Unlike the rulers of the fore-mentioned three families of ancient Kaliṅga, Viśākhavarman has not been endowed with the title of "Lord of Kaliṅga". Thus his relation with these rulers cannot be determined with any degree of certainty at present. It is, however, believed by some scholars that he was probably a feudatory under the kings of Piṣṭapura.[13] But there is no evidence

11. *EI*, Vol. XXI (1931-32), pp. 23-25.
12. *IO*, Vol. I, Pt. 2 (1958), p. 3.
13. *HCIP*, *The Classical Age* (1954), p. 213.

to corroborate such an assumption. The locality which Viśākhavarman granted is stated in his record to have been situated in Kōrāsōḍaka-*pañcāli*, identified with the present Koroshanda in Parlakhimedi taluk in Ganjam district, which is also the findspot of the charter. The gift village Tampōyaka has been identified with the present village of Tampa near Koroshanda in the same taluk. Scholars are of the opinion that the modern town of Vishakhapatnam, which is said to be named after the god Viśākhasvāmin worshipped there, is probably due to this king Viśākhavarman who perhaps built a temple and named the god after his name. But it is not possible to accept this assumption in the absence of any corroborative evidence. Viśākhavarman seems to have been overthrown by the Eastern Gaṅgas of Kaliṅganagara who occupied the region during the first part of the sixth century A.D.

General Nature of the Records of the Māṭharas, the Vāsiṣṭhas and the Pitṛbhaktas

The epigraphic records of the ruling families known so far to the scholarly world are all in the form of copper-plate grants. These may be included in the category of official records containing royal orders issued by kings in respect of grants made apparently for the purpose of attaining religious merit. These copper-plates are more or less of uniform nature, and only a few exceptions are noticeable in specific cases. Each record consists of three plates strung together on a copper ring with the royal seal soldered on its joints. The plates are generally rectangular in shape and are made of thin sheets of copper. The size of the plates usually varies from 5" to 7.6" in length and 2" to 3" in breadth. The royal seal is of bronze cast from mould. The seals are usually without any dynastic emblem, with the exception of two charters (Nos. 5 and 6) of the Vāsiṣṭha family which bear seals with the emblem of a conch in low relief along with some indistinct object inside it. The remaining charters bear seals with legends in one, two or four lines of writing. The seals are usually oval in shape, measuring 3" and 2.5", 2" and 0.5" or 1.5" and 1.25". The oval seals have a rectangular incuse containing the legend in very low relief cast in mould.

Almost every record is seen to follow a more or less definite order. The usual symbol for *siddham*, found incised at the beginning of a record as a mark of auspicious invocation, is conspicuous by its absence in the majority of these records. The symbol is not found in the grant Nos. 1, 2, 3, 4, 8, 9, 10, 11 and 17. But the word *svasti* has been used in all the records in order to indicate the auspicious beginning. The inscription generally begins with the name of the place of issue of the grant, followed by an introduction to the reigning king with his epithets and achievements. The records of some of the Māṭhara and Vāsiṣṭha rulers furnish a genealogy of three generations of the reigning king (Nos. 2, 5 and 6). This is followed by a royal address to different officers and cultivators of the locality to be granted. The name of the gift village is invariably mentioned without reference to the district or division in which it was situated. Some of the records (Nos. 1, 4, 6, 7, 9 and

17), however, mention the district or division comprising the gift village. This is followed by a reference to occasional taxes in some inscriptions (Nos. 2, 14 and 15).

Almost all the records, however, contain references to regular or usual taxes payable in cash and kind. Very few records specify the boundaries of the gift village (Nos. 2 and 14). The inhabitants of the gift village are directed to pay the usual taxes without obstruction. The date of the grant in the regnal reckoning of the reigning king is given in the record, which is followed by the names of some royal officers responsible for executing the grant. The name of the writer or engraver is usually mentioned at the end of the grant. Sometimes the king himself is mentioned as the executor of the charter (such as Nos. 1, 8 and 13). The records conclude with some verses of an imprecatory and benedictory nature, which emphasize the virtue of making land-grants. These verses are generally stated to have been quoted from Vyāsa.

While giving the date in the regnal years of the respective kings, different systems of reckoning are found to have been used in the records. In some records, the specification of a day is given as belonging to one of the eight fortnights of a season. This system of *cāturmāsī* reckoning was prevalent in different parts of Kaliṅga during the fifth century A.D., as revealed by these copper-plate charters. The records of Nandaprabhañjanavarman (No. 13) and Caṇḍavarman (No. 15) of the Pitṛbhakta family and that of Viśākhavarman (No. 17) are dated according to this system. They seem to have adopted the system of *cāturmāsī* reckoning from the early south Indian royal families, like the Sātavāhanas, the Ikṣvākus, and so on. The use of this system of reckoning is not found in the epigraphic records of the subsequent period, after the decline of these Kaliṅga kings.

Only one record of the Vāsiṣṭha family (No. 5) is found to have been dated according to Jupiter's Twelve Year Cycle. This system of reckoning is associated with the movement of the planet Jupiter. The year is named after the lunar months, such as Caitra and Vaiśākha, and the *nakṣatra* or lunar mansion in which Jupiter enters. The word *mahat* is usually used as a prefix to the name of the lunar month to indicate the year of the cycle. Thus the year *mahāśvayuja*, mentioned in the charter of Anantavarman (No. 5), begins with Jupiter's reappearance in the *nakṣatras* of Revatī, Aśvinī or Bharaṇī in the lunar month of Āśvina, after which the year is so named with the prefix *mahat*. This system of reckoning has now become obsolete. It occasionally occurs in the epigraphic records of northern and southern India of about the fifth century A.D. It has been found particularly in a few epigraphs of the Parivrājaka kings of central India and the Kadambas of the south in the fifth century A.D.

The majority of the records under discussion, especially those of the Māṭharas, are found to have followed the system of calculating the date according to the lunar month and the *tithi* or the lunar day, indicating the popularity of the *purṇimānta* system. According to this system, a lunar month consisting of two fortnights or *pakṣas* of fifteen days each, namely, *kṛṣṇa* or *bahula* (dark fortnight) and the *śukla-pakṣa* (bright fortnight), is counted from *kṛṣṇa-pakṣa* or *bahula-dina* 1 (abbreviated in epigraphic records as *badi* 1) to *śukla-pakṣa* (*śudi*) 15. Some of these records, like the grant of Anantavarman of the Vāsiṣṭha family (No. 6), show the use of luni-solar reckoning. This charter is dated the thirteenth *tithi* or the lunar day when there was the *uttarāyaṇa* or summer solstice, though the fortnight to which the *tithi* is to be referred to cannot be determined due to the damaged condition of the charter. According to the luni-solar system of reckoning, the lunar days (regulated by the movement of the moon) are made equal to the calculation of a solar year, to have considerable religious importance. A lunar *tithi* is not counted until the occurrence of a *saṅkrānti*, that is, the sun's entry into a *rāśi* or a sign of the Zodiac (Meṣa, Vṛṣa, and so on). The lunar month, having no *saṅkrānti*, is called the *adhika* or *mala*. When a lunar month has two *saṅkrāntis*, it is called a *kṣaya* or *nija* month.

A majority of the records under discussion show the dates, which are generally mentioned in words as well as numerical symbols for the year. The number of *tithis*, and so on, are also mentioned though abbreviations (such as the use of *di* for *dina*) are occasionally used (Nos. 10, 11 and 15).

The scripts used in the records are generally accepted as belonging to the group of post-Gupta Brāhmī alphabet of the southern variety, prevalent during the fifth and sixth centuries A.D., resembling the archaic characters adopted in the records of the other ruling families of south India, such as the Śālaṅkāyanas, the Viṣṇukuṇḍins and those found in other records of the same period coming from the ancient Kaliṅga region. Many of the letters in these records are written in cursive style. The cursive letters, such as *l, n, kṛ, jña, su* and *pu*, appear to be more developed than the other letters of the records. Some are peculiarly formed. The serif of letters indicated by a dot or dots in some of the Māṭhara copper-plates, especially those found in the Ragolu charter (No. 1) of Śaktivarman and the Andhavaram charter (No. 3) of Anantaśaktivarman, is a peculiarity of the style of writing adopted in the area in that period. It may be noted that the above charters were written by two different persons. Peculiarities are also found in the formation of certain letters, and the dissimilarity (such as in the formation of *t* and *n*) is seen in the records of Anantaśaktivarman. In some cases, *t* is looped and *n* is without a loop but with a curve while, in other cases, the reverse forms of these letters have been noticed. This peculiarity is also noticeable in the records of the Śālaṅkāyanas.[14] Similar cursive letters, such as, *l, n* and *kṛ* of our records, have also been found in the inscriptions of the early Eastern Gaṅgas of Kaliṅganagara.[15] These peculiarities in the form of writing may not be considered irregular in determining the palaeographical dating. They were mainly due to the peculiar styles adopted by the scribes which may be presumed to have developed in the area during the fifth century A.D.

---

14. *JAHRS*, Vol. I (1926), p. 94, Plate; *EI*, Vol. XXV, p. 46, Plate.
15. *EI*, Vol. XXV (1940), p. 281, Plate.

The separate signs for *b* and *v* have been indicated in the records under discussion. But the sign for *b* became obsolete in the epigraphic records of Orissa in the subsequent period. The later records of the Pitṛbhakta king Umāvarman (Nos. 9, 10 and 11) have the thick-set ductus writing. The characters tend to assume either a square or round shape. It is likely that all the three later grants of Umāvarman were engraved by Mātṛvara, son of Haridatta, though the portion containing the name of the engraver in the grant No. 9 is lost. In some cases, the letters *m* and *v* in the earlier grants of Umāvarman (No. 8) seem rounder as compared to those in his later grants which appear angular.

The signs for *jihvāmūlīya* (No. 6) and *upadhmānīya* (No. 5) occasionally occur in the records of the Vāsiṣṭhas and Pitṛbhakta kings. The use of these signs in the record became rare from the seventh century A.D. onwards. The sign for *upadhmānīya* has been used in place of the *visarga* in the Siripuram plates of Anantavarman.

The correction of a wrong word is indicated by a small mark resembling the English sign "X" (No. 9, lines 3 and 4). Sometimes inter-punctuation is indicated by a small horizontal stroke (No. 10, line 2; No. 11). In some of the records, the mark for punctuation (usually indicated by two vertical strokes and generally called double *daṇḍas*) is totally absent. This sign has been rarely used in the records (Nos. 4, 10, 11, 12 and 16). Sometimes, two sets of triple *daṇḍas*, with a floral design in-between, have been used to indicate the end of the charter (No. 3).

The language of the records is Sanskrit, though not always free from grammatical and other errors. With the exception of a few usual imprecatory and benedictory verses in the *anuṣṭubh* metre, the records are written throughout in prose.

As regards orthography, consonants preceding *r* are generally doubled, as in the case of *varmma, vikkrama, gōttra* and *puttra,* which are found in almost all the records under discussion. The orthographical errors found in the records are mainly due to the inadvertence of the scribe as well as the influence of faulty local pronunciation. A few examples may be cited here, for instance, *ātrā* for *ātreya* (No. 5, line 12); *samvyatsara* for *saṁvatsara* (No. 7, line 21); *yuddhiṣṭhira* for *yudhiṣṭhira* (No. 8, lines 14-15); *kriṣṇacandra* for *kṛṣṇcandra* (No. 13, line 17); *yātvā* for *gatvā* (No. 14, lines 13, 16, 19 ff.); and *siṅgha* for *siṁha* (No. 2, line 1; No. 4, line 1). There are also instances of the use of *b* for *v*, as in *barṣa* (No. 4, line 3) and *v* for *b* as in *valādhikṛta* (No. 4, line 8). Perhaps the confusion in the pronunciation between *v* and *b* induced the scribes in subsequent times to use a single sign for these letters. The confusion in the spelling of *v* and *b* occurs more frequently in the records of the subsequent period.

Administration

A perusal of the epigraphic records of the Māṭharas, the Vāsiṣṭhas and the Pitṛbhaktas would enable us to have an idea of the administrative system prevalent in the Kaliṅga region during the period under review. The records reveal that a major part of the kingdom of Kaliṅga was under the direct rule of the kings of these royal families. No record of the feudatories or subordinate kings of these rulers has been discovered so far. Only one record of Umāvarman (No. 7) of the Pitṛbhakta family refers to one Mahārājādhivarman, who was the executor of the grant. But this may also denote the king himself. The monarchical system of government prevailed in Kaliṅga, the king being the head of the central administrative hierarchy. The system was hereditary, as is evident from the records, the reigning king being described as meditating or as a devotee at the feet of his father and, sometimes, his father and grandfather being endowed with the royal title of *mahārāja*. Occasionally, however, the reigning king is credited with having acquired the kingdom by his own valour. In several records the king is described as having acquired his body, kingdom, prosperity and prowess through devotion at the feet of his father (Nos. 3 and 4).

Though there is no clear reference to the existence of a royal court consisting of ministers and other high officials who helped the king in the central administration, it may be presumed that some of the officers mentioned in connection with the land-grants must have acted in the capacity of ministers and other dignitaries in the royal court. We have a reference to *amātya* (No. 1), presumably denoting a minister who prepared the draft of the charter. The same person has been designated as the *deśākṣapaṭalādhikṛta* in a later grant (No. 4). It seems that a minister or *amātya* was also in charge of the office of the Accountant-General, who at the same time served as the chief of the keepers of royal records. This is evident from a grant (No. 7) of the Pitṛbhakta king Umāvarman, which describes the writer of the charter as *deśākṣapaṭalādhikṛta* as well as *amātya*. The official designation of *deśākṣapaṭalādhikṛta* has been regarded as Accountant-General by some scholars and by others as the chief of the office of the record-keepers. But, it seems, both the offices were in charge of the same officer or minister in ancient Kaliṅga during the period under discussion.

The royal order relating to the grant of a village was sometimes executed and issued by the reigning king himself, as known from the expression *svayam-ājñapti* (Nos. 1, 9, 13, 14, 15 and 16). But the order was often conveyed through an intermediary, who was generally a high officer called *dūtaka* (literally meaning "the messenger"). Śivabhōjaka and Vasudatta were *kumārāmātyas* in the court of the Māṭhara king Anantaśaktivarman, and both of them acted as *dūtakas* when the king issued his Sakunaka grant (No. 4). Both of them were also high officers in the king's army, designated as *mahābalādhikṛta* and *daṇḍanetṛ*. *Kumārāmātya* was perhaps the designation of a minister or the governor of a division of the kingdom, who was generally a member of the royal family. It appears that *daṇḍanetṛ* and *daṇḍanāyaka* are synonymous, and were popular designations among the army officers in the south Indian inscriptions.[16] In many cases, the designation indicated a provincial governor as well as the chief of the army. The officer designated

---

16. D.C. Sircar, *Ind. Ep.*, pp. 35-54.

as the *mahādaṇḍanāyaka* in the grants (Nos. 2 and 3) may have denoted the chief of the *daṇḍanāyakas* or the chief of the army generals who acted as a provincial governor. A person endowed with several designations in the Māṭhara kingdom would indicate that he was associated with various responsibilities relating to the administration of a division or a province. This may also reveal interesting facts about the development of the feudal system in the Kaliṅga region.

Another official designation denoting high rank was *mahāpratihāra* (No. 2), originally meant to be an officer-in-charge of palace gates. This designation in the Māṭhara records may have denoted the superintendent of the troops in charge of the defence of the gates of the palace and capital. The officer, possibly, served as a bodyguard to the king. The person in charge of the office of *mahāpratihāra* also held the office of *mahādaṇḍanāyaka,* which may indicate that he was a royal dignitary having the power of a provincial governor.

Another official status is indicated by the expression *bhōgika,* originally meaning the owner or enjoyer of a territorial unit called *bhōga.* A *bhōgika* was sometimes regarded as the village headman. The designation is also often found prefixed with the name of the *bhōga* or the locality, for instance, Acaṇṭapura-*bhōgika* (No. 6). The record also reveals the interesting fact that the brāhmaṇa, a *bhōgika* who was responsible for the administration of Acaṇṭapura-*bhōga,* was granted another village as an *agrahāra.* The *bhōgika* sometimes acted as the executor of the land-grant issued by the king (No. 17). Another expression, *bhōjaka,* perhaps with the same meaning, is mentioned along with the agriculturist householders of the village of Rāgōlaka in a charter of the Pitṛbhakta king Nandaprabhañjanavarman (No. 14). It may be the same as the village proprietor or a *jāgīrdār* of the medieval Muslim rule, enjoying rent-free holding for his services to the king.

At least some of the offices were hereditary in nature. This is known from the reference to Haridatta, the *deśākṣapaṭalādhikṛta,* who was succeeded by his son Mātṛvara (No. 10) to the same office during the reign of Umāvarman. Mātṛvara was again succeeded by his son Rudradatta to the office of *deśākṣapaṭalādhikṛta* during the reign of Umāvarman's son or successor Caṇḍavarman of the Pitṛbhakta family (No. 15).

For the purpose of civil administration, the kingdom of Kaliṅga was divided into various units, as the records of the different royal families of the period would reveal. These divisions are: *viṣaya, bhōga, madamba, pañcāli, grāma, chēda* and *vāṭaka* or *pāṭaka.*

The *viṣaya* seems to have been the largest territorial division in Kaliṅga during the period under discussion. It may have denoted a district comprising a number of smaller territorial units called *bhōgas.* There are references to a number of *viṣayas* included in Kaliṅga, such as, Kaliṅga-*viṣaya* (No. 1); Tellavalli-*viṣaya* (No. 6); and Bhiliṅga-*bhōga-viṣaya* (No. 7). Besides, there are references to two other divisions: Mahendra-*bhōga* (No. 9) and Varāhavarttani (No. 4). Though they have not been specifically stated to be *viṣayas,* they may be presumed to have been the same territorial units.

Both these units are found later in the records of the early Eastern Gaṅgas as *viṣayas*.[17] The district or *viṣaya* named after the kingdom of Kaliṅga is first known from the charter of the Māṭhara king Śaktivarman.

The term *bhōga*, literally meaning "enjoyment", seems to have denoted a group of villages while a group of *bhōgas* possibly constituted a *viṣaya*. Sometimes a *viṣaya* was named after its principal *bhōga*, such as, Bhiliṅga-*bhōga-viṣaya*. The names of several *bhōgas* are found in the records, such as, Pattana-*bhōga* (No. 5), Acaṇṭapura-*bhōga* (No. 6), Dantayavāgu-*bhōga* (No. 10), Bhiliṅga-*bhōga* (No. 7), and Mahendra-*bhōga* (No. 9).

Another territorial division found in the records is called *madamba*. There are references to two *madambas*: Kharapurisa-*madamba* (No. 5); and Dantayavāgu-*madamba* (No. 11). The terms *bhōga* and *madamba* seem to be synonymous, as the *madamba* called Dantayavāgu in the Temburu grant (No. 11) of Umāvarman has been mentioned as a *bhōga* in the Bṛhatproṣṭha grant (No. 10) of the same king. There is a reference to *madamba* in medieval literature as constituting a group of eleven villages.[18] During the reign of the early Eastern Gaṅga king Indravarman, Dantayavāgu constituted a village.[19]

The territorial unit called *pañcāli* probably referred to a smaller division than the *bhōga* and *madamba*. There is a lone reference to this term, named Kōrōṣōḍaka-*pañcāli*, in the record of Viśākhavarman (No. 17). The same geographical unit was later included in the Eastern Gaṅga kingdom, as known from the Chicacole plates of Indravarman of Gaṅga year 146 (*c*. A.D. 644-45).[20] The expression, like *madamba*, is typical of the Kaliṅga region. These two terms are not to be found in the inscriptions of northern Orissa. *Pañcāli*, perhaps, denoted part of a *viṣaya* or *madamba* and consisted of a group of five villages.

The *grāma* or a village was, perhaps, the lowest unit in the territorial arrangements in ancient Kaliṅga during the period under discussion. Villages which were made free holdings and granted to brāhmaṇas or a religious institution were called *agrahāras*. The names of a large number of *agrahāras* are known from these records, such as Rākaluva, Niṅgōṇḍi, Āndōreppa, Tiritthāṇa-*vāṭaka*, Akṣat-*āgrahāra*, Kaliṅg-*āgrahāra* and Varaṅg-*āgrahāra*. Besides, we come across the names of several *agrahāras* in the specification of the boundaries of the gift village in the grant of Nandaprabhañjanavarman (No. 14), such as Dusi, Chili, Gōndya and Hōjamyaka. The *agrahāra* Kaliṅga, named after the kingdom, was created by Umāvarman during his 40th regnal year, by separating a portion from the *madamba* called Dantayavāgu. A village was often divided into several parts and called *cheda, vāṭaka* or *pāṭaka*. Sometimes *cheda* and *vāṭaka* were prefixed with the name of the locality. *Cheda* also sometimes denoted the specific boundary of a village. The Niṅgōṇḍi grant of Prabhañjanavarman (No. 2) refers to *grāma-cheda*

---

17. *EI*, Vol. XXIII (1935-36), pp. 62 ff.; Vol. III (1894-95), pp. 127 ff.; *IO*, Vol. II (1960), pp. 15, 25.
18. *EI*, Vol. XXIV (1937-38), p. 49, fn. 4.
19. *EI*, Vol. XXV (1940), pp. 194-98; *IO*, Vol. II (1960), pp. 29 ff.
20. *IA*, Vol. XIII (1884), pp. 122 ff.; *IO*, Vol. II (1960), pp. 48, 75 ff.

while specifying the boundaries of the gift village. That a particular area of a village inhabited by a particular caste organization or community used to be named after that caste prefixed with *cheda* is seen in the records of the subsequent period in the Kaliṅga region, as in the case of Kumbhāra-*cheda* mentioned in a copper-plate charter of the Śailōdbhava dynasty.[21] Like *cheda*, *vāṭaka* probably denoted a particular quarter of a village or a hamlet, often suffixed with the name of the locality, as in the case of Tiritthāṇa-*vāṭaka* mentioned in the grant of Caṇḍavarman (No. 15), which was later made an *agrahāra* by him in his 4th regnal year.

It is, however, difficult to form an idea about the extent of a *viṣaya*, *madamba*, *bhōga* or *pañcāli* from these copper-plate records. Their area may have varied from time to time during the reign of different rulers of the Māṭhara, Vāsiṣṭha and Pitṛbhakta families.

Revenue

The copper-plate charters of the Māṭharas, the Vāsiṣṭhas and the Pitṛbhaktas contain a few terms informing us about the system of revenue collection prevalent in Kaliṅga. A few inscriptions specify the boundaries of the gift villages, the privileges to be enjoyed by the donee or donees in respect of the sources of revenue from the villages. While creating rent-free holdings or *agrahāras* in favour of the brāhmaṇas, some copper-plate charters (Nos. 1, 3, 5, 6 and 7) record the grant of land or a village together with the exemption of all taxes to be paid by the donee, including free entry of the royal agents (*a-bhaṭa-praveśya*), and all the *parihāras* i.e., all the exemptions to be enjoyed by the donee or donees.

A majority of the copper-plate grants record an exemption on all taxes. But, at the same time, the inhabitants of the gift village are directed to pay the donee the *meya* and *hiraṇya*. The expression *meya* is generally taken to be the king's share of grain and *hiraṇya* is taken to be the usual taxes paid in cash or in metallic money. The Siripuram grant (No. 5) of Anantavarman of the Vāsiṣṭha family records that the gift village was made free from all taxes, but at another place it is specifically mentioned that a small amount of tax was to be paid by the donees. The Varanga grant of Umāvarman (No. 7) records that the gift village was made free from all taxes, but the inhabitants of the village were directed to pay the donee, besides the usual *meya* and *hiraṇya*, periodic offerings of other produce from the locality. Some records of the Māṭharas and the Pitṛbhaktas (Nos. 2, 14 and 15) refer to the annual taxes to be paid in advance in a specified amount as was usually fixed as in the case of all other *agrahāras*. The expression in the records *ṣaṭtriṁśad-agrahāra-sāmānyaṁ kṛtvā* has been interpreted in the sense of "many" or "all" for "thirty-six *agrahāras*", in a general sense. It appears from this that the usual custom was to grant *agrahāras* on payment of a nominal cess or rent in advance, as the expression *agrahāra-pradeyāṁśa* would suggest though, at times, the grant was declared rent-free.

21. See Section IV, No. 46 in this volume.

The Ragolu grant of Nandaprabhañjanavarman (No. 14) further mentions that the grant was made free from all taxes, but the donee was required to pay, annually, 50 *paṇas* in advance, together with 20 *paṇas* levied towards fines for various offences. *Paṇa,* an ancient Indian coin-name, is frequently found in the early medieval epigraphic records of different parts of the Indian sub-continent. The term has been used in a general sense for various metallic coins in inscriptions. It was also regarded as one of the units of calculation of metallic coins and cowries. It is now well-known, according to ancient and medieval Indian literary texts, that 80 cowries were equal to one copper coin called *paṇa.*[22] Nothing can, however, be said definitely; whether the donee of this record was required to pay the amount in copper coins called *paṇa* or in the form of cowrie shells, which amounted to 4,000, together with another 1,600 cowries towards fines. Likewise, in the *Niṅgōṇḍi* grant of the Māṭhara king Prabhañjanavarman (No. 2) and in the Bobbili grant of the Pitṛbhakta king Caṇḍavarman, the donees were directed to pay 200 *paṇas* for each grant towards annual nominal rent. The amount was equal to 16,000 cowrie shells. It seems probably that the donees were required to pay the amount in copper *paṇas,* as the number of cowries was too large to handle in bigger transactions. Copper coins were not rare in the Kaliṅga region during the period under discussion. The well-known Purī-Kuṣāṇa, or the imitation Kuṣāṇa type copper coins, which have been assigned to the fifth and sixth centuries A.D., are abundantly found throughout Orissa, including the region ruled by the Māṭharas and other dynasties of Kaliṅga. These hoards of copper coins are reported to have been found at Bhilingi,[23] the ancient Bhiliṅga-*bhōga-viṣaya* of the epigraphic records of the Pitṛbhaktas of Kaliṅga, as well as other areas bordering present Andhra Pradesh and Orissa.

Unfortunately, we do not have any reference to the types of weights and measures used to determine the amount of land, agricultural produce or the weight of metal and liquid items. Nor do we find adequate reference to the system of irrigation on the basis of which a clear picture of agriculture in Kaliṅga during the period under discussion could be drawn. The large number of brāhmaṇa settlements in different parts of Kaliṅga, no doubt, helped in the growth and development of the cultivated area. The Ragolu grant of Nandaprabhañjanavarman (No. 14), while specifying the boundaries of the gift land, refers to some *pālyas* or irrigation channels, *vāpīs* or stepped wells, and *taṭākas* or tanks or water reservoirs, which may have been used for irrigating lands and, at the same time, serving other requirements of the inhabitants of the locality. There are references in this inscription to some bridges constructed for the purpose of crossing the water courses of the streams or channels, and trenches filled with water evidently for irrigation. There are also references to some reservoirs from which channels were dug obviously for the purpose of irrigation. Besides, there were natural reservoirs

---

22. S. Tripathy, *Early and Medieval Coins and Currency System of Orissa,* pp. 14, 20ff.
23. Ibid., pp. 43 ff.

and the brāhmaṇas were endowed with the privilege of using them (No. 14, lines 22-23). The inscriptions tend to show that new *agrahāras* were created by the kings by reclaiming the uncultivated lands and separating them from different territorial divisions. The increase in human settlements by the creation of *agrahāras* and the increasing desire of brāhmaṇas for material progress served in various ways to bring the fallow and forest land under cultivation, as Kaliṅga during this period followed a mainly agrarian type of economy.

Religion and Society

Sectarian epithets indicating the religious persuasion of the rulers of Kaliṅga are often noticed in their records. The Māṭharas were often followers of the Vaiṣṇavite faith (Nos. 2 and 3) and have been described in their respective grants as devout worshippers of Nārāyaṇa (Viṣṇu). Besides, another epithet for them is *paramadaivata,* which may either be interpreted as "a devout worshipper of the gods" or may apparently indicate "a devotee of the Vaiṣṇava faith". The Pitṛbhakta kings were also followers of Vaiṣṇavism, and the religious epithets for them are known to be *paramabhāgavata* (Nos. 12, 13, 15 and 17) and *paramadaivata.* But the Vāsiṣṭha kings appear to be followers of the Śaivite faith (Nos. 5 and 6), as known from their religious epithet *paramamāheśvara,* though the dynastic emblem of a conch indicating a Vaiṣṇavite symbol is known to have been adopted by them for their royal seals.

The inscriptions show that the brāhmaṇas (or the priestly class) occupied the highest position in society. The creation of *agrahāras* and the establishment of brāhmaṇa settlements by granting rent-free lands on a large scale in different parts of Kaliṅga would reveal the great honour shown to the learned brāhmaṇas, who were regarded as the spiritual as well as the religious leaders of the society. All the extant epigraphic records of the Māṭharas, the Vāsiṣṭhas and the Pitṛbhaktas are grants relating to the creation of *agrahāras* made to brāhmaṇas of various *gōtras,* who were well-versed in the study of the sacred scriptures and in the performance of Vedic sacrifices. They received royal patronage in every respect, including the grant of rent-free holdings for preserving the sacred tradition of the study of the Vedas and other sacred texts and maintaining a pious life. The Siripuram charter of Vāsiṣṭha Anantavarman (No. 5) was issued to eighteen brāhmaṇas of the Ātreya *gōtra* in order to establish a brāhmaṇa settlement and, at the same time, to provide all facilities to the brāhmaṇa donees in their pursuit of sacred knowledge, to enable them to perform *yajña* (Vedic sacrifices), *yājana* (performance of Vedic rites for others), *adhyayana* (study of sacred scriptures) and *adhyāpana* (teaching others the Vedic scriptures); and to make and receive donations. Viśākhavarman of the Siripuram grant (No. 17) is also known to have established an *agrahāra* for a number of brāhmaṇas of the Ātreya *gōtra.* The brāhmaṇas, as men of learning, teachers, religious preceptors, litterateurs and specialists in sacrificial lore, wielded great influence over the ruling authorities. They helped to establish religious institutions and monasteries, all of which became centres of learning and new socio-religious movements which affected the entire kingdom in the subsequent periods of history. It is to be noted in this context that the Māṭharas and other rulers used to donate a village either to a group of brāhmaṇas of different *gōtras* or a particular *gōtra* along with their sons and brothers. The expression *brāhmaṇa-kulebhy-ātisṛṣṭa* in the grant of Anantaśaktivarman may be noted in this context. Among the Pitṛbhakta kings, Nandaprabhañjanavarman and Caṇḍavarman established settlements of the brāhmaṇa community.

The inscriptions of these early rulers of Kaliṅga, however, do not provide us with any clear and definite idea about the immigration of the brāhmaṇas and other castes of the social hierarchy then prevalent, though considerable light is shed on the brāhmaṇas and their *gōtras* and the different branches of the Vedic *śākhās* or *caraṇa* they studied. The inscriptions rarely refer to the *pravaras* along with the name of the *gōtra* of the brāhmaṇa donees. The Ragolu plates of Śaktivarman (No. 1), however, refer to the Pañcārṣeya *pravara* and Vājasaneya *caraṇa* along with the *gōtra* of the donee and his sons. We find the following *gōtras* along with the *caraṇa* or *śākhā* in the inscriptions:

Gōtra	*Pravara*	*Śākhā* or *Caraṇa*	*Inscription*
Sāvarṇa	Pañcārṣeya	Vājasaneya	Grant No. 1
Kātyāyana	—	Taittirīya	Grant No. 4
Ātreya	—	—	Grant Nos. 5, 17
Kauśika	—	Taittirīya	Grant No. 6
Kāśyapa	—	—	Grant Nos. 7, 8
Vatsa	—	Chāndōgya	Grant No. 9
Upamanyu	—	Bahvṛca	Grant No. 10
Vasiṣṭha	—	Taittirīya	Grant No. 11
Devarāta	—	—	Grant No. 12
Kauṇḍinya	—	—	Grant No. 14
Bhāradvaja	—	Vājasaneya	Grant No. 16

The epigraphic records of these rulers tend to distinguish the names of persons belonging to different *varṇas* or classes of the society, which appear to have been followed according to the traditions established by the ancient law-codes like the *Manusmṛti*.[24] For example, all the names of the kings and their predecessors have been suffixed with *varman*, indicating that they originally belonged to the kṣatriya clan of the society. A majority of their records refer to the names of the brāhmaṇas having the appellation of *śarman*, while a few names of the brāhmaṇa donees, as in the Dhavalapeta grant of Umāvarman (No. 9) and in the Chicacole grant of Nandaprabhañjanavarman (No. 12) of the Pitṛbhakta family, are suffixed with the appellation of *svāmin*.

24. II, vv. 31-32.

SECTION II

We have seen from the inscriptions of the previous section that the history of Kaliṅga during the fifth century A.D. was marked by the rise and fall of several families claiming to be "lords of Kaliṅga". A number of epigraphic records of some unknown royal families of about the same period and of the subsequent centuries ruling from the same localities have also come to light. Their existence is known only from a few copper-plate charters issued by some rulers, of whom some are known to have enjoyed independent status while others appear to have ruled small principalities in the Kaliṅga region as feudatory chiefs under some unknown overlords.

Of these inscriptions, the copper-plate charter of Mahārāja Śatrudamanadeva may be the earliest one, which is known to have been issued from the well-known Siṁhapura, the chief city of Kaliṅga at the time of the Māṭharas, the Pitṛbhaktas and the Vasiṣṭhas. The characters used in this record closely resemble those in the charters of the Māṭharas and the Pitṛbhaktas of Kaliṅga. Unfortunately, the seal attached to the charter is completely defaced and neither the legend nor any dynastic emblem can be restored from it, which could have thrown interesting light on the royal family to which the issuer of the record belonged. Palaeographically, as well as from some internal evidences furnished by this charter, this ruler would appear to have flourished during the first half of the fifth century A.D.

Śatrudamanadeva has been called in his charter *mahārāja* and *bhaṭṭāraka-pāda-parigṛhīta*, literally meaning "favoured by the feet of the overlord". This may indicate that he was ruling the central part of Kaliṅga, with Siṁhapura as its headquarters, in the capacity of a feudatory chief under the control of a paramount ruler. But the use of his own regnal reckoning instead of his overlord's in any era would also indicate, at the same time, that he possibly enjoyed a semi-independent status.

The Allahabad pillar inscription of Samudragupta mentions that the Gupta emperor, during his southern campaign, defeated a king named Damana who was ruling Eraṇḍapalla, which at the time formed a principality. This locality has been identified with the present Erandapalle near Srikakulam in Andhra Pradesh. The city of Siṁhapura has also been identified with the present Singupuram near Srikakulam and Narasarapeta in Srikakulam district. The feudatory epithet stated above, applied to *mahārāja* Śatrudamana, reminds us of similar epithets used by some of the feudatory rulers of the Gupta emperors.[25] The supremacy of the Guptas in different parts of Orissa is known to have been acknowledged from several epigraphic records of the subsequent period of history. There is reason to believe that Śatrudamana also acknowledged the suzerainty of a Gupta emperor, or his provincial viceroy entrusted with the administration of the Kaliṅga region forming a part of the Gupta empire. It is also possible to assume that Damana of Eraṇḍapalla, a contemporary of Samudragupta, may have been a near

25. D.C. Sircar, *Sel. Ins.*, Vol. I, pp. 283, 285, 310, 324, 338 ff.

predecessor of the family of Śatrudamana, as his namesake and the area of his rule would tend to suggest. Śatrudamana, however, could not have ruled for long from Siṁhapura, as the area soon became a bone of contention for several rulers of the Māṭhara and Pitṛbhakta families of Kaliṅga in the subsequent period.

Only one copper-plate charter of Śatrudamana is known to have been discovered so far. The kingdom (or part of it) that he ruled that was known from this charter was Giri-Kaliṅga (literally meaning the hilly region of Kaliṅga). The *agrahāra* named Vardhamāna was situated in this part of Kaliṅga. The locality seems to be the same as that mentioned in the records of the Pitṛbhaktas of Kaliṅga as one of the chief towns during their rule. Of the three localities donated to the brāhmaṇas of the Kauṇḍinya *gōtra* and students of Taittirīya (*śākhā*), the village called Duhā-*grāma* has been identified with the present Pedda-Dugam, the findspot of this charter, and is situated near Srikakulam. The other two villages, though still unidentified, were evidently situated in the vicinity of Pedda-Dugam. The grant was made a *brāhmaṇa-deya* (gift to the brāhmaṇas) and made free from all taxes, though the usual share of the king of the produce of the field (*meya*) as well as tax in cash (*hiraṇya*) or metallic money were to be paid by the farmers to the donees regularly.

The system of dating adopted in this record is what is called the solar system of reckoning. This system was prevalent then in some parts of northern and southern India. According to this system, twelve months of a year are counted according to the twelve *rāśis* or constellations. In Orissa, the solar month (that is, the sun's passage from the beginning up to the end of a *rāśi*) begins on the day of *saṅkrānti* (that is, the sun's entry into a new *rāśi*). In some southern states like Tamil Nadu, the same system is followed, whereas in Bengal and a few other northern regions, the solar month is counted from the day following the *saṅkrānti*. According to this system, the days of a solar month are counted from 1 to 29 or 30.

The executor or the *dūtaka* of the grant of Śatrudamana was a physician (*vaidya*). He seems to have served as a physician in the royal court, but no information is forthcoming regarding his official designation. He also seems to have prepared the draft of the charter.

The gift villages were divided into different shares (*vṛttis*) among the group of brāhmaṇas, who were residents of another village named Paṭṭuva-*grāma*. The villages appear to have been previously granted by some other ruler as they were already included in the *agrahāra* or the revenue-free area of Vardhamāna[*pura*].

After the Vāsiṣṭhas and the Māṭharas, the area around Piṣṭapura seems to have been separated from the kingdom of Kaliṅga. An independent principality was established with Piṣṭapura as its headquarters during the last part of the fifth century A.D. This is known from the two copper-plate grants issued by a king named Pṛthivī Mahārāja, son of the Vikramendra and grandson of Mahārāja Raṇadurjaya. One of these charters was issued from Piṣṭapura and the other from Virajā-*nagara*. Unfortunately, the royal seals attached to both the charters are lost, which would have enabled us to have some idea of the history of the family of Pṛthivī Mahārāja. In both the records, the king has been credited with having acquired fame and extending the kingdom by his own valour. His father Vikramendra is not known to have assumed any royal title, though his grandfather had the title of *mahārāja*. It seems that either his father predeceased him or the kingdom, which was lost to him due to some political disturbance, was regained by his son. Pṛthivī Mahārāja has been described in his grants to have belonged to the Kāśyapa *gōtra* and been a worshipper of gods (*paramabrahmaṇya*). The expression Śrī-Rāma used before the *gotra* name of the king as well as with the name of the executor of the grants is an interesting feature to be noted, though its significance in the context of the *gōtra* cannot be explained with any degree of certainty. Both the grants were issued by Pṛthivī Mahārāja in favour of learned brāhmaṇas, who were known to be great scholars of their times. They are stated to have studied, taught and commented on the three thousand sciences. They performed various Vedic sacrifices and mastered the *Śruti* (*Vedas*), *Vedāṅgas* and *Dharmaśāstras* and attained expertise in the study of the *Purāṇas*, the epics and in many other fields. They are also known to have sincerely followed the various Vedic rituals. The brāhmaṇa donee of his Tāṇḍivāḍa grant (No. 19), dated in his 46th regnal year, is stated to have belonged to the Kāmakāyana *gōtra*. It is to be noted in this context that the *gōtra* name is encounted in the inscriptions of Orissa, though brāhmaṇas belonging to this *gōtra* are now known to have settled in different parts of Orissa.[26]

There is no evidence to show the existence of any relationship between the family of Pṛthivī Mahārāja and those of the Māṭharas and the Vāsiṣṭhas of Kaliṅga. Nor is there any clue in the inscriptions of this king to indicate the exact period of his rule as they are dated in his regnal years. The language, phraseology and other formal elements in his records would induce us to assign him to a period more or less contemporaneous to the Vāsiṣṭhas of Kaliṅga. It is to be noted that the name of his kingdom is not found in his charters. The name of Kaliṅga is not found either, though Piṣṭapura seems to have been the headquarters of the dominions he rūled. During the rule of the Vāsiṣṭhas and the Māṭharas, Piṣṭapura was an integral part of Kaliṅga, as their epigraphic records have revealed. The Aihole inscription of the Western Cālukyan king, Pulakeśin II[27] and other records of south India would have us believe that the region of Piṣṭapura passed over to the Eastern Cālukyas and remained under their control for a long time. This may also indicate that after the decline of the Vāsiṣṭhas and the Māṭharas, the region was for some time occupied by the *śrī-rāma* Kāśyapa family of Raṇadurjaya and Pṛthivī Mahārāja, who held Piṣṭapura till it was ultimately conquered by the Cālukyas.

26. Several brāhmaṇa families belonging to this *gōtra* are now known to have settled in the well-known pilgrim centre at Puri since several centuries and migrated to other parts of Orissa during the Mughal and Marāṭhā rule in the late medieval period.
27. *EI*, Vol. VI (1900-1), pp. 4 ff.; Vol. IX (1907-8), pp. 317 ff.

The second extant copper-plate record of Pṛthivī Mahārāja was issued in his 49th regnal year from his residence at Virajā-*nagara*, which has been described as the *vijaya-skandhāvāra* (literally meaning a victorious camp). Virajā-*nagara* was evidently a renowned centre of pilgrimage in Orissa, the present name of which is Jajpur in Cuttack district. It was well-known since long past and the Āraṇyaka Parvan of the *Mahābhārata*, describes it as follows:

tatō vaitaraṇīṁ gatvā nadīm pāpa-pramōcanīm /
virajāṁ tirtham=āsādya virājati yathā śaśī //

Some scholars, on the basis of the reference in the charter, believe that Pṛthivī Mahārāja extended his kingdom as far as Jajpur in Cuttack district in Orissa up to the river Mahanadi. But it is now well-known that the Guptas of northern India had installed their subordinates in different parts of Orissa during the sixth century A.D.[28] The indirect rule of the Guptas in Orissa, including the Kaliṅga region, seems to have continued till the rise of Śaśāṅka of Gauḍa in the first part of the seventh century A.D. Moreover, it is to be noted that Pṛthivī Mahārāja, unlike his predecessors the Vāsiṣṭhas and the Māṭharas in the area of his rule, did not claim to be a "Lord of Kaliṅga", though he is believed to have extended his dominions up to Uttara Tōsali and made the city of Virajā one of his victorious camps. There is reason to believe that he issued the second grant while he was on pilgrimage to the holy city of Virajā. The gift villages mentioned in both his grants were presumably situated in the area of his rule, around Piṣṭapura. There are several instances in the early medieval epigraphic records of Orissa referring to the grant of lands to brāhmaṇas by rulers of different royal families while on pilgrimage, which were far from the area of their rule.[29]

The two copper-plate records show that Pṛthivī Mahārāja had a long reign of about fifty years. It is to be noted that unlike the inscriptions of northern Orissa, these records of the southern part of ancient Kaliṅga appear to have adopted the system of luni-solar reckoning in the dates of the grants. The years of the records are, however, given in the regnal years of the reigning king.

It appears from inscription No. 21 that while the kingdom of Pṛthivī Mahārāja extended up to the Parlakhemidi region in the southern part of Ganjam district in Orissa, the northern part of the same district was under the control of one of the viceroys of the Guptas of northern India. Though the name of the Gupta overlord is not known from this inscription, his subordinate was Pṛthivīvigraha who was then ruling Kaliṅga-*rāṣṭra*. The charter is one of Dharmarāja, a feudatory of Pṛthivīvigraha, installed in the region around Khallikote in the northern part of Ganjam during the Gupta year 250 (*c.* A.D. 569-70). We have seen that the kingdom of Kaliṅga extended

28. See Section IV in this Volume.
29. *EI*, Vol. XI (1973), pp. 113-17; *IHQ*, Vol. XII (1936), pp. 489-93.

up to East Gōdāvarī district in the south during the rule of the Māṭharas and the Pitṛbhaktas. But, after their decline, the region around Srikakulam came under the Eastern Gaṅgas with their headquarters at Kaliṅga-*nagara*, or the present Mukhalingam in Srikakulam district. They sometimes claimed to have conquered the whole of the Kaliṅga kingdom. Pṛthivīvigraha seems to have been a contemporary of the early Eastern Gaṅga kings, Hastivarman and Indravarman, who were ruling the above region during the Gaṅga year 79-80 (corresponding to about A.D. 577-78) and claimed to have acquired sovereignty over the whole of Kaliṅga.[30] This would tend to suggest that the so-called Kaliṅga-*rāṣṭra* of Pṛthivīvigraha was probably confined to the region comprising the northern part of Ganjam district and the area around Chilka lake in Puri district. It seems that the Vigrahas were subordinates of the Later Guptas of Magadha and practically ruled independently, but without officially throwing off the Gupta yoke, as indicated by the use of the Gupta era in the record under discussion.

Dharmarāja claims in this record to have belonged to the family of Abhaya. Scholars have tried to associate the family with the Śailōdbhava dynasty that ruled as an independent power in the subsequent period of history in the same region.[31] The rulers of this dynasty assumed the epithets suffixed with *bhīta* or *abhīta*, such as Raṇabhīta and Yaśōbhīta, which were similar in meaning to the expression *abhaya*. Moreover, a later member of this dynasty was named Dharmarāja, which induced scholars to assume that the issuer of the present charter was one of the distant ancestors of the dynasty. If this assumption is taken to be correct, it may be held that the earlier members of this family were petty chieftains under the Vigrahas. During the Vigraha rule, these chieftains had not adopted a definite nomenclature for their family like "Śailōdbhava".

The charter of Dharmarāja is attached with a seal made of brass. This contains on its counter-sunk surface an emblem resembling a *tōraṇa* or gateway and the legend *mahārāja-dharmma*. The record is in prose, with the exception of a few imprecatory and benedictory verses at the end. The introductory part of the record is found to have been adopted in a number of inscriptions of the period. The script used is generally called the Gupta script assigned to about the sixth century A.D. Separate signs for *b* and *v* have been used in some cases, but in others they have been confused (as in words like *vappa* for *bappa* in line 5, *vahu* for *bahu* in line 17). The confusion is obviously due to faulty pronunciation of the letters frequently noticed in the inscriptions of a slightly later period.

The system of reckoning adopted in this charter is luni-solar in character, with the era of the Guptas as the year 250. The grant was issued on the sacred occasion of the *uttarāyaṇa*, falling on the eleventh lunar day (*tithi*) of the dark fortnight of the month of Māgha. The date of the grant has been taken to have corresponded to 20 December A.D. 569.

---

30. *EI*, Vol. XVII (1923-24), pp. 330 ff.; Vol. XXIII (1935-36), pp. 62-67; *JAHRS*, Vol. III (1925-26), pp. 49-53; *IO*, Vol. II (1960), pp. 14, 19.
31. See Section V in this book.

Dharmarāja appears to have been a contemporary of Śambhuyaśas, a sovereign of the Mudgalą family then ruling in the Uttara and Dakṣiṇa Tōsali in the northern part of Orissa, extending up to the northern part of Puri district.[32] Possibly, there was some rivalry between the Vigrahas of Kaliṅga-*rāṣṭra* and the Mudgalas of Tōsali, which is corroborated by the epigraphic record of another Vigraha ruler[33] controlling Dakṣiṇa Tōsali during the Gupta year 280 (corresponding to about A.D. 599-600). But, by this period, Kaliṅga-*rāṣṭra* appears to have been in a state of turmoil and the Vigraha family was no longer powerful enough to control this kingdom. Part of it had already fallen into the hands of the Eastern Gaṅgas of Kaliṅga-*nagara*. From the ruins of this Kaliṅga-*rāṣṭra* had then emerged a new kingdom comprising the northern part of Ganjam and the region round Chilka lake in Puri district, and came under the control of one Charamparāja.

A copper-plate charter of this king has been discovered from Khallikote taluk in Ganjam district (No. 22). The kingdom he ruled is known from this charter as Kōṅgōda-*maṇḍala*, which he is stated to have acquired by his own valour. The area of his rule was the same as that previously occupied by Dharmarāja under the suzerainty of Pṛthivīvigraha. Though the dynasty of this king is not known from the record, the name of the king suffixed with *rāja* as well as the area of his rule would tend to suggest that Charamparāja was probably a scion of the Abhaya or the early Śailōdbhava family of Dharmarāja. The palaeography of his record closely resembles the Sumandala plates of Dharmarāja (No. 21), though the medial signs in a few cases look more developed. The charter is stated to have been issued from Kōṅgōda, evidently the chief city of the kingdom of the same name. The same locality is known to have formed the capital of the kingdom of Kōṅgōda-*maṇḍala* of the Śailōdbhavas in the subsequent period. The district or *viṣaya* of Khiṇḍiṅgahāra, in which the gift village is stated to have been situated, is also found in the Śailōdbhava records.[34] This has been identified with the present Khidingi in Kodala taluk of Ganjam district. The practice of enumerating the names of the officers associated with the execution of the grant in verse, which is usually found at the end of the records of Mādhavavarman II of the Śailōdbhava dynasty,[35] is also found to have been adopted in the charter of Charamparāja. It is also to be noted that the engraver of his grant seems to have been the same person who engraved the charters of Mādhavavarman II as they have the same versified introduction. In all his records, including the present record of Charamparāja, this person has been designated as a *bhōgin* and served as the engraver. This observation may suggest that Charmaparāja was not far removed from Mādhavarāja or Mādhavavarman II of the Ganjam charter of the Gupta year 300, the first record to reveal the name of the dynasty as Śailōdbhava.

The royal seal attached to the copper-plate charter of Charamparāja bears

---

32. See Section IV in this book.
33. Ibid.
34. See Section V, No. 54 in this book.
35. See Section V, Nos. 47-50 in this book.

the emblem of a couchant bull, which is also known to be the dynastic emblem of the Śailōdbhavas in the subsequent period.

A copper-plate charter, paleographically assigned to about the eighth century A.D., is known from the area contiguous to the kingdom of Kōṅgōda of Charamparāja in Ganjam district. The name of the king mentioned in this record is Neṭṭabhañja. This name was popular in ancient Orissa among the Bhañja kings of Khiñjali-*maṇḍala* of the later period. But the present inscription reveals that this Neṭṭabhañja belonged to the family of Drumarāja (Drumarāja-*kula*). The palaeography of the record suggests that he belonged to an earlier period than the earliest known members of the different branches of the Bhañja dynasty ruling in different parts of Orissa. Unlike the Bhañjas of Khiñjali-*maṇḍala* of the later period, the charter does not give any legendary account of the origin of the dynasty of Neṭṭabhañja, nor does it refer to the place of issue of the Bhañja charters. Unfortunately, due to corrosion, no emblem or any legend can now be traced on the royal seal attached to this charter.

Vārāḍḍā, the place of issue of the charter of Neṭṭabhañja, has been described as a *vijaya-skandhāvāra*. But the vivid description of the locality, which has been stated to have been endowed with gardens, groves and beautiful temples, would have us believe that it was the capital of the king, though the name of the kingdom is not known from his record. The purpose of the land-grant mentioned in this charter is also interesting to note. It seems to have been made on behalf of the queens named Kṣatridevī and Kaivartadevī and the princess Meghāvalīdevī, for their easy access to heaven. The names of the two queens have induced scholars to believe that they belonged to particular communities of the society. If it is accepted that they belonged respectively to the kṣatriya and *kaivarta* (or fisherman) communities, as their names would indicate, then we have interesting information relating to the working of the social order in ancient Orissa, and particularly in the Ganjam region.

The charter of Neṭṭabhañja is dated in his regnal year, which may indicate that he enjoyed a sort of independent status. The reference to the month and day of the issue of the charter, usually found in the early medieval Orissan records, is not given in the inscription. No royal title has been used for the king, though he has been endowed with the religious title of *paramabrahmaṇya* and *paramamāheśvara*. He was a Śaivite king, as known from this religious title as well as from the verse in adoration to god Śiva at the beginning of his charter. The title of *paramabrahmaṇya* sometimes taken to mean one who respected the brāhmaṇas or a devout worshipper of Brahman. The record describes him as representing the hundredth generation of the ancient royal family called Drumarāja. The area of his rule, as known from this record, comprised a part of northern Ganjam district around Russelkonda and Bhañjanagar. This region is known from the later records of the Bhañja dynasty of Khiñjali-*maṇḍala* of about the ninth and tenth centuries, to have been included in their dominions. It seems probable that he was a contemporary of the later Śailōdbhava kings of Kōṅgōda-*maṇḍala*, which was contiguous to the Khiñjali-*maṇḍala* kingdom of the Bhañjas. Besides Neṭṭabhañja, no king of the family of Drumarāja is known so far. Probably, after his downfall, the area of his rule came under the control of the Bhañjas who named their kingdom Khiñjali-*maṇḍala* and were feudatories of the Bhauma-kara rulers of Tōsali and Utkala (*c.* eighth to tenth century A.D.). Neṭṭabhañja ruled for at least twenty-six years, as known from his record.

The titles and designations of the feudatory rulers and the royal officers found in the charter of Neṭṭabhañja are similar to those found in the other records of the sixth and seventh centuries A.D. The writer of the charter was one Vandya-Devabhadra. The expression *vandya* as a prefix to the name is believed to be originally a surname of a class of brāhmaṇas of Bengal having the appellation Vandyōpādhyāya. But, in the absence of any evidence to show the specific caste organization to which the writer of the said charter belonged, it cannot be definitely said that the person was actually a brāhmaṇa of Rāḍhā (Bengal) and that he or his predecessors migrated to the Ganjam region during the eighth century A.D. It may be pointed out here that the origin of the *kulīna* classes having the brahmanical cognomens (such as Vandyōpādhyāya and Caṭṭōpādhyāya) is known to have been of a later date. These cognomens are specifically known to have originated in Bengal, and not in Orissa. They became regular among a class of Bengal brāhmaṇas at a later date, who became known as *kulīnas*.

SECTION III

Some copper-plate records prove the existence of a number of royal families in the western and south-western parts of Orissa, comprising Kalahandi and Koraput districts and parts of Bastar and Chhattisgarh regions in Madhya Pradesh, while the northern and southern parts of Orissa were under the control of the Vigrahas and the Mudgalas and subsequently under Śaśāṅka of Gauḍa. Although the region, from the earliest period, formed a part of the ancient Kōsala country as known from some epigraphic records (including the Allahabad pillar inscription of Samudragupta), these ruling families do not mention in their records the name of their kingdom. Besides the well-known royal families (like those of the Śarabhapurīyas or the *Amarārya-kula* and the Nalas) who held sway over these regions, a few epigraphic records of some hitherto unknown families would reveal their existence in different parts of Kalahandi and Bastar in Orissa and Madhya Pradesh respectively during the sixth century A.D.

It is now a well-known fact that after the southern invasion of Samudragupta, several royal families rose to power and held sway over different parts of Orissa, forming petty principalities and often enjoying a sort of semi-independent status. One such ruler was Nandarājadeva. His single copper-plate grant is known to have been discovered from Kalahandi district in the western part of Orissa and he seems to have been an independent king of this region. The palaeography of the inscription is very similar to that of the charter of Charamparāja (No. 22). Based on palaeographical evidence, it can be assigned to a period not earlier than the sixth century A.D. In this context, it may be pointed out that some of the letters in the charter have been written very carelessly. Very often, the same letter has been written in several different forms. *D* looks like *y* (line 5). The *ā mātrā* is written in two different ways: sometimes it is formed by slightly lengthening downwards the stroke at the right end of the serif and sometimes it is indicated by a top vertical stroke to the right above the line. The medial *e* is also indicated by a top vertical stroke to left above the line. Punctuation is indicated by two vertical lines, the first being smaller than the second.

The charter is stated to have been issued from a place called Parvatadvāra by the king Nandarāja who is known for the first time from this record. The locality seems to be the capital of the king, as can be inferred from its description in the first plate of the charter. Its reference is found in another contemporary inscription of the area under discussion, though it cannot be identified at present. There is no pedigree of the king nor is the dynasty to which he belonged mentioned. He is stated to have granted a village called Prajñātapadraka, situated in the division of Cikkhalikā. The royal order in this regard was addressed to the inhabitants of the locality of Cikkhalikā. The grant was made in favour of three brāhmaṇas, though the *gōtras* and *pravaras* of the donees have not been furnished by it as is usually found in other contemporary records. The grant was made a permanent endowment. It was issued in the 3rd regnal year of the king. The month in which it was issued is not given, though day nine of a month is mentioned. The usual admonitions and the imprecatory verses found at the end of a grant are conspicuous by their absence in this record.

The locality called Cikkhalikā has been mentioned in a number of copper-plate records from Bastar in Madhya Pradesh and Ganjam district in Orissa. A locality called Cikhali (or Cikhali-*pañcāli*) is found in the epigraphic records of the early Eastern Gaṅgas of Kaliṅga-*nagara*. The Santabommali plates of the Eastern Gaṅga king Nandavarman of the Gaṅga year 221 (*c.* A.D. 718-19) refer to Cikhalikā, situated in Phareyabhukti *viṣaya*, as the gift village of his charter.[36] The same locality seems to have formed a territorial division called *pañcāli* at the time of Madhukāmārṇava[37] of the same dynasty during the Gaṅga year 526, which included the locality called Cikhali-*pāṭnāpura*, indicating perhaps a port town. But, at present, it is quite uncertain whether this place can be considered the same as that which is mentioned in the charter of Nandarājadeva. It may, however, be the same as Cikhali of the Kanker plates of Pamparājadeva,[38] which has been identified with its namesake, situated at a distance of about twenty-one miles from Kanker in the Chhattisgarh division of Madhya Pradesh. It is now included in the Dhamtari tahsil of the same division. If this identification is taken to be

36. *JAHRS*, Vol. II (1927-28), pp. 185-89; *IO*, Vol. II (1960), p. 90.
37. *JAHRS*, Vol. VIII (1935-36), pp. 168-80.; *IO*, Vol. II (1960), pp. 174 ff.; *JBORS*, Vol. XVIII (1932), pp. 272-75.
38. *EI*, Vol. IX (1907-8), p. 168.

correct and Parvatadvāra, the capital of Nandarājadeva, is assumed to have been situated somewhere in Kalahandi district, it may be presumed that he had an extensive territory under his control comprising the Chhattisgarh region in Madhya Pradesh and Kalahandi district in Orissa. There are places in the Chhattisgarh division, like Rajnandgaon and Nandur (Sanskrit, Nandapura), which may have been named after the king Nandarāja of the present record. But this cannot be considered a fact at the present state of our knowledge.

Another copper-plate grant (No. 25), discovered from the same Kalahandi district, is also highly significant in this context. The charter contains two grants: one issued by Mahārāja Tuṣṭikāra of an unknown royal family and the other by the queen-mother named Kaustubheśvarī. The endorsement engraved on the first side of the first plate contains the subject-matter of the grant of a plot of land made by the queen-mother, written in the manner of a summary of the grant. The brief nature of the record is due possibly to the need to adjust it in the space on the outer side of the plate. An attempt was first made to engrave the endorsement on the outer side of the third plate, but it seems to have been given up after engraving only one line. An attempt was also made to erase the line. These letters appear to have been written by someone other than the scribe of the main document of the king. The engraver of the endorsement of the queen-mother also seems to have been a different person who had little acquaintance with the scripts and language of the period, as numerous errors in both drafting and engraving are noticed in this part of the inscription. It seems that, at first, the person was engaged in engraving the endorsement on the blank side of the third plate, which was left blank after the king's document was completed on the inner side of the same plate. But, later, it was given up due to the inadvertence of the engraver. A different engraver, who had little knowledge of the scripts prevalent in the area, was later entrusted with the task of engraving the endorsement on the outer side of the first plate.

The grant of Tuṣṭikāra contains the scripts popularly known as the Kaliṅga variety of the southern alphabet of about the sixth century A.D., resembling those in the early copper-plate records of the Gaṅga kings of Kaliṅga-*nagara*.[39] They may also be compared with the scripts used in the grants of the Pitṛbhakta king Umāvarman.[40] It is to be noted that the characters of the queen-mother's grant belong to the well-known box-headed variety of the central Indian alphabet that was prevalent in the western part of Orissa in the region comprising the districts of Kalahandi, Koraput and Bolangir. But the letters have been incised very carelessly. The numerous errors in both the drafting and engraving of the endorsement may tend to suggest that it is a forgery by the donee in the name of the queen-mother in order to acquire an additional plot of land. But this cannot be said with any certainty at present.

---

39. *JAHRS*, Vol. III (1925-26), p. 51 and plate.
40. *EI*, Vol. XXVIII (1949-50), p. 298 and plate.

Mahārāja Tuṣṭikāra issued the grant from a place called Tarabhramaraka. This has been identified with the present locality of Talabhamara, situated about two miles south of the archaeological site of Belkhandi-Rajpadar on the bank of a small river called Utei, a tributary of the river Tel. But the grant of the queen-mother, Kaustubheśvarī, is stated to have been issued from Parvatadvāra, which is identical with that mentioned as the place of issue of the charter of Nandarājadeva (No. 24). Tuṣṭikāra and his mother are described as the devotees of the goddess Stambheśvarī, the tutelary deity of the royal family to which they belonged.

Tuṣṭikāra and his mother, like Nandarājadeva of Parvatadvāra, are not known from any other source. The expression *śri-śōbhinnā* before the name of the queen-mother (*rāja-jananyā*) seems to be an epithet used for the queen-mother and not the name of a king as sometimes believed. There are instances of charters being issued by the reigning king along with his family members. The copper-plate charter of Raṇabhañja and Narendrabhañja, of the Bhañja dynasty of Khijjiṅgakōṭṭa (*c.* tenth century A.D.), may be cited here, which was issued by the reigning king Raṇabhañja along with his elder brother in favour of the same donee, granting two different villages.[41] Tuṣṭikāra granted the village named Prastara-*vāṭaka*, while a piece of land (probably situated in the same village) was granted by his mother to the same donee, named Drōṇasvāmin of the Kāśyapa *gōtra*. Parvatadvāra was evidently the capital or the chief city of the king. He issued the declaration of the charter while he was residing at Tarabhramaraka, which comprised the gift village.

At present, it is not possible to ascertain the extent of Tuṣṭikāra's kingdom from this single record which is so far known to have been discovered. It would apparently indicate that he ruled the area now comprising the district of Kalahandi in Orissa. Though the locality called Parvatadvāra is now known from the two records of Nandarāja as well as Tuṣṭikāra, it cannot be identified with certainty with its present namesake. It was apparently situated near Tel river, a tributary of the river Mahanadi. The gift village, Prastara-*vāṭaka*, seems to have been situated near the present locality of Terasingha on the Tel river, which is the findspot of the charter of Tuṣṭikāra.

The record would have us believe that Tuṣṭikāra enjoyed an independent status and assumed the title of *mahārāja*. Neither the genealogy of the king nor the date of the record is given.

The official designation, *rahasika*, found in the charter of Tuṣṭikāra, is no doubt the same as *rahasyādhikṛta* of the early Indian inscriptions. This designation was popular in the Nala kingdom of Koraput and Bastar during the sixth century A.D. as known from their records. Subandhu, the writer of the record, acted apparently as the *rahasika* or the "privy counsellor" of Tuṣṭikāra.

The antiquity of the worship of the tribal goddess, Stambheśvarī, is apparent from this charter of Tuṣṭikāra. The deity was the family goddess

---

41. S. Tripathy (ed), *IO*, Vol. VI (1974), pp. 14-19, 20-24.

of a number of early medieval royal families of Orissa, as revealed by the epigraphic records.[42] It is already known that the worship of the goddess had its origin in the practice of worshipping a wooden post or pillar by the aboriginal people of Orissa, especially in the western part.[43] Reference to this tribal deity is frequently found in the inscriptions of the area in the subsequent period.

The south-western part of Orissa, comprising parts of Koraput district and Bastar (Madhya Pradesh), is known to have been under some independent rulers claiming to be of the Nala family during the first part of the sixth century A.D. Our knowledge about these kings is mainly derived from a few of their inscriptions incorporated in this volume. Besides, the discovery of some repousse-type gold coins, known to have been issued by some of these rulers, corroborate their supremacy in this region.

The earliest king of the dynasty seems to be Varāharāja, whose gold coins have been discovered along with those of the other Nala kings.[44] Unfortunately, so far no epigraphic record of this king has come to the notice of scholars. The discovery of his gold coins in association with the coins of other Nala kings, their uniform weight, the dynastic emblem of the bull and crescent and the palaeography of the legend on them giving the name of the issuers in the box-headed characters of about the sixth century A.D. have induced scholars to believe that Varāharāja was a king of the Nala dynasty. Besides Varāharāja, repousse-type gold coins of the same weight standard and with the same dynastic emblem with the names of the two issuers called Nandanarāja and Stambha in the so-called box-headed scripts have also been discovered in the Chhattisgarh division of Madhya Pradesh. These two kings, hitherto unknown from any other source, in all probability belonged to the Nala family of the region and period under discussion. The two other Nala kings whose coins have been discovered along with Varāharāja are Arthapati and Bhavadatta, who are also known from their epigraphic records. Varāharāja evidently enjoyed a sovereign status as his gold coins would tend to indicate though, however, it cannot be definitely said that he was the founder of the dynasty. Scholars believe that he was the earliest king of the family on the basis of the palaeography of the legend on the gold coins of all the above Nala kings. The task of arranging these rulers in a chronological order is, however, beset with difficulties. This is mainly due to the fact that no epigraphic record of the issuers of these gold coins, such as Varāharāja, Stambha and Nandanarāja, are known yet, which would have revealed important information on this point as well as about the dynasty to which they belonged.

Another ruler of the family who is known both from his gold coins as well as inscriptions is Mahārāja Arthapati. Only one copper-plate grant (No.

42. *EI*, Vol. XXVIII (1949-50), pp. 111-12.
43. See B.C. Majumdar, *Orissa in the Making*, pp. 107 ff. for a detailed account of the worship of the goddess in the western part of Orissa.
44. *JNSI*, Vol. I (1924), pp. 29 ff.; S. Tripathy, *Early and Medieval Coins and Currency System of Orissa*, pp. 74 ff.

26) so far is known to have been discovered. This was issued by this king from the locality called Puṣkarī, apparently the capital of the royal family. This locality, as will be seen below, seems to have been situated in the Podagadh region of Koraput district in Orissa. The characters used in this record are of the "scooped out" type of the southern variety of the so-called "box-headed" scripts, prevalent in different parts of central India during the fifth and sixth centuries A.D.

The inscription, dated in the 7th regnal year of Arthapati, records the grant of the village called Keśalaka by the reigning king in favour of the brāhmaṇas belonging to the Kautsa *gōtra*. The locality has been identified with the present village of Kesaribeda under Umarkot Police Station in Koraput district, which is also the findspot of the charter. The gift village was exempted from paying all taxes and from the obligation of supplying conveyance to the royal officials on tour, as the expression *a-vaha* would tend to suggest. The villagers were further directed to be careful about their obligations to the donees, in accordance with the customs prevalent in the kingdom, and to regularly pay the usual dues, such as the annual rent for land payable in metallic money (termed *hiraṇya*) besides the share of agricultural produce. The record states that the sincerity on the part of the villagers to serve the donees would lead to the satisfaction of the *bhaṭṭāraka-rāja*, evidently indicating Arthapati-*bhaṭṭāraka*. The word *bhaṭṭāraka* seems to have been regarded as an integral part of the king's name. The draft of the charter was prepared by an officer named Culla, who served the king as a *rahasyādhikṛta*. This official designation has been taken to denote the Privy Counsellor, which is also known from other records of the region and the period under discussion.

Arthapati has been described as *maheśvara-mahāsen-ātisṛṣṭa-rājya-vibhava*. The expression has been interpreted differently by scholars. It is generally taken to mean "one upon whom has been bestowed the glory of royalty by Maheśvara [Śiva] and Mahāsena [Skanda-Kārttikeya]". It is also interpreted as, "one who has dedicated his kingdom and wealth to the gods Śiva and Skanda".[45] Arthapati has been described as *nala-nṛpati-vaṁśa-prasūta,* which is also interpreted as "one who has descended from Nala", the ancient king of Niṣadha, known from the epic and Purāṇic literature. But, in the absence of any such reference to the ancient king of Niṣadha, it may at present be interpreted, like other dynasties (such as the Māṭharas), that Arthapati had simply referred to the name of the royal family, that is, the family of the Nala kings. The king's banner is stated to have borne the emblem of *tri-patāka,* explained as the representation of the "hand with three fingers stretched out or three pennons". It cannot, however, be said definitely whether Varāharāja was succeeded by Mahārāja Arthapati to the throne of the Nalas. There is no reference to his predecessor in the record of Arthapati.

The next ruler of the Nala family known his gold coins as well as a

45. *EI*, Vol. XXVIII (1949-50), p.13 and fn. 2.

copper-plate charter is Mahārāja Bhavadattavarman. Reference to this king is also found in his successor's record. The copper-plate grant issued by Bhavadattavarman (No. 27) was discovered from Rithapur in Amaraoti district of the Vidarbha region of Maharashtra. The palaeography of this record is of the southern variety of the so-called "box-headed" characters of the angular type, and not the scooped-out type that has been used in the charter of Arthapati-*bhaṭṭāraka,* although both the records are known to have been written by the same person. It appears that two different engravers were employed for the incision of these records, though the engraver's name in the record of Arthapati is not given. The engraver of the record of Bhavadatta was one Bōppadeva.

The charter refers to this king as Bhavattavarman, which seems to be a scribal mistake though it is sometimes taken to be "a partly Prakritized form" of the name of Bhavadattavarman, which is the correct form of the name as found in his own gold coins as well as in his son's record (No. 28). The charter is stated to have been issued from Nandivardhana during the eleventh year of the king's reign. The drafting of the charter is very similar to that of the charter of Arthapati-*bhaṭṭāraka* so far as the description and epithets of the issuer of the record are concerned. No pedigree of the king is given. Bhavadatta is also called *nala-nṛpa-vaṁśa-prasūta,* "born in the family of the Nala kings", and is said to have acquired the kingdom through the grace of Maheśvara and Mahāsena and whose banner had borne the *tri-patāka.* The charter records the donation of the village Kadambagiri to a brāhmaṇa of the Parāśara *gōtra* and his eight sons, whose names have been given in the grant, for blessings to himself and his queen. It is stated to have been issued while the king and his queen were staying as pilgrims at Prayāga (Allahabad), the holy place at the confluence of the rivers Ganga and Jamuna. The concluding part of the record is stated to have been actually endorsed by Arthapati-*bhaṭṭāraka,* who has been called the *āryaka* or the father of the reigning king. The expression *āryaka,* though sometimes taken to mean "grandfather" is also regarded as an epithet of Bhavadatta himself.[46]

It is sometimes believed, on the basis of the gold coins as well as the statement in the concluding part of the Rithapur grant,[47] that Arthapati succeeded Bhavadatta. Some scholars even believe that Bhavadatta was the grandfather of Arthapati on the basis of the expression *āryaka* in the Rithapur grant, and the year 11 mentioned in it has been taken as the regnal year of Arthapati.[48] But this is contradicted by the internal evidences furnished by both the charters of Arthapati and Bhavadattavarman. It is also sometimes believed that Arthapati was the younger brother of Skandavarman of the Podagadh stone inscription (No. 28), who has been mentioned as the son of

46. *EI,* Vol. XIX (1927-28), p. 102.
47. *EI,* Vol. XXVI (1942), pp. 49 ff.; D.K. Ganguly, *Historical Geography and the Dynastic History of Orissa,* pp. 255 ff.
48. *EI,* Vol. XXVIII (1949-50), p. 13.

Bhavadatta.[49] But it should be noted that while we have several gold coins of Arthapati and Bhavadatta, no such currency has yet been attributed to Skandavarman. The gold coins of the above two Nala kings have been found along with those of Varāharāja, but no coin of Skandavarman is so far known to have been found in these hoards. Skandavarman clearly mentions in his record that he is the son of Bhavadatta and not of Arthapati. It may also be noted that the draft of the charters of Arthapati and Bhavadatta was prepared by the same person named Culla, whereas the record of Skandavarman was written by the son of Culla.

The charter of Bhavadatta records that the village named Kadambagiri was granted to the brāhmaṇas as a permanent rent-free holding, along with certain rights to acquire ten *nivarttanas* of land to plough, and to use the village orchards and paths. Further, the grant was exempted from *śulka* or the levies and taxes. The ancient land measure called *nivarttana* is known from several early Indian inscriptions as well as ancient literary texts.[50] The exact area measuring a *nivarttana* in a particular region cannot be ascertained, as the measure differed from place to place. It was also very popular in different parts of south India from the days of the Sātavāhanas, as known from their epigraphic records. The expression *śulka* is sometimes interpreted as tolls and different kinds of customs duties. The term *viraka*, mentioned while specifying the boundaries of the gift village, seems to indicate a portion or division of a particular locality, like *cheda* or *pāṭaka* mentioned in the records of the Māṭharas and other families of Kaliṅga.

Bhavadatta's gold coins are known to be of the same type as those issued by his father, Arthapati. He was succeeded by his son, whose name has been doubtfully read as Skandavarman from his Podagadh stone inscription. Podagadh, the findspot of this record, is situated in Koraput district of Orissa, not far from the region of Bastar in the central provinces and the city of Puṣkari has been located by scholars in the region round Podagadh. Skandavarman, described as the son of Bhavadatta of the Nala family, is credited with having recovered the lost glory of the Nala family and re-peopled the deserted city of Puṣkarī. The inscription records the construction of a shrine of Viṣṇu by this Nala king, apparently at Podagadh.

The inscription reveals valuable information relating to the chronology of the Nala kings as well as the political condition of the region comprising the dominions of this family. The earlier belief that Arthapati of the Kesaribeda plates (No. 26) was the son of Skandavarman, cannot be accepted, as it is now clear that he was an earlier member of the family and may have been the grandfather of Skandavarman. The genealogy of the Nala kings, so far known from the extant epigraphic records as well as the gold coins, may be reconstructed thus:

---

49. D.K. Ganguly, op. cit., pp. 255 ff.
50. D.C. Sircar, *Ind. Ep.*, pp. 409 ff.

Varāharāja

↓

Arthapati

↓

Bhavadattavarman

↓

Skandavarman

Though we do not yet know the exact relationship between Varāharāja and the other rulers of the family in the absence of any epigraphic records, the close resemblance in their respective gold coins, the use of the same dynastic emblem and the scripts used on these coins have induced scholars to assume that he was an earlier member of the family. Moreover, his coins were discovered from a locality situated close to the region of Podagadh, which has been identified as one of the headquarters of the Nalas.

The city of Puṣkarī seems to have been the earlier capital of the Nalas. It was the chief city of the Nalas during the rule of Arthapati from where he issued his copper-plate charter. It was probably during the rule of Bhavadattavarman that there occurred some political disturbances which compelled him to abandon the city. It seems that during the time of Bhavadatta, Nala power was extended towards the north. Here the Nalas came into conflict with the Vākāṭakas of the main branch. But while Bhavadatta was busy annexing the heart of the Vākāṭaka kingdom, the region round Puṣkarī was probably attacked by the Western Cālukyas under the leadership of Kīrttivarman I (*c.* A.D. 567-97), who claimed to have destroyed the Nalas and their residence (*nilaya*).[51] The Nalas have sometimes been regarded as traditional enemies in the records of the Western Cālukyas. Inscriptions of the time of Cālukya Vikramāditya I (*c.* A.D. 655-80) refer to the home of the Nalas as Nalavāḍi-*viṣaya*,[52] identified with the modern Ratnagiri in Bellary district of Karnataka. The Aihole inscription[53] credits Kīrttivarman I with the destruction of the Nalas. The fact that Bhavadatta's Rithapur charter was issued from Nandivardhana instead of Puṣkarī, the original headquarters of the Nalas, seems to suggest that they had extended their sway, for at least a short period, to ancient Vidarbha and Nandivardhana, which was the capital of the Vākāṭakas before the foundation of Pravarapura.[54] This is corroborated by the record of Vākāṭaka Pṛthivīsena II, who is stated to have restored the glory of his family, apparently by subduing the Nalas and even carrying arms into the enemy's territory. It was probably, the Vākāṭakas or the Western Cālukyas under Kīrttivarman I who were responsible for the attack on the Nala capital Puṣkarī and its devastation.

---

51. *EI*, Vol. XXI (1931-32), p. 155; *EI*, Vol. VI (1900-1), pp. 4 ff.
52. *Bombay Gazetteer*, Vol. I, Pt 2, pp. 181, 363.
53. *EI*, Vol. VI (1900-1), p. 4.
54. *EI*, Vol. XXVI (1942), pp. 49 ff.

Skandavarman seems to have maintained the suzerainty of his ancestral kingdom and restored the royal fortune which had fallen into the hands of the adversaries for a brief period. But there is no epigraphic record yet to show the continuity of Nala rule after Skandavarman in the region round Puṣkarī (that is, in the Bastar and Koraput regions).

The writer of the Podagadh inscription seems to be the son of the writer of the charters of Arthapati and Bhavadatta. Their references as father and son in these three records would also suggest that the dynasty continued to rule the region, presumably since the time of Varāharāja, though there were occasional political skirmishes between the rival powers like the Western Cālukyas from the south and the Vākāṭakas of the Central Provinces. At present, it cannot be said with any certainty how their power declined, but their existence at a later date is known from a stone record from Rajim (No. 29) in Raipur district of Madhya Pradesh. Although we cannot determine the exact relationship of these Nalas with the earlier dynasty of Arthapati, Bhavadatta and Skandavarman, it is clear from this record and the names of the rulers mentioned therein that they belonged at least to one of the later branches of the same family, ruling a territory confined to a small area in the Chhattisgarh region of Madhya Pradesh.

The palaeography of the Rajim record has been assigned to the seventh or eighth century A.D. The script of this record has been found to be similar to those used in the record of Mahāśivagupta Bālārjuna of the Pāṇḍuvaṁśins. The record is not dated. It refers to a king Vilāsatuṅga of the Nala family, apparently described as the son of Virūparāja and grandson of Pṛthvīrāja. These kings are described as born into the family of Nala, the well-known legendary king of epic fame. It is to be noted that these kings flourished during the period when the Pāṇḍuvaṁśins had established themselves in the region called Kōsala or South Kōsala, comprising the Chhattisgarh region of Madhya Pradesh. They appear to have succeeded in reclaiming a small territory in the Chhattisgarh region, but were probably ousted by the Pāṇḍuvaṁśins within a short time. We do not have any other epigraphic record of this family to show their existence in the Bastar-Koraput or Chhattisgarh region after the eighth century A.D.

The record has been called a *praśasti* and, in fact, contains a eulogistic description of the Nala kings, Pṛthvīrāja, Virūparāja and the reigning king Vilāsatuṅga. The last named king has been credited in this record with having erected an excellent and lofty temple for god Viṣṇu. The main objective of building, the temple was to increase the religious merit of his son, whose name is not found in the inscription. This line of the Nala kings appear to have been followers of Viṣṇu.

The records of Arthapati and Bhavadatta indicate that they were devotees of Śiva, which is also corroborated by their respective gold coins. The Śaivite symbol of the couchant bull was the dynastic emblem adopted by these Nalas. But they also patronized the followers of other religious cults, especially Vaiṣṇavism, as is evidenced from the installation of the footprints of Viṣṇu in a Vaiṣṇavite temple by Skandavarman. He is also credited with having granted land in favour of the said temple for its maintenance as well as making provisions for a *satra* to feed the brāhmaṇas, ascetics and destitutes.

The extent of the Nala kingdom during the time of Arthapati and Bhavadatta cannot be ascertained from their records. But the gold coins issued by these kings would indicate that the Nalas enjoyed sovereignty. It was perhaps during the rule of Arthapati, or his predecessor Varāharāja, that the Nalas, at the height of their power, launched successful military expeditions against the Vākāṭakas and annexed a vast area of Vidarbha, including Nandivardhana which was one of the chief cities of the Vākāṭakas during Prabhāvatīgupta and Pravarsena II. Bhavadatta seems to have inherited a vast kingdom from his father. By the time he issued his Rithapur grant, the Nala kingdom included a large part of the Central Provinces and Berar, including the Bastar and Koraput region. Probably towards the end of his reign, Bhavadatta suffered reverses at the hands of the enemies, the Vākāṭakas, as well as the Western Cālukyas who claimed to have destroyed the residence of the Nalas. Skandavarman, his son and successor, however, succeeded to some extent in restoring the lost glory of the family by reclaiming the ancestral kingdom comprising Bastar and Koraput, including the original Nala capital of Puṣkarī. But his kingdom seems to have been greatly circumscribed, confined only to small areas in Bastar and Koraput. The later Nala family of Vilāsatuṅga was probably ousted by the Pāṇḍuvaṁśins.

The rulers of Śarabhapura, who claimed to have belonged to the *Amarārya-kula,* were probably contemporaries of the Nalas. The repousse-type gold coins issued by the earlier Śarabhapurīyas, like Mahendrāditya, Kramāditya and Prasannamātra, closely resemble the repousse-type coins of the Nalas mentioned earlier. The general fabric of the coins of both the dynasties is very much the same. The Śarabhapurīyas had their territory to the north of that of the Nalas of Bastar and Koraput. The districts of Durg and Raipur-Bilaspur in Madhya Pradesh and parts of Kalahandi in Orissa formed the kingdom of the Śarabhapurīyas, as revealed by their coins and epigraphic records. It is possible to assume that they were also adversaries of the Nalas and contributed to their ultimate downfall.

SECTION IV

The epigraphic records covered in this section, ranging from the beginning of about the sixth century to the end of about the seventh century A.D., provide valuable information about the history and culture of the northern part of Orissa. They reveal that various parts of northern Orissa were occupied by subordinate kings of different royal families controlled by suzerain powers. These inscriptions indicate the spread of the cultural influence of the Guptas of northern India in these regions of Orissa.

It is sometimes believed, on the basis of these epigraphs, that a sort of Gupta supremacy was acknowledged here during the fifth and sixth century

A.D., although no such direct evidence in this regard has yet come to notice. This has already been observed in the case of Kaliṅga-*rāṣṭra*, ruled by Pṛthivīvigraha, originally owing allegiance to the Guptas but later enjoying independent status in the second half of the sixth century A.D. The use of the era introduced by the Gupta monarchs as well as their influence on other aspects of history, noticed in the epigraphic records of northern Orissa during the period, would suggest that the Guptas held certain parts of Orissa through some of their subordinate kings or viceroys till the middle of the sixth century. But the disintegration of the Gupta empire in northern India during this period paved the way for these viceroys to assert independence in their respective areas of rule. The inscriptions under this section would also reveal that these newly independent rulers, claiming to belong to different royal houses, vied with each other so as to expand their area of influence. The existence of rivalry among them further facilitated the advent of another paramount power from Gauḍa (Bengal) named Śaśāṅka, who is also believed to have asserted independence after the fall of the Guptas and followed a policy of expansion at the cost of these newly independent rulers.

The earliest of the inscriptions under review is a eulogistic record of a hitherto unknown king named Śatrubhañja of Nāga dynasty (No. 30). This is the only epigraphic record of the king so far known to have been discovered, and the only source of information about the king and his family. The inscription is reported to have been unearthed from Asanpāṭ village in Keonjhar district. It has been incised on a stone slab under the image of an eight-armed Naṭarāja-Śiva in the dancing posture.[55] The characters used in this record may be regarded as the earliest of the class called the Gupta script so far as some of the letters (namely, *l*, *h*) and conjuncts are concerned, which bear close similarity to those used in the Allahabad pillar inscription of Samudragupta.[56] But some letters, like *y* (line 8), *s* (line 3) and, in some cases, the elongated medial *i* (*bhikṣu* in line 10, *parivrājaka* in line 9, and so on) resemble later characters. This would indicate a date for the record not earlier than the first part of the sixth century A.D. The orthography of the inscription points to the same supposition, as we find *v* in some cases represented by the sign for *b* (cf. *vṛhaspa-* in line 7). Such confusion between the two signs is frequently noticed in the inscriptions of Orissa from about the sixth century A.D. From about the seventh century onwards, the sign for *b* is not to be found and the sign for *v* is used for both *b* and *v*. The *anusvāra* before *ś* and *s* has been changed to *ṅ* (cf. *vaṅśō* in line 4) and *n* (as in *mīmānsā* in line 11), which seems to be due to the influence of local pronunciation. A similar orthographical peculiarity is noticed in the word *bhāratha* for *bhārata* (line 11). A punctuation mark is seen only in one case (line 2), in the form of a small slanting stroke after the word *kīrtti*. The

55. For details about the image, see *OHRJ*, Vol. XIII, No. 2 (1965), pp. 1 ff.; *EI*, Vol. XL (1973), pp. 121 ff. and plate. A large number of stone slabs used in the building of a temple, presumably the same as mentioned in the inscription, is also reported to have been discovered in the vicinity of the findspot of the above inscribed slab.

56. *CII*, Vol. III (1888), pp. 1 ff. and plate.

omission of a word is indicated by a small mark resembling a cross given above the line, and the omitted word is seen inserted below the same line (line 6). The writer of the eulogy, though his name is not known from this record, seems to have acquired much knowledge of the long phraseologies found in the inscriptions of the Gupta emperors. The record of Śatrubhañja is found to have contained long phrases very similar to those of the Guptas.[57]

Śatrubhañja of this inscription was the son of Mahārāja Mānabhañja and the queen Mahādevī Damayantī of the Nāga family. He has been described as the lord of Vindhyāṭavī and as having acquired fame by virtue of his own valour. Vindhyāṭavī seems to have been a forest state and the hilly jungle region around Keonjhar district was probably the kingdom ruled by Śatrubhañja of our record, though it was not a part of the Vindhya range of mountains. Some of the early medieval rulers are known to have assumed the titles of *vindhyeśvara, vindhya-nareśa* and *sakala-vindhyādhipati*, which were considered prestigious, though the region round the Vindhyas had nothing to do with their respective kingdoms.[58] It is believed that "all the ranges running east to west or west to east in the central belt of India were known as the Vindhyas".[59]

The suffix *bhañja* to the names of Śatrubhañja and his father of the Nāga family have induced scholars to believe that they belonged to one of the different branches of the Bhañja dynasty of early medieval Orissa and that this dynasty was an "offshoot of the Nāga clan".[60] But these rulers have specifically referred to the name of the family to which they belonged. References to several kings bearing the name Śatrubhañja are to be found in the epigraphic records of the Bhañjas that ruled different parts of Orissa during the ninth and tenth centuries, but all of them claim to belong to the Bhañja family. This is the earliest known reference to the same name, though the dynasty of the king differs. The epithet *mahārāja* applied to his father's name would suggest that he also ruled the kingdom for some time, enjoying perhaps an independent status. The introductory part of the record contains two verses describing the king and his achievements in an eulogistic manner. The rest of the epigraph is in prose. Śatrubhañja is stated to have fought hundreds of battles and claimed to have travelled widely and made gifts at holy places like Pāṭalīputra (or the modern Patna in Bihar), Gayā, Krimila (or the present Rajauna-Valgudar near Luckeesarai in Monghyr district of Bihar), Lalāvardhana (not identified), Puṇḍravardhana (or the present area around Burdwan in West Bengal), Gōkkhaṭi, Khadraṅga, Tāmralipti (or the present Tamluk in Midnapore district of West Bengal) and at the holy places of Ubhaya Tōsali, i.e., northern and southern Tōsali of early medieval Orissa. He appears to have visited these places on pilgrimage. Some of these places are not yet known from any other sources. Names such as Lalāvardhana, Gōkkhaṭi and Khadraṅga have not been identified. But references to

57. Ibid., pp. 1 ff.
58. *EI*, Vol. IV (1896-97), pp. 41 ff.
59. D.C. Sircar, *SGAMI*, p. 56 and n. 6; *EI*, Vol. XL (1973), p. 124.
60. *EI*, Vol. XL (1973), p. 123.

Pāṭalīputra, Gayā, Krimila, Tāmralipti and Ubhaya Tōsali are, however, well-known from several early medieval inscriptions. It is believed that Śatrubhañja travelled to these places as a feudatory of the contemporary Gupta emperor[61] because some of these places were situated in Bengal and Bihar comprising the Gupta dominions. Although it cannot be definitely said whether Śatrubhañja was a feudatory of the Gupta emperors, his kingdom was evidently surrounded by the Gupta territories.

Besides the above Gupta dominions in Bengal and Bihar, the kingdom of Ubhaya Tōsali also seems to have been dominated by the Gupta subordinates. Ubhaya Tōsali, as is known from several inscriptions of the period, consisted of Uttara Tōsali and Dakṣiṇa Tōsali, the river Mahanadi being the dividing line between the two territories. Uttara Tōsali denoted the present Cuttack and Balasore regions to the north of the river in Orissa and the south-western region of Midnapore district in West Bengal, then known as Daṇḍabhukti. It seems that the present districts of Dhenkanal, Keonjhar and Mayurbhanj in Orissa situated in this division were also sometimes included in the territory of Uttara Tōsali. Dakṣiṇa Tōsali, as has already been observed elsewhere, comprised of Puri and the northern part of Ganjam district up to the river Rsikulya or at least up to Chilka lake. The region around the Rsikulya was sometimes included in the kingdom of Kaliṅga, as known from the inscription of the time of Pṛthivīvigraha (No. 21). The subordinates earlier ruling these areas subsequently declared independence following the downfall of the Guptas of Magadha. It seems that Śatrubhañja of our record, who controlled the territory around Keonjhar district situated contiguous to the Balasore region of Uttara Tōsali, was originally a feudatory of the Gupta emperors but later threw off the Gupta yoke and formed a separate kingdom which was not included in the kingdom of Ubhaya Tōsali. It is now a well-known historical fact that Samudragupta succeeded in defeating the Nāga rulers of Kauśāmbī, Padmāvatī (Padam Pawaya) and perhaps the regions comprising the Vindhya mountain ranges in Madhya Pradesh during his campaign against the rulers of Āryāvarta. Several branches of the Nāga family were driven from their original settlements to the hilly forest regions of the Vindhyas. One of these branches of the Nāgas may have been the ancestors of the family of Śatrubhañja, who possibly established a principality in the hilly jungle region around Keonjhar district following the invasion of the Gupta monarch and named it after the jungle state of the Vindhyas. The name of the king suffixed with the word *bhañja* is typical of that used by the early medieval kings of Orissa. It is probable that the family of this king had settled in the region since the days of the Gupta invasion of the Nāga kingdom and was influenced by the culture and tradition of Orissa by the time Śatrubhañja came to rule the territory.

The inscription also describes the catholicity of Śatrubhañja by referring to the fact that he made dwellings and monasteries for various recluses belonging to the brāhmaṇical, Buddhist, Jain and other communities. He

61. Ibid., p. 124.

also gave alms to the heretics. He was a learned king who studied the *Mahābhārata, Purāṇa,* history, grammar (*vyākaraṇa*), *sāṁkhya,* logic (*mīmāṁsā*), the metrical science, Vedas and the sacred scriptures of the Buddhists. He has been described as an expert in the arts and a storehouse of superior knowledge. The actual purpose of the epigraph was to commemorate the construction of a temple for god, evidently Śiva, by Śatrubhañja, which is stated at the end of the eulogy.

Śatrubhañja is stated in the record to have made gifts of lakhs of *hiraṇya,* denoting some metallic money or currency then prevalent in the region and its surroundings. The reference to the numerical unit called *lakṣa* used before *hiraṇya* and the cows he donated to several religious institutions may be noted. The expression is found in an inscription of Orissa for the first time. *Hiraṇya* may have denoted here the gold coins prevalent during the period. It is well-known that gold coins circulated by the Gupta monarchs were popularly accepted as coinage throughout the country due mainly to their high metallic value. Besides, copper coins of the imitation Kuṣāṇa type were abundantly available throughout Orissa, including in the region around Keonjhar which actually formed the coinage of Orissa during the fifth and sixth centuries A.D.[62] This currency is now believed to have been introduced in Orissa through the viceroys of the Gupta emperors, who held sway over different parts of the region during the period under discussion.

A short record (No. 31) below a tempera painting[63] on a rock-shelter, found at Sītābhiñji in Keonjhar district, indicates the name of a king as Mahārāja Diśābhañja. We do not have any historical information about this king from any other source. The suffix *bhañja* to his name has induced scholars to assign him to one of the Bhañja families of early medieval Orissa.[64] The palaeography of the inscription suggests that it cannot be earlier than the sixth century and the above-mentioned Asanpat inscription of Śatrubhañja. The elongated medial sign of *i* and the formation of consonants like *bh* and *ha* would also indicate that it is later than the record of Śatrubhañja. Scholars sometimes assign it to about the fourth century A.D. on the basis of other associated antiquities discovered at Sītābhiñji. Though the painting is now greatly damaged, it shows the artistic influence of the Gupta period. This short inscription does not furnish any information on the dynasty to which Diśābhañja belonged. One can assume, in view of the area and the similarity in the nomenclature of the kings, that Diśābhañja of our record was a descendant, more probably a successor, of Śatrubhañja of the Nāga family of the previous record. The royal procession depicted in the rock-painting as well as the title *mahārāja* assumed by Diśābhañja would have us believe that he was an independent king of the area like his predecessors. Several archaeological antiquities have been discovered in the vicinity of this rock painting assignable to about the fifth or sixth century

62. S. Tripathy, *Early and Medieval Coins and Currency System of Orissa,* pp. 35 ff., 58 ff.
63. For a detailed description of the painting and inscription, see *JAHRS,* Vol. XIX (1948-49), p. 191.
64. HCIP, *The Age of Imperial Unity,* Vol. IV (1964), p. 74.

A.D. having considerable Gupta cultural influence. Moreover, the Asanpat inscription of Śatrubhañja, discussed above, has shown that this Nāga king was ruling more or less contemporaneously with the later Gupta kings, who held sway over different parts of Orissa through their semi-independent viceroys during the period under discussion. Several independent kings having *bhañja* suffixed to their names are thus known from these records, though they are not specifically known to have belonged to the so-called Bhañja dynasty of the later period. Several branches of this dynasty, which flourished during the ninth and tenth centuries, may have originated from the later descendants of these Nāga rulers bearing the names of some later Bhañja kings.

During the first part of the sixth century, a part of northern Orissa seems to have been under the control of a sovereign ruler of Bengal named Gōpacandra. A copper-plate grant of one of his feudatories named *mahārāja* Acyuta has been discovered from the locality called Jayarampur in Balasore district, situated on the border of Balasore and Midnapore districts of Orissa and Bengal respectively. The charter reveals that during the first regnal year of *mahārājādhirāja* Gōpacandra, the area called Daṇḍabhukti was ruled by his feudatory *mahārāja* Acyuta, who had the feudatory title of *mahāsāmanta*. He purchased a piece of land situated in a village called Śvetavālikā-*vīthi* of Daṇḍabhukti in the presence of several royal officers and village elders. The said *vīthi* was under the administrative control of the *kumārāmātya-rājanaka* named Vijayavarman. The land was donated by Mahārāja Acyuta in favour of the *ārya-bhikṣu-saṁgha* of the *mahāvihāra* situated at Bōdhipadraka in order to establish a Buddhist monastery (*vihāra*), and for the maintenance of the *ārya-bhikṣu-saṁgha* as well as for supplying materials for the worship of the Buddhist deity Avalōkiteśvara.

Gōpacandra, the donor's overlord who had assumed the sovereign title of *mahārājādhirāja*, is known from several epigraphic records found in different parts of Bengal. All these inscriptions belong to different subordinate chiefs who acknowledged his supremacy. One of these records belongs to *mahārāja* Vijayasena,[65] who ruled Vardhamāna-*bhukti* (or the present Burdwan region in West Bengal) as a feudatory of Gōpacandra during his 3rd regnal year. Another copper-plate grant was issued by one of his administrative officers (*viṣayādhikaraṇa*) from Vāraka-*maṇḍala* (or the present Faridpur region in Bangladesh) during the 18th regnal year of Gōpacandra.[66] All these records would show that Gōpacandra had an extensive region under his rule, which included the western part of Bangladesh up to a part of northern Balasore in Orissa.

Scholars have different opinions on the period of Gōpacandra's rise to power. One of his vassal chiefs, Vijayasena, has been identified with the person of the same name mentioned in the Gunaighar plate of Vainyagupta, dated in the Gupta year 188 (*c.* A.D. 507), as his *mahāsāmanta* and *dūtaka*.[67]

65. *EI*, Vol. XXIII (1935-36), pp. 159 ff.
66. *IA*, Vol. XXXIX (1910), pp. 204 ff.
67. D.C. Sircar, *Sel. Ins.*, Vol. I, pp. 331 ff.; *IHQ*, Vol. VI (1930), pp. 53 ff.

If this identification is accepted, the period of Gōpacandra's rule may safely be assigned to the first part of the sixth century A.D. Gupta rule in different parts of Bengal seems to have come to an end during this period. The local rulers, who may have been feudatories of the Gupta rulers, assumed independence following their decline. Gōpacandra was possibly one such local ruler who threw off the Gupta yoke. The south-western part of Bengal is known to have formed an integral part of the Gupta empire since at least the time of Samudragupta. But the use of regnal years instead of the Gupta era and the sovereign title from at least the first part of the sixth century in the epigraphic records of these local rulers would support the assumption that they enjoyed the status of suzerainty.

Gōpacandra seems to have had a short reign of about twenty years. During his 18th regnal year, one Nāgadeva served him as the *kumārāmātya, uparika* as well as the *mahāpratihāra* in the division of Vāraka-*maṇḍala* of his kingdom.[68] The same person is known to have served as the *mahāpratihāra* and *uparika* of the same division, under the rule of another independent king named Dharmāditya.[69] This would indicate that the Faridpur region of Gōpacandra's kingdom was lost to him soon after his 18th regnal year. It seems that by the middle of the sixth century A.D., Bengal was ruled by several independent kings like Gōpacandra, Dharmāditya and then Samācāradeva. After these rulers, the region round Burdwan and south-western Bengal (including the district of Midnapore) appear to have passed into the hands of Śaśāṅka of Gauḍa. The northern part of Orissa (including Balasore district) appears to have been split up into different principalities and ruled by different rulers, some of them enjoying a semi-independent status. As is known from their inscriptions, the region round Balasore (which was included in the division of Uttara Tōsali, also called Utkala) was included in the kingdom of Śaśāṅka. The epigraphic records of his time, as will be seen below, reveal that Daṇḍabhukti and Utkala constituted two different geographical units, Daṇḍabhukti being the present south-western part of Midnapore district in West Bengal. But during Gōpacandra's rule, Daṇḍabhukti seems to have included the region north of the river Suvarṇarekhā in Balasore district as well as the area round the present Dantan in Midnapore district. This region was in the charge of his feudatory *mahāsāmanta mahārāja* Acyuta. From the records of the subsequent period, this division is known to have formed a *maṇḍala*, presumably denoting a province.

The locality called Śvetavālikā has been termed as a *vīthi*. The expression seems to denote a subdivision of a district often situated on the seashore or on the bank of a river. A number of *vīthis* perhaps formed a *bhukti* or a province. The village Śvetavālikā seems to have been named after the *vīthi* in which it was situated, as it has been called a *grāma* at one place (line 25) in the inscription.

---

68. Sircar, *Sel. Ins.*, Vol. I, pp. 357 ff.
69. Ibid., pp. 354 ff.

The charter of Acyuta gives a list of the officers associated with the transaction of the land-grant in the said village. They are *kārtākṛtika; kumārāmātya; rājanaka; tadāyuktaka; viṣayapati; hiraṇya-sāmudāyika; bhōgin; pustapāla; mahāmahattara; kāyastha; karaṇika; sthānapāla; viṣayādhikaraṇa*; and *gṛhādhikṣaka*.

The *kārtākṛtika* seems to be the superintendent or manager of state affairs. The designation of *kumārāmātya* was usually regarded as similar to the status of an *amātya* or minister, enjoying the status of a prince of royal blood. The designation of Vijayavarman, the chief of administration of the *vīthis* (including the *vīthi* of Śvetavālikā) was *kumārāmātya*. He seems to have belonged to a kṣatriya royal family, as the appellation *varman* suffixed to his name would suggest. The *rājānaka* seems to be of the same rank as that of the *kumārāmātya*, but perhaps indicated a son of a feudatory. The reference to *tadāyuktaka* after *viṣayapati* may indicate that the officer was employed by the *viṣayapati* (or the chief of a district) to look after the district administration. The *viṣayādhikaraṇa* seems to have been of the rank of a clerk under the administration of the *viṣayapati*.

Another official designation noticed in an epigraph of Orissa for the first time is *hiraṇya-sāmudāyika*, which may have been the collector of taxes in metallic money (*hiraṇya*). The designation *bhōgin* is derived from *bhōga*, which is generally regarded as a subdivision of a district or one or more villages constituting a *bhōga*. The person as the head of administration of a *bhōga* was designated as *bhōgin* and often *bhōgika*. The *pustapāla* often denoted the keeper of official records of a district. The term *kāyastha* usually indicated the writer of records. The *kāyasthas* were originally a professional class of scribes, which later crystallized into a caste, though in the early medieval inscriptions as well as in the medieval lexicons the terms *karaṇa* and *kāyastha* have been used as synonyms, meaning a scribe or a member of the writer class. In some early copper-plate inscriptions of Orissa, such as the present one, the terms appear to have been used in a different sense. *Karaṇa* or *karaṇika* seems to have been used in the sense of subordinate officers and assistants to higher officers. The *sthānapāla* perhaps looked after the holy places of the district. It may have also indicated an officer-in-charge of a police or military outpost. The *viṣayādhikaraṇa* obviously denoted the officers of different grades employed in a district or *viṣaya*. The *gṛhādhikṣaka* apparently indicated a superintendent of the royal household. Besides, we have references to *mahattaras*, who were apparently headmen or elders of different villages. The term *pradhāna* was presumably used in the sense of a headman of a particular mercantile community. The *pradhānas* of different communities probably constituted the village council.

The inscription throws considerable light on the currency prevalent in the area ruled by *mahārāja* Acyuta. The annual rent fixed for the village was one hundred *aripiṇḍaka-cūrṇikā*, to be paid to the ruling authority, though the grant was declared free from all kinds of dues. The term is known for the first time from this copper-plate charter. The coin-name *cūrṇikā* was often used in the sense of cowrie-shell, which was regarded as the lowest unit in the calculation of metallic coins in ancient times. It was also frequently used in the sense of the well-known silver punch-marked coins. One copper coin called *paṇa*, weighing one *karṣa* or 80 *ratis*, was regarded as equal to 80 cowrie-shells. The *cūrṇikā* in this inscription seems to have been used in the sense of some metallic coins, not the cowries, as the value of one hundred cowries for *cūrṇikā* would be too small to be fixed as annual dues. It may have referred to the silver or copper coins termed *aripiṇḍaka*.

The expression seems to have been associated with the Buddhist monastery, and possibly had significance with regard to the Buddhist religious rites. It is well-known from the currency history of the area and period in question that the silver punch-marked coins of the earlier period continued to be in use for higher business transactions and regarded as currency. At the same time, during the fifth and sixth centuries, various coins cast in moulds as well as die-struck pieces imitating the devices of the earlier Kuṣāṇa currency, were prevalent in different parts of Orissa, including the region of Daṇḍabhukti. Of them, the well-known Puri-Kuṣāṇa or the imitation Kuṣāṇa type of copper coins were prevalent throughout Orissa, including the adjoining regions of Singhbhum (Bihar), Midnapore (West Bengal) and parts of Srikakulam (Andhra Pradesh), as known from their discovery in several hoards. It is probably these coins of the imitation Kuṣāṇa type that have been referred to in the charter of Acyuta.

The catholicity of Gōpacandra is known from the records of his feudatories. Though he was a follower of Śaivite faith and had borne the religious epithet of *paramamāheśvara*, he allowed his feudatories to construct *vihāras* for the Buddhists and follow different religious faiths. It is believed that one of his feudatories, *mahārāja* Vijayasena, was a Buddhist king, but he donated land to the brāhmaṇas to perform sacrifices in his kingdom of Vardhamāna-bhukti.[70]

We do not have any information regarding the religious faith followed by his other feudatory, *mahārāja* Acyuta. Probably he was a follower of Buddhism. During the period under discussion, Mahāyānic Buddhism received great impetus under the patronage of several ruling families in different parts of Orissa, as is evidenced from a number of inscriptions as well as several Buddhist *vihāra* sites which have been brought to light as a result of archaeological excavations.[71] The charter of Acyuta at least informs us that a *mahāvihāra* was in existence in the area of his rule, and the locality was called Bōdhipadraka. It was probably located somewhere near the present village of Jayarampur, the findspot of the charter. A vast area in and around Jayarampur has yielded huge archaeological remains, which may suggest

70. *EI*, Vol. XXIII (1935-36), pp. 157 ff.
71. A large number of clay seals having the Mahāyānic *dhāraṇīs* and Buddhist sculptures have recently been discovered at Abhaṇā, Soro, Gaṇḍiberh and adjoining places in Balasore district. Besides, recent excavations in 1987 by the Archaeological Survey of India at the Udayagiri Buddhist site in Cuttack district have brought to light the existence of an *ārya-bhikṣu-saṁgha* at the *mahāvihāra* of the locality called **Mādhavapura. A large** number of clay seals of the said *saṁgha* have been discovered, **which bear the legend** *Mādhavapura-mahāvihāra-ārya-bhikṣu-saṁghasya*.

the existence of the said Buddhist monastery here. A colossal mound, now overgrown with trees and bushes, still exists in the middle of the village and is popularly called *āhuti-kuṇḍa*. The copper-plate charter under review was discovered from this site. Besides some Mahāyānic Buddhist antiquities (including a chlorite image of Tārā, a bronze Buddha and a large number of burnt bricks) are still found in and around the village which have been utilized by the villagers for building their houses. Mahāyānic deities were worshipped like those of the Hindus, as is evidenced from the reference to the provisions made for the supply of *bali, caru, gandha, puṣpa* and *pradīpa*, and so on, for the worship of the installed deity Avalokiteśvara in the said *mahāvihāra*. Mahārāja Acyuta is also credited with having built several temples, *maṭhas, vihāras* and *āvasathas* (or guest-houses) for the gods as well as for the monks of different religious creeds.

The copper-plate charter of Acyuta is dated in the regnal year of his overlord *mahārājādhirāja* Gōpacandra, as the first year of his reign. The day and the month of the year one is mentioned in the solar system of reckoning as the twentieth day of the month of Phālguna. There is no reference to the lunar day, neither the dark nor the bright fortnight.

The name of another sovereign ruler is known from three copper-plate grants (Nos. 33, 34 and 36) which are presumably dated in the Gupta era. Śambhuyaśas of these records, like Gōpacandra and Pṛthivīvigraha, appears to have risen to power on the ruins of the Gupta empire. While Gōpacandra used his regnal year instead of adopting the era of the Guptas, Śambhuyaśas and Pṛthivīvigraha used it conventionally, though they were virtually independent monarchs. It is to be noted in this context that Śambhuyaśas has not specifically mentioned the name of the era. This had led scholars to speculate on the dates mentioned in his records.

Śambhuyaśas has been described in all the three grants as having belonged to the Mudgala family. Of the three charters, two (Nos. 33 and 34) were issued by him from two different military camps situated in Dakṣiṇa Tōsali and Uttara Tōsali. The third charter (No. 36) was issued by one of his feudatories from Dakṣiṇa Tōsali. The earliest known copper-plate record (No. 33) of Śambhuyaśas is dated in *samvat* 235 as an unspecified era, issued from the victorious camp (*jayaskandhāvāra*) at Hāndaka, and situated in Dakṣiṇa Tōsali. His second charter (No. 34) was issued from the victorious Tamparavaḍama, situated in Uttara Tōsali, in *samvat* 260. The locality of Hāndaka has presumably been taken to have been situated in Puri district while the other one is considered to be somewhere near Soro in Balasore district. The third charter (No. 36) was issued by a feudatory king named Śivarāja, from a locality called Vōrttanōka situated in Dakṣiṇa Tōsali. It is stated to have been issued in the year 283, when the Māṇa family was ruling (*pravarttamāna-māṇa-vaṃśa-rājya-kāle*) under Śambhuyaśas of the Mudgala family. The name of Śivarāja's family is not mentioned in this record.

Apart from his own records, the grant of his feudatory furnishes the evidence that Śambhuyaśas enjoyed the status of a paramount ruler and held sway over a wide tract of country called Tōsali, which was divided into two divisions roughly covering the districts of Balasore, Cuttack, Puri and a portion of northern Ganjam. He had assumed the full sovereign titles of *paramabhaṭṭāraka* and *paramadaivatādhidaivata*. His feudatory Śivarāja was endowed with the royal title of *mahārāja*. As is known from other records of the Gupta period, the subordinate kings, the feudatories and the subordinate allies of the Gupta monarchs enjoyed the title *mahārāja* and were often called *paramabhaṭṭāraka-pād-ānudhyāta*, that is, meditating on or favoured by the feet of the overlord. It is also known that the Gupta monarchs popularized among the independent rulers in different parts of their rule the imperial titles of *paramabhaṭṭāraka* and *mahārājādhirāja*. The titles used for Śambhuyaśas in his feudatory's grant remind us of the use of similar epithets in relation to the independent monarchs of the Gupta period. Besides, in his own grants, he has been endowed with the paramount title of *paramadaivata*.

The record of Śivarāja (No. 36) reveals that he was installed as a feudatory of Śambhuyaśas in the division of Dakṣiṇa Tōsali. The district or *viṣaya* of Vorttanoka in which the gift village of this charter was situated during this time, included in this division of Dakṣiṇa Tōsali. The locality has been identified with the place of the same name in the Athgarh taluk of Ganjam district. It seems to be the same as the *viṣaya* of Vartini mentioned at a later period in the Śailōdbhava grants[72] as well as in the Badakhimedi plates of Jayavarmadeva[73] of the Śvetaka branch of the Gaṅga dynasty. But it was later included in the dominions of Kōṅgōda-*maṇḍala*.

The dates mentioned in the copper-plate grants of Śambhuyaśas, as well as in his feudatory's grant, have been a matter of controversy among scholars. Though he has not expressly mentioned the name of the era like his contemporaries, the Vigrahas, it is likely that same era was also used in his records. But the date in his feudatory's grant has been specifically called the Māna year, when the rule of the Māna-*vaṁśa* was in existence, though the overlord of Śivarāja has been expressly mentioned as belonging to the Mudgala-*kula*. The reference to the Māna year in this record has led scholars to believe that Śambhuyaśas was a scion of the Māna dynasty and the dates mentioned in all the grants were different from the Gupta era. It is to be noted that Śambhuyaśas has never referred to this family name in his own grants. Moreover, we do not have any other evidence to show the existence of Māna rule in any part of Orissa during the period of the fifth and sixth centuries A.D. It seems that the Gupta era, which was prevalent in different parts of Orissa during the period, has been confounded in his grant with the era of the Māna family, which never existed in this part of the country.

The Sumaṇḍala charter of Dharmarāja has revealed that during the Gupta era 250, the Vigrahas were ruling independently over the southern part of Orissa then known as Kaliṅga-*rāṣṭra*. During this period, Śambhuyaśas controlled the northern part of Orissa with both the Tōsalis. But continued

72. See Section V, No. 56 in this book.
73. *IO*, Vol. II (1960), pp. 258 ff.

rivalry for supremacy over Tōsali seems to have existed between these two independent royal families. It is known from Śivarāja's grant that during the year 283 (*c.* A.D. 602-3), he ruled Dakṣiṇa Tōsali under the overlordship of Śambhuyaśas. But, during the Gupta year 280 (*c.* A.D. 599-600), a scion of the Vigraha family is known to have ruled Tōsali, which comprised eighteen forest states. This Vigraha king named Lōkavigraha is known from his single extant record (No. 35), issued from a locality called Muṭida or Uṭida in Dakṣiṇa Tōsali. The charter describes him as a *parama-devat-ādhidaivata*, and as ruling over the Tōsali region comprising eighteen forest states, in the Gupta year 280, corresponding to about A.D. 599-600. The purpose of Lōkavigraha's grant was to make endowments to the monastery dedicated to the illustrious Maṇināgeśvara-*bhaṭṭāraka* of Ekāmbaka and the maintenance of the brāhmaṇas of different *gōtras* who were students of the Maitrāyaṇīya branch of *Yajurveda*. These brāhmaṇas are stated to have resided in this monastery or the college attached to the temple of the said deity. It is to be noted that the grant was actually made by the royal officers of the district of Uṭida or Muṭida, situated in Dakṣiṇa Tōsali, with the permission of the *parama-devat-ādhidaivata, paramabhaṭṭāraka* Lōkavigraha during the Gupta year 280. The gift village, ṝdhvaśṛṅga, was situated in the said district. This seems to be in the same locality as the present Olasing in Puri district. It is stated in this grant that the gift village had land which was uncultivated for long (*cira-khila-śūnya*). A reference to this locality and a grant made in favour of the same deity and the monastery is known from another charter, issued a few years after the downfall of the Vigrahas, as will be shown below.

It appears from the different dates furnished by the records of Śambhuyaśas, Śivarāja as well as that of Lōkavigraha, that this Vigraha king temporarily succeeded in capturing parts of Tōsali country from Śambhuyaśas. It should be noted in this context that Lōkavigraha, unlike his predecessor, does not claim to have had control over Kaliṅga-*rāṣṭra* but the Tōsali country. His grant was issued somewhere near the Khurda-Nayagarh region in Puri district, then included in Dakṣiṇa Tōsali. Lōkavigraha's claim to suzerainty over the kingdom of Tōsali seems to have ended some time after the Gupta year 280. By A.D. 603-4, the Vigrahas had been ousted by the Mudgalas from the Tōsali region, including the area ruled by Śivarāja which later came to be known as Kōṅgōda. The Gupta rule in Orissa, though not direct, is thus rightly believed to have been brought to an end by the family represented by Śambhuyaśas. Śivarāja, owing allegiance to Śambhuyaśas, seems to be a later member of the Abhaya family, which was represented by Dharmarāja ruling under Pṛthivīvigraha, acknowledging the Gupta suzerainty during the Gupta year 250 in the same region. He was also probably one of the earlier members of the Śailōdbhava family which flourished in the same region subsequently, by assuming the new nomenclature for the dynasty.

The Soro plate (No. 34) refers to the name of a land-measure called *timpira*, which is known for the first time from this charter. But, unfortunately, the origin of this measure is still doubtful and nothing is known about the exact area indicated by the term. This is now known to have been prevalent only in the southern part of Orissa, as revealed by the records of the Śailōdbhava family at a slightly later period.[74] It seems, perhaps, that Śambhuyaśas introduced the land-measure in the northern part of Orissa, but it did not remain current for long in this region. Śambhuyaśas's grant reveals that cultivated land was measured in the *timpira* standard whereas homestead land was measured by a unit called *hasta*. This unit of measurement was the cubit often measured by the length of the forearm of a particular individual. While *timpira* (relating to a land-measure) was typical of Orissa, the measure called *hasta* was prevalent in different parts of the Indian sub-continent.

While granting land, certain specifications were made regarding some of the privileges to be enjoyed by the donee or donees, as noticed from the records of the period. The grants of Śambhuyaśas refer to expressions like *uparikara* and *uddeśa*, found to have been mentioned along with other specifications. *Uparikara* has been taken to be, "a tax levied on cultivators having no proprietory right on the soil".[75] But, at the same time, it has been specified that the granted land was made free from all obstructions. The expression *uddeśa* is generally taken to mean the space above the ground, that is, the gift land was granted to the donee along with the right to utilize the space above the ground.

There are references to a number of officers who acted in various capacities under the king and his feudatories. The feudatories or subordinate rulers of the king, who were installed in different parts of the kingdom, have been described as *mahāsāmanta-mahārāja, rājaputra, kumārāmātya* and so on. Of the officials, *aṁśa-bṛhadbhōgika* seems to be the same as the head of a number of villages who enjoyed the status of a partner or joint-head of the *bhogas* or a group of villages. The designation of *vaiśvāsika* is rarely found in the records of Orissa, but is generally believed to be a privy counsellor or one in charge of secret and confidential communications. Another designation, *draṅgapāla,* is not usually found in the inscriptions of Orissa, but in other states of India[76] it is mentioned as *drāṅgika*. According to Sanskrit lexicon, the expression *draṅga* is a synonym for *udraṅga*. This is generally taken to be a kind of tax levied on the share of the produce payable to the king.[77] Thus, *draṅgapāla* of the present charter seems to be an officer-in-charge of collecting *udraṅga* for the king.

Epigraphic evidence, however, implies that Mudgala rule continued for some time in the Tōsali region through some subordinate rulers, though the reference to Śambhuyaśas or his successor is not to be found in the records of these rulers. A number of copper-plate grants of these rulers have been found in Orissa, particularly in the northern part of the state. These copper-plate records belong to the kings named Bhānudatta and Sōmadatta. Three

74. See Section V in this book.
75. D.C. Sircar, *Ind. Ep.*, p. 394.
76. D.C. Sircar, *Sel. Ins.*, Vol. I, pp. 433 ff.
77. *CII*, Vol. III (1888), p. 97 and fn. 6.

copper-plate grants of Bhānudatta have been discovered so far. All of them are dated in the 5th regnal year of this king and the draft of all the three is same. Bhānudatta has been endowed with the feudatory titles of *mahārāja, mahāpratihāra* and *mahāsāmanta* in all his records, which refer to his overlord as *paramabhaṭṭāraka* without specifically mentioning the name. Bhānudatta's feudatory status is further indicated by the epithet *paramabhaṭṭāraka-pad-ānudhyāta*, "one who is devoted at the feet of his overlord". All the three grants were heated for affixing the royal seals by one Pratiṣṭhitacandra, who acted as the *peḍāpālaka* or the officer-in-charge of keeping official records. The vague reference to his overlord as well as the use of his own regnal year seem to suggest that Bhānudatta enjoyed a sort of semi-independent status. His earliest known record seems to be the Olasing (No. 37) plates issued from Andhaśṛṅga or Ūrdhvaśṛṅga in his 5th regnal year during the month of Āśvina. The locality seems to be the same as Ūrdhvaśṛṅga, the gift village mentioned in the record of Lōkavigraha (No. 35) and identified with the present Olasing, the findspot of Bhānudatta's charter. The purpose of both this charter of Bhānudatta and that of Lōkavigraha is the donation of land in favour of the deity named Maṇināgeśvara-*bhaṭṭāraka* of Ekāmbaka and the brāhmaṇa residents of the monastery attached to the temple of the said deity, who were students of the Maitrāyaṇīya school of *Yajurveda*. The charter seems to suggest that soon after the Gupta year 280 (*c.* A.D. 599-600), the region round Ūrdhvaśṛṅga or Andhaśṛṅga, stated to have been situated in Dakṣiṇa Tōsali in the Kanas plate (No. 35), came under the control of another paramount ruler, probably Śambhuyaśas, as indicated by the grant of his feudatory, Śivarāja. The region around Olasing in Puri district was then entrusted with Bhānudatta as a feudatory of Śambhuyaśas. The absence of the name of his overlord in his grants during his 5th regnal year is probably due to the fact that, during this period, there was no paramount ruler to control these feudatories. Śambhuyaśas appears to have died by this time and the successor to the throne of the Mudgala family of Tōsali may have been a weak ruler having no control over them. The kingdom of the Mudgalas in Tōsali may have been in a state of chaos and confusion during this period.

Bhānudatta ruled virtually independently, though for a short period. His second record (No. 38) was issued from an area around Balasore in the same regnal year, in the month of Mārgaśira, only a month after his first charter. The third plate of this king was issued two months after the second one in the same regnal year, from his residence at Virajā. The third plate appears to have been issued during the king's pilgrimage to the holy centre at Virajā (or the present Jajpur in Cuttack district). Both his second and third plates suggest that he no longer had control over Dakṣiṇa Tōsali, but shifted to the region round Soro in Balasore district in Uttara Tōsali. But his rule seems to have been short-lived as we know from other copper-plate records of the region issued by another feudatory, who seems to have belonged to the family of Bhānudatta. It is interesting to note that Bhānudatta has not mentioned Uttara Tōsali or Dakṣiṇa Tōsali, though the localities mentioned in his charters were situated in these divisions, as known from the records of his successors and the other contemporary records such as those of Śambhuyaśas and Lōkavigraha. This would indicate that he wielded authority over a petty principality first in the division of Dakṣiṇa Tōsali, and later in Uttara Tōsali in the capacity of a feudatory chief assuming the subordinate titles of *mahāpratihāra, mahārāja* and *mahāsāmanta.*

Three copper-plate records of another feudatory ruler named Sōmadatta, presumably of the same family as that of Bhānudatta, are known to have been found in Balasore region. These reveal interesting facts relating to the development of the political situation during the period under discussion. All the three charters reveal that Sōmadatta ruled the northern part of Orissa, comprising Balasore district and the region called Daṇḍabhukti (or south-western Midnapore district in West Bengal). The general characteristics of the copper-plate records of both Bhānudatta and Sōmadatta tend to indicate that they belonged to the same family.

The subordinate royal titles used by Sōmadatta in two of his charters are *mahābalādhikṛta, antaraṅga* and *mahāsāndhivigrahika*. These two charters are dated in his 15th regnal year and issued from the *viṣaya* of Sarephahāra, now identified with the area round Soro in Balasore district. Both the records, like those of Bhānudatta, do not specify the name of the overlord, only the vague reference to his existence is known from such expressions as *paramadaivatādhidaivata* and *paramabhaṭṭāraka-pad-ānudhyāta*. The earliest of his extant charters (No. 40) refers to Ōḍra-*viṣaya* included in Uttara Tōsali. The gift village is stated to have been situated in Sarephahāra *viṣaya,* which was again included in Ōḍra. Ōḍra-*viṣaya,* or Orḍra-*deśa,* has generally been taken to be another name for the entire Tōsali country, that is, the present coastal districts of Orissa. Ōḍra-*viṣaya* in this record presumably referred to the erritory ruled by Śambhuyaśas, and comprised the entire Tōsali country.

Both the above records of Sōmadatta have been issued in favour of brāhmaṇas of Vatsa *gōtra,* who are also found to be the donees of the two Balasore charters of Bhānudatta (Nos. 38 and 39). The village of Vahir-*vāṭaka* in Sarephahāra district mentioned in the grant of Bhānudatta is also the subject-matter of Sōmadatta's grant (No. 40). It is to be noted that the land in the said village, as mentioned in the record of Bhānudatta, remained uncultivated (*cira-khila-śūnya*) when he granted it. This may mean that the area was not developed into a locality when he issued his grant. It was, at that time, situated in Sarephahāra-*viṣaya.* The same area had developed into a locality, along with the division in which it is stated to have been situated (Varukōṇa-*viṣaya*), by the time Sōmadatta came to rule the area. It is also to be noted that, while the Soro grant of Bhānudatta enumerates the names of all the donees who were granted land in the village of Vahir-*vāṭaka,* the grants of Sōmadatta (Nos. 40 and 41) do not give all the four names but indicate this by the expression "and others". Of the four donees known from Bhānudatta's charters, Priyamitra, Vāṭamitra, Dhruvamitra and Āruṅgamitra, the last two names are found in the records of Sōmadatta along with the expression "and others". This may indicate that Bhānudatta was succeeded by Sōmadatta in the region of Uttara Tōsali, or that he was a near contemporary to the former. Scholars, however, believe that Sōmadatta preceded Bhānudatta.[78]

It should be noted, however, that all the three charters of Bhānudatta issued from different parts of Uttara Tōsali and Dakṣiṇa Tōsali do not expressly refer to Śaśāṅka as his overlord, as found in the later records of Sōmadatta. It seems that Bhānudatta enjoyed a higher status in the rank of a feudatory than Sōmadatta, as indicated by their respective titles specified in their four records discovered from Soro and Balasore (Nos. 38, 39, 40 and 41). While Bhānudatta styles himself as *mahārāja-mahāsāmanta* and *mahāpratihāra*, Sōmadatta's titles (*mahābalādhikṛta, antaraṅga* and *mahāsandhivigrahika*) are indicative of a somewhat lower rank. The title *mahābalādhikṛta* originally denoted the great commander of the army, a designation used for the military officer. A person having this designation was sometimes appointed as a minister and regarded as a higher officer than the *senāpati*, during about the sixth and seventh centuries A.D. The title of *antaraṅga* seems to suggest that Sōmadatta was originally the Privy Counsellor in the court of his overlord and also acted as the minister for war and peace.

That both the above feudatories originally acknowledged the suzerainty of the Mudgalas under Śambhuyaśas, or a weak successor of the family, is also indicated by the general, nature of their records. All their records of the period—from the Gupta year 250 (that is, the date of the Sumaṇḍala charter of the time of Pṛthivīvigraha)[79] till the end of the Gupta year 300 when the Śailōdbhavas rose to power under the suzerainty of Śaśāṅka of Gauḍa and his hegemony over the coastal regions of Orissa—reveal the history of a short period of only fifty years. During this period, the Vigrahas were ousted by the Mudgalas. The Mudgalas, in their turn, seem to have been driven out as a result of the rise of Śaśāṅka. This fact is confirmed by the discovery of another copper-plate grant of Sōmadatta, dated in his 19th regnal year. In this grant he is stated to have been ruling Utkala and Daṇḍabhukti as a feudatory under the suzerainty of Śaśāṅka, assuming the subordinate royal title of *sāmanta-mahārāja*. In the light of this charter, it may be presumed that the two earlier charters of his 15th regnal year were issued when he was a semi-independent ruler, acknowledging the overlordship of the Mudgalas who were then in a state of decline and finally subdued by Śaśāṅka. It was after the 15th year of his reign that he acknowledged the suzerainty of Śaśāṅka. He was raised to the rank of a *sāmanta-mahārāja* and made the ruler of Daṇḍabhukti and Utkala. Daṇḍabhukti is generally considered to be the region around Dantan in south-western Midnapore district in West Bengal. Utkala, as we know from several early medieval inscriptions, is the same as northern Tōsali, that is, the coastal districts of Balasore and Cuttack in Orissa. The inscriptions of the subsequent period indicate that Utkala in

78. HCIP, *The Classical Age*, Vol. III (1954), pp. 92 ff.; *EI*, Vol. XXVIII (1949-50), p. 333.
79. See Section II, No. 21 in this volume.

Uttara Tōsali also included the present districts of Mayurbhanj, Keonjhar and Dhenkanal. It is interesting to note that the same coastal region called Utkala has been mentioned as Ōḍra-*viṣaya* in one of the Soro plates of Sōmadatta.

Śaśāṅka, the king of Gauḍa with his capital at Karṇasuvarṇa (situated somewhere in Midnapore district of West Bengal), rose to power during about the first part of the seventh century. He greatly influenced the political events that followed in eastern India. He seems to have gradually extended his sway over Orissa as far as Kaliṅga, which is evidenced from the above charter of Sōmadatta. There remains little doubt that within a few years Śaśāṅka wielded his authority over southern Tōsali or Dakṣina Tōsali and Kōṅgōda, as can be seen from the study of the inscriptions incorporated in Section V below. The evidence from these inscriptions would have us believe, however, that Śaśāṅka did not wait long to establish his suzerainty over the adjoining regions of Orissa, that is, the districts of Cuttack, Puri and Ganjam. Śaśāṅka's occupation of Orissa led to the establishment of a new ruling family called the Śailōdbhavas in the southern part of Tōsali, with a separate kingdom named Kōṅgōda.

Another feudatory chief contemporary to Sōmadatta, though having a lower rank, under the control of Śaśāṅka, was Śubhakīrtti, who was installed in the region of Daṇḍabhukti. The Midnapore grant (No. 43) of this feudatory is dated in the 8th regnal year, which is believed to be the regnal year of Śaśāṅka, his overlord. But there are reasons to believe that the date mentioned in this charter as well as that of Sōmadatta's charter, dated in his 19th year, are in the regnal years of the issuers of the respective grants. Śubhakīrtti was endowed with the title of *mahāpratihāra,* and was entrusted with the smaller principality of Daṇḍabhukti. It is to be noted that the general nature of the two Midnapore grants (Nos. 42 and 43) of Sōmadatta and Śubhakīrtti, respectively, is the same. Both the records are written in verse. The gift village named Mahākumbhārapadraka mentioned in the grant of Sōmadatta, donated in favour of a brāhmaṇa named Bhaṭṭeśvara of the Kāśyapa *gōtra,* is also found in the grant of Śubhakīrtti. This is stated in his grant to have been situated in the *deśa* or division of Ketakapadraka. A plot of homestead land measuring 4 *drōṇas* and another plot of one *drōṇavāpa* were donated in favour of a brāhmaṇa named Dāmyasvāmin of the Bhāradvāja *gōtra.*

The two Midnapore charters of Sōmadatta and Śubhakīrtti have shed much light on the system of local administration. The seals attached to these two charters have the legend reading *tāvir-ādhikaraṇasya.* This may be interpreted as the administrative officers of the locality. Probably, the headquarters of a division in the kingdom was termed *tāvira.* It seems to have been the headquarters of a district. The charters of Sōmadatta and Śubhakīrtti reveal that this administrative office at the *tāvira* was constituted by learned people headed by brāhmaṇa elders. Prakīrṇadāsa, the *amātya* or the minister of Sōmadatta, was the head of this institution of the *tāvira.* The grant of a village and the transactions relating to the sale and purchase of land in the locality were announced from this office.

Another interesting fact to be noted here is that the conventional imprecatory verses containing admonitions to those born into the family of the donor, evidently referring to the royal family, are not in keeping with the context in these two charters, which is related to the *adhikaraṇa* or the administrative officer of the *tāvira*.

The land measure mentioned in the charter of Śubhakīrtti, termed *drōṇa* and *drōṇavāpa*, was popular in different parts of India during the fifth and sixth centuries A.D. The expression *drōṇa* was also used as a measure for grain and seems to have been derived from the measure of capacity. It was, however, not the same in different periods and localities. One *drōṇa* measure of seed is generally taken to be equal to about one and a half or two maunds. *Drōṇa* and *drōṇavāpa* are taken to be synonymous. It is known to have varied in length in different parts of the country. One *drōṇa* is sometimes taken to be a little less than 7 acres.[80] The land measure seems to have been derived from the requirement of one *drōṇa* measure of seed-grain to be sown on the land.

SECTION V

As many as sixteen copper-plate records covered in this section reveal the existence of a dynasty of kings called the Śailōdbhavas. The kingdom they ruled was called Kōṅgōda-*maṇḍala*, with its capital at Kōṅgōda. As discussed earlier in the context of the records of Pṛthivīvigraha and Śambhuyaśas, the kingdom grew out of the ruins of Kaliṅga-*rāṣṭra* of the Vigraha family and Dakṣiṇa and Uttara Tōsali of the Mudgalas. The three main events that occurred during about the later part of the sixth century and the first quarter of the subsequent century of the Christian era were the collapse of the Vigrahas in Kaliṅga, apparently caused by the Mudgalas of Tōsali who were themselves extirpated by the Gauḍas of West Bengal; the rise of Śaśāṅka, the king of Gauḍa (West Bengal), then ruling from Karṇasuvarṇa and dominating the whole of eastern India (comprising Bihar, Bengal and Orissa); and the downfall of the Mudgalas from Dakṣina Tōsali, the region which subsequently formed part of the kingdom of Kōṅgōda of the Śailōdbhavas. These main events of the history of Orissa were actually responsible for the rise of the Śailōdbhavas, by carving out a new kingdom at the expense of declining powers like the Vigrahas and the Mudgalas. The downfall of the Mudgalas paved the way for Śaśāṅka of Gauḍa, whose capital was at Karṇasuvarṇa in the southern part of Midnapore district in West Bengal, to undertake a policy of expansion towards the southern part of Orissa.

The epigraphic records covering a short period of fifty years (from about A.D. 570-71 to A.D. 620-21) reveal that the Vigrahas from Kaliṅga-*rāṣṭra* and the Mudgalas from both the Tōsalis were ousted as a result of the Gauḍa hegemony under Śaśāṅka. By the Gupta year 300, Śaśāṅka's suzerainty is known to have been acknowledged by a feudatory named Mādhavarāja of

---

80. D.C. Sircar, *Sel. Ins.*, Vol. I, p. 286 and fn. 9.

the Śailōdbhava dynasty, in the region which was earlier ruled by Dharmarāja of the Abhaya family as a feudatory of Pṛthivīvigraha during the Gupta year 250. It has already been shown that the principality previously ruled by Dharmarāja and subsequently occupied by a semi-independent king named Charamparāja came to be known as Kōṅgōda-*maṇḍala*. It also included the region comprising Vartini-*viṣaya* in the southern part of Dakṣiṇa Tōsali, identified with the Bugudā-Pōlasarā region in the present Ganjam district, which was previously held by a feudatory named Śivarāja under Śambhuyaśas. The name Kōṅgōda, the place of issue of Charamparāja's copper-plate record (No. 22) apparently indicating the chief city of his kingdom, appears for the first time in this grant, though the name of the kingdom and the family to which he belonged cannot be ascertained from it. It has also been suggested earlier that the above-mentioned feudatories were possibly members of a line of kings striving for power and looking for an opportunity to assert independence, whose successors subsequently claimed to belong to the family called Śailōdbhava. The close similarity in the names of the Śailōdbhava kings and the feudatories named Dharmarāja, Śivarāja and Charamparāja, and the region they ruled, would have us believe that these feudatories were the predecessors of the Śailōdbhavas who flourished before Kōṅgōda formed a part of Śaśāṅka's empire and when the specific name of the kingdom, Kōṅgōda-*maṇḍala*, was not in existence. It was Śaśāṅka of Gauḍa who, after his conquest of Orissa, installed a scion named Mādhavarāja from this line of kings by forming the province of Kōṅgōda-*maṇḍala* with Kōṅgōda as its headquarters. This feudatory of Śaśāṅka was endowed with a somewhat higher status than that of his predecessors, who acknowledged the suzerainty of the Virgrahas as well as the Mudgalas, as mentioned above. This Mādhavarāja is known to have been the first king to claim the establishment of the dynasty called the Śailōdbhavas and name his kingdom Kōṅgōda-*maṇḍala*. The history of the Śailōdbhava dynasty practically begins with the rule of Mādhavarāja *alias* Sainyabhīta, the feudatory of Śaśāṅka of Gauḍa, who appears to be its real founder.

The study of the history of the Śailōdbhavas began with the study of the copper-plate charters issued by different kings of this dynasty. The first known charter was edited by F. Kielhorn in the pages of *Epigraphia Indica*.[81] The study was then continued by R.D. Banerji, Pt. Binayak Misra, E. Hultzsch, G.M. Laskar, N.G. Majumdar, N.P. Chakravarty, H.P. Shastri, Y.R. Gupte, D.C. Sircar, R.C. Majumdar, S.N. Rajaguru and, till recently, by S.C. Behera. These scholars have contributed valuable historical articles on the Śailōdbhava dynasty based on these copper-plate records. The study of the sixteen copper-plate records of the dynasty, which are the only source of information, have revealed interesting facts relating to the history and culture of the Śailōdbhavas, though there are other sources (such as, the ancient monuments and accounts of foreign travellers) which have corroborated these epigraphic evidences.

81. Vol. III (1903), pp. 41-46.

Mādhavarāja, who began his career as a feudatory of Śaśāṅka of Gauḍa, is known to be the second king bearing this name in the family of the Śailōdbhavas. As many as six copper-plate records of this king have been discovered so far, which reveal interesting pieces of information relating to the history of the southern part of Orissa during the seventh century A.D. Mādhavarāja issued his earliest copper-plate charter (No. 45) in the Gupta year 300 (corresponding to *c.* A.D. 620-21) when he was a feudatory king under Śaśāṅka, the Gauḍa monarch of eastern India.

The extant copper-plate records of this king may be classified into two groups, as the earlier and later charters, on the basis of the nature of the records. The two copper-plate records, including the present one under discussion, were issued during the early part of his reign and written in prose. The four later records, however, were issued when he asserted independence and played an important part in the politics of southern Orissa during the later part of his life. The introductory part of the present charter (No. 45), written in prose, is similar to that found in the Sumaṇḍala plates of Dharmarāja of the Gupta year 250 and that of Lōkavigraha of the Gupta year 280. The royal seal attached to this charter bears the legend *śrī-sainyabhītasya,* indicating that he was endowed with a secondary or coronation name. This is also corroborated by his later records issued in the subsequent years of his reign. The grant is stated to have been issued from the locality called the "victorious Kōṅgōda", which was presumably the headquarters of his kingdom. Though the name of the kingdom is not stated in this record, the subsequent records of this king reveal that the territory ruled by him was called Kōṅgōda-*maṇḍala*. The city of Kōṅgōda, the place of issue of the charter, is stated to have been situated on the banks of the river Sālimā. The charter records the grant of a locality called Cchavalakkhaya, situated in the district (*viṣaya*) of Kṛṣṇagiri, in favour of a brāhmaṇa named Charampasvāmin of the Bhāradvāja *gōtra,* on the occasion of the solar eclipse. Though the localities and the river have been tentatively identified with their present namesakes by previous scholars, this has been contradicted by recent observations on the subject, which will be discussed later.

The pedigree of the donor Mādhavarāja has been given in the record. This is presented below:

Mahārāja Mahāsāmanta Mādhavarāja I

↓

Mahārāja Ayaśōbhīta[82]

↓

Mahārāja Mahāsāmanta Mādhavarāja II
alias Śrī-Sainyabhīta (the donor)

82. The name has been variously read by scholars as Ayaśōbhīta or Yaśōbhīta.

The above table shows that Mādhavarāja II was the son of Ayaśōbhīta and the grandson of Mādhavarāja I. That he was a subordinate chief is corroborated by his feudatory titles Mahārāja Mahāsāmanta. His predecessors were also feudatories, as known from the feudatory titles affixed to their names in the record. But it cannot be definitely said if Mādhavarāja I and his son Ayaśōbhīta were feudatories under Śaśāṅka. No epigraphic records of these kings are known so far to corroborate this view, though they have been quite vaguely referred to in the records of their successors.

It is already known from the Sumaṇḍala plates of Pṛthivīvigraha that one Dharmarāja of *Abhay-ānvaya* was in charge of administration as a feudatory, during the Gupta year 250, in the region around Khallikote in Ganjam district, fifty years before the issue of the present Ganjam plates of Mādhavarāja II. Unfortunately, we do not find the names of his father and grandfather from this grant of Dharmarāja. It seems that this Dharmarāja was succeeded by Mādhavarāja I as a feudatory in this region, which later came to be known as Kōṅgōda-*maṇḍala* under his grandson Mādhavarāja Sainyabhīta II. Mādhavarāja I was succeeded by his son Ayaśōbhīta, who was also a feudatory. Attempts have been made[83] to identify Ayaśōbhīta with Charamparāja of the Khaṇḍipadā-Nuāpalli grant, which was discovered from a locality contiguous to the findspot of the Sumaṇḍala plates. But it cannot be said definitely as to who was the overlord of Mādhavarāja I and Ayaśōbhīta, as we find one Charamparāja intervening between them as a semi-independent king for a short period. It may also be presumed that Mādhavarāja I and his son had a short reign, if they ever succeeded to the throne of Kōṅgōda.

The second copper-plate charter (No. 46) of Mādhavarāja II was also issued from Kōṅgōda. The royal seal attached to this charter contains, like his first one, the figure of a bull with the legend *śrī-sainyabhītasya.* It confirms that he had the secondary name Sainyabhīta. The genealogy stated in this charter, and furnished below, would show that Mādhavarāja I, the grandfather of the donor of the grant, also had the secondary name of Sainyabhīta, who may thus be Sainyabhīta I.

Śrī-Mādhavarāja-Sainyabhīta I

↓

Śrī-Ayaśōbhīta

↓

Śrī-Mādhavarāja-Sainyabhīta II

The scripts used in this record closely resemble those found in the Ganjam grant (No. 45) of the same king as well as the Sumaṇḍala plates (No. 21), though the drafting of the introductory part of this charter is altogether

83. S.C. Behera, *Rise and Fall of the Śailōdbhavas*, pp. 58-59.

different from his first record. The charter records the grant of a locality called Kumbhāraccheda, situated in the village of Arahanna in Thorana district. Kumbhāraccheda constituted a part of the said village, perhaps inhabited by the potters (the *kumbhakāras*). The expression *cheda* signifies a portion of a village, as known from several earlier epigraphic records as cited in Section I. There is no reference to any officer responsible for the execution of the charter. The same is also found in the case of the Ganjam grant. The practice of referring to some of the officers executing the grant is known to have been followed in the later charters of the king. The present record, unlike the Ganjam grant, is not dated. It also does not refer to the overlord of the reigning king, Mādhavarāja II. He is, instead, endowed with the prestigious royal title of "Lord of the whole of Kaliṅga" (*sakala-kaliṅgādhipati*) in this record.

The Ganjam grant of Mādhavarāja II was issued on the occasion of the solar eclipse. As regards the date of this charter, F. Kielhorn worked out the two nearest possible dates which could have corroborated the Gupta year mentioned in this record. According to him, the two solar eclipses visible in Ganjam district were on 4 November A.D. 617 and on 2 September A.D. 620. Evidently, the possible date of the grant is the latter one, when Mādhavarāja II was a feudatory of Śaśāṅka. It seems that immediately after A.D. 620, Mādhavarāja possibly assumed independence. After this date, Śaśāṅka was no more in the political arena of Orissa when Mādhavarāja II issued his Khurda grant (No. 46) which describes him as "lord of the whole of Kaliṅga".

During about A.D. 634, the Chinese pilgrim Hiuen-Tsang visited eastern India. According to his accounts, Śaśāṅka appears to have died by this date.[84] The epigraphic records of the Vigrahas and the Mudgalas would have us believe that Śaśāṅka's invasion of Kōṅgoda was accomplished after the Gupta year 283 (*c.* A.D. 603-4) and thus he occupied Orissa for a short period of about twenty years. It is sometimes believed, on the basis of the pilgrim's account, that Harṣavardhana, the Puṣyabhūti king of Kanauj, invaded and subjugated Utkala and Kōṅgōda soon after Śaśāṅka's death in about A.D. 625. But his victory over these regions, particularly over Kōṅgōda, seems to have been more formal than real, as we know from the subsequent records of Mādhavarāja and his successors that the Śailōdbhavas enjoyed independent status after Śaśāṅka's death.

The Khurda and later records of Mādhavarāja do not refer to any overlord reigning in the Kōṅgōda region. Mādhavarāja had also abandoned the use of the Gupta era in his later records. It is, however, to be presumed that if at all Harṣa invaded Kōṅgōda, his hold over it must have been short-lived. The Aihole inscription[85] of the Western Cālukyan king Pulakeśin II has us believe that Harṣa suffered reverses at his hands some time before A.D. 634.

84. Samuel Beal, *Life of Hiuen-Tsang*, pp. 159, 172; T. Watters, *On Yuan Chwang's Travels in India*, Vol. II, pp. 197-98.
85. *EI*, (1900-1), Vol. VI, pp. 1 ff.

Harṣavardhana, with Bhāskaravarman of Kāmarūpa as his ally, is known to have defeated the Gauḍa king Śaśāṅka when the Chinese pilgrim visited eastern India apparently some time before A.D. 634. Thus, it is apparent that Harṣa's defeat at the hands of Pulakeśin II must have occurred after the former's victory over Śaśāṅka. All these events took place within a short period of about twenty years after A.D. 620-21 when Mādhavarāja II asserted independence. The Khurda grant, issued without any reference to his overlord and the date, seems to have belonged to a period of political turmoil, perhaps due to the invasion of Pulakeśin II and Harṣa. Mādhavarāja also took this opportunity to assume the prestigious title of *sakala-kaliṇgādhipati,* though evidence is not available to show his conquest of the entire Kaliṅga country, which was then under the control of the early Eastern Gaṅga dynasty with their headquarters at Kaliṅganagara (the present region round Mukhalingam in Srikakulam district in Andhra Pradesh). Whether he assumed such a royal title by expanding the boundaries of his kingdom cannot be said with any degree of certainty. The total silence in respect of Kaliṅga in his later records shows, however, that even if he succeeded in wresting some portions of the Gaṅga kingdom of Kaliṅga his success was purely temporary. The contemporary Gaṅga king during or after A.D. 620 seems to have been Indravarman, who issued a charter from his capital at Kaliṅganagara in the Gaṅga year 128 (corresponding to *c.* A.D. 626-27) claiming to have acquired the whole of the kingdom of Kaliṅga.[86] Though there is no tangible evidence to prove such an assumption, Mādhavarāja II probably came into conflict with this Gaṅga king and temporarily snatched away a portion of Kaliṅga and boasted of the prestigious title.

Besides the above two charters (Nos. 45 and 46) which are written in prose, there are four more copper-plate records issued by this Śailōdbhava king in the later part of his reign when he was firmly established as an independent ruler by considerably consolidating his kingdom. It is interesting to note that these four later records are written in verse. A versified introduction of the kings of the Śailōdbhava dynasty, from its very inception, is to be found in these charters. It is also known to have been copied by the successors of Mādhavarāja II in their own records. Moreover, a legendary account of the origin of the dynasty is to be noticed in this introduction for the first time. The style of this versified introduction seems to have close affinity with the one that has been adopted in the Aihole inscription of the Western Cālukyan king Pulakeśin II. The first verse in this inscription invokes lord Jinendra, the following verse introduces the reigning king and then the verses describe the history of the Cālukyan family from the very beginning of the dynasty. Likewise, the first verse in the later records of Mādhavarāja-Sainyabhīta II is in adoration of lord Śiva, which is followed by a verse introducing the reigning king endowed with the epithet Mādhavendra.

The following verses in the introductory part delineate the history of the

86. *IA*, Vol. XIII (1884), pp. 120-23; *IO*, Vol. II (1960), pp. 43 ff.

Śailōdbhava family from the very beginning. The history begins with a legendary account of the origin of the family, which first introduces one legendary person named Pulindasena, described as famous among the people of Kaliṅga and a devotee of lord Svayambhū (Śiva). But the person does not seem to be directly associated with the family of the Śailōdbhavas. He is stated to have obtained a boon from god Śiva as a result of his worship. The god is stated to have created, apparently out of rocks, the eponymous king named Śailōdbhava. This king became famous as the founder of the family of kings known as the Śailōdbhavas. The next verse speaks of his descendant named Araṇabhīta or Raṇabhīta. The following several verses have been devoted to exhibiting the pedigree of the family and its descendants, listing their achievements and magnifying the importance of the kings. Raṇabhīta had a son named Sainyabhīta, who has been identified with Mādhavarāja I *alias* Sainyabhīta I of the Ganjam and Khurda plates. He was succeeded by Yaśōbhīta or Ayaśōbhīta. In some of the records, this king has been described in the versified genealogy as the descendant and not the son of Sainyabhīta I. Together with this, his son and successor Sainyabhīta has been named Mādhavavarman, who is the same as Mādhavarāja II of the Ganjam and Khurda grants. Moreover, in a verse, he has been introduced as Mādhavendra. There are controversies among scholars that Yaśōbhīta or Ayaśōbhīta was a descendant of Sainyabhīta I *alias* Mādhavavarman I. But he is clearly mentioned as the son of Mādhavarāja I in the Ganjam and Khurda grants as well as in the pedigree given in some of the later records of Mādhavavarman's successors. Moreover, there are several literary as well as epigraphic instances of the son being represented as a descendant of the father.[87]

Of the six copper-plate grants, the Ganjam and the Khurda charters were earlier issued in the name of Mādhavarāja II *alias* Sainyabhīta II, and written in prose. The other four charters were issued by the same king in the name of Mādhavavarman II *alias* Sainyabhīta II. The third charter attributed to this king is the Buguḍā grant (No. 47) which is not dated. This seems to be the first record of the king to have been written in verse. Besides, the other three later charters of this king written in verse—the Puri charter (No. 49), the Purushottampur charter (No. 48) and the Cuttack Museum charter (No. 50)—are dated in his regnal years. Most of the verses are common in all these four grants of Mādhavavarman II or Mādhavarāja II, composed for the first time presumably by a court poet of his time. The Purushottampur and Puri grants (Nos. 48 and 49 respectively) of the king are dated in his 13th regnal year, though the date in the Puri grant has been doubtfully read by R.G. Basak[88] as 23. The last known grant, that is, the Cuttack Museum charter, is dated in his 50th regnal year.

With the exception of this grant, all the other records were issued from Kōṅgōda, which was evidently the capital or the chief city of the kingdom bearing the same name. The last grant (No. 50) was issued from a locality

87. *EI*, Vol. XXIX (1951-52), p. 35 and fn. 2.
88. *EI*, Vol. XXIII (1935-36), pp. 122-31 ff.

called Mādhavapura, evidently named after Mādhavavarman II. The other three grants refer to one of his epithets as Śrinivāsa in a verse which is not to be found in his Cuttack Museum plates. There is a reference to mount Mahendra in one of the verses of this charter, which has been described as a *kulagiri*. It seems that the mountain formed the southern boundary of the kingdom of Kōṅgōda-*maṇḍala*, and the family of the Śailōdbhavas originally hailed from the region around this mountain. It is known to have been intimately associated with the kingdom of Kaliṅga from several literary as well as epigraphic records. The epigraphs of the early Eastern Gaṅgas of Kaliṅganagara refer to the mountain as the abode of lord Gokarṇeśvara (Śiva), the presiding deity of the Gaṅga family.[89] The epigraphic records of the Māṭhara and the Pitṛbhakta kings refer to a district named Mahendra-*bhoga*, situated in their kingdom of Kaliṅga and presumably named after the mountain.[90]

Thus, the above four later records of Mādhavavarman II furnish the following genealogy, tracing it from a legendary or eponymous king up to his time.

Śailōdbhava

↓

Raṇabhīta

↓

Sainyabhīta I

↓

Ayaśōbhīta

↓

Sainyabhīta II *alias* Mādhavavarman II

Mādhavavarman II, as known from these grants, abandoned the use of the Gupta era as soon as he assumed independence. He ruled Kōṅgōda-*maṇḍala* for at least fifty years enjoying an independent status. The four later grants dated in his regnal years reveal that he performed the horse sacrifice (*aśvamedha*) and certain other sacrifices. These must have been performed some time after A.D. 620-21 when he threw off the Gauḍa yoke. The performance of several sacrifices, including the *aśvamedha*, would indicate the recent assumption of independence for the dynasty. Probably after the death of Śaśāṅka, he embarked upon a policy of expansion and also extended the boundaries of his kingdom at the cost of the Eastern Gaṅgas and others. He performed the *aśvamedha* and other sacrifices, perhaps to commemorate his victories. His rule in Kōṅgōda may have continued till about A.D. 670-71.

---

89. *IO*, Vol. II (1960), pp. 10, 44, 49, 54, 59 ff.

90. See Section I in this volume.

As a mark of his independent status, Mādhavavarman II seems to have adopted the practice of enumerating the history of the Śailōdbhava family with a fabulous genealogy in verse, going back to the legendary ancestors of the reigning king fabricated by the court poet with a poetic imagination. This fabricated genealogy is not found in his two earlier charters. The tradition of tracing the origin of different royal families to mythical or legendary personages had become common during the early medieval period. The practice of fabricating a respectable genealogy, tracing descent from a number of mythical and imaginary personages, is often noticed in the early medieval times in some well-known dynasties of different parts of India, like the Gurjara-Pratihāras claiming descent from the Solar dynasty, the Rāṣṭrakūṭas from the Yādava dynasty of Purāṇic and epic fame, and the Eastern Gaṅga dynasty of Orissa claiming descent from the Lunar dynasty of the Purāṇas and the epics. Legends were often fabricated by the court poets to claim such a respectable descent and also to explain the name of the royal family, as is the case of the Śailōdbhavas. The tendency was to associate the founder of the family with an eponymous hero, in order to maintain a high status among the other royal families. The principal motive behind such exaggerated legendary accounts was to legitimize the authority of the new ruler and to consolidate the rule of his dynasty.

The real origin of the Śailōdbhavas, thus, seems to have been indicated by this conventional exaggeration. They appear to have originally belonged to an aboriginal stock of the region called the Pulindas, living around Mahendra mountain in the southern Ganjam area. The petty chieftains of this tribal stock gradually accumulated power and were eager to be merged into sophisticated Hinduism. The process of state formation in ancient Orissa, as elsewhere in India, had its genesis in the tribal areas, as is revealed by the legendary accounts found in the records of various royal families, (such as the Bhañjas and the Eastern Gaṅgas) while enumerating their origin. The process seems to have been adopted in different tribal areas of Orissa with the commencement of the political career of the Śailōdbhavas. The petty tribal chiefs, who later claimed to be Śailōdbhavas, launched a bid for supremacy in the process of socio-cultural transformation that led to their social promotion from their tribal origin to the Hinduized elements. Thus, they claimed the miraculous origin of their founder from inanimate rocks through the grace of god Śiva and assumed the name Śailōdbhava (born out of rocks) for their family. They were eager to elevate themselves socially and politically by imposing upon the people and the respectable ruling families the conception of a miraculous origin of the founder so that they could claim a respectable status in society as well as among the other Kṣatriya clans.

The introductory verses, though dealing with some historical personages who are believed to be identical with persons bearing the same names as found in the earlier records, are shadowed by poetical, eulogistic and conventional elements. The verse devoted to the introduction of Raṇabhīta as a descendant of the legendary figure Śailōdbhava would have us believe that he was the first historical king of the dynasty. He has been considered by some scholars to have flourished during about the sixth century A.D.[91] But nothing is known about this person from any other source. He is sometimes represented as the father of Mādhavavarman I *alias* Sainyabhīta I. Raṇabhīta seems to be a secondary name, his first name being unknown from any other source. It is to be noted in this context that Raṇabhīta was an epithet assumed by the early Eastern Gaṅga king Hastivarman, as known from his copper-plate records dated in the Gaṅga years 79 and 80 (*c.* A.D. 577 and A.D. 580)[92].

The Śailōdbhavas presumably adopted this epithet for themselves in order to elaborate the fabricated genealogy. Moreover, it is to be noted that this secondary name is not known to have been adopted by any of the successors of this early Śailōdbhava king, though we are acquainted with such secondary names as Ayaśōbhīta and Sainyabhīta invariably adopted by the Śailōdbhava rulers.

One of the interesting facts revealed by the Buguḍā plates (No. 47) of Mādhavavarman II is in respect of its palaeography. The characters used in the charter look more developed. They do not tally with the scripts used in other grants of the king or with the scripts prevalent in Orissa during the seventh and eighth centuries A.D. Moreover, according to F. Kielhorn who edited the charter, "these plates originally bore another inscription, the letters of which probably were beaten in to make room for the inscription here edited. But some letters of the older inscription may still be recognized even in the ink impression, especially on the second side of the second plate."[93] Traces of this earlier inscription may have belonged to a Śailōdbhava charter of about the seventh or eighth century A.D.

The later scripts, according to Kielhorn, belong to the northern variety of the alphabet of about the tenth century A.D. As has been rightly pointed out by him, they closely resemble the scripts used in the grants of Neṭṭabhañja *alias* Kalyāṇakalaśa and Vidyādharabhañja of the Bhañja dynasty of Khiñjali-*maṇḍala* who ruled from Vañjulvaka during about the tenth century A.D. It may be pointed out that the later scripts in the Buguḍā charter of Mādhavavarman II and in the Ganjam[94] and Komanda[95] charters of Neṭṭabhañja were incised by the same person. The original writing on the Buguḍā charter seems to have been beaten in and re-engraved on the same plate at a later date, evidently during the time of Neṭṭabhañja *alias* Kalyāṇakalaśa of the Bhañja dynasty of Vañjulvaka. Almost all the extant copper-plate charters of Neṭṭabhañja are known to have been engraved by one Durgadeva, designated as an *akṣaśālin*. The interesting point to be noted is that the letters incised by Durgadeva in the Bhañja copper-plate grants are

---

91. *JAHRS*, Vol. X (1936-37), pp. 1-15.
92. *EI*, Vol. XXIII (1935-36), pp. 62-67; Vol. XVII (1923-24), pp. 330-34; *IO*, Vol. II (1960), pp. 14-21.
93. *EI*, Vol. III (1894-95), p. 41.
94. *EI*, Vol. XVIII (1925-26), pp. 290 ff. and plate.
95. Ibid., Vol. XXIV (1937-38), pp. 173 ff. and plate.

very similar to those engraved in the Bugudā plates of Mādhavavarman. This tends to suggest that the same person re-incised the Bugudā plates during about the tenth century A.D. when Neṭṭabhañja came to rule the region around Bugudā and Bhañjanagar in Ganjam district, which was earlier included in the kingdom of Kōṅgōda-*maṇḍala* of the Śailōdbhavas.

In this context, we may refer to the two incomplete palimpsests[96] (No. 60) discovered in the region called Dharakote near Aska in the same district, which would corroborate our assumption in this regard. This palimpsest record, having two copper-plates without the ring and the royal seal, is now preserved in the Orissa State Museum, Bhubaneswar. Each plate contains, on one side, the introductory part of the grants of the Bhañja king named Kalyāṇkalaśa, evidently the secondary name of Neṭṭabhañja. The other side is engraved with the introductory verses of a record of the Śailōdbhava dynasty. Both the records are incomplete as the third plate is lost, which formed the middle plate of the grant of Kalyāṇakalaśa and the last plate of the Śailōdbhava king. It is not possible to determine the name of the Śailōdbhava king whose grant these stray plates contained. The interesting point to be noted in these plates is that both the records appear to have been engraved by the same person, Durgadeva, whose name is found to have been mentioned along with other officers at the end of the plate containing the record of Kalyāṇakalaśa.[97] It is also to be noted that the sides containing the earlier Śailōdbhava record were beaten in to make space for the Bhañja grant. The writings of the earlier record are clearly seen in the plates as well as in the photographs. It appears that the plates contained an earlier record of a Śailōdbhava king, which were later beaten in to engrave the record of land granted by a Bhañja king during about the tenth century A.D.

The reason behind re-engraving the earlier record at a later date, as found in the Bugudā plates, may presumably be attributed to the loss or damaged condition of the plates of the set issued by Mādhavavarman II. It was, presumably, re-engraved on the request of the successors of the donee during the reign of Neṭṭabhañja, in order to establish the authenticity of the ownership of the grant, which evidently continued to exist since the earlier period, and which he inherited from his predecessors. The Dharakote plates also tend to suggest that the family of the donee which enjoyed the grant made by the Śailōdbhava king, was later endowed with either the grant of newly reclaimed land by the Bhañja king or the grant previously made by the Śailōdbhava ruler was confirmed. It seems it was not the paucity of copper-plates which induced the scribe-engraver to re-engrave both the grants in one plate but to preserve both the records of ownership of the gift lands for future convenience.

The officers responsible for the execution of the original charter of Mādhavavarman II, as given in the Bugudā plates, are also found in his later charters (Nos. 48, 49 and 50). The engraver of the original charter, named

96. See plate V.
97. The name of some of these officers mentioned in this record are also found in other extant records of this Bhañja king. See S. Tripathy, *IO*, Vol. VI (1974), pp. 171-75.

Daḍḍibhōgin of the Buguḍā plates, was also the engraver of these records. His name has been differently spelt in different charters as Cheḍḍibhōgin and Chaḍḍibhōgin. Durgadeva of the time of Neṭṭabhañja, who re-engraved the Buguḍā plates of Mādhạvavarman and the Dharakote plates of the unknown Śailōdbhava king, appears to have been directed to copy the records exactly as they were in their original form. This would also indicate that the charter was re-engraved for a renewal of the grant by the donee's descendants, in order to establish their ownership over it.

It is to be noted that the officers usually associated with the execution of the copper-plate records are conspicuous by their absence in the two earlier charters of Mādhavavarman II, while his later three charters in verse refer to a number of officers in two verses at the end of the grants. All these three records are stated to have been drafted by Upendrasiṁha, the son of Kuṇḍabhōgin. Though no official designation has been used for this person, his father seems, however, to have been a *bhōgin*, or the head of a *bhōga*. These three records are endowed with seals (*lāñchita*) by one Jayasiṁha who is also not designated. All the records, except the Cuttack Museum plates (No. 50), have been engraved by Chaḍḍibhōgin or Daḍḍibhōgin who appears to have been endowed with the administration of a *bhōga*. The chief executor of all these three charters is named Gaṅgabhadra. He acted as a *dūtaka* and was designated as the *pratihāra*. The officers named Jayasiṁha and Upendrasiṁha appear to have served Mādhavavarman II till the end of his reign. Jayasiṁha has been credited with having heated (*tāpita*) the charter for affixing the seal in his last known record, which seems to be the same as *lāñchita* in his other grants. The *dūtaka* of the Cuttack Museum plates was Guhacandra.

The Cuttack Museum charter of Mādhavavarman II adds a new verse at the end of the record, referring to a person, presumably a feudatory king, named Śrī-Varamōra. This name seems to have occurred on a broken stone slab at the ruined temple site at Baṅkāḍagaḍ. But the reading is doubtful as the letters of this slab are very carelessly engraved. The above copper-plate record states that the king favoured his feudatory Śrī-Varamōra, and had been graciously disposed towards him. Mādhavavarman has been described as Lōkanātha in this verse. This seems to be an epithet for Mādhavavarman II like Śrīnivāsa. Controversies prevail among scholars relating to the identification of Lōkanātha. Scholars believe that Mādhavavarman II allied himself with a king named Lōkanātha of Śrīdharapura, on the basis of the reading of the text furnished by N.G. Majumdar.[98] Lōkanātha has been identified with the king of the same name ruling in the Samataṭa region in Bengal. But what has been read by Majumdar as *śrīdharapōraḥ*, and corrected as *śrīdharapauraḥ*, actually seems to have been written as *śrīvaramōraḥ* indicating the name of the feudatory king whom Mādhavavarman had shown favour by friendly gestures and perhaps by agreeing to grant land which was situated in the dominion of this feudatory chief.

98. *EI*, Vol. XXIV (1937-38), p. 150; S.C. Behera, *Rise and Fall of the Śailōdbhavas*, pp. 82-83; *IO*, Vol. I, Pt 2 (1958), p. 260.

The palaeographic peculiarity found in the Bugudā plates, together with the change of the king's name in his later records in verse (as Mādhavavarman instead of Mādhavarāja of his earlier grants in prose), have aroused suspicion among scholars about the identity of the ruler. Moreover, Ayaśōbhīta, father of Mādhavavarman II, has sometimes been mentioned as a descendant and sometimes as a son of Mādhavavarman I in the versified genealogy of the later records of the successors of this king. They have suggested, on the basis of the above information, that there existed two distinct groups of Śailōdbhava kings, and have accordingly designated them as "earlier" and " later".[99] According to them, Mādhavavarman-Sainyabhīta II of the versified records was a later Śailōdbhava king and ruled in about A.D. 850. He may have been the third ruler of the same name in the family. But the recent observations on these points would tend to suggest that Mādhavarāja-Sainyabhīta II was later endowed with the name of Mādhavavarman-Sainyabhīta II when he acquired sovereign status. The date attributed to this king would also clash with some of the known facts of history, as it is now a well-known fact that during the latter half of the eighth century A.D., the Buddhist kings of the Bhauma-kara dynasty of Tōsali and Utkala had already occupied the kingdom of Kōṅgōda-*maṇḍala* and the Śailōdbhavas had fallen into obscurity by that period.

It is now known that the predecessors of Mādhavavarman II were all feudatories who held petty principalities in the Ganjam region, first under the Vigrahas, then for some time under the Mudgalas. Mādhavarāja or Mādhavaraman I, described as the grandfather of Mādhavavarman II, is not yet known to have issued any charter. He is known only from his grandson's records and those of his successors. Presumably, Mādhavavarman I and his son Ayaśōbhīta had a very short reign, if they ever succeeded to the throne of Kōṅgōda. In view of the political disturbances that followed the downfall of the Vigrahas and the invasion of Śaśāṅka, it is quite probable that Ayaśōbhīta or his father could hardly find time to consolidate their power and position.

One of the important events during the reign of Mādhavavarman II is the visit by the Chinese pilgrim Hiuen-Tsang to Kōṅgōda in about A.D. 638. Interesting facts are known from his travel accounts relating to the political and socio-economic conditions of Kōṅgōda during the time. Mādhavavarman II was evidently on the throne of Kōṅgōda during that period, though there is no reference to the contemporary king of this country in the pilgrim's account. Hiuen-Tsang speaks highly of the people of Kōṅgōda. The relevant passage from his travels has been translated by Samuel Beal as follows:

> Within the limits of this country there are several tens of small towns which border on the mountains and are built contiguous to the sea. The cities themselves are strong and high; the soldiers are brave and daring; they rule by force the neighbouring provinces, so that no one can resist them. . . . This country, bordering on the sea, abounds in

99. *JAHRS*, Vol. X (1936-37), pp. 1-15.

> many rare and valuable articles. They use cowrie-shells and pearls in commercial transactions.[100]

Watters has put this somewhat differently: "As the towns were naturally strong, there was a gallant army which kept the neighbouring countries in awe, and so there was no powerful enemy."[101] The pilgrim also observed that "Rare and precious substances of various kinds from the sea-ports are bartered for merchandise."[102] Thus, the people of Kōṅgōda enjoyed a period of peace and prosperity during the reign of Mādhavavarman II-Sainyabhīta.

Mādhavavarman II was succeeded by his son Madhyamarāja *alias* Ayaśōbhīta, as known from his two extant copper-plate records (Nos. 51 and 52). The name Madhyamarāja assumed by the Śailōdbhava kings is known for the first time from these charters, though the secondary or coronation name Ayaśōbhīta seems to have been adopted from the grandfather of this king who is mentioned in the genealogy of the Śailōdbhavas in almost all their records. Madhyamarāja was thus the second king of the family to assume the name and may be called Ayaśōbhīta II. Unfortunately, one of these charters (No. 51) is incomplete. That the issuer of this charter was Madhyamarāja-Ayaśōbhīta II can only be known from a verse on the reverse of the second plate describing his achievements, the third plate being engraved with half a line of writing meant for introducing, in prose, the customary list of officials and others belonging to Kōṅgōda-*maṇḍala*. It is not known why the last plate was abandoned without the grant portion being engraved. The charter is reported to have been discovered in Banpur in Puri district. There are altogether twenty verses, of which twelve are already known from the records of Mādhavavarman II, the father of this king. The verse introducing king Mādhavendra, first found in the charters of his father and known to be one of his epithets, is also found to have been quoted in both the charters of his son Madhyamarāja. This has induced scholars to believe that the epithet found in the charters of the son and grandson of Mādhavavarman II was also used for all the kings of the dynasty, and all of them bore *Mādhavendra* or Mādhavavarman as a secondary name.

However, the verse seems to have been quoted from the predecessor's charter quite unintentionally, indeed, carelessly, only to introduce the predecessors of the issuers of the grants, as in the case of other subsequent verses which are also quoted from the earlier grants. For example, the third verse of the present grant of Madhyamarāja, introducing mount Mahendra as the *kulagiri*, seems to have been copied from the Cuttack Museum plates (No. 50) of Mādhavavarman II. Verses 4-12 of the charter are common to all the later records of Mādhavavarman II as well as his successors, dealing with the fabricated origin and the genealogy of the predecessors of Ayaśōbhīta II. Verses 13-20 of this record, which are also common to his other extant charter (No. 52), describe the career and achievements of

100. *Buddhist Records of the Western World*, pp. 206-7.
101. *On Yuan Chwang's Travels in India*, Vol. II, pp. 196-99.
102. Ibid., Vol. I, p. 178.

Ayaśōbhīta II. These eight verses are again found quoted in his successor's records. The language of these verses is defective in both his grants when compared to the other verses referring to his predecessors.

The royal seal attached to this charter (No. 51) contains the legend *śrī-madhyamarājaḥ* and the emblem of a couchant bull facing proper right. The palaeography, language and orthography of this inscription closely resemble his second extant charter (No. 52) discovered in Parikud in Puri district. The second grant was issued from Kaṭaka, though the reading of the name is doubtful due to the corroded nature of the plate. But the gift village is again stated to have been situated in Kaṭakabhukti *viṣaya* (district). Some scholars identify the locality with the modern town of Cuttack situated in the Mahanadi delta. On the basis of this assumption, they have attempted to stretch the northern boundary of the kingdom of Kōṅgōda-*maṇḍala* as far as the lower valley of the Mahanadi river.[103] It is now a well-known fact that the present locality of Cuttack was established long after the decline of the Śailōdbhavas, during the period of the imperial line of the Eastern Gaṅga dynasty in about the Śaka year 1152 (*c.* A.D. 1230), as known from epigraphic records. It has been rightly identified by Behera with the region around Purushottampur-Jaugaḍa in Ganjam district.[104] The locality of Pūrvakhaṇḍa, the division in which the gift village is stated to have been situated, can thus be identified with the region round Purushottampur, situated to the east of Aska town in the same district and still known by the same name. This division called Pūrvakhaṇḍa is now known to have been on the eastern side of the river Baḍanai or the Mahanadi of the Māṭhara records, which is why it seems to have been so named. Unfortunately, the name of the gift village in the copper-plate is lost due to corrosion. The date of the charter is given in the 26th regnal year of the king, written in words, which is repeated in numerical signs at the end of the record, though it is largely obliterated.

The genealogy of the Śailōdbhava kings furnished by these two grants of Madhyamarāja may thus be arranged in a tabular form:

Śailōdbhava
↓
Raṇabhīta
↓
Sainyabhīta I
↓
Ayaśōbhīta I
↓
Sainyabhīta-Mādhavavarman II-Śrīnivāsa
↓
Ayaśōbhīta II-Madhyamarāja

103. *JAHRS*, Vol. X (1936-37), pp. 1-15.
104. S.C. Behera, *Rise and Fall of the Śailōdbhavas*, p. 23.

This king has also been credited in his own grants to have performed the *aśvamedha* and other sacrifices. Like his father, he is stated to have taken an *avabhṛtha* bath in connection with the celebration of these sacrifices. A separate passage in both his records, ascribing the celebration of sacrifices to this king, would tend to indicate that Madhyamarāja ruled the kingdom with peace and prosperity for at least twenty-six years without any political disturbances. Nothing is known, however, about his political activities from these charters. He is described as a devout worshipper of the god Śiva, which is corroborated by the Śaivite symbol adopted in the seal attached to his charter.

The Parikud plates (No. 52) of this king refer to a land-measure called *timpira* (or *ṭimpira*) prevalent in different parts of the kingdom of Kōṅgōda-*maṇḍala.* This land-measure has also been referred to in a charter of Śambhuyaśas,[105] discovered in the northern part of Orissa. But frequent references to this measure in the grants of the Śailōdhavas would indicate that the land-measure was more popular in the southern part of Orissa during the seventh and eighth centuries A.D. The origin of the term *timpira* is, however, uncertain. It seems to have been prevalent in the region comprising the northern part of Ganjam district together with the part of Puri district around Chilka lake. Earlier, this region, as known from the records of Śambhuyaśas, was included in the kingdom of the Mudgalas during about A.D. 603.[106] The contemporary records of other regions in Orissa are silent about this land-measure, with the exception of the grant of Śambhuyaśas issued from the Balasore region. The early rulers of the Eastern Gaṅga dynasty of Kaliṅganagara, who are known to have been ruling contemporaneously in southern Ganjam and Srikakulam districts, have not referred to this land-measure in their epigraphs. It seems to have been originally confined to the region of Kōṅgōda-*maṇḍala.* It was introduced into the region of Uttara Tōsali by Śambhuyaśas for some time, though the term became obsolete here with the end of his rule. The Śailōdbhavas continued to follow this land-measure as long as they ruled Kōṅgōda-*maṇḍala,* as revealed by their epigraphs. The Cuttack Museum plates of Mādhavavarman (No. 50) refer to 23 *timpiras* of land donated to twenty-four brāhmaṇas. The Parikud plates of his son refer to 12 *timpiras* of land donated to twelve brāhmaṇas of different *gōtras*, each brāhmaṇa receiving one *timpira* of land.

Madhyamarāja ruled up to about the end of the seventh century A.D. It is to be noted that unlike the later charters of his father containing a versified introduction of the officers associated with the execution of the grants, his own records introduce the officers in prose. The same practice seems to have been followed by his successors, as known from the subsequent records of the family. The name of the engraver of the Parikud plates of this king has been doubtfully read as Dṛḍḍha or Dṛddha, which is the last part of his name. The correct name of the person seems to be Sthaviravṛddha, who was also the engraver of many of the copper-plate charters of Madhyamarāja's

105. See Section IV, No. 34 in this volume.
106. See Section IV, No. 36 in this volume.

son and successor. Moreover, the close resemblance in the letters engraved in all these grants of Madhyamarāja and his son would also corroborate this assumption.

Madhyamarāja-Ayaśōbhīta II was succeeded to the throne of Kōṅgōda-*maṇḍala* by his son Dharmarāja. Altogether, six copper-plate charters of this king have been discovered so far. They reveal that he had the secondary or coronation name of Mānabhīta. Moreover, they furnish important information on the political events that took place during the accession of this king. His earliest known record is the Ranpur grant (No. 53), issued during his 3rd regnal year from a locality called Mātṛcandra-*pāṭaka*. The name Mātṛcandra seems to have been very popular in the Kaliṅga region since earlier times. A person named Mātṛvara was associated with several copper-plate grants of the Māṭharas and the Pitṛbhaktas of about the fifth century A.D. A locality or *pāṭaka* may have been created by naming it after this person. Besides, there are references to one Mātṛcandra, the father of the writer of several early Eastern Gaṅga copper-plate records, during the last part of the seventh century A.D.[107] The locality seems to have been situated in the region of northern Kaliṅga, that is, in the Ganjam area, which later comprised the kingdom of Kōṅgōda-*maṇḍala* of the Śailōdbhavas.

All the six charters of Dharmarāja merely contain a selection of introductory verses referring to the legendary origin of the Śailōdbhava dynasty and the predecessors of the king, copied from his predecessors' grants. Only the verses describing the achievements of Dharmarāja have been added in these records. One of these verses, which is found quoted in all his six charters, gives us valuable historical information about the political situation at the time and about the Śailōdbhava kingdom when Dharmarāja ascended the throne. According to this verse, Dharmarāja had an elder brother named Mādhava. Dharmarāja claims that Mādhava had some ill-will against him and tried to usurp the throne of Kōṅgōda. Mādhava revolted and was defeated by Dharmarāja on the Phāsikā battlefield. Mādhava then fled and took shelter with a king named Tīvara. But Dharmarāja claims, in this verse, to have defeated and killed both Tīvara and Mādhava in a battle fought at the foot of the Vindhyas. The verse would clearly indicate that Dharmarāja was the younger brother of Mādhava, the legitimate successor of Madhyamarāja-Ayaśōbhīta II, though scholars have taken Mādhava to be the younger brother and the usurper of the throne of Kōṅgōda. The name Mādhava would evidently indicate that he was named after his grandfather Mādhvavarman II. He was the lawful heir to the throne of Kōṅgōda as he was the eldest son of his father Ayaśōbhīta II. The verse would tend to indicate that soon after the death of Ayaśōbhīta II, a fratricidal war followed between his two sons. But Mādhava, who may be taken as Mādhavavarman III, proved to be a weak ruler who could not hold his own against Dharmarāja in this struggle for succession. Thus, with the end of Madhyamarāja's rule, the main line of the Śailōdbhava dynasty started by Mādhavavarman II

---

107. *IO*, Vol. II (1960), pp. 63-85.

came to an end in Kōṅgōda. Dharmarāja, however, proved to be powerful and took advantage of the weakness of Mādhavavarman III. Though he executed a coup, he seems to have maintained the sovereignty of the kingdom throughout his period of rule, as revealed by his copper-plate grants. Other than his grandfather, he was the second known ruler of the dynasty to have issued the maximum number of copper-plate grants.

Dharmarāja assumed the secondary or coronation name of Mānabhīta, presumably after he captured the throne of Kōṅgōda. Neither the name Dharmarāja nor Mānabhīta assumed by any other ruler of the dynasty is to be found in the genealogical chart furnished by the Śailōdbhava records. The Sumaṇḍala charter of the time of Pṛthivīvigraha (No. 21) is known to have been issued by one Dharmarāja; but he is presumed to have been a remote ancestor of the Śailōdbhavas who flourished during the period when the dynastic name Śailōdbhava was unknown to the family.

Dharmarāja ruled for at least thirty years, as is known from his latest grant dated in his 30th regnal year (No. 58). All his grants are dated in his regnal years. He is known to have issued all the six charters from different places. Two of these charters (Nos. 53 and 56) were issued from the victorious Mātṛcandra-*pāṭaka*. His Nivina grant (No. 54) was issued from a locality named Alatālaṅghapura. The Banpur grant (No. 55) was issued from the locality called Āsiliḍa. The Chandeswar grant (No. 57) was issued from the royal residence at Kōntalayi. His Kōṇḍeḍḍā grant (No. 58) was issued from his victorious residence at Saumyapura. Unfortunately, none of these localities have been satisfactorily identified. S.C. Behera has, however, tried to identify Alatālaṅghapura with a locality called Loṅghara, situated about one mile from the Khallikote railway station.[108] All these places appear to be temporary residences of the king. Frequent references to Kōṅgōda as the chief city of the Śailōdbhava kingdom in the records of his predecessors are conspicuous by their absence in the charters of Dharmarāja.

Of the six copper-plate grants of Dharmarāja, four were engraved by Sthaviravṛddha, the same person who engraved one of the grants of his father (No. 52). The Banpur charter (No. 55) was engraved by Ādityadeva the *akṣaśālin*, while the engraver of the Nivina charter (No. 54) of this king was Chaḍḍibhōgin. The name of the engraver in the last-mentioned plates has been doubtfully read as Chaḍḍibhaya, although the correct name should be Chaḍḍibhōgin. This is the same person as the one mentioned in the Buguḍā and Purushottampur grants of Mādhavavarman II, the grandfather of Dharmarāja. Curiously, the letters of the Buguḍā plates of Mādhavavarman and the Nivina plates of Dharmarāja, which are similar to each other, do not tally with the letters of the other plates of Mādhavavarman II engraved by Chaḍḍibhōgin. It has already been discussed, while dealing with the palaeography of the charters of Mādhavavarman II, that the Buguḍā plates of this king were later re-engraved by Durgadeva of the time of Neṭṭabhañja of the Bhañja dynasty. The Nivina grant of Dharmarāja, similarly, was re-

108. S.C. Behera, *Rise and Fall of the Śailōdbhavas*, p. 24.

engraved at a later date, its palaeography closely resembling those found in the grants of Neṭṭabhañja and Vidyādharabhañja of the Bhañja family.

The distinction between the scripts used in this grant and the rest of the charters of Dharmarāja has not been emphasized earlier due to an oversight. Every letter in it belongs to a far later date and is similar to those prevalent in about the tenth century A.D. Further, the record has the general appearance of being fabricated at a later date. It seems to have been a mixed copy of the introductory verses from the charters of Mādhavavarman II and Dharmarāja's other records. The drafting of the passage dealing with the grant and the specification of the boundaries of the village is so defective that it is not possible to make out the real meaning of the words. The concluding portion, containing the names of the officers associated with the execution of the grant, seems to have been copied partly from a grant of Mādhavavarman II and partly from that of a charter of Dharmarāja. All the other charters of Dharmarāja refer to the *dūtaka* of the grant and, unlike the records of his grandfather, the officers are mentioned in a prose passage. But, in the case of the Nivina grant, it is observed that the scribe has attempted to copy the names of the officers from a draft of Mādhavavarman's record, as the expression *tanaya* after *mahākṣapaṭala. . . deva,* which is in verse, would indicate. The second part of a verse found at the end of Mādhavavarman's charters has been copied here. This is written as follows: *lāñchitaṁ jayasiṁhena utkīrṇam (c-ōtkirṇaṁ) chaḍḍibhōgin* [ǁ]. The first part of the verse in the grants of his grandfather reads: *likhit-ōpendrasiṁhena tanayaḥ kuṇḍa-bhōginaḥ* [।] which is conspicuously found omitted in this charter of Dharmarāja. Thus, the names of the writer and the real engraver of the charter are not given here. It may be pointed out here that Jayasiṁha, who affixed the seal in all the charters of Mādhavavarman II, as well as the engraver Chaḍḍibhōgin, are not found in any other extant charters of Dharmarāja. There is also no reason to believe that these two persons were different from those mentioned in the records of his grandfather as there is a long time gap between the two kings of the dynasty. This incomplete stanza was undoubtedly copied from the king's predecessors' records, which seems to be a deliberate attempt to forge the document at a later date. This is corroborated by another discrepancy found in the record under discussion. The number of year in the portion with the date of the record after the word *samvat* has been either deliberately or inadvertently omitted by the engraver. Further, the word *samvat* and the occasion of the grant have been incised before the imprecatory and benedictory verses and along with the description of the boundaries of the gift land, which is not usually found in other records of Dharmarāja. All his other records mention the date at the end. The name of the month and the fortnight have also been mentioned in a peculiar manner, giving the impression of being fabricated later. After the name of the month Vaiśākha, the bright night is mentioned as *śudi.* Again, it is written as *prathama pakṣa* or the first fortnight and then the day is given as the second day of the said fortnight. The sign for the final *t* of the word *samvat* has, however, been mistaken for the numerical symbol for 9 by the editor of the grant. It seems likely that the portion enumerating the grant of land in Nivina village situated in Khiṇḍiṅg-*ahāra* district, as well as the specification of the boundaries of the gift land which is hopelessly unintelligible, were fabricated when the grant was copied by an unknown engraver. Though the names of the localities may be genuine, it cannot be said with certainty if the name of the donee was fabricated.

The above observations on the Nivina grant of Dharmarāja would tend to suggest its spuriousness and the possibility that it was forged during the reign of the Bhañja kings in about the tenth century A.D., when they occupied a part of the kingdom of Kōṅgōda in the Ganjam region. Instances are not rare in early Indian history regarding the forgery of documents, especially for the purpose of establishing one's title over a plot of land. The alleged spuriousness of the Nalanda and Gaya plates of Samudragupta is already known to scholars.[109] The bad quality of the orthography in the passage relating to the grant of land and the specification of the boundaries, the portion of the body text misplaced (as in line 47) and the jumbled content would tend to indicate its spuriousness. It is possible that the Nivina charter was fabricated in order to legitimize the claim of the donee, whose name has been mentioned in the grant, over the land specified.

The religious title assumed by Dharmarāja was *paramamāheśvara,* a devout worshipper of lord Śiva, unlike his grandfather, whose only one grant revealed that he had the title of *paramabrāhmaṇya* when he was a feudatory of Śaśāṅka. It is, however, known from the royal seals attached to the grants of the Śailōdbhava kings that they were Śaivites. Ayaśōbhīta II is also known to have assumed the title of *paramamāheśvara*. It is interesting to note that the Nivina grant of Dharmarāja, unlike his other grants, omits this title and, instead, mentions the epithet of *parameśvara* for the king. It is also to be noted that the king in this grant has been endowed with the royal epithets of *paramabhaṭṭāraka, mahārājādhirāja* and *parameśvara,* which are conspicuous by their absence in other grants of the same king as well as in his predecessors' grants. The practice of using these epithets is frequently seen in the records of about the tenth century onwards. The absence of these epithets is a common feature of the Śailōdbhava records. The royal seal attached to the Nivina charter, according to the editor of the grant, is presumed to have contained the legend *śrī-mānabhītasya,* though the seal is stated to be a corroded one.

There is a reference to a road named after Dharmarāja in a copper-plate charter of Sāmantavarman of the Śvetaka branch of the Eastern Gaṅga dynasty,[110] which is stated to have led to Kaliṅga. This Dharmarāja has been taken by scholars to be the Śailōdbhava king of the same name. The provenance of this record is a locality called Kamā-Nalinākṣapur, situated in the vicinity of Jaugaḍa-Purushottampur in Ganjam district, which was earlier included in the kingdom of the Śailōdbhavas. This would evidently have us believe that the road was constructed in the name of Dharmarāja, the

109. D.C. Sircar, *Sel. Ins.*, Vol. I, pp. 262-66.
110. *OHRJ*, Vol. VII, No. 2 (1958), pp. 86-90; *IO*, Vol. II (1960), pp. 318 ff.

Śailōdbhava king. But nothing can be said with certainty in the absence of any other corroborative evidence. The genealogy of the dynasty, as furnished by the copper-plate charters of Dharmarāja as well as his predecessors, is furnished here in a tabular form:

Śailōdbhava
↓
Raṇabhīta
↓
Mādhavavarman-Sainyabhīta I
↓
Ayaśōbhīta I
↓
Mādhavavarman-Sainyabhīta II-Śrīnivāsa
↓
Madhyamarājā Ayaśōbhīta II
↓

↓ Mādhavavarman III ↓ Dharmarāja-Mānabhīta

We do not have any record of the successor of Dharmarāja-Mānabhīta except a stray copper-plate grant of one Madhyamarāja. This incomplete charter, however, sheds considerable light on the last days of Śailōdbhava rule in the Ganjam region. The forces of disintegration had already started during the last days of Dharmarāja's rule, as is evidenced from this stray grant. It furnishes a genealogy of the later Śailōdbhavas from Dharmarāja onwards, the other two plates containing an account of his predecessors now being lost. The record is known to have been found in the Tekkali region (now in Andhra Pradesh).

It is not possible to know the place of issue of the record due to its stray nature. It, however, states that Dharmarāja-Mānabhīta was succeeded by his son Madhyamarāja, having the secondary name Ayaśōbhīta. Thus, he seems to have been the third ruler bearing this coronation name of Ayaśōbhīta in the genealogical history of the dynasty. He also assumed the epithet of Raṇakṣōbha. It is stated in this grant that this Madhyamarāja, who may be taken as Madhyamarāja II, had no son to succeed to the throne of Kōṅgōda. He had a cousin-brother, a son of his uncle (*pitṛvya*) named Allaparāja. Evidently, this Allaparāja was the son of the Mādhava or Mādhavavarman III, the deceased elder brother of Dharmarāja-Mānabhīta who was defeated and killed at the foot of the Vindhyas. Allaparāja is stated in this record to have had a son named Tailapanibha, the crown prince (*yuvarāja*). We have no evidence to show if this Allaparāja or his son Tailapanibha ever ascended the throne of Kōṅgōda and, possibly, they died a premature death. Madhyamarāja III, who issued this charter, seems to be the son of Tailapanibha. Unfortunately, this stray charter does not tell us anything about the area that these later members of the family, ruled or the extent of the kingdom during the rule of Madhyamarāja III. The name of Kōṅgōda, the kingdom of the Śailōdbhavas or the place of its issue, is not to be found in this incomplete grant. Only a few verses found in the records of Dharmarāja-Mānabhīta that have been quoted in this grant, enable us to attribute it to the Śailōdbhava family. It furnishes the genealogy which is continued from Dharmarāja up to Madhyamarāja III. It is further known from this record that Madhyamarāja III became king when he was a boy, but it cannot be said how long he continued to rule. The record would have us believe that the kingdom, which had been greatly circumscribed after the rule of Dharmarāja-Mānabhīta, again passed over to the descendants or Mādhava or Mādhavavarman III, who belonged to the main line of the Śailōdbhava dynasty. Thus, the genealogy of the Śailōdbhava kings obtained from all these records would stand as follows:

Śailōdbhava
↓
Raṇabhīta
↓
Mādhavavarman I-Sainyabhīta I (or Mādhavarāja I)
↓
Ayaśōbhīta I
↓
Mādhavavarman II-Sainyabhīta II (or Mādhavarāja II)
↓
Madhyamarāja I-Ayaśōbhīta II
↓

Mādhava (or Mādhavavarman III)	Dharmarāja-Mānabhīta
↓	↓
Allaparāja	Madhyamarāja II-Ayaśōbhīta III
↓	
Yuvarāja Tailapanibha	
↓	
Madhyamarāja III	

Dharmarāja-Mānabhīta possibly ended his rule sometime during A.D. 726-27, if we take the date mentioned in his last known grant (No. 58) to be correct. His son Madhyamarāja II assumed the coronation name of Ayaśōbhīta III. He, perhaps, did not rule for long, as the political situation of the region during this period would tend to suggest. It seems, that Madhyamarāja III, the last known king of the dynasty, also could not have resisted the forces of disintegration. Possibly, during this period, the kingdom of Kōṅgōda-*maṇḍala* was annexed to the dominions of the Bhauma-karas, who were steadily gaining ground in the northern parts of Orissa at the time. They are known to have started an era of their own, which has now been proved to have commenced from about A.D. 736-37. Kōṅgōda-*maṇḍala* at first seems to have become a part of the kingdom of the Śvetaka branch of the Eastern Gaṅga dynasty, which was for some time under the control of the Bhauma-kara king Unmattakeśarin ruling from Virajā or the present Jajpur in Cuttack district. This is known from a copper-plate grant of the Gaṅga king Jayavarmadeva of Śvetaka, issued in *samvat* 50, when Unmattakeśarin was ruling from Virajā. The kingdom of Śvetaka, with its headquarters of the same name, comprised the Aska, Dharakote and Chikiti regions of Ganjam district on the left bank of the Baḍanai (or the ancient Mahanadi), and contiguous to the kingdom of the Śailōdbhavas. The capital of Śvetaka has been identified with the present locality of Chikiti in Ganjam district. The above *samvat* mentioned in the charter of Jayavarmadeva has been taken as the Bhauma era, corresponding to A.D. 786-87.[111] The record refers to a king named Rāṇaka Viṣavārṇava, who was installed as a feudatory in charge of the administration of Kōṅgōda-*maṇḍala*. It is known to have remained a *maṇḍala* or province under the control of the Bhauma-karas till the end of their rule. References to this *maṇḍala* frequently occur in the records of the Bhauma-karas[112] and it is known to have been governed by a feudatory king all along. After the decline of the Bhauma kingdom during about the first half of the tenth century A.D., the province of Kōṅgōda-*maṇḍala* passed into the hands of the Sōmavaṁśins of Kōsala and Utkala.[113] The latest reference to Kōṅgōda-*maṇḍala* is found in the Banpur grant of the Sōmavaṁśin king Indraratha, wherein the king is stated to have made a grant of land situated in this *maṇḍala*.[114] After the Sōmavaṁśins, the name of Kōṅgōda-*maṇḍala* was lost in obscurity. Thus, by the year A.D. 730, the downfall of the Śailōdbhavas was already imminent after the death of Dharmarāja-Mānabhīta. By the middle of the fourth decade of the eighth century, they were completely annihilated by the Bhauma-karas of Tōsali who had installed their own feudal chiefs in the region previously ruled by the Śailōdbhavas.

---

111. *IHQ*, Vol. XII (1936), pp. 489-93; *IO*, Vol. II (1960), pp. 258-63. The reading of the date in this grant is doubtful, though it is certain that Kōṅgōda was at that time already included in the Bhauma-kara kingdom.
112. *JAHRS*, Vol. IV (1929-30), pp. 189-94: *EI*, Vol. VI (1900-1), pp. 133 ff.; B. Misra, *Orissa Under the Bhauma Kings*, pp. 60-67.
113. *JBORS*, Vol. II, Pt 1 (1916), pp. 53 ff.
114. *JASB*, Vol. VIII, No. 4 (1966), pp. 271-76.

The chief city or the capital of the Śailōdbhavas during the early period of their rule was called Kōṅgōda, presumably named after the kingdom they ruled. The Ganjam grant of Mādhavarāja II (No. 45), issued from this city, gives a picturesque description of it. It is stated to have been situated on the bank of the river Sālimā. The river is now identified with the present Sāliā which runs past the township of Banpur in Puri district and flows into Chilka lake. Banpur is situated only four kilometres north-west of this lake. The town is now noted for several ancient temples and sculptures and for other antiques of great historical importance. It has also yielded a number of copper-plate records of the Śailōdbhavas (incorporated in this volume), the Bhauma-karas[115] as well as the Sōmavaṁśins.[116] Besides, the present township of Banpur and the area around it is full of archaeological remains ranging from about the seventh century A.D. to medieval times.

Hiuen-Tsang's description of the capital of Kōṅgōda states that it "is about 20 *li* in circuit which borders on a bay" (angle of the sea).[117] The bay here obviously denotes Chilka lake. Hiuen-Tsang's description of the capital of the Śailōdbhavas admirably points to the location of the township of Banpur, though some scholars are induced to identify Kōṅgōda with the recently discovered temple complex site at Baṅkāḍa at the foot of the hill of the same name in Puri district, which is situated at a distance of about 25 miles from Banpur and Chilka lake. Though the site is near the Sāliā river, it does not fit the description of the Chinese pilgrim. Rather, the town of Banpur, like the other ancient townships of Bhubaneswar and Jajpur, gives the impression, with all its archaeological remains, that the locality continued to flourish for a long time, at least since the time of the Śailōdbhavas.

As many as ten divisions or districts (*viṣayas*) of Kōṅgōda-*maṇḍala* are known from the inscriptions of the Śailōdbhavas. Their identification would tentatively determine the extent of the kingdom. The *viṣaya* or the district called Kṛṣṇagiri, mentioned in the record of Mādhavarāja II (No. 45), was obviously named after the hill of the same name, situated at a distance of about 18 miles from the present township of Khallikote in Ganjam district. The area around the hill formed a district during the rule of the Śailōdbhavas. Several archaeological remains, including old caves and temples, have been found at the foot of the hill. Of these, a Śaivite temple complex consisting of about twelve ruined temples is worthnoting. The gift village Chavalakkhaya, situated in this district, has been identified with the present locality of Chāilu in Khallikote tahsil.[118]

The *viṣaya* called Thōraṇa has been referred to in a number of copper-plate charters of the Śailōdbhava kings. The two grants of Mādhavavarman II (Nos. 46 and 49) and the Banpur grant of his grandson (No. 55) refer to this locality as a *viṣaya* or district. The area around the present locality of

115. *JBORS*, Vol. V (1919), pp. 571 ff.
116. *JASB*, Vol. VIII, No. 4 (1966), pp. 271 ff.
117. Samuel Beal, *Buddhist Records of the Western World*, pp. 206-7; T. Watters, *On Yuan Chwang's Travels in India*, Vol. II, pp. 196-97.
118. *IHQ*, Vol. VII (1931), p. 665.

Sōraṇa near Banpur in Puri district has been identified with this *viṣaya*. Villages known from these records to have been included in this *viṣaya* cannot be definitely identified with their present locations, although scholars have attempted to do so.[119]

The *viṣaya* called Guḍḍa found in the charter of Mādhavavarman II (No. 47) is obviously the area around the present township of Buguḍā in Ganjam district. The *pāṭaka* called Khadira-*pāṭaka*, indicating a division of the said *viṣaya*, has been mentioned in the record to have comprised the gift village Puipiṇō. Khadira-*pāṭaka* has been identified by B. Misra as the modern Khairaputi, situated about five miles to the north of Buguḍā. The gift village cannot be identified at present.

Devagrāma-*viṣaya*, mentioned in the Purushottampur plates (No. 48) of Mādhavavarman II, has been taken to be the same as Degam in the Kodala tahsil of Ganjam district. Jayapura-*viṣaya* of the Cuttack Museum plates (No. 50) is the area around the locality bearing the same name, and situated on the bank of the river Ṛṣikulyā near Purushottampur in the same district. This locality is also mentioned as Jayakaṭaka-*viṣaya* in the Dharakote charter of Śubhākaradeva[120] of the Bhauma-kara dynasty, which succeeded the Śailōdbhavas in the region during the subsequent period of history.

Kaṭakabhukti-*viṣaya* has so far been taken to be the present city of Cuttack. But it has already been pointed out that the present city of Cuttack was founded much later, during about Śaka 1152 (A.D. 1230-31). The record probably meant the locality called Jayakaṭaka, or the same Jayapura on the eastern bank of Ṛṣikulyā river mentioned in the Cuttack Museum plates (No. 50). Pūrvakhaṇḍa, stated to have included in this *viṣaya* in the Parikud grant of Madhyamarāja-Ayaśōbhīta II (No. 52), is still known by the same name, which comprised the area around Purushottampur on the eastern bank of the river Ṛṣikulyā in Ganjam district.

Some of the *viṣayas* and other divisions mentioned in the Śailōdbhava charters could not be identified due to the defective reading of the texts and also due to the bad preservation of the charters. The district name read as Kirātatalaka in the Chandeswar plates (No. 57) has remained unidentified due to the doubtful reading of the name. Though the reading of the *viṣaya* called Tanekaṇḍrā mentioned in the Ranpur grant of Dharmarāja (No. 53) is doubtful, it has been tentatively identified with Kaṇḍarāsiṅgi or Keraṇḍa-Tāṅgi near Ranpur in Puri district.[121] The gift village called Usavāṭaka has been accordingly identified with the present Ustapada near Ranpur in the same district, which is also reported to be the findspot of the said charter.

The Nivinā (No. 54) and Kōṇḍeḍḍā (No. 58) charters of Dharmarāja-Mānabhīta mention the *viṣaya* name Khiṇḍiṅg-*ahāra,* identified with the area around the present village of Khidiṅgi in the Kodala taluk of Ganjam district.

---

119. S.C. Behera, *Rise and Fall of the Śailōdbhavas*, p. 21.
120. *JAHRS*, Vol. IV (1930), pp. 189-94.
121. S.C. Behera, op. cit., p. 23.

The gift village Nivinā is the same as the modern Nimina, which is situated in the same area and is also the findspot of the record of Dharmarāja. The *viṣaya* is found in a number of copper-plate inscriptions of the later period and in the area under discussion.[122] It was also included as a *viṣaya* in the kingdom of Kōṅgōda earlier ruled by Charamparāja.[123]

The Puri plates of Dharmarāja (No. 56) refer to Vartini *viṣaya,* which is the present locality bearing the same name situated in the Athgarh taluk of Ganjam district. The same *viṣaya* is found mentioned in the Patiakela grant of Śivarāja, the feudatory of the Mudgala king Śambhuyaśas. During his time, the *viṣaya* was included in Dakṣiṇa Tōsali.[124] The area around the *viṣaya* is of great archaeological importance. Quite a number of copper-plate inscriptions of the subsequent period have been discovered in this region, which include those of the Bhañjas of Khiñjali-*maṇḍala* and different branches of the Gaṅga dynasty of Kaliṅga.[125] Besides, the ruins of ancient temples are found here.

The records of the Śailōdbhavas would have us believe that mount Mahendra, described as the *kulagiri,* marked the southern boundary of Kōṅgōda. Hiuen-Tsang refers to the kingdom of Kōṅgōda as "bordering on a bay". The epigraphic records also corroborate this statement that the eastern boundary of the kingdom was the Bay of Bengal and Chilka lake. The localities mentioned in the copper-plate grants would tend to suggest that the south-western boundary of the kingdom was the river Ṛṣikulyā. To the south of this river was the hilly tract of Śvetaka, comprising the present Chatrapur-Chikiti regions, the kingdom of one of the branches of the early Eastern Gaṅgas. This was the south-western frontier of the kingdom of Kōṅgōda-*maṇḍala.* The western boundary of this kingdom was the present Baḍanai or the river Mahanadi of earlier times, which joins the Ṛṣikulyā near Bhañjanagar. The western bank of this river comprised a separate kingdom later known as Khiñjali-*maṇḍala,* the kingdom of the Bhañjas. The northern part of Puri district, up to at least Khurda subdivision, formed the northern boundary of Kōṅgōda. Thus, the region round Chilka lake comprising the two districts of Puri and Ganjam was the kingdom of the Śailōdbhavas.

Some scholars correlate the Śailōdbhavas of Kōṅgōda with the Śailendra dynasty, which established a powerful empire in the Malay Peninsula and Malay Archipelago in the eighth century A.D. It is believed that the Śailōdbhava probably migrated from Kōṅgōda and established a new empire with the dynasty named Śailendra.[126] Some scholars have even attempted to connect the Śailōdbhavas with the royal family called Śailavaṁśa who

122. The *viṣaya* and its contiguous areas seem to have formed a principality known as Khiṇḍiraśṛṅga-*maṇḍala* ruled by the kings named Bhīmasena and Narendradhavala of a later Nala family during the first part of the eleventh century A.D. See *OHRJ,* Vol. VI, No. 1 (1957), pp. 11 ff.; Vol. XXII (1976), pp. 53-57.
123. See Section II in this volume.
124. See Section IV, No. 35 in this volume.
125. *EI,* Vol. XXIV (1937-38), pp. 15-20; *IO,* Vol. VI (1974), pp. 215-19; *JAHRS,* Vol. III (1925-26), pp. 30 ff.; *EI,* Vol. XXVIII (1949-50), pp. 63 ff.
126. *HCIP,* Vol. III, *The Classical Age,* (1954), p. 147.

established a kingdom in the region around Balaghat district in Madhya Pradesh. The kings of this family are stated to have originally lived in the Kailās region and later came to be known as the lords of the Vindhyas.[127] Both these hypotheses lack definite evidence.

127. *EI*, Vol. IX (1907-8), p. 41.

I

INSCRIPTIONS OF THE MĀṬHARAS, THE VĀSIṢṬHAS AND THE PITṚBHAKTAS OF SOUTHERN ORISSA

NO. 1: RAGOLU PLATES OF ŚAKTIVARMAN, YEAR 13

Provenance	:	Ragolu, Chicacole district, Andhra Pradesh.
References	:	E. Hultzsch, *EI*, Vol. XII (1913-14) pp.1-3 and Plates; and S. N. Rajaguru, *IO*, Vol. I, Pt. 2, pp. 21-24.
Language	:	Sanskrit, in prose, except the three verses at the end.
Metre	:	Verses 1-3 *anuṣṭubh.*
Script	:	Southern variety of about the fifth century A.D.
Date	:	13th regnal year, the full-moon day of the month of Vaiśākha.

TEXT[1]

First Plate: Second Side

1 सिद्धिरस्तु ।। स्वस्ति विजय**पिष्टपुरा**त्कलिङ्गाधि-
2 पतिर्म्माठ[र][2] कुलालङ्करिष्णुर्व्वासिष्ठीपुत्रो
3 **महाराजश्री श[क्ति]वर्म्मा** कलिङ्गविषये
4 राकलुवग्रामे सर्व्वसमन्वागतान्गृहपतिकान्[3]

Second Plate: First Side

5 आज्ञापयति [।*] अस्त्येष ग्रामकोस्माभिः स्वपु-
6 ण्यायुर्ब्बलवृद्धये आचन्द्रतारकादग्रहारं
7 [कृत्वा सावर्ण्ण]सगोत्रपञ्चार्षेयवाजसनेयि-
8 ब्राह्मणकुमारशर्म्मणेष्टाभ्यश्च पु[त्रेभ्य]

Second Plate: Second Side

9 एवमेतस्मै गोत्राय दत्तः अभटप्रावेश्यः
10 सर्व्वकरप्रदेयैश्च परिहृतस्तज्ज्ञात्वा युष्माभिः
11 पूर्व्वप्रवृत्तया मर्य्यादयोपस्थानङ्कर्त्त-

1. From the facsimile in *EI*, Vol. XII (1913-14), pp. 2-3.
2. Hultzsch reads र्म्माग[ध].
3. Hultzsch reads. . . गतान्तहपतितान्.

12 व्यम्मेयहिरण्याद्यञ्चोपनेयम् [।*]

Third Plate: First Side

13 अस्मद्गोत्रजाश्च वाच्या: [।*] य: प्रमादाल्लोभाद्वास्य
14 लोपं कुर्य्यात्स पञ्चमहापातकसंयुक्तो भवेत् [।*]
15 ये चान्ये राजानस्तांश्च विज्ञापयति [।*] राजधर्म्मोय-
16 मित्यनुपालयितव्य: [।*] भवन्ति चात्र प्रागभिहिता:

Third Plate: Second Side

17 श्लोका: [।*] बहुभिर्व्वसुधा दत्ता वसुधा वसुधाधिपै: [।*]
18 यस्य यस्य यदा भूमिस्तस्य तस्य तदा फलम् [।।*१]
19 षष्टि वर्षसहस्राणि स्वर्ग्गे वसति भूमिद: [।*]
20 आक्षेप्ता चानुमन्ता च तान्येव नरके वसे[त्] [।।*२]

Fourth Plate: First Side

21 पूर्व्वदत्तान्द्विजातिभ्यो यत्नाद्रक्ष युधिष्ठिर [।*]
22 महीम्महिमतां श्रेष्ठ दानाच्छ्रेयोनुपालनमिति [।।*३]
23 **स(सं)वत्सरे त्रयोदशे वैशाखपोर्ण्णमास्याम्** [।*]
24 स्वयमाज्ञा(ज्ञ)प्तिरमात्यार्जुनदत्तेन लिखितम् [।।*]

ABSTRACT

Lines 1-4 of the charter refer to the reigning king **Mahārāja Śaktivarman,** the ornament of the Māṭhara family, the son of Vāsiṣṭhī, who issued the royal order from the victorious Piṣṭapura, addressing the inhabitants accompanied by all others of the village of Rākaluva, situated in the *viṣaya* of Kaliṅga. This is followed by the grant of the said village, in lines 5-12, by the king, for the increase of his own merit, life and power, having made it an *agrahāra,* to the brāhmaṇa Kumāraśarman and to his eight sons who belonged to the Sāvarṇa *gōtra*, *pañcārṣēya* (*pravara*) and the Vājasanēya (*śākhā*), as long as the moon and the stars exist. The donees were exempted from all taxes and dues, and the soldiers were restricted from entering the gift village. The inhabitants were further directed to attend to the donees and pay them the usual *mēya* (share of the produce) and *hiraṇya* (tax in cash), according to the established rule. Lines 13-14 refer to the donor's admonition to his descendants that whosoever confiscates the grant would be guilty of five great sins. Lines 15-16 refer to the donor's request to other kings to preserve the grant as their own duty. Lines 17-22 contain three of the usual imprecatory and benedictory verses. Line 23 refers to the **date** of the grant in the **regnal year** of the king as **the year 13, the full-moon day of the month of Vaiśākha**. Line 24 mentions that the order relating to the grant was given by the king himself and the charter was written by the *amātya* (minister) Arjunadatta.

NO. 2: NIṄGŌṆḌI GRANT OF PRABHAÑJANAVARMAN

Provenance	:	Parlakhimedi, Ganjam district, Orissa.
References	:	L. N. Jagadev, *Vaitaraṇī* (in Oriya), Vol. IV (1930); D.C. Sircar, *EI*, Vol. XXX (1954), pp. 112-18 and Plates; and S. N. Rajaguru, *IO*, Vol. I, Pt. 2 (1958), pp. 44-47.
Language	:	Sanskrit, in prose, except three of the imprecatory and benedictory verses at the end.
Metre	:	Verses 1-3 *anuṣṭubh*.
Script	:	Southern variety of the alphabet of about the fifth century A.D.
Date	:	The twelfth day of the bright fortnight of the month of Kārttika.

TEXT[1]

First Plate

1 स्वस्ति [।।*] विजयसिङ्ह(सिंह)पुरात् भगव[त्*] स्वामि नारायणपादानुध्यात: मा-
2 ठरकुलकीर्त्तिवर्द्धनकर[:] श्रीशङ्करवर्म्मण[:*]पौत्र[:*] कृष्णवेन्नाम-
3 हानद्यन्तर(रं) स्वप्रजाधर्म्मेण(णा)नुशासिन[:*]श्रीशक्तिवर्म्मण[:] पुत्र[:*] स्व-
4 कुलालङ्करिष्णुस्सकलकलिङ्गाधिपति[:] **श्रीमहाराजप्रभञ्जनवर्म्मा**

Second Plate: First Side

5 अस्ति होणरामग्रामे[2] सर्व्वसमवेता[न्*]कुटुम्बिन[:*] समाज्ञापयति [।*] य एष ग्रा-
6 माछे(च्छे)द्येन उत्तरेण रुक्मपति[:*] पश्चिमेण(न) व्याघ्रप्रस्तरशाल्मलीवृ-
7 क्षस्यु(स्था)यिवा(व)ल्मीक(क:) दक्षिणेन समुद्र एभिर्व्वे[3] सीमै[:*] आचन्द्रतारकप्रति-
8 ष्ठं निङ्गोण्डि[:*] अग्रहारं कृत्वा नानाविधगोत्त्रश्च(च)रणेभ्य[:*][4] संप्र[द*]त्त: [।*]

---

1. From the facsimile in *EI*, Vol. XXX (1954), pp. 116-17; the charter is now preserved in the Orissa State Museum, Bhubaneswar.
2. D.C. Sircar reads अस्तिहोणरामग्रामे; he believes अस्तिहोण and रामग्राम are two adjacent places. The locality seems to be the same as Hoṇareṅga of the charter of Umāvarman (No. 5).
3. Read एभिरेव.
4. The scribe has dropped the word ब्राह्मणेभ्य: ।

Second Plate: Second Side

9 तदेवं विदित्वा युष्माभि[:*] पूर्व्वोचितमर्य्यादयोपस्थानं कर्त्तव्यमिति मेयहिर-

10 न्या(ण्या)दि चोपनेयं [5]भविष्यराज्ञश्च संपूजया सुधर्म्मक्रमविक्रमाभ्यां

11 दानमनुपालनञ्चेति[।*][5] एष खलु स्वधर्म्म[:*] अपि चात्र व्यासगीता:(तान्)

12 श्लोकानुदाहरन्ति [।*] बहुभिर्व्वसुधा दत्ता:(त्ता) वसु(हु)धा वसुधाधिपै[:*।] यस्य य-

Third Plate

13 [स्य यदा] भूमि [स्*] तस्य [तस्य] तदा फलं(लम्) [।।*१] स्वदत्ता(त्तां) परदत्तां वा यत्नाद्रक्ष यु[धि]ष्ठि[र । म]-

14 हीं महीमतां श्रेष्ठ दानाच्छ्रेयोनुपालनं(नम्) [।।*२] षष्टिवर्षसहस्राणि स्वर्गे मोदति भूमिद[:*] आ-

15 क्षेता [चा]नुमन्ता च तान्येव नरके वसेत् । [।*३] सा(सां)वत्सरिककरपणाग्रशतौ द्वौ[6] [।*] **कार्त्ति-**

16 **कशुक्लपक्षदिवसो द्वादशी**[7] [।*]आज्ञप्ति[:*] महाप्रतीहारदूतो महादण्डनायक [ज्येष्ठ][:*।।]

ABSTRACT

The charter begins with the word *svasti* and a reference to the victorious city of Siṁhapura, the place of its issue, in line 1. It then introduces, (lines 1-4) the reigning king, the illustrious **Mahārāja Prabhañjanavarman,** the donor of the grant. He is described as the son of Śaktivarman and the grandson of Śaṅkaravarman, a devotee of Bhagavat-svāmi-Nārāyaṇa, as the increaser of the fame of the Māṭhara family, and as the lord of the entire Kaliṅga country. Line 5 refers to the king's order regarding the grant, to the farmers assembled at the locality called Hōṇarāma. The boundaries of the village Hōṇarāma are specified in lines 6-7 as bounded by Rukmapati in the north, Vyaghra-prastara and a Śālmalī tree together with a mole-hill in the west and the sea in the south. The area granted was named as Niṅgōṇḍi and made a permanent *agrahāra* till the moon and the stars exist. The grant was made in favour of some brāhmaṇas belonging to different *gōtras* and *caraṇas*. The cultivators are advised in lines 9-10 to attend on the donees according to the established custom and to regularly

5. The passage in other records reads भविष्यतश्च राज्ञो विज्ञापयामि; धर्मक्रमविक्रमाणामिदं दानम् सद्धर्ममनुपश्य-द्भिरेषोग्रहारोनुपाल्य: ।

6. Read शते द्वे.

7. The absence of the year seems to be due to the inadvertance of the scribe of the charter or the engraver of the plates.

offer them *mēya* (share of the produce) and *hiraṇya* (tax in cash). Future rulers are then requested to protect the grant by taking it as the *sva-dharma* of the kings. Three of the usual imprecatory verses are next quoted from Vyāsa. In line 15, reference is made to the annual rent fixed at two hundred *paṇas* to be payable for the grant. Lines 15-16 refer to the **date** as **the twelfth day of the bright fortnight of the month of Kārttika** when the grant was issued. The charter ends with the mention of the *ājñapti* or executor of the grant named Jyēṣṭha, designated as *mahādaṇḍanāyaka*, who acted as a *duta* or representative of the *mahāpratihāra*.

NO. 3: ANDHAVARAM PLATES OF ANANTAŚAKTIVARMAN, YEAR 14

Provenance	:	Andhavaram, Srikakulam district, Andhra Pradesh.
References	:	R. Subrahmanyam, *EI*, Vol. XXVIII (1949-50), pp. 175-79 and plate; and S.N. Rajaguru, *IO*, Vol. I, Pt. 2 (1958), pp. 13-16.
Language	:	Sanskrit, in prose, except for the two benedictory verses at the end.
Metre	:	Verses 1-2 *anuṣṭubh*.
Script	:	Southern variety of about the fifth century A.D.
Date	:	14th regnal year, the fifth day of the bright fortnight of the month of Śrāvaṇa.

TEXT[1]

First Plate

1 स्वस्ति [।*] महाहस्त्यश्वस्कन्धावाराद्विजय[**सिंह** *] पुराद्भगवतᳵक-
2 मलनिलयाक्रान्तवक्षसो नारायणस्वामिनᳶपादभक्तः
3 परमदैवत[:*] बप्पभट्टारकपादप्रसादावाप्तशरीर-
4 राज्यविभवप्रतापो माठरकुलालङ्करिष्णुः कलिङ्गाधिप-

Second Plate: First Side

5 ति**श्श्रीमन्महाराजानन्तशक्तिवर्म्म** [।*] आन्दोरेप्पग्रामे[2]सव्व(र्व्व)स-
6 मन्वागतान्कुटुम्बिनस्समाज्ञापयति [।*] अस्त्यवनिपयथोक्त-
7 धर्म्मावस्थानविजितत्रिविष्टपैरार्य्यकशक्ति भट्टारकपा-
8 दैः नानागोत्रचरणेभ्यो[3] ब्राह्मणेभ्यः पूर्व्वदत्त इत्यस्मा-

---

1. From the facsimile in *EI*, Vol. XXVIII (1949-50).
2. This village has been mentioned as आन्दोरक in the Andhavaram plates of the Eastern Gaṅga king Indravarman (*EI*, Vol. XXX (1954), pp. 37-42). This locality has been identified with the present Andhavaram in Srikakulam district, Andhra Pradesh.
3. Subrahmanyam reads नानागोत्रनानाचरणेभ्यो, but the word नाना is not in the facsimile.

Second Plate: Second Side

9 भिरपि स्वपुण्यायुर्य्यशोभिवृद्धये आसहस्रांशुशशितार-
10 कादग्रहारङ्कृत्वा सर्व्वपरिहारैश्च परिहृत्यैभ्यो ब्राह्मणकु-
11 लेभ्योतिसृष्टः [।।*]तदेवं ज्ञात्वा युष्माभिरुचितोपस्थानङ्क-
12 र्त्तव्यम् [।*] भविष्यद्राजांश्च विज्ञापयति युष्माभिरपि प्रवृत्तकम्

Third Plate: First Side

13 इमन्दानधर्म्मनुपश्यद्भिरेषोग्रहारोनुपाल्यः [।*]
14 अपि चात्र मनुव्यासगीतौ श्लोकौ भवतः [।*] बहुभिर्व्वहुधा द-
15 त्ता वसुधा वसुधाधिपैः[।*] यस्य यस्य यदा भूमिस्तस्य
16 तस्य तदा फलम् [।।*१] पूर्व्वदत्तान्द्विजातिभ्यो यत्नाद्रक्ष युधिष्ठिर [।*]

Third Plate: Second Side

17 महिम्महिमतां श्रेष्ठ दानाच्छ्रेयोनुपालनमिति ।। आज्ञप्तिः
18 महादण्डनायकाः [।*] **संवत्सरश्चतुर्द्दशः १०.४ श्रावण-**
19 **शुक्लपञ्चम्याम्** ५ [।*] देशाक्षपटलाधिकृत दण्डनायक-
20 मातृवरेण लिखितमिति ।।। ।।।[4]

ABSTRACT

After the word *svasti,* lines 1-6 of the charter record that the reigning king **Mahārāja Anantaśaktivarman**, an ornament of the Māṭhara family, a devout worshipper of the lotus feet of the god Nārāyaṇa, an inheritor of the body, kingdom, prosperity and prowess through devotion at the feet of the Lord, the father, and the lord of Kaliṅga, issued the royal order addressing the residents of the village of Āndōreppa, from the army camp Vijaya-(Siṁha*?)pura. Lines 6-11 record that the gift village was made an *agrahāra,* free of all taxes and donated to a number of brāhmaṇa families belonging to various *gōtras* and *caraṇas,* to whom the village was earlier granted by *Āryaka*-Śakti-*bhaṭṭāraka,*[5] described as the conqueror of the celestial beings by the incessant practice of *dharma.* The future rulers are then requested, in lines 12-13, to honour and maintain the gift. This is followed by two of the usual benedictory verses said to have been quoted from

---

4. There is floral design between the two sets of triple *daṇḍas* and a wavy line at the end.
5. A number of brāhmaṇa residents of the said village are known to have been donees of the Andhavaram plates of the Eastern Gaṅga king Indravarman of the Gaṅga year 133 (*EI,* Vol. XXX (1954), pp. 41 ff.).

Manu and Vyāsa (lines 14-17). Lines 17-18 mention the executor or *ājñapti* of the grant to be one *mahādaṇḍanāyaka* (commander-in-chief). Lines 18-19 state the **date** of the issue of the grant as **the 14th regnal year** of the king, **the fifth day of the bright fortnight of the month of Śrāvaṇa**. Lines 19-20 state that the record was written by Mātṛvara, who acted as the *daṇḍanāyaka* and *dēśākṣapaṭalādhikṛta* (record-keeper of the district).

NO. 4: MADRAS MUSEUM PLATES OF ANANTAŚAKTIVARMAN, YEAR 28

Provenance	:	Not known, now preserved in the Government Museum, Madras.
References	:	M. Venkataramayya, *EI*, Vol. XXVIII (1949-50), pp. 227-35 and plate; S.N. Rajaguru, *IO*, Vol. I, Pt. 2 (1958), pp. 17-20.
Language	:	Sanskrit, in prose, except the imprecatory verses in lines 13-17.
Metre	:	Verses 1-3 *anuṣṭubh*.
Script	:	Southern class of alphabet of about the fifth century A.D.
Date	:	28th regnal year, the tenth day of the bright fortnight of the month of Phālguna.

TEXT[1]

First Plate

1 स्वस्ति [।*] व(वि)जय**सिङ्ह(सिंह)**पुरात्त(त्प)रमदैवतबप्पभट्टारकपादप्रसा-
2 दावात्तशरीरराज्यविभव:[2] माठरकुलालङ्का(ङ्क)रिष्णुकलिङ्गाधिप-
3 ति**श्रीमन्महाराज**[3] **अनन्तशक्तिवर्म्मा** ब(व)राहवर्त्तन्या आविपारिश्वे
4 सकुणक[4] ग्राम(मे) सर्व्वसमवेताङ्कु(न्कु)टुम्बिना(न:) समाज्ञापयति [।*] अ-
5 स्त्येषग्रामोस्माभिआ(रा)त्मन: पुन्या(ण्या)युर्य्यशोभिवृद्धये[5] अस्मै

Second Plate: First Side

6 कात्यायनसगोत्राय तेतृ(त्तिरी)य सब्रह्मचारिब्राह्म-
7 णनागशर्म्मणे दुर्ग्गशर्म्मणेभ्यो द्वौ भ्रातरौ[6] आचन्द्रतारक-
8 प्रतिष्ठमग्ग्रहारं कृत्वातिसृष्ट: [।*] तदेव(वं)विदित्वा यु-
9 ष्माभिर्य्यथोचितमर्य्य(र्य्या)दयोपस्थान(नं) कर्त्तव्य:(व्यम्) [। *] भविश्य(ष्य)तश्च

1. From the facsimile in *EI*, Vol. XXVIII (1949-50), pp. 234 and 235.
2. The rule of *sandhi* is not observed here.
3. The rule of *sandhi* is not observed here.
4. There seem to be two illegible letters after ण and क.
5. *Sandhi* is not observed here.
6. The correct reading shoud be दुर्ग्गशर्म्मणे चाभ्यां द्वाभ्यां भ्रातृभ्याम्.

10 राज्ञो विज्ञापयति धर्म्मक्क्रमविक्क्रमाणामन्यतमयोगा-

Second Plate: Second Side

11 दवाप्य महीमनुशासनाम् प्रवृत्तकमिमन्दानधर्म्ममनुप-

12 श्यद्भि:[7] एषोग्रहारोनुपाल्य[:] [।*] भवति(न्ति) चात्र व्यास[गी]ता [:*] श्लोका[:*।] ब-

13 हुभिर्व्वहुधा दत्ता वसुधा वसुधाधिपै[:*।] यस्य यस्य

14 यदा भूमिस्तस्य तस्य तदा फलम् [।*१] षष्ठि(ष्टि)वर्षसहस्रा-

15 णि स्वर्ग्गे वसति भूमिद: [।*] आक्षेप्ता चानुमन्ता च तान्येव न-

Third Plate

16 रके वसेत् [।।२*] पूर्व्वदत्तां दिजातिभ्यो यत्नाद्रक्ष युधिष्ठिर [।*] महि-

17 म्महिमता(तां) श्रेष्ठ दानाच्छ्रेयोनुपालनमिति [।।*३] दूतौ कु-

18 मारामातौ(त्यौ) महाव(ब)लाधिकृतदण्डनेतृशिवभोजक-

19 वसुदतौ(त्तौ) **।। संवत्सरम् २०८ फ(फा)ल्गुण(न)शुक्लपक्ष दश[म्यां]** लि]-

20 खितम् देशाक्षपटलाधिकृत[त*]लवरार्ज्जुनदत्तेन ।।

ABSTRACT

The inscription begins with the word *svasti.* Lines 1-4 state that the reigning king **Anantaśaktivarman** of the Māṭhara dynasty, who has been described as *paramadaivata* and credited to have obtained his body, kingdom and prosperity through the grace of his father, and to have borne the title of the lord of Kaliṅga, issued the order from the victorious **Simhapura**, addressing the inhabitants of the village of Sakuṇaka, situated in the district of Varāhavartani. The order relating to the grant of the said village is recorded (lines 5-8) to have been made in favour of the two brāhmaṇa brothers named Nāgaśarman and Durgaśarman of Kātyāyana *gōtra* and Taittirīya (*śākhā*) by the king for obtaining religious merit, which was to last as long as the moon and the stars exist. The gift village was converted into an *agrahāra*. The inhabitants, as well as the future rulers, were requested to honour the gift in lines 8-12. This is followed by three of the usual imprecatory and benedictory verses in lines 12-17. The names of the two *dūtakas,* who were the executors of the royal gift, are given (lines 17-19) as Śivabhōjaka and Vasudatta who have been designated as *kumārāmātya, mahābalādhikṛta* and *daṇḍanetṛ*. The grant is stated in line 19 to have been issued in **the 28th regnal year of the king, on the 10th day of the bright fortnight of the month of Phālguna.** In line 20, the record is stated to have been written by the *deśākṣapaṭalādhikṛta* and *talavara* named Arjunadatta.

7. *Sandhi* has not been observed here.

NO. 5: SIRIPURAM PLATES OF ANANTAVARMAN

Provenance : Siripuram, Srikakulam district.
References : G.V. Srinivasa Rao, *EI*, Vol. XXIV (1937-38), pp. 47-52 and plate; M. Narasimham, *Bhāratī* (Telugu), September 1931; and S.N. Rajaguru, *IO*, Vol. I, Pt. 2 (1958), pp. 31-32.
Language : Sanskrit, in prose.
Script : Southern variety of about the fifth century A.D.
Date : *Mahāśvayuja*, on the full-moon day in the month of Māgha.

TEXT[1]

First Plate

1 सिद्धम्[2] स्वस्ति [।।*] विजय**देवपुरा**द्वासिष्ठविपुलामलसकलचन्द्रमसो
2 विभ्रत्भू(द्भू)हिरन्य(ण्य)[3] गोसहस्राद्यनेकदानधर्म्माभिरतस्य शक्तित्रयो-
3 पनतराज्यसंप्प(म्प)दस्य[4] अत्यु(त्य)ता(न्ता)मलशरच्चन्द्रचन्द्रिकावदातोरु-
4 यशस[:*] श्री[मन्]महाराजगुणवर्म्मण: आत्मजन्मनोनेकगुणगणा-
5 भ्यलंकृतस्य श्रीमां(मन्) महाराजप्रभज्ज(ञ्ज)नवर्म्मण: सूनुर्ण्ण(र्न्न)यविनय-
6 सत्यशौचाचारत्यागौदार्य्यदाक्षिण्योत्स्सा(त्सा)हसात्वसप्पनो[5] स्वभुज-

Second Plate: First Side

7 विक्रमोपार्ज्जितभू ≍ प्रजाहिततरतो(त:)परममाहेश्वर(रो)मातापि-
8 तृपादानुध्यातो(त:)**श्रीकलिङ्गाधिपतिरनं(न)न्तवर्म्मा** तोण्टापरेस्सम[6]
9 वेतां(तान्)कुटुम्बिनस्समाज्ञापय[त्य*]स्त्येष:(ष) पूर्व्वमेवाग्रहार: खरपुरि-
10 मदम्वसामान्य:(न्य) कर:(र)प्रद: तेभ्य एवस्स[7] इदानीमस्माभि: पुन्यायुर्य्य-

1. From the facsimile in the *EI*, Vol. XXIV (1937-38), pp. 50-51.
2. Expressed by a symbol.
3. The letter न्य is inserted below the line with a small cross above the line.
4. Read सम्पद: .
5. Read सत्त्वसम्पन्न: .
6. Read तोण्टापरे सम-.
7. Read एव स.

11 षसामभिवृद्धये[8] यजनयाजनयाजनाध्ययन(ना)ध्यापनदान:[9](न)प्रति-
12 ग्रहनिरतेभ्यो(भ्य) आत्रगोत्रचरणेभ्यो[10] ब्राह्मणेभ्य: अष्टाश्शक[11] संख्येभ्य[:]

Second Plate: Second Side

13 **महाश्वयुजे स(सं)व्व(व)त्सरे माघमासपौर्ण्णमास्या[मु*]**दकपूर्व्वं कृत्वा
14 सर्व्वकरपरिहारै≍परिहृत्य खरपुरिषमदम्बविनिर्ग्गतं
15 पत्तनभोगविनिर्गतंञ्च(तञ्च) कृत्वा आचन्द्रार्ककाल≍(काल)प्रतिष्ठमग्र-
16 हारं कृत्वा विधिवस्सं(त्सं)प्रदत्त: इत्यवगम्य ग्रामफलमु-
17 पनीय सर्व्वादरेण वचन≍(न)प्रेषणोपस्थानं कर्त्तव्यमिति:(ति)
18 आज्ञा अप्युत्तरकालभाविराजभिश्च धर्म्मदानस्यानुपालने[12]

ABSTRACT

The charter begins with the symbol for *siddham* and the word *svasti.* This is followed by a reference to the victorious **Devapura** whence the royal order was issued by the reigning king, *kaliṅgādhipati śrī-Anantavarman*, who was the son of Mahārāja Prabhañjanavarman and grandson of Mahārāja Guṇavarman of the family of Vāsiṣṭha. The reigning king has been described as a devotee of Mahēśvara (Śiva), endowed with wisdom, refineness, courtesy, heroism and strength, devoted to the welfare of his subjects and who acquired the earth by the strength of his own arms. Lines 8-16 refer to the royal order relating to the grant of the village Tōṇṭāpara, addressed to the farmers and others of the said village, which had already been an *agrahāra* enjoying the privileges applicable to the group of villages in Kharapuri-*madamba.* The grant was made in favour of eighteen brāhmaṇas belonging to the Ātrēya *gōtra* on the **full-moon** day **in the month of Māgha in the year Mahāśvayuja**. The gift village was exempted from all kinds of taxes after making it a separate *agrahāra* from the division of Kharapuri-**madamba** and the division of Pattana-*bhōga*. This was made permanent, so as to last as long as the moon and the sun endure. The cultivators were then advised (line 17) to attend on the donees. The future rulers were also requested (line 18) to protect the grant.

8. Read पुण्यायुर्यशसामभिवृद्धये.
9. याजन has been written twice.
10. Read आत्रेय.
11. Possibly अष्टादश was intended to mean eighteen brāhmaṇas. G.V. Srinivasa Rao suggests अष्टांशक.
12. The third plate is missing.

NO. 6: SRUNGAVARAPUKOTA PLATES OF ANANTAVARMAN

Provenance	:	Srungavarapukota, Vishakhapatnam district, Andhra Pradesh.
References	:	M. Narasimham, *JAHRS*, Vol. VIII (1935-36), pp. 153-60 and plate; R.C. Majumdar, *EI*, Vol. XXIII (1935-36), pp. 56-61 and plate; and S.N. Rajaguru, *IO*, Vol. I, Pt. 2 (1958), pp. 35-39.
Language	:	Sanskrit, in prose, except the three imprecatory verses at the end.
Metre	:	Verses 1-3 *anuṣṭubh*.
Script	:	Southern variety of the alphabet of about the fifth century A.D.
Date	:	The thirteenth day of the summer solstice.

TEXT[1]

First Plate

1 सिद्धम्[2] स्वस्ति [।।*] विजय**पिष्टपुराधिष्टाना**न्महीमण्डलव्यापिशारदेन्दुकरनिर्म्मलगुणस्य
2 देवराष्ट्राधिपतेरनेकसमरसंघट्टविजयाधिगतयशसो महाराजश्रीगु-
3 णवर्म्मण ≍ परमपौत्र: शक्तित्त्रयोपनतराज्यसम्पदो वासिष्ठकुलचन्द्रम-
4 स: श्रीमहाराजप्रभजंनवर्म्मण:[3] प्रियपुत्त्रस्स्वबलविक्का(क्र)मोपार्ज्जितभूर्न्न-
5 यविनयसत्त्वसम्पन्नाधिगतयशा देवद्विजातिगुरुजनानुद्धयानसं-

Second Plate: First Side

6 वर्द्धितमहिमा परममाहेश्वरो मातापितृपादानुध्यात ※ कलिङ्गाधिपतिश्री-
7 **महाराजानन्ता(न्त)वर्म्मा** तेल्लवल्लिविषये किण्डेप्पग्रामे सर्व्वसमवेतान्कुटु-
8 म्बिन: समाज्ञापयत्यस्ति एष ग्रामोस्माभिरुत्ता(त्त)रायणेस्मत्पुण्यभिवृद्ध-
9 ये एतस्मै कौशिकसगोत्त्राय तैत्तिरि(री)यस ब्रम्ह(ह्म)चारिणे अचण्टपुरभोगि-
10 कमातृशर्म्मणे आचन्द्रार्कतारकप्रतिष्ठमग्रहारं कृत्वा सर्व्वकरभरै:

---

1. From the facsimile in *EI*, Vol. XXIII (1935-36), pp. 60 and 61.
2. Expressed by a symbol.
3. Read प्रभञ्जन.

Second Plate: Second Side

11 परिहृत्य सम्प्रदत्तस्तदेवमवधृताज्ञैर्भवद्भिस्तदाज्ञानुविधायिभि ᳵ प्रत्यह-
12 मुपस्थातव्यम् [।।*] ब्राह्मणेन चात्मनोग्रहार: पुत्रपौत्रिकमुपभुज्यमा-
13 नो न कैश्चिद्वल्लभदुर्ल्लभैरुपहन्तव्य: [।।*] आगामिभिरपि राजर्षि-
14 भिर्वृत्तमनुपालयद्भिर्य्यथास्य धर्म्मप्रसवस्याविच्छेदेन प्रवृ-
15 त्तिर्भ्भ(र्भ)वति तथानुष्ठेयं एवञ्च सति तत्र तेषामपि धर्म्मेणाभिसम्व-

Third Plate: First Side

16 न्द्धस्स्मर्यते ।। बहुभिर्व्वसुधा दत्ता बहुभि . . . .[4]
17 स्य तस्य तदा फलं [।।*१] स्वदत्ताम्परदत्तां वा यन्ना . . . .[5]
18 च्छ्रेयोनुपालनं(नम्) [।।*२] षष्टिं वर्षसहस्राणि स्वर्ग्गे . . . .[6]
19 न्येव नरके वसेत् [।।*३] प्रवर्द्धमानया राज्यश्रिया राजव . . . . **[त्र*]-**
20 **योदश्यामुत्तरायणे** धर्म्मप्रदानं कृतमिति भ . . . .

ABSTRACT

The charter begins with a symbol for *siddham* and the word *svasti*. Lines 1-7 refer to the reigning king **Mahārāja Anantavarman** and his predecessors. He has been described as the lord of Kaliṅga who acquired the earth by his own strength and valour, who was the son of the glorious Mahārāja Prabhañjanavarman of the Vāsiṣṭha family and the grandson of glorious Mahārāja Guṇavarman, who was the lord of Dēvarāṣṭra. The king is stated (lines 7-8) to have issued an order from his residence in the victorious city of **Piṣṭapura**, addressing the cultivators of the village of Kiṇḍēppa in Tēllavalli district. Lines 8-12 refer to the grant of the said village during the summer solstice, for the sake of increasing the religious merit by the king, in favour of the brahmacārin Mātṛśarman of the Kauśika *gōtra*, a student of Taittirīya (*śākhā*) and who was the *bhōgika* of Acaṇṭapura. The grant is stated to have been made a permanent *agrahāra* to last as long as the sun, the moon and the stars endure and exempted from all burdens of taxation. Lines 12-16 refer to the advice to the inhabitants of the village to attend on the donee who was to enjoy his own *agrahāra* in hereditary succession and who should not be hindered in any way by any officer, however eminent. The future rulers were also requested in the passage to preserve the grant following the traditional usage. Lines 16-19 contain three of the usual imprecatory verses. Lines 19-20 contain the **date** of the issue of the grant as the **thirteenth day, during the summer solstice.**[7]

4. The right half of this plate is broken and missing. R.C. Majumdar reads the rest of the line as श्चानुपालिता । यस्य यस्य यदा भूमिस्त-.
5. Majumdar reads द्रक्ष युधिष्ठिर । महीं महीमतां श्रेष्ठ दाना-.
6. Majumdar reads मोदति भूमिद: । आक्षेप्ता चानुमन्ता च ता-.
7. The year, presumably given in the regnal reckoning of the king, is now lost as the plate is damaged.

NO. 7: BARANGA GRANT OF UMĀVARMAN, YEAR 6

Provenance	:	Baranga, Ganjam district, Orissa.
References	:	S.C. Behera, *OHRJ*, Vol. VI, Pt. 3 (1957), pp. 106-9 and plate; and S.N. Rajaguru, *IO*, Vol. I, Pt. 2 (1958), pp. 75-77.
Language	:	Sanskrit, in prose, except the three imprecatory and benedictory verses at the end.
Metre	:	Verses 1-3 *anuṣṭubh.*
Script	:	Southern variety of the alphabet of about the fifth century A.D.
Date	:	6th regnal year, the fifth day of the bright fortnight of the month of Vaiśākha.

TEXT[1]

First Plate: Second Side

1 सिद्धम्[2] स्वस्ति [।।*] विजय**सुनगरा**त्परमदैवतबप्पभट्टारकपाद-
2 भक्तः कुशली **महाराजोमवर्म्मा** भिलिङ्गाभोगविषये
3 हेमण्डकग्रामे सर्व्वसमवेतान्कुटुम्बिनस्समा-
4 ज्ञापयत्यस्त्येष ग्रामोस्माभिः स्वपुण्यायु-
5 र्य्य(र्य)शोभिवृद्धये आसहस्त्रा(स्त्रां)शुशशिताराग(ग्र)हप्रतिष्ठ-
6 मग्रहारङ्कृत्वा सर्व्वकरपरिहारैश्च परिहृत्य

Second Plate: First Side

7 काप्यस[3] गोत्राय ब्राह्मणविष्णुशर्म्मण(णे)प्रदत्तः [।।*]
8 तदेव ज्ञात्वा भवद्भिः पूर्व्वोचितमर्य्यादया सर्व्वोप-
9 स्थानं करणीयं मेयवरिमादि[4] च समुत्पाद्य-

1. From the photographs in *OHRJ*, Vol. VI, Pt. 3 (1957) pp. 108 and 109, and from the original plates; the charter is now preserved in the Orissa State Museum, Bhubaneswar.
2. Expressed by a symbol.
3. Read काश्यप.
4. Read मेयहिरण्यादि as in the other grants of the Māṭhara family.

10 मानद्रव्यमुपनेयमिति [।।*] भविष्यतश्च राज्ञो
11 विज्ञापयत्यन्यतमयोगादवाप्य महीमनुशासद्भि-
12 रेषोग्रहारोनुपालयितव्यः [।।*] भवन्ति चात्र व्यासगीता

Second Plate: Second Side

13 श्लोकाः [।*] बहुभिर्व्वसुधा दत्ता वसुधा वसुधाधिपैः [।*]
14 यस्य यस्य यदा भूमिस्तस्य तस्य तदा फलम् [।।*१]
15 स्वदत्तां परदत्तां वा यन्नाद्रक्ष युधिष्ठिर [।*]
16 महीम्महीमतां श्रेष्ठ दानाच्छ्रेयोनुपालनम् [।।*२]
17 षष्टि(ष्टिं)वर्षसहस्राणि स्वर्ग्गे मोदति भूमिदः [।*]
18 आक्षेप्ता चानुमन्ता च तान्येव नरके वसेदिति [।।*३]

Third Plate: First Side

19 आज्ञा महाराजाधिवर्म्मा लिखितं देशाक्ष-
20 पटलाधिकृतामात्यकुमारदेवेनेति ।।
21 **षष्ठसंव्य(व)त्सरस्य वैशाख शुक्ल**
22 **पञ्चम्या(म्यां)** [।।*]

ABSTRACT

The charter begins with a symbol for *siddham* and the word *svasti.* Lines 1-7 state that from the victorious city of Sunagara, **Mahārāja Umāvarman**, a devout worshipper at the feet of his father, made the declaration before all the inhabitants of the village named Hēmaṇḍaka, situated in the district of Bhiliṅga-*bhōga,* relating to the grant of the said locality by making it an *agrahāra* and free from all kinds of taxes, in favour of the brāhmaṇa named Viṣṇuśarman of the Kāśyapa *gōtra.* The inhabitants were then directed (lines 8-10) to attend on the donee according to established custom and to offer him regularly the usual *mēya* (share of the produce) and *hiraṇya* (tax in cash) as well as other produce of the locality. The future rulers were also requested (lines 10-12) to protect the grant. Lines 13-18 contain the usual imprecatory and benedictory verses quoted from Vyāsa. The charter is stated (line 19) to have been issued by order of Maharāja Ādhivarman.[5] Lines 19-20 state that the charter was written by the *dēśākṣapaṭalādhikṛta* Kumāradēva. The grant is stated (lines 21-22) to have been issued in **the 6th regnal year** of the king, **on the fifth day of the bright fortnight of the month of Vaiśākha.**

5. The name perhaps denotes the reigning king Umāvarman.

NO. 8: TEKKALI PLATES OF MAHĀRĀJA UMĀVARMAN, YEAR 9

Provenance	:	Tekkali, Visakhapatam district, Andhra Pradesh.
References	:	G.H. Jagadev, *JAHRS*, Vol. VI (1931-32), pp. 53 ff; M. Venkataramayya, *EI*, Vol. XXVIII (1949-50), pp. 298-302 and plate; and S.N. Rajaguru, *IO*, Vol. I, Pt. 2 (1958), pp. 4-6.
Language	:	Sanskrit, in prose, except three verses at the end.
Metre	:	Verses 1-3 *anuṣṭubh*.
Script	:	Southern variety of the alphabet of about the fifth century A.D.
Date	:	9th regnal year, the seventh day of the dark fortnight of the month of Māgha.

TEXT[1]

First Plate

1 स्वस्ति [।*] विजय**वर्द्धमानपुरा**[त्] पितृपादानुध्यातः **श्रीमहारा़जो**-
2 **मवर्म्मा** अस्ति हवेरग्रामे[2] सर्व्वसमवेतां(तान्) कुटुम्बिनस्स-
3 माज्ञापयत्यस्तु वो विदितम् [।*] अस्माकं स्वपुन्या(ण्या)युर्य्य(र्य)शो-
4 भिवृद्धये आचन्द्रतारकार्क्कप्रतिष्ठमग्रहारं कृत्वा अ-

Second Plate: First Side

5 [क]रग्राहिकग्रामञ्च कृत्वा सर्व्वकरभरपरिहारै[:*] परिह[त्य]
6 य[श]शर्म्मणे काश्यपगोत्ताय सम्प्र[द*]त्तः [।*] तदेवं विदित्वा
7 युष्माभिः पूर्व्वोचितमर्य्यादयोपस्थानं कर्त्तव्यमिति
8 [मे]यहिरण्यादि चोपनेयमिति भविष्यद्राज्ञश्च विज्ञाप-

Second Plate: Second Side

9 यामि धर्म्मक्क्रमविक्क्रमाभ्य[3] दानमनुपालनञ्चेति ए-

---

1. From the facsimile in *EI*, Vol. XXVIII (1949-50).
2. D.C. Sircar takes the name of the village to be Astihavera, (*EI*, Vol. XXX (1954), p.117).
3. Read धर्म्मक्रमविक्रमै:

10 ष खलु स धर्म्मः । अपि चात्र व्यासगीता[न्*] श्लोकानुदा-
11 हरन्ति [।*] बहुभिर्व्वसुधा दत्ता वसुधा वसुधाधिपै[: *।] य-
12 स्य यस्य यदा भूमि[:*] तस्य तस्य तदा फलम् [।।*१] षष्टिंवर्षस

Third Plate: First Side

13 हस्राणि स्वर्ग्गे मोदति भूमिद[:*।] आक्षेप्ता चानुमन्ता च तान्येव
14 नरके वसेत् [।।*२] स्वदत्तां(त्तां) परदत्तां वा यत्नाद्रक्ष युद्धि(धि)-
15 ष्ठिर [।*] महिम्महिमता(तां) श्रेष्ठ दाना[च्*]छ्रेयोनुपालनम् [।।*३] **माघस्य कृ-**
16 **ष्णादिवसो(से) सप्तमी**[4] **सम्वत्सर(रे) नवम(मे)** स्वयमाज्ञा [।।*]

Third Plate: Second Side

17 राज्ञा स्वहस्तलिखितं शासनं पापनाशनमिति [।*]
18 पिष्टपुरवास्तव्येन केशवदेवेन लिखित[मिति] [।*]

ABSTRACT

The charter begins with the word *svasti*, which is followed by a prose passage in lines 1-3 stating that the reigning king **Mahārāja Umāvarman** issued the royal order from **Vardhamānapura**. It was addressed to the cultivators assembled at the locality called Havēra.[5] The king has been described as a devotee at the feet of his father. The charter records (lines 3-6) the grant of the said locality by the king, as a permanent and rent-free *agrahāra* for accruing religious merit for himself. The gift was made in favour of a brāhmaṇa named Yaśaśarman of the Kāśyapa *gōtra*. The residents of the locality were then advised (lines 6-9) to attend on the donee according to established custom and to regularly offer him a share of the produce (*mēya*) and tax in cash (*hiraṇya*). Future rulers were also requested to protect the grant. Such a protection of grants made by previous rulers is said to be the *sva-dharma* of kings. There are three usual benedictory and imprecatory verses stated to have been quoted from Vyāsa. In lines 15-16 at the end, reference is made to the **date** of the grant, given in words as **the seventh day of the dark fortnight of the month of Māgha**, in **the ninth year of** the king's reign. In lines 16-18, the record is stated to have been written by the king himself. Also Kēśavadēva, a resident of Piṣṭapura, is stated to have been the writer of the charter.

---

4. Read सप्तम्यां.
5. The name of the locality has been doubtfully read by the editor of the grant as Astihavēra or *asti*-Havēra. Some scholars take it to be Astihavera and identify it with Atava in Visakhapatam district (see *EI*, Vol. XXVIII (1949-50), p. 301).

NO. 9: DHAVALAPETA PLATES OF MAHĀRĀJA UMĀVARMAN

Provenance : Dhavalapeta, Srikakulam district, Andhra Pradesh.

References : M. Narasimham, *JAHRS*, Vol. X (1936-37), pp. 143-44 and plates; R.K. Ghoshal, *EI*, Vol. XXVI (1942), pp. 132-35 and plates; and S. N. Rajaguru, *IO*, Vol. I, Pt. 2 (1958), pp. 7-9.

Language : Sanskrit, in prose.

Script : Southern variety of about the fifth century A.D.

TEXT[1]

First Plate

1 सिद्धम्[2] स्वस्ति [।।*] **सुनगरात्** परमदैवतबप्पभट्टारकपादा-
2 नुध्यातः **श्रीर्म्महाराजोमवर्म्मा** महेन्द्रभोगे कुत्तु-
3 रग्रामे सर्व्वसमन्वागतान्कुटुम्बिनस्समाज्ञाप-
4 [यति][।*] अस्त्येष ग्रामोस्माभिरात्मन[3][:*] पुण्यायुय[4](र्य)शोभिवृद्ध-

Second Plate: First Side

5 ये वत्ससगोत्राय छन्दोगसब्रह्मचारिणे ब्राह्म-
6 णखल्लस्वामिने आसहस्रांशुशशि[5]तारकप्रतिष्ठ-
7 मग्रहार(रं) कृत्वा सर्व्वकरपरिहारैश्च परिहृत्य
8 संप्रदत्तस्सहवाटकेन [।*] तदेवं विदित्वा युष्माभिः

Second Plate: Second Side

9 पूर्व्वोचितमर्य्यादा(द)योपस्थानं कर्त्तव्यम् [।*] यच्चात्र

---

1. From the facsimile in *EI*, Vol. XXVI (1942), pp. 134-35.
2. Expressed by a symbol which is incised at the beginning of line 2.
3. The letter *na* has been inserted at the foot of the line.
4. The letter *ya* has been inserted below *so* and the correction has been indicated by a small 'x' mark above the line.
5. The word शशि has been inserted at the top of the line.

10 किंचिदुत्पद्यते मेयहिरण्यादि तत्सर्व्वमु-
11 पनेयं [।*] भविष्यतश्च राज्ञो विज्ञापयति [।*] धर्म्मक्रम-
12 [विक्र]माणामन्यतमयोगादवाप्य महीमनुशासता[6]-

ABSTRACT

The charter begins with a symbol for *siddham* and the word *svasti*. Lines 1-3 refer to the king **Mahārāja Umāvarman**, described as *paramadaivata* and meditating at the feet of his father who issued the royal order from the city of **Sunagara**, addressing the cultivators of the village Kuttura situated in the division of Mahēndra-*bhōga*. Lines 4-8 refer to the grant of the said village by the king to the brāhmaṇa Khallasvāmin who belonged to the Vatsa *gōtra* and Chandōga (*caraṇa*), described as a brahmacārin, in order to obtain religious merit, longevity and fame for the donor himself. The village was made a permanent *agrahāra*, which was to last as long as the sun, the moon and the stars would endure and exempted from the liability of paying all taxes. The cultivators were then advised (lines 8-11) to attend on the donee and to pay him the usual *mēya* and *hiraṇya* according to established custom. The future rulers were also requested (lines 11-12) to protect the gift.

---

6. The third plate containing the rest of the text is now lost.

NO. 10: BṚHATPROṢṬHĀ GRANT OF UMĀVARMAN, YEAR 30

Provenance : Palakonda, Andhra Pradesh.
References : E. Hultzsch, *EI*, Vol. XII (1913-14), pp. 4-6 and plate; S.N. Rajaguru, *IO*, Vol. I, Pt. 2 (1958), pp. 10-12.
Language : Sanskrit, in prose, except the three imprecatory verses in lines 11-15.
Metre : Verses 1-3 *anuṣṭubh*.
Script : Southern variety of the alphabet of about the fifth century A.D.
Date : 30th regnal year, the twentieth day of the month of Mārgaśīrṣa.

TEXT[1]

First Plate: Second Side

1 सिद्धम्[2] स्वस्ति [।।*] विजयसी(**सिं**)हपुराद्बप्प[भट्टारक*]पादभक्त ※ कलिङ्गाधिपति**श्रीमहाराजो**-
2 **मवर्म्मा**-[3] बृहत्प्रोष्ठाग्रामे सर्व्वसमवेतान्कुटुम्बिनस्समाज्ञापय-
3 त्यस्त्येष ग्रामोस्माभिरौपमन्यम(व)सगोत्ताय बह्वृचसब्रह्मचारि-
4 णे ब्राह्मणहरिदत्तायासहस्रांशुशशितारकप्रतिष्ठमग्रहारं

Second Plate: First Side

5 कृत्वा सर्व्वकर[परिहारैश्च परिहृत्य द]न्तयवागुभोगादुद्धृत्य
6 षट्त्रिंशदग्रहारसामन्यङ्कृत्वा भोगसम्ब[न्द्धनिर्व्व]चनीयम्प्र[द*]त्तः[4] [।*]
7 तदेवं विदित्वा युष्माभिः पूर्व्वोचितमर्य्यादयोपस्थानङ्कर्त्तव्यम्
8 मेयहिरण्याद्यञ्चोपनेयम्भविष्यतश्च राज्ञो विज्ञापयति [।*] धर्म्म-

1. From the facsimile in *EI*, Vol. XII (1913-14), pp. 4 and 5.
2. Expressed by a symbol.
3. This mark of a hyphen was probably intended for punctuation.
4. Hultzsch reads म्प्रत्तः [।*].

Second Plate: Second Side

9 क्रमविक्रमाणामन्यतमयोगादवाप्य महीमनुशासताम्प्रवृत्त-
10 कमिदन्दानं सद्धर्म्मम[5]नुपश्यद्भिरेषोग्रहारोनुपाल्य: [।*] भवन्ति
11 चात्र व्यासगीताश्लोका: [।*] बहुभिर्व्वसुधा दत्ता वसुधा वसुधाधि-
12 पै: [।*] यस्य यस्य यदा भूमिस्तस्य [त]स्य [तदा]फलम् [।।*१] स्वदत्ताम्परदत्तां[6]

Third Plate: First Side

13 वा यन्नाद्रक्ष युधिष्ठिर [।*] महीम्महिमतां श्रेष्ठ दानाच्छ्रेयोनुपालन[म् ।। *२]
14 षष्टिं वर्षसहस्राणि स्वर्ग्गे वसति भूमिद: [।*] आक्षेप्ता चानुमन्ता च
15 तान्येव नरके वसेत [।।*३] आज्ञा वासुदेव: [।*] **संवत् ३० मार्ग्गशीर्षा(र्ष)दि २०** [।*]
16 देशाक्षपटलाधिकृत[7] हरिदत्तसूनुना मा[तृ*]वरेण लिखितमिति ।।

ABSTRACT

The charter, issued from **Siṁhapura**, begins with a symbol for *siddham* and the word *svasti*. The reigning king **Mahārāja Umāvarman** is then introduced (lines 1-6) as a devotee at the feet of his father and the lord of Kaliṅga. He is stated to have issued the order informing the cultivators and others of village Bṛhatproṣṭhā about the grant of the said village in favour of the brāhmaṇa Haridatta of the Aupamanyava *gōtra* and Bahvṛca (*caraṇa*), after having made it an *agrahāra* and separating it from the division of Dantayavāgu like any other *agrahāra*. The grant is stated to have been made permanent so as to last as long as the sun, the moon and the stars would endure and exempted from all taxes. The cultivators were then advised (lines 7-8) to attend on the donee according to established custom and to regularly offer him the usual *mēya* and *hiraṇya*. The future kings were then requested (lines 8-10) to honour and protect the grant as their own duty. Lines 11-15 contain three of the usual imprecatory and benedictory verses. Line 15 gives the **date** of the record in the **regnal year** of the king as **saṁvat 30, the twentieth day of the month of Mārgaśīrṣa**. The charter is stated (line 16) to have been written by Mātṛvara, son of Haridatta, designated as the *dēśākṣapaṭalādhikṛta*.

---

5. This may be read as स्व धर्म्म as in other plates of the Māṭhara family.
6. Read स्वदत्तां परदत्तां.
7. Read कृतेन.

NO. 11: TEMBURU PLATES OF UMĀVARMAN, YEAR 40

Provenance	:	Temburu, Patapatnam taluk, Srikakulam district, Andhra Pradesh.
References	:	B.N. Shastri, *Bharati*, Vol. 44, Pt. 12, 1967, pp. 13 ff.: G.S. Gai, *EI*, Vol. XXXVII (1947-48), pp. 337-40 and plates.
Language	:	Sanskrit, in prose, except the customary verses at the end.
Metre	:	Verses 1-3 *anuṣṭubh*.
Script	:	Southern variety of about the fifth century A.D.
Date	:	40th regnal year, the twentieth day of Vaiśākha.

TEXT[1]

First Plate

1 [सिद्धम्[2] [।*] स्वस्ति विजय][3] **सिंहपुराद्बप्पपादभक्तः** कलिङ्गाधिपतिः

2 **[श्रीम]हाराजोमवर्म्मा** ।[4] होणरेङ्गग्रामे सर्व्वसमवेतान्

3 कुटुम्बिनस्समाज्ञापयत्यस्त्येष ग्रामोस्माभिः पुत्र-

4 वसुषेणराजस्य पुण्ययशोभिवृद्धये वासिष्ठसगो-

5 त्राय तैत्तिरीयसब्रह्मचारिणे ब्राह्मणभातृशर्म्मणे

Second Plate: First Side

6 आसहस्रांशुशशितारकप्रतिष्ठमग्रहारङ्कृत्वा दन्त-

7 यवागुमदम्वाद्विनिष्कृष्य कलिङ्गाग्रहारसामान्यं कृत्वा

8 सर्व्वकरपरिहारैश्च परिहृत्य प्रदत्तः [।*] तदेवं विदित्वा

9 युष्माभि[ः पूर्व्वो]चितमर्य्यादयोपस्थानङ्कर्त्तव्यं मेयहिर-

10 ण्या[द्यञ्चोपनी]यम्भविष्यतश्च राज्ञो विज्ञापयति [।*] धर्म्म-

---

1. From the facsimile in *EI*, Vol. XXXVII (1947-48), pp. 338 and 339.
2. Expressed by a symbol.
3. Traces of these damaged letters are slightly visible.
4. The punctuation mark indicated by a horizontal stroke is redundant.

Second Plate: Second Side

11 क्रमविक्रमाणामन्यतमयोगादवाप्य महीमनुशासतां
12 प्रवृत्तकमिदन्दानं सद्धर्म्म(र्म्म)मनुपश्यद्भिरेषोग्रहारोनु-
13 पाल्यः [।*] भवन्ति चात्र व्यासगीताः श्लोकाः [।*] बहुभिर्व्व-
14 हुधा(सुधा) दत्ता वसु(हु)धा वसुधाधिपैः [।*] यस्य यस्य यदा भूमिः
15 तस्य तस्य तदा फल[म्] [।।*१]स्वदत्तां परदत्तां वा यन्नाद्रक्ष युधि-

Third Plate

16 ष्ठि[र][।*] महीम्महिमतां श्रेष्ठ दानाच्छ्रेयोनुपालनम् ।। [२*]
17 षष्टिं वर्षसहस्राणि स्वर्गे वसति भूमिदः [।*] आक्षेप्ता चा-
18 नुमन्ता च तान्येव नरके वसेत् [।।*३] आज्ञा वासुदेवः
19 **संवत् ३०.१० वैशाखा(ख)दी(दि)२०** देशाक्षपटलाधिकृत-
20 हरिदत्तसूनुना मा[तृ]वरेण लिखितमिति ।।* ।।[5]

ABSTRACT

The charter begins with the symbol for *siddham* and the word *svasti*, followed by a prose passage in lines 1-8 stating that **Mahārāja Umāvarman**, the lord of Kaliṅga, a devotee at the feet of his father, issued the royal order from the victorious **Simhapura**. The order was addressed to the cultivators of Hōṇarēṅga village, relating to the grant of the said village, after having made it an *agrahāra* and naming it Kaliṅg-*āgrahāra*, separating it from the division of Dantayavāgu. The grant was issued in favour of the brāhmaṇa Bhātṛśarman of the Vāsiṣṭha *gōtra* and Taittirīya (*śākhā*), by making it a permanent holding and free from all kinds of taxes, which was to exist till the sun, the moon and the stars would endure. The purpose of the grant was to increase the religious merit and fame of prince Vasusēṇarāja. Line 9 refers to the king's advice to the inhabitants of the gift village to attend on the donee and to pay him the usual *mēya* and *hiraṇya*. The future rulers were then requested (lines 10-12) to honour and protect the grant by taking it as their own *dharma*. Lines 13-18 contain three of the usual imprecatory and benedictory verses. Line 18 refers to one Vāsudēva, on whose instruction the grant was executed. Line 19 refers to the **date** of the grant stated as **the 40th year, the twentieth day of the month of Vaiśākha**. Lines 19-20 refer to the writer of the document named Mātṛvara, the son of Haridatta, the *dēśākṣapaṭalādhikṛta*.

5. A floral design is engraved between the two sets of double *daṇḍas*.

NO. 12: CHICACOLE PLATES OF NANDAPRABHAÑJANAVARMAN

Provenance	:	Chicacole, Srikakulam district, Andhra Pradesh.
References	:	J.F. Fleet, *IA*, Vol. XIII, (1884), pp. 48-50 and plates; S.N. Rajaguru, *IO*, Vol. II, Pt. 2 (1958), pp. 40-43.
Language	:	Sanskrit, in prose, except the three imprecatory and benedictory verses at the end.
Metre	:	Verses 1-3 *anuṣṭubh*.
Script	:	Southern variety of the alphabet of about the fifth century A.D.
Date	:	Undated.

TEXT[1]

First Plate

1 स्वस्ति[2] [।*] विजय**सारपल्लिवास**कात्परमभागवतो मातापितृपादा-
2 नुद्धया(ध्या)तस्सकलकलिङ्गाधिपति[:*] **श्रीमहाराजनन्दप्रभ-**
3 **ञ्जनवर्म्मा** डेयवाटे[3] कुटुम्बिनमाज्ञापयति [।*] विदितम-
4 स्तु अक्षताग्रहारीयब्राह्मणहरिश्चन्द्रस्वामिने उद-

Second Plate: First Side

5 कपूर्व्वे(र्व्वे)ण अकरं भरवाणवर्ज्जम् पुण्यायुय्य(र्य्य)शसामभिवृद्धये
6 आचन्द्रदा(ता)रकार्कप्रतिष्ठितमग्रा(ग्र)हारं कृत्वा सर्व्वकरपरिहा-
7 रैश्च परिहृत्य देवं[4]रातगोत्रचरणेभ्यो(भ्य:) प्रदत्तं [।*] एवं
8 ज्ञात्वा युष्माभि: पूर्व्वोचितमर्य्यादया सर्व्वोपस्थानं कर्त्तव्यं

Second Plate: Second Side

9 मेयं हिरण्याद्यं चोपनेय(यं) [।*] भविष्यतश्च राज्ञो विज्ञापयामि

---

1. From the facsimile in *IA*, Vol. XIII (1884), pp. 48-49.
2. The word is written slightly below the line in the left margin of the plate.
3. Fleet suggests alternately अड़ेयवाटे.
4. The *anusvāra* is superfluous.

10 धर्म्मं[5] क्रमविक्रमाणां[5] मन्यतमयोगादवाप्यमनुशासतां
11 प्रवृत्तकमिदं दानं स्वधर्म्ममनुपश्यद्भि[:*] स्तददतितिवा[6]-
12 यमग्रहारा(रो)नुपाल्य[:*।।] अपि चात्र व्यासगीताश्लोकानुदाह-

Third Plate

13 रिष्यामि ।। बहुभिर्व्वसुधा दत्ता राजानै:[7] वसुधाधिपै:[8] [।*] यस्य
14 यस्य यदा भूमि[:*] तस्य तस्य तदा फलम् [।।*१] स्वदत्तां पर-
15 दत्तं(त्तां) वा यन्नाद्रक्ष युधिष्ठिर:[9][।*] महीमता[न*]च्छ्रेस्ठ(ष्ठ) दाना-
16 च्छ्रेयोनुपालनमुत्तमं[10] [।। *२] षष्टिं वर्षसहस्त्राणि स्वर्ग्गे मोदति भू-
17 मिद[:*।] आक्षेप्ता चानुमन्ता च तान्येव ना(न)रक्षे(के) वसेन् ।। [३*]

ABSTRACT

After the word *svasti*, the record mentions (lines 1-3) that the reigning king **Mahārāja Nandaprabhañjanavarman**, the lord of the whole of Kaliṅga, who assumed the title of *paramabhāgavata*, issued the order from the victorious residence of **Sārapalli**, addressing the cultivators of Ḍēyavāṭa. Lines 4-7 state that the said village (Ḍēyavāṭa) was granted by the reigning king to the brāhmaṇa Hariścandrasvāmin of the Akṣat-*āgrahāra*, who belonged to the Devarāta *gōtra* and *caraṇa*, with the libation of water, by making it free from paying taxes, and permanent as long as the moon, the stars and the sun would endure. The purpose of the grant was to obtain religious merit. The cultivators were then instructed (lines 8-9) to attend on the donee, according to established custom, and to offer him regularly the usual *mēya* and *hiraṇya*. In lines 9-12, the future kings are requested to protect the grant, taking it as their own duty. The charter ends with three of the usual imprecatory and benedictory verses, stated to have been quoted from Vyāsa.

---

5. The *anusvāra* is superfluous.
6. Read स्वदत्तिरिवा.
7. Read राजभि: .
8. It may be सगरादिभि:
9. The *visarga* is redundant.
10. The usual reading is महीं महीमतां श्रेष्ठ दानाच्छ्रेयोनुपालनं.

NO. 13: BARANGA PLATES OF NANDAPRABHAÑJANAVARMAN, YEAR 15

Provenance : Baranga, Ganjam district, Orissa.
References : S.C. Behera, *OHRJ*, Vol. VI, No. 2 (1957), pp. 106-14 and plate; S.N. Rajaguru, *IO*, Vol. I, Pt. 2, (1958) pp. 78-80.
Language : Sanskrit, in prose, except the four imprecatory and benedictory verses at the end.
Metre : Verses 1-4 *anuṣṭubh*.
Script : Southern variety of the alphabet of about the fifth century A.D.
Date : 15th regnal year, the first fortnight of Grīṣma, the thirteenth day.

TEXT[1]

First Plate: Second Side

1 [स्वस्ति] [।*] [विज]**यवर्द्धमाना**त्परमदैवतबप्पभट्टारक-
2 पादभक्तः सकलकलिङ्गाधिपती(तिः) श्रीमान् **महाराजन-**
3 **न्दप्रभंजनवर्म्मा** सिङ्घलग्रामे सर्व्वसमवेता[न्*] कु[2]-
4 कुटुम्बिनः समाज्ञापयत्यस्त्येषग्रामोस्माभी(भि)रात्म-
5 न[ः*] पुण्यायुर्य्यशसामभिवृद्धये आसमुद्रार्कतारकप्रति-

Second Plate: First Side

6 ष्ठमग्रहारं कृत्वा सर्व्वकरपरिहारैश्च परिहृत्य नानागोत्रचरणे-
7 भ्यो वरङ्गाग्रहार[3] ब्राह्मणेभ्यः प्रदत्तः ।। तदेवं ज्ञात्वा भवद्भिः
8 पूर्व्वोचितमर्य्यादया सर्व्वोपस्थानं कर्त्तव्य[म्*] मेयहिरण्याद्य(दि)
9 चोपनेयमिति [।।*] भविष्यतश्च राज्ञो विज्ञापयामि धर्म्मक्रमविक्रमा-
10 णामन्यतमयोगादवाप्य महीमनुशासति [।।*] प्रवृत्तकमिदन्दानं

1. From the original and the facsimile in *OHRJ*, Vol. VI, No. 2 (1957). The charter is now preserved in the Orissa State Museum, Bhubaneswar.
2. The letter is redundant.
3. This is probably intended for वरङ्गाग्रहारं कृत्वा.

Second Plate: Second Side

11 सद्धर्म्ममनुपश्यद्भि:[4] रेषोग्रहारोनुपाल्य[:* ।।] अपि चात्र व्यासगीता[न्]
12 श्लोकानुदाहरन्ति [।।*] बहुभिर्व्वसुधा दत्ता वसुधा वसुधाधिपै:[।*] य-
13 स्य यस्य यदा भूमि: तस्य तस्य तदा फल:(लम्) [।।*१] स्वदत्ताम्परदत्ता[5]-
14 म्वा(त्तां वा) यन्नाद्रक्ष युधिष्ठिर [।*] महीम्महीमता(तां) श्रेष्ठ दानाच्छ्रेयोनुपालनं(नम्)
[।।*२]
15 षष्टि(ष्टिं) वर्ष सहस्राणि स्वर्ग्गे मोदति भूमिद: [।*] आक्षेप्ता चानुमन्ता च

Third Plate

16 तान्येव नरते वसेत् [।।*३] स्वदत्तां परदत्तां वा यो हरेत वसु-
17 न्धरां [।*] स विष्ठायां क्रि(कृ)मिर्भूत्वा पितृभि: सह पच्यते [।।*४] क्रि(कृ)ष्णचन्द्रे[ण]
18 लिखितं स्वयमाज्ञा **सम्वत्सर [6]१०.५ पंचदशमे ग्रीष्मपक्ष**
19 **प्रथम दिवस: त्रयोदशी १०.३** [।।*]

ABSTRACT

The charter begins with a prose passage recording that the reigning king **Mahārāja Nandaprabhañjanavarman,** the lord of Kaliṅga, a devotee at the feet of his father, issued the order relating to the grant from the victorious **Vardhamānapura**, and addressed it to the cultivators and other inhabitants assembled at the village called Siṅghala. Lines 5-7 record the grant of the said village by making it an *agrahāra*, naming it Baraṅga, to the brāhmaṇas of different gotras and *caraṇas*. The inhabitants were then directed (lines 7-9) to attend on the donees according to established custom and to regularly pay them *mēya* and *hiraṇya*. The future rulers were then requested (lines 9-11) to protect the grant and such an act of protection is stated to have been regarded as *sad-dharma*. Lines 12-17 deal with four of the usual imprecatory and benedictory verses stated to have been quoted from Vyāsa. The grant is stated to have been written by Kṛṣṇacandra, by order of the king himself in his **15th regnal year on the thirteenth day of the first month of summer (*grīṣma*).**

---

4. The *visarga* is redundant.
5. Read स्वदत्तां परदत्तां.
6. The two numerical symbols for 10 and 5 are written below the line, virtually in line 19, after the symbols for 10 and 3 which are meant for the days.

NO. 14: RAGOLU PLATES OF NANDAPRBHAÑJANAVARMAN, YEAR 24

Provenance	:	Ragolu, Srikakulam district, Andhra Pradesh.
Reference	:	N. Mukunda Row, *Three Grants from Ragolu*, pp. 1-7 and plates.
Language	:	Sanskrit, in prose, except the three benedictory verses at the end.
Metre	:	Verses 1-3 *anuṣṭubh*.
Script	:	Southern variety of the alphabet of about the fifth century A.D.
Date	:	24th regnal year, the month of Phālguna.

TEXT[1]

First Plate

1 सिद्धम्[2] [।*] विजयसिङ्गपुराद्बप्पभट्टा[रक]पादभक्तस्सकलकलिङ्गा[धि*]-
2 पतिः **श्रीमा(म)न्महाराज नन्दप्रभञ्जनवर्म्मा** [।*] रागोलकग्रामे[3] सर्व्वस[म*]-
3 वेतान्कुटुम्बिनो भोजकंश्च समाज्ञापयति अस्तियोत्र ग्रामे नक्षत्रिका[4]-
4 कभूमिः[।।*] यानिवास्या भूम्यनन्तराणि नन्दिशर्म्मणः पूर्व्वाग्रा(ग्र)हारस्थल-
5 क्षेत्राणि च मध्यसीमया द्वौ व(वि)प्रक्षेत्रौ तोयश्च परिवर्त्तकमन्या वाटक(कं)
6 च प्रत्येमिरित्येतद्वास्यार्थं यमेकम्वाटकनिबन्द्धान् कृत्वास्माभिरात्मनः पुण्या[यु र्यश*]-
7 सामभिवृद्धये आसमुद्रार्क्कतारक(कं) प्रतिष्ठमग्रहारं कृत्वा सर्व्वकरपरि[हारैश्च प]-

Second Plate: First Side

8 रिहत्य षट्तिंन्शद[5]ग्रहारं सामान्यं चाग्रहारं प्रदेय(यं) साम्वत्सरिकम्पंचा[6]शत्पणाश्चशग्रदे[7]-

1. From the photographs in N. Mukunda Row's *Three Grants from Ragolu*, pp. 4-5, 6-7.
2. Expressed by a symbol.
3. The same village is written as Rākaluva in the charter of Śaktivarman (No. 1); *EI*, Vol. XII (1913-14), pp. 1-3.
4. One letter is lost.
5. Read षट्त्रिंशद-.
6. Read पञ्चा-.
7. The intended reading may be पणाश्चाग्रदे[यं].

9 दण्डपणाश्च विंशदुपनिवन्द्ध्य ग्रामस्य वक्तव्यम्विनिर्ग्गतङ्कृत्वास्मा[भि:*] ये(ए)व धर्म्मसञ्ज्ञया सद्ब्रह्म-

10 चारिणे कौण्डिन्यसगोत्र(त्रा)[य*] ब्राह्मणनन्दिशर्म्मणे सम्प्रदत्त: [।*] अपि चात्र भवद्भि: होजम्यक

11 दुसि छिलि गोण्डयाग्रहाराणान्नगरत्तोर(रे) निडिंजेरुव होंसरेवबलभङ्गग्रामाणान्तद् क-

12 ण्डक(का) [वृ*]क्षकस्य[8] च समक्षम्प्रदर्शितसेतव: उत्तरेण होजम्याग्रहार सीमान्तस्तत [:*]

13 करंजतटाकिकापाल्या पूर्व्वाग्रश्रृंङ्गद्दक्षिणेन या(ग)त्वा तिमिरखात: [।*] तस्मात्मासौपवासक्षेत्र ।। पाद्य [:]

14 तस्योत्तर(रे) सेतुना गत्वा पूर्व्वेण वापि पाल्यामतिक्रम्य मारिचवृक्षस्तत्पूर्व्वेण सूहिगुल्मस्तद्दक्षि-

15 णेन गर्त्ता [।*] तत: कौछलिकनुम्मिकक्षेत्रोत्तर स(से)तुभिरतिक्रम्य पूर्व्वदक्षिणेन विटपो वल्मीकाश्च

Second Plate: Second Side

16 तत्पश्चिमेन गर्त्तायां या(ग)त्वा पुनद्द(र्द)क्षिणेन हुट्टशिरु प्राग्दक्षिणेनातिक्रम्य हलन्दवल्मीक: त[द्*]-

17 दक्षिणपश्चिमेन मन्दारवल्मीकस्तद्दक्षिणेन विटपपंक्तिमतीत्य निम्वाखोचा [।*] तस्यान्दक्षिणेन

18 पुरुरषश्छाया(य)या[9] गत्वा गर्त्ता सा(तस्या:) पश्चिमेन गत्वा पुनस्संकरार्य्यक खण्ड[:*] तद्यद्दक्षिणेन श्रृङ्गवृक्ष[:*] तत:

19 करण्डकक्षेत्रोत्तरे सेतुना पूर्व्वेण या(ग)त्वा धर्म्मपट्टक्षेत्रप्रसे(दे)षे(शे) उत्कूलन्दिका वल्मीक-

20 स्ता[व*?]रक क्ष(क्षे)त्रं प्राप्य दक्षिणेन करण्ड़क स्थावरकसंकरार्य्यक क्षेत्रान्तर सेतुभिर्य्या(र्ग)त्वा त(ति)मिर

21 गर्त्तां गच्छतितया गर्त्तया पश्चिमेन या(ग)त्वा ज्व[1]ग्रहारसीमान्तानाग्रे लेनिनदी [।*] तामतिक्र[म्य*]

22 दुस्यग्रहार सीमान्तात्पुनस्सैव होजाम्याग्रहारसीमान्तेति पर्व्वतामरगत्तोद[क]-

23 तटाकोदक (को)व(वा) विप्रस्यात: पूर्व्वोचितमेव देयं तदेवम्विदित: युष्माभिरसौ

Third Plate

24 ब्राह्मणौ यथालिखित[म्*] मर्य्यादया सेतुनिबन्द्धेनेतद्वाट्टक-[11]

25 भवि[ष्य]द्राजभिश्च धर्म्मक्रमव(वि)क्रमाणां अन्यतमयोगादवाप्य-[12]

26 मिदन्दा[13]नमेष सतान्द्ध[14]म्मेति अनुपश्यद्भिरेषोग्रहारानुपाल्य:. . . .

---

8. The intended reading may be करण्डक वृक्षस्य-.
9. One letter is not legible.
10. The letter is not legible.
11. The rest of the letters are lost as the plate is broken here.
12. The rest of the letters are lost as the plate is broken here.

27 बहुभिव(र्व्व)हुधा दत्ता वसुधा वसुदा(धा)धिपः [।*] यस्य.यस्य य. . . .

28 फलं [।।*१] स्वदत्ताम्परदत्ताम्वा[15] यत्नाद्रक्ष युधिष्ठिर [।*] महीम्महिम. . . .

29 पालन[म्*।।२] षष्ठिं(ष्टिं) वर्षसहस्राणि स्वर्ग्गे वसति भूमिदः [।*] आक्षेप्ता चानु. . . .

30 नरके वसेदिति [।।*३] स्वयमाज्ञि(ज्ञ)प्तिः [।*] **सम्वत्सर २४ फाल्गुण (न) दि.** . . . .

31 दत्तसूनुना मातृवरेण[16] लिखितमिति ।।*।।

ABSTRACT

The charter begins with the symbol for *siddham*. This is followed by two lines introducing the reigning king, **Nandaprabhañjanavarman,** a devotee at the feet of his father and the lord of the entire Kaliṅga. He is stated to have issued the charter from the victorious **Siṅgupura.**[17] Lines 2-3 refer to the king's order relating to the grant of a piece of land which was addressed to the cultivators and royal officers assembled at the village called Rāgōlaka. Lines 4-10 mention that a piece of homestead land was granted to brahmacārin Nandiśarman of the Kauṇḍinya *gōtra* in the said locality, in exchange for the previous *agrahāra* donated. The gift land is stated to have been situated between two lands belonging to the brāhmaṇas (*vipra-kṣētra*) and the area was made a *vāṭaka* (part of the village or *pāṭaka*). The gift was made free from all kinds of taxes for the increase of merit and fame of the king himself. It was, however, indicated (lines 8-9) that the donee was required to pay annually, in advance, a sum of fifty *paṇas*, as well as another twenty *daṇḍa-paṇas* towards fines, to the village committee, as in the case of all other *agrahāras*.

The boundaries of the gift land are enumerated in lines 10-23. To the north of the localities called Hōjamyaka, Dusi, Chili and Gōṇḍya are situated the villages named Niḍiṁjeruva, Hoṁsareva and Valabhaṅga, and the tree called Kaṇḍaka (or Karaṇḍaka?) in front of which is located the bridge. There is a pond called Karañja-*taṭāka* and a moat on the northern boundary of the *agrahāra* called Hōjamya. Then, to the south, the boundary line of the gift village crosses a deep ditch. Then there is a plot of land meant for the performance of monthly fasting. Further north, going up to the bridges and to the east, crossing a drain of the well, the boundary line reaches a *marica* tree and, to the east of it, the *suhi* bush. To the south of it are the ditches. Then there is the plot of land called Kautcchali-Kanummika-*kṣetra*,

---

13. Read मिदं दा-.
14. Read सतां धर्मे-.
15. Read त्तां वा .
16. Mātṛvara is known from the Bobbili plates of Caṇḍavarman to be the son of Haridatta [*EI*, Vol. XXVII (1947-48), pp. 33-36].
17. This is obviously Siṁhapura, one of the chief cities of the Māṭhara kingdom, known from their copper-plate records and identified with the present Singupuram in Srikakulam district, Andhra Pradesh.

to its north; crossing the bridges towards south-east, are the trees, ant-hills. Still to their west, going up to the ditches, then again, to the south, is situated the *mart* named Siru. Crossing it towards the south is the ant-hill called Halanda and to its south-west, is the ant-hill called Mandāra. To its south, after crossing a row of trees, are the trees known as *nimva* and *khōcā*. To their south, going up to a human memorial (a tomb or statue), there are ditches and, to their west, is the tank situated in the area belonging to Śaṅkarāryaka. To its south is the *sṛṅga* tree. To the north of the Karaṇḍaka-*kṣetra* is the bridge. To the east, the boundary line reaches the plot of land known as Dharmmapaṭṭa-*kṣetra*, the ant-hill called Utkulandikā, and the plot of land called Stāvaraka-*kṣetra*. Then the boundary line proceeds south after crossing the plots of land called Karaṇḍaka, Stāvaraka and Śaṅkarāryaka as well as the bridges and after them the ditches, and again proceeds west and reaches the end of the boundary, where there is the river called Leni. After crossing it, the boundary of the *agrahāra* (the gift village) reaches the boundary lines of the villages (*agrahāras*) of Dusi, then the *agrahāra* of Hojamya, at the end of which there are ditches filled with water from the mountains and the tanks. The brāhmaṇa donee is then directed to pay the usual taxes according to established custom. The future rulers are also then requested to maintain and honour the grant of the *vāṭaka* (part of the village) in lines 24-27. This is followed by three of the usual imprecatory and benedictory verses in lines 27-30. The grant is stated to have been executed by the king himself in line 30. The **date** of the grant is given in the same line as the **24th regnal year**, and **the month of Phālguna.** The scribe's name is lost, but may be restored as Rudradatta, son of Mātṛvara.

NO. 15: BOBBILI PLATES OF CAṆḌAVARMAN, YEAR 4

Provenance	:	Bobbili, Srikakulam district, Andhra Pradesh.
References	:	R.K. Ghoshal, *EI*, Vol. XXVII (1947-48), pp. 33-36, and plate; S.N. Rajaguru, *IO*, Vol. I, Pt. 2 (1958), pp. 25-27.
Language	:	Sanskrit, in prose, except the three customary verses at the end.
Metre	:	Verses 1-3 *anuṣṭubh*.
Script	:	Southern variety of about the fifth century A.D.
Date	:	4th regnal year, the fifth day of the second fortnight of summer.

TEXT[1]

First Plate

1 सिद्धम्[2] स्वस्ति [।। *] विजय**सिङ्घ[3]पुरा**[त्]परमभागवत[:*] पितृपादानुध्यात[:*]
2 कलिङ्गाधिपति**श्रीमहाराजा(ज)चण्डवर्म्मा** तिरित्थाणग्रामे सर्व्व-
3 समवेतान्कुटुम्बिन:(नो) भोजका(कां)श्च समाज्ञापयत्यस्त्येषो(ष)ग्राम(मो)-
4 स्माभिरात्मन[:] पुण्यायुर्य्यशसामभिवृद्धये [आ]समुद्रादृ(द्रि) शसि(शि)तारकार्क-
5 प्रतिष्ठमग्रहारं कृत्वा सर्व्वकरपरिहारैश्च परिहृत्य षट्ंत्रिड्श (ट्त्रिंश)-

Second Plate: First Side

6 दग्रहारसामान्यञ्चाग्रहार[:*] प्रदेय(यं) साम्वत्सरिकं स(प)णाग्रं शतभु(द्व)[4]-
7 यञ्चाशंचोपनिवन्द्धय:[5] तिरित्थाणवाटकाग्रहारब्राह्मणानाम्
8 नानागा(गो)त्रसब्रह्मचारिणाम् सम्प्रत्त: [।*] तदेवं ज्ञात्वा
9 युष्माभि: पूर्व्वोचितमर्य्यादया सर्व्वोपस्थानं कर्त्तव्यम्
10 मेयहिरण्याद्यञ्चोपनेयम् [।*] भविष्यतश्च राज्ञो

---

1. From the facsimile in *EI*, Vol. XXVII (1947-48), pp. 34-35.
2. Expressed by a symbol.
3. Read सिंह-.
4. R.K. Ghosal reads सणाग्रं; C.R. Krishnamacharlu suggests पणा त्रंशत्.
5. The *visarga* is redundant.

Second Plate: Second Side

11 विज्ञाम(प)यामि [।*] धर्म्मक्रमविक्रमाणामन्यतमयोगा-
12 दवाप्य महीमनुशासताम् प्रवृत्तकमिदन्दानम्
13 सद्धर्म्मममनुपश्यद्भिरेषोग्रहामा(रो)नुपाल्य[:*।] अपि चात्र
14 व्यासगीतानि(न्) श्लोकानुदाहरन्तिः(न्ति) [।*] बहुभिर्व्वद्वं[6] दत्ता वसु(हु)धा
15 [व]सुधाधिपैः [।*] यस्य यस्य यदा भूमिः तस्य तस्य तद(दा) फलं(लम्) [।।*१]

Third Plate

16 [स्वद]त्ताम्परदत्ताम्वा[7] यन्नाद्रक्ष्व[8] युधिष्ठिर [।] महीन्म(म्म)हीमतां श्रेष्ठ
17 [दानाच्छ्रेयो]नुपालनं (नम्) [।।*२] षष्टिं वर्षसहस्राणि स्वर्ग्गे वसति भू-
18 मिद[:] [।*] आक्षेप्ता चानुमन्ता च तान्येव नरके वसेदिति[9]
19 स्वयमाज्ञापना [।*] देशाक्षपटलाधिकृतेन मातृवरस्य
20 सूनुना रुद्रदत्तेन लिखितमितिः(ति) [।*] **सम्वत्सरं चउतम ४ ग्रीष्म २ दि ५** [।।*]

ABSTRACT

The charter begins with a symbol for *siddham* and the word *svasti*, followed by a passage in lines 1-3 introducing the reigning king **Mahārāja Caṇḍavarman**, the lord of Kaliṅga. He issued the charter from **Siṁhapura**, addressing the cultivators and tenants of the village Tiritthāṇa that the said village was granted, having been made into an *agrahāra*, in favour of a number of brāhmaṇas, who were brahmacārins, belonging to different *gōtras*. The grant was made a permanent *agrahāra*, so as to last as long as the ocean, the mountains, the moon and the stars exist, after having exempted it from all taxes and having registered the amount payable for the *agrahāra*, in advance, annually at 200 *paṇas*, as in the case of all other *agrahāras*. The cultivators were then directed (lines 9-10) to attend on the donees according to established custom and to offer them the usual *mēya* and *hiraṇya*. The future rulers were also requested (lines 10-13) to maintain and protect the grant. Lines 14-18 contain three of the usual imprecatory verses stated to have been quoted from Vyāsa. Lines 19-20 mention the writer of the charter as Rudradatta, who has been designated as the *dēśākṣapaṭalādhikṛta* and the son of Mātṛvara. The **date** of the grant is given at the end as **the 4th regnal year** of the king, **the fifth day of the second fortnight of Grīṣma**.

---

6. Read बहुभिर्वसुधा.
7. Read स्वदत्तां परदत्तां वा.
8. Read यत्नाद्रक्ष.
9. Read वसेत् [।।*३] इति.

NO. 16: KOMARTI PLATES OF CAṆḌAVARMAN, YEAR 6

Provenance	:	Komarti, Srikakulam district, Andhra Pradesh.
References	:	E. Hultzsch, *EI*, Vol. IV (1929-30), pp. 142-45 and plate; S.N. Rajaguru, *IO*, Vol. I, Pt. 2 (1958), pp. 28-30.
Language	:	Sanskrit, in prose, except the imprecatory verses in lines 13-19.
Metre	:	Verses 1-3 *anuṣṭubh*.
Script	:	Southern variety of about the fifth century A.D.
Date	:	6th regnal year, the fifth day of the bright fortnight of the month of Caitra.

TEXT[1]

First Plate

1 सिद्धम्[2] स्वस्ति [।।*] विजय**सिंहपुरा**त्परमदैवत:(तो) बप्पभट्टारकपादभक्त:
2 कलिङ्गाधिपति **श्रीमहाराजा चण्डवर्म्मा**[3] कोहेतुरे सर्व्वस-
3 मवेतात्कुटुबिन:[4] समाज्ञापयत्यस्त्येष ग्रामोस्माभि:
4 आत्मन:[5] पुण्यायुर्य्यशसामभिवृद्धये(य) आसह-
5 स्त्रांशुशशितारकाप्रतिष्टमग्रा(ग्र)हारं कृत्वा सर्व्वकर-

Second Plate: First Side

6 परिहारैश्च परिहृत्य भारद्वाजसगोत्राय वाजिस-
7 तेय[6]सब्रह्मचारिणे ब्राह्मणदेवशर्म्मणे प्रत्त: [।*]
8 तदेवं विदित्वा पूर्व्वोचितमर्य्य(र्य्या)दयोपस्थानं कर्त्त-
9 व्यं मेयहिरण्यादि चोपते(ने)यं(यम्) [।*] भविष्यतश्च राज्ञ:(ज्ञो)
10 विज्ञापयति [।*] धर्म्मक्रमविक्रमाभ्याम्

---

1. From the facsimile in *EI*, Vol. IV (1929-30), pp. 144 and 145.
2. Expressed by a symbol.
3. Read महाराजश्चण्ड.
4. Read -तान्कुटुम्बिन:
5. Read -स्माभिरात्मन:
6. Read वाजसनेय.

Second Plate: Second Side

11 अन्य[7]तमयोगादवाप्य च महीमनुशासता प्रवृत्तक-
12 मिदं दानं सद्ध[8]र्म्ममनुपश्यद्भिरेषोग्रहारोनुपाल्यः [।*]
13 अपि चाग्र(त्र) व्यासा(स)गीतात्श्लोका[9]नुदाहरन्ति [। *] बहुभिर्व्वसु-
14 धा दत्ता वसुधा वसुधाधिपैः [।*] यस्य यस्य यदा भूमि-
15 [स्*] तस्य तस्य तदा फलम् [।।*१]

Third Plate

16 स्वदत्तां परंदत्तां[10] वा यत्न(त्ना)द्रक्ष युधिष्टिर [।*] महीम्महि-
17 मतां श्रेष्ठो(ष्ठ) दाता(ना)च्छ्रेयोनुपालनं [।।*२] षष्टिं वर्ष-
18 सहस्त्राणि स्वर्ग्गे मोदति भूमिदः [।*] आक्षेप्ता
19 चानुमत्ता(न्ता) च तान्येव नरके वसेमिति[11] ।। [३*] स्वमुखां[12]ज्ञा [।*]
20 **संवत्सरः षष्ठः ६ चैत्रमासशुक्लपंचमि(मी)दिवसः ।।**

ABSTRACT

The record begins with the symbol for *siddham* and the word *svasti*. Lines 1-7 record that the reigning king **Mahārāja Caṇḍavarman**, the lord of Kaliṅga, a devout worshipper of the gods and devoted to the feet of his father, addressed the royal order issued from the victorious **Siṁhapura** to the inhabitants of the village of Kōhētura. The order related to the grant of the said village by converting it into an *agrahāra* and exempting it from all taxes, to the brāhmaṇa Dēvaśarman of the Bhāradvāja *gōtra*, a student of the Vājasanēya (*caraṇa*). The grant is stated to have been made permanent so as to last as long as the sun, the moon and the stars exist. In lines 8-9 the tenants were directed to pay the usual share of *mēya* and *hiraṇya* to the donee according to the established custom. In lines 9-12 the king has requested the future rulers to honour and preserve the gift. This is followed by three of the usual benedictory and imprecatory verses (lines 13-19). Lines 19-20 state that the charter was written at the command of the king himself in his **6th regnal year on the fifth day of the bright fortnight of the month of Caitra**.

7. Hultzsch suggests विक्रमाणामन्य-.
8. Read स्वधर्म-.
9. It should be गीतान्श्लोका-.
10. Read परदत्तां.
11. Read वसेदिति.
12. The *anusvāra* is superfluous.

NO. 17: KOROSHANDA PLATES OF VIŚĀKHAVARMAN, YEAR 7

Provenance	:	Koroshanda, Ganjam district, Orissa.
References	:	S.N. Rajaguru, *JBORS*, Vol. XIV, Pt. 2 (1928), pp. 282-84; S.N. Rajaguru, *IO*, Vol. I, Pt. 2 (1958), pp. 1-3; and G. Ramdas, *EI*, Vol. XXI (1931-32), pp. 23-25 and plate.
Language	:	Sanskrit, in prose, except the two imprecatory verses at the end.
Metre	:	Verses 1-2 *anuṣṭubh*.
Script	:	Southern variety of about the fifth century A.D.
Date	:	7th regnal year, the twentieth day of the seventh fortnight of Hēmanta.

TEXT[1]

First Plate

1 स्वस्ति [।।*] विजय**श्रीपुरा[त्*]** परमदैवत[:*] बप्पभट्टारकपादभक्त: **श्रीमहाराज**-

2 **विशाखवर्म्मा** कोरासोडकप(पं)चाल्या(ल्यां) तंपोयकग्रामे कुटुम्बिन:

3 समाज्ञापयति अस्त्येष ग्रामोस्माभिरस्मद्बप्पभट्टारकपादानां

Second Plate: First Side

4 सुरलोकादप्रच्युतानां भूय≍पुण्याप्यायनाय आचन्द्रतारार्क्कप्रति-

5 ष्ठमग्रहारं कृत्वा सर्व्वकरभरैश्च परिहृत्य आत्रेयसगोत्रे-

6 भ्य: शबरभेण्डक विष्णुशर्म्मश्रेष्ठिशर्म्मअग्निशर्म्मनागशर्म्मशिवशर्म्मे(र्म्म)-

Second Plate: Second Side

7 भ्य[:] संप्रदत्तस्तदेवमवेत्य पूर्व्वोचितमर्य्यादाभिस्सर्व्वोपस्थानं

8 कर्त्तव्यमिति [।।*] आज्ञाभोगिकबोढुदेव[:] **स(सं)व्वत**[2] **७ हेमं ७**

9 अत्र च व्यासगीतौ द्वौ श्लोकौ **दिवस २०**[3]

---

1. From the facsimile in *EI*, Vol. XXI (1931-32), pp. 24 and 25.
2. Ramdas reads [सं]व्वत् ; the final *t* is written in a smaller character below the line.
3. This portion of the date was perhaps inserted later due to the inadvertance of the scribe.

Third Plate

10 बहुभिर्व्वहुधा दत्ता वसुधा वसुधाधिपैः [।*] यस्य यस्य

11 यदा भूमि[स्तस्य] तस्य तदा फल[म्* ।।] [१*] षष्टिं वर्षसहस्राणि

12 स्वर्ग्गे मोदति भूमिद[:] [।*] आक्षेप्ता चानुमन्ता च तान्येव नरके वसेत् [।।*२]

ABSTRACT

The charter begins with the word *svasti*. This is followed by the passage in lines 1-8 recording that **Mahārāja Viśākhavarman**, who was devoted at the feet of his father, issued the order from the victorious **Śrīpura**, addressing the cultivators of village Tampōyaka in Kōrōṣōḍaka-*pañcālī*. The order relates to the grant of village Tampōyaka to the brāhmaṇas named Viṣnuśarman, Śrēṣṭhiśarman, Agniśarman, Nāgaśarman and Śivaśarman of the Ātrēya *gōtra* and belonging to (the locality?) Śabarabheṇḍaka, by making it a permanent *agrahāra* till the moon, the stars and the sun exist, and making it free from all kinds of taxes. The cultivators were also directed to attend on the donees according to established custom. The purpose of the grant was to obtain further religious merit for his father. Line 8 mentions the name of the executor of the grant as Bōḍhudēva, designated as the *ājñā-bhōgika*. The **date** of the grant is given in the same line in the **7th regnal year** of the king, **the seventh fortnight of Hēmanta, on the twentieth day**. Lines 9-12 contain two of the usual imprecatory and benedictory verses, stated to have been quoted from Vyāsa.

II

INSCRIPTIONS OF THE MISCELLANEOUS UNKNOWN ROYAL FAMILIES OF SOUTH AND SOUTH-EASTERN ORISSA

NO. 18: PEDDA-DUGAM PLATES OF ŚATRUDAMANA, YEAR 9

Provenance	:	Pedda-Dugam, Srikakulam district, Andhra Pradesh.
References	:	V. Bhanumurty, *JAHRS*, Vol. XXI (1950-52), pp. 159 ff.; D.C. Sircar, *EI*, Vol. XXXI, (1955-56), pp. 89-93 and plate; and S.N. Rajaguru, *IO*, Vol. II (1960), pp. 237-41.
Language	:	Sanskrit, in prose, except for four of the imprecatory and benedictory verses at the end of the charter.
Metre	:	Verses 1-4 *anuṣṭubh*.
Script	:	Southern variety of the alphabet of about the fifth century A.D.
Date	:	9th regnal year, tenth day of the month of Āṣāḍha.

TEXT[1]

First Plate

1 सिद्धम् [।*][2] विजय**सिङ्ह(सिंह)**पुराद्भगवतो दमनेश्वर-
2 स्वामिनः पादानुध्यातो भट्टारकपादपरिगृ-
3 हीतो **महाराजश्रीशत्रुदमनदेवः** गिरि-
4 कलिङ्गवर्द्धमानाग्रहारे दुहाग्रामे वसुवाटके

Second Plate: First Side

2[3]

5 गोवाटके स(च) व्रा(ब्रा)ह्मणपुरोगा[4]द्ग्रामाञ्छरीरादिकुशलं
6 स्पृष्टवा[5] लिखित्यस्त्येते मया ग्रामका [आ*]त्मनः पुन्या(ण्या)प्यायन-
7 निमित्तं ब्राह्मणानां(भ्यां) पट्टुवग्रामवास्तव्याय(भ्यां)
8 कौण्डिन्यसगोत्राय(भ्यां) तैत्तिरीयसब्रह्मचारिणे(भ्यां)

---

1. From the facsimile in *EI*, Vol. XXXI (1955-56), pp. 92 and 93.
2. Expressed by a symbol.
3. This numerical figure represents a modern Telugu-Kannaḍa and Oriya numeral for 2; a similar figure for 1 is found on the blank side of the first plate.
4. Read पुरोगान्.
5. पृष्ट्वा.

9 यज्ञशर्म्मणः पुत्र(त्राभ्यां) बप्पशर्म्मणाय शर्व्वशर्म्म-

Second Plate: Second Side

10 णाय च[6] त्रीण्यपि[7] ग्रामका दत्ता आभ्यां ब्राह्मणदेयं कृत्वा
11 द्विजभोगे विसृषृस्तद्युष्माभि[:*] श्रोतव्यमाज्ञा[8] च कर्त्तव्या[।*]
12 अत्र च शर्व्वशर्म्मणाय(णे)वृत्तिद्वय(यं) व(ब)प्पशर्म्मणाय(णे)
13 च वृत्तिरेका[।*] सर्व्वे च समुचितग्रामाणां प्रत्याय-
14 मेयादिमुपनेस्य(ष्य)थ [।*] भवन्ति चात्र श्लोका[:*।] य: [illegible] कियां धर्म्म-
15 संयुक्तां मनसाप्यभिनन्दति[।*] वर्द्धते स चात्र यथेष्टेन(षृञ्च)

Third Plate: First Side

3[9]

16 शुक्लपक्षे(क्ष) इवाङ्शु(वांशु)मां(मान्)।।[१*] व(ब)हुभिर्व्वसुधा दत्ता
17 वसु(हु)धा वसुधाधिपै:[।*] यस्य यस्य यदा भूमि[:*]
18 तस्य तस्य तदा फलं(लम्)।। [२*] पूर्व्वदत्तां दिजातिभ्यो
19 यन्नाद्रक्ष युधिष्ठिर । महीम्महिमतां श्रेष्ठ
20 दानाच्छ्रेयोनुपालनं(नम्)[।।*३] षष्टिं वर्ष्व(र्ष) सहस्त्रणि

Third Plate: Second Side

21 स्वग्गे(र्गे) मोदति भूमिद: [।*] आक्षेप्ता चानुमन्ता च
22 तान्येव नरके वसे[त्*] ।। [४*] इत्येवं लिखित **सम्ब(संव)त्सरो**
23 **नवमो ९ आषाढमासदिवसो दशमो**
24 दूतो वैद्यकृष्णदत्त[:*।।]

ABSTRACT

The charter begins with a symbol for *siddham*. This is followed by a passage in prose (lines 1-11) recording that the reigning king **Śatrudamanadēva**, who was favoured by the feet of his overlord (*bhaṭṭāraka-pāda-parigṛhīta*) and was a devotee of lord Damanēśvara-svamin, issued the order from the victorious **Siṁhapura** addressing the

6. Read बप्पशर्म्मणे शर्व्वशर्म्मणे च.
7. Read त्रयोपि.
8. Read श्रोतव्या.
9. This numerical figure resembling the modern Oriya 3 is engraved in the left margin near the beginning of lines 17-18.

inhabitants headed by the brāhmaṇas and others, residing at the three villages named Duhā-*grāma,* Vasu-*vāṭaka* and Gō-*vāṭaka,* situated within the *agrahāra* called Vardhamāna in the district of Giri-Kaliṅga. These three villages[10] were granted in favour of the two brāhmaṇas named Bappaśarman and Śarvaśarman, who were the sons of Yajñaśarman and belonged to the Kauṇḍiṇya *gōtra* and Taittirīya (*śākhā* of the *Yajurvēda*). They were residents of Paṭṭuva-*grāma.* The gift was made by the king in order to acquire religious merit. The gift villages were made *brāhmaṇa-dēya* and granted to the donees as *dvija-bhōga.* Lines 12-14 stated that the gift was divided into three shares (*vṛttis*), two of which were granted to Śarvaśarman and one to Bappaśarman. The villagers were enjoined to abide by the orders of the donees and were directed to pay them their dues as rent or taxes (*pratyāya*) and give them a share of the produce of the fields (*mēya*). This is followed by four imprecatory and benedictory verses (lines 14-22). Lines 22-23 refer to the **date** of the charter issued on **the tenth day of the month of Āṣāḍha in the 9th regnal year** of the king. The charter ends with a reference (line 24) to Kṛṣṇadatta, the *vaidya* (physician), who was the *dūta* or the executor of the grant.

10. These three villages appear to have been reallotted to the brāhmaṇas by the king, as the localities are known to have been already included under the revenue-free area or the *agrahāra* of Vardhamāna.

NO. 19: TANDIVADA GRANT OF PṚTHIVĪ MAHĀRĀJA, YEAR 46

Provenance	:	Not known.
References	:	R.S. Panchamukhi, *EI*, Vol. XXIII (1935-36), pp. 88-98, and plates; S.N. Rajaguru, *IO*, Vol. I, Pt. 2 (1958), pp. 48-52.
Language	:	Sanskrit, in prose, except the three imprecatory verses at the end.
Metre	:	Verses 1-3 *anuṣṭubh*.
Script	:	South Indian alphabet of about the sixth century A.D.
Date	:	46th regnal year, the full-moon day of Kārttika.

TEXT[1]

First Plate

1 स्वस्ति[2] [।*] श्रीमत्पिष्टपुरात्सकलजगदवनसमुद्भूतकीर्त्ति-
2 चारुचन्द्रिकासमुद्यो(द्‌यो)तितदिगत्त(न्त)रस्य म-
3 हाराजरणदुर्ज्जयस्य सूनोस्समति-
4 शयितशक्रविभूतेर्व्विक्रमेन्द्रस्य प्रियतनय[:*]

Second Plate: First Side

5 प्रवर्द्धमानप्रतापोपनतसमस्तसामन्तमण्डल(लो) निज-
6 भुजविजयोदयाधिगतयशोविशेषभूषण: श्रीरम(राम)-
7 काश्यपसगोत्र: परमब्रह्मण्यो मातापितृपा-
8 दानुद्धया(ध्या)त[:] **श्रीप्रि(पृ)थिवीमहाराज:** पागुणारविषये ताण्डि-
9 वाड़ग्राममधिवस्सतसेर्व्व[3]समवेतान्कुटि(टु)म्बिनस्स[मा]ज्ञाप-

Second Plate: Second Side

10 यति यथा । श्रुतिम्मृ(स्मृ)तिपारदृश्वन:[4] यथावदनुष्ठिताग्न(ग्नि)ष्टो-

---

1. From the facsimile in *EI*, Vol. XXIII (1935-36), pp. 96 and 97.
2. The word is incised in the left margin near line 3 of the text.
3. Read. . .वसतस्सर्व्व. . . .
4. The Parlakhimedi plates of the same king read पारगाय.

11 मादिक्रियापूतात्मनो विष्णुशर्म्मणः पु(पौ)त्राय असकृदिज्या-
12 प्रयोग[5]प्ररायमाणद्रविणसूचितर्त्विकस-
13 दस्यसमृद्धेः त्रिसहस्रविद्याध्ययनप्रवचनव्याख्यान-
14 शीलिनः प्रि(पृ)थिवीशर्म्मणः पुत्राय वेदवेदाङ्गन्याय(यो)प-

Third Plate: First Side

15 निषद्योग(गा)वबोधनिर्म्मलीकृतबुद्धये विविधाध्वरावभृथा-
16 म्भःपवित्रीकृतविग्रहाय देवपितृमनुष्यसमर्चन-
17 समानित(नीत)रात्रिन्दिवाय कोण्डमञ्चिग्रामनिवासिने
18 त्रिसहस्रविद्याय विंशतिव्याख्यानाय कामकायनस-
19 गोत्राय छन्दोगसब्रह्मचारिणे भवशर्म्मणे अस्मदायु-

Third Plate: Second Side

20 रारा(रो)ग्ययशोभिवृद्धये सर्व्वकरपरिहारेणाग्रहारी-
21 कृत्य ग्रामोन्दत्तः[6] न कैश्चिदपि बाधा करणीया [।*] प्र-
22 **[व*]र्द्धमानविजयराज्यसंवत्सरे षट्चत्वारी(रिं)शे**
23 **कार्त्तिकपौर्ण्णमास्यान्द्धर्म्मप्रदान**मेतत् [।*] आज्ञप्तिः श्रीराम-
24 लेणृराजः[7] [।*] अत्र व्यासगीता[:*] श्लोकाः [।*] बहुभिर्व्वसुधा दत्ता

Fourth Plate

25 बहुभिश्चानुपालिता[।*] यस्य यस्य यदा भूमित(स्त)स्य तस्य
26 तदा फलम् [।।*१] स्वदत्तां परदत्ता(त्तां) वा यत्नाद्रक्ष युधिष्ठिर ।
27 मर्ही महीमतां श्रेष्ठ धर्म्माछ्रेयोनुपालनं [।।*२]
28 आस्फोटयन्ति पितरो वल्गन्ति प्रपितामहाः[8] ।। (।)
29 भूमिदाता कुले जातः ।[9] स नस्त्राता भविष्यति ।। [३*]

ABSTRACT

The charter begins with the word *svasti*. This is followed by the prose passage in lines 1-8 describing the reigning king **Pṛthivī Mahārāja** and his

---

5. Read पराय. . . .
6. Read ग्रामो दत्तः
7. Rajaguru suggests लेन्दुराजः and opines that the name might have been connected with one of the capitals of the Viṣṇukuṇḍins named Lendulura; *IO*, Vol. I, Pt. 3 (1958), p. 50 and fn. 4. But the correct name of the locality is Deṇḍaluru.
8. Read प्रवल्गन्ति पितामहाः
9. The punctuation mark is superfluous.

predecessors. The king has been described as the son of Vikramēndra and the grandson of *Mahārāja* Raṇaḍurjaya, and as one who meditated on the feet of his parents. He was extremely pious and belonged to the Śrī-Rāma-Kāśyapa *gōtra*. Lines 8-21 refer to the royal order relating to the grant, addressed to the cultivators and other inhabitants of Tāṇḍivāḍa village situated in the *viṣaya* of Pāguṇāra. The said village is stated to have been granted, by making it an *agrahāra* and free from all imposts, to Bhavaśarman of the Kāmakāyana *gōtra* and a student of Chandōga (*śākhā*), who had studied three thousand sciences and (wrote) twenty commentaries and resided in Kōṇḍamañci village. The donee is stated to have been the son of Pṛthivīśarmaṇ, who studied, taught and commented on the three thousand sciences and whose prosperity was revealed among the priests. The donee was the grandson of Viṣṇuśarmaṇ, who performed the *agniṣṭōma* and other sacrifices and mastered the *Śruti* and *Smṛti*. Lines 22-23 refer to the **date** of issue of the grant, given in the regnal year of the king as the **46th year** of his prosperous and victorious reign, and **the full-moon day of the month of Kārttika**. The grant is stated (lines 23-24) to have been executed by Śrī-Rāma-Leṇṛurāja. Lines 24-29 contain three of the customary verses.

NO. 20: PARLAKHIMEDI PLATES OF PṚTHIVĪ MAHĀRĀJA, YEAR 49

Provenance	:	Parlakhimedi, Ganjam district, Orissa.
References	:	S.C. De, *EI*, Vol. XXXV, (1963-64), pp. 221-23 and plates; and, S.N. Rajaguru, *IO*, Vol. I, Pt. 2 (1958), pp. 54-56.
Language	:	Sanskrit, in prose, except the three verses at the end.
Metre	:	Verses 1-3 *anuṣṭubh*.
Script	:	Southern variety of about the sixth century A.D.
Date	:	49th regnal year, the eighth day of the bright fortnight of the month of Jyēṣṭha.

TEXT[1]

First Plate

1 स्वस्ति[2] [।*] श्रीविजयस्कन्धावारात् **विरजोनगराधिवासकात्**सकलजगदवनसमुद्भू-
2 तकीर्त्तिचारुचन्द्रिकासमुद्यो(द्यो)तितदिगन्तरस्य महाराजरणदुर्ज्जयस्य
3 सूनोस्समतिशयितशक्रविभूतेर्व्विक्रमेन्द्रस्य प्रियतन-
4 यः प्रवर्द्धमानप्रतापोपनतसमस्तसामन्तमण्डलः निज-
5 भुजविजयोदयाधिगतयशोविशेषभूषणः श्रीराम-

Second Plate: First Side

6 काश्यप[सगो]त्रः परमब्रह्मण्यो मातापितृपादानुध्यातः **श्री[पृथिवी]**-
7 **महाराजः** कुद्धावती[3] विषये गोल्लवल्लीग्राममधिवसतः सर्व्वस-
8 मवेतां(ता)न्कुटुम्बिनः समाज्ञ(ज्ञा)पयति यथा मातृशर्म्मणः पौत्रा-
9 य दामोदरशर्म्मण ≍ पुत्राय वेदवेद(दा)ङ्गप(पा)रगाय षट्कर्म्मनिर-
10 ताय यमनियमपरायणाय पुराणरामायणधर्म्मशास्त्रा-

---

1. From the facsimile in *EI*, Vol. XXXV (1963-64), pp. 222 and 223.
2. The word is incised in the left margin near line 3 of the text.
3. Rajaguru reads रुद्रावती ; S.C. De reads it as कुद्रावती and D.C. Sircar suggests रुद्रावली; the *viṣaya* may be the same as रुप्यवती found in the Tekkali plates of early Eastern Gaṅga kings, Indravarman of the Gaṅga year 154 and Devendravarman of the Gaṅga year 310 [*IO*, Vol. II (1960), pp. 58 ff. and 128 ff.] This *viṣaya* probably comprised the area round Tekkali (now in Andhra Pradesh) and Parlakhimedi in Ganjam district.

Second Plate: Second Side

11 द्यनेकविद्यापारदर्श(र्शि)ने भृगुसगोत्राय तैत्तिरि(री)य[सब्रह्मचारिणे]
12 पद्मशर्म्मणे ग्रामोयमस्मत्पुण्यायुरारोग्यजययशोभिवृद्धये
13 सर्व्वकरपरिहारेणाग्रहारीकृत्य दत्तः [।*] न कैश्चिदपि बाधा क-
14 रण(णी)या [।*] **प्रवर्द्धमानविजयराज्यस(सं)वत्सरे नवाधिकच[त्वारिं]श्र(शे)**
15 **जेष्ट[4] मासशुक्ल पक्षाष्टम्यां** धर्म्मप्रदानमेतदाज्ञप्तिः श्रीराम-

Third Plate

16 लेणृराजः[5] [।*] अत्र व्यासगीताः श्लोकाः [।*] [बहुभिर्व्वसुधा दत्ता बहु][6]-
17 भिश्चानुपालिता [।*] यस्य [यस्य यदा भूमिस्तस्य तस्य]
18 तदा फलं(लम्) [।।*१] आस्फोटय[न्ति पितरो प्रवल्गन्ति पितामहाः ।]
19 भूमिजा(दा)ता कुले जातस्स न स्त्राता भवि[ष्यति [।।*२] षष्टिं वर्षसहस्त्राणि स्वर्गे]
20 मोदति भूमिदः [।*] आक्षेप्ता चानुम[न्ता च तान्येव नरके वसेत्] [।।*३]

ABSTRACT

The charter is stated in line 1 to have been issued from the victorious camp at **Virajā-nagara**. Lines 1-6 of the charter describe the reigning king **Pṛthivī Mahārāja,** who was the son of Vikramēndra and the grandson of Mahārāja Raṇadurjaya, who belonged to the Śrī-Rāma-Kāśyapa *gōtra.* He has been described as *paramabrāhmaṇya* and is stated to have acquired fame by his own valour. Lines 7-13 record the royal declaration before the cultivators assembled at the village named Gōllāvallī in Kuddhāvatī district. This village is stated to have been granted in favour of Padmaśarmaṇ, son of Dāmōdaraśarmaṇ and grandson of Mātṛśarmaṇ, who belonged to the Bhṛgusa *gōtra* and Taittirīya (*śākhā*) and who had studied the *Vēdas* and *Vedāṅgas* and gained expertise in the study of the *Purāṇas, Rāmāyaṇa, Dharmaśāstras* and many other related fields and sincerely followed the *ṣaṭ-karmas* and other rituals. The grant is stated to have been made free from all taxes, after being turned into an *agrahāra,* in order to obtain religious merit and longevity and fame for the donor. Lines 14-15 refer to the **date** of the grant as **the 49th year of the victorious reign of the king and the eighth day of the bright fortnight of the month of Jyēṣṭha.** Lines 15-16 refer to Śrī-Rāma-Leṇṛrāja, who is stated to be the executor of the grant. Lines 16-20 contain three of the usual imprecatory and benedictory verses, said to have been quoted from *Vyāsa.*

4. Read ज्येष्ठ
5. S.C. De reads लेन्थुराजः
6. The right half of the plate containing the words shown in square brackets in lines 16 to 20 is broken and lost.

NO. 21: SUMANDALA PLATES OF THE TIME OF PRTHIVĪVIGRAHA-*BHAṬṬĀRAKA*, GUPTA YEAR 250

Provenance	:	Sumandala, Ganjam district.
References	:	S.N. Rajaguru, *OHRJ*, Vol. I (1952), pp. 66-69; *idem*, *IO*, Vol. I, Pt. 2 (1958), pp. 113-16 and plates; and D.C. Sircar, *EI*, Vol. XXVIII (1949-50), pp. 79-85 and plates.
Language	:	Sanskrit, in prose, except four of the imprecatory verses at the end.
Metre	:	Verses 1-4 *anuṣṭubh*.
Script	:	Gupta variety of script of about the sixth century A.D.
Date	:	Gupta year 250, the eleventh day of the dark fortnight of the month of Māgha.

TEXT[1]

First Plate

1 सिद्धम्[2] स्वस्ति [।*] चतुरुदधिमेखलायां सप्तद्वीपपर्व्वतसरित्पत्त[न]-
2 भूषणायाम्व(यां व)सुन्धरायाम्व(यां **व**)**र्त्तमानगुप्तराज्ये वर्षशतद्वये**
3 **पञ्चाशदुत्तरे** कलिङ्गराष्ट्रमनुशासति **श्रीपृथिवीविग्रह**-
4 भट्टारके तत्पादानुध्यात: पद्मखोल्यां महाराजोभयान्वयो
5 व(ब)प्पदेव्यामुत्पन्नतनु: सहस्त्ररश्मिपादभक्तो **महाराजधर्म्मरा**-
6 **ज:** कुशली परक्खलमार्ग्गविषये वर्त्तमान भविष्यत्साम[न्त]-

Second Plate: First Side

7 महाराजराजपुत्रकुमारामात्त्योपरिकतदायुक्तकदाण्डवासिक[3]स्थान (ना)-
8 न्तरिकानन्यांङ्श्च[4] वल्लभजातीयान्राजपादोपजीविनो व्य[व]हारिवैषे(ष)-
9 यिकाङ्श्च (कांश्च) यथार्हम्मानयत्त्यादिशति च विदितमस्तु वो यथा-

1. From the original plates. The charter is now preserved in the Orissa State Museum, Bhubaneswar.
2. Expressed by a symbol.
3. The intended reading is दाण्डपाशिक.
4. Read न्यांश्च.

10 स्माभिः **माघकृष्णस्यैकादश्यामुत्तरायने(णे)** एतद्विषयसं-
11 ट्टिव्य[5]र्द्धाकमण्डुकग्रामश्चन्दनवाटक सहितोग्रहारीकृत्य होम्वकाग्र-
12 हारीयब्राह्मणोपाध्यायमट्टुस्वामिप्रमुखानां नानागोत्रचरणा-

Second Plate: Second Side

13 नां वृत्ताद्ध्यनवतां ब्राह्मणानां(ना)माचन्द्रार्क्कसमकालस्थित्त्याताम्र[प]-
14 ट्टाभिलिखितः सर्व्वकरपीडावर्ज्जितः सोद्देशः सोपरिकरः मा[ता]-
15 पित्रोरात्मनश्च पुण्याभिवृद्धये प्रतिग्रहेण प्रतिपादितः [।*]
16 तदेषास्मद्दत्तिर्द्धर्म्मगौरवात्प्रतिपालनीयेति । उक्तञ्च धर्म्म-
17 शास्त्रे । व(ब)हुभिर्व्वसुधा दत्ता राजभिस्सगरादिभिः [।*] यस्य यस्य य-
18 दा भूमिस्तस्य तस्य तदा फलं(लम्) । [।१*] षष्टिम्व(ष्टिं व)र्षसहस्राणि स्वर्ग्गे मोदति

Third Plate

19 भूमिदः [।*] आक्षेप्ता चानुमन्ता च तान्येव नरकं(के) वसेत् । [।*२] मा भूदफ-
20 [6]लशङ्का वः परदत्तेति पार्थिवाः [।*] स्वदानात्फलमानन्त्यं परदा-
21 नानुपालनं (ने) । [।*३] स्वदत्तां परदत्ताम्वा(त्तां वा) यो हरेत वसुन्धरां(राम्) । स विष्ठा-
22 यां कृमिर्भूत्वा पितृभिस्सह पच्यते । [।*४] लिखिताधिकरणि-
23 कदासुकेन । लक्षणस्वामिना[7]
24 तापितमिति ।।[8]

ABSTRACT

The inscription begins with the symbol for *siddham* and the word *svasti.* A prose passage follows in lines 1-6, referring to the reigning king **Mahārāja** ***Dharmarāja,*** a descendant of Mahārāja Abhaya and born of Bappadevī, who issued the royal order from **Padmakhōli,** when his overlord **Śrī-Pṛthivīvigraha-bhaṭṭāraka** was ruling Kaliṅga-*rāṣtra* in **the Gupta year 250**. The royal order is said to have been addressed to the present and future kings and officers connected with the administration of the *viṣaya* of Parakkhalamārgga. Lines 7-9 refer to the officers, such as the *sāmanta, mahārāja, rājaputra, kumārāmātya, uparika, tadāyuktaka, dāṇḍapāśika, sthānāntarika, vyavahārin* and *vaiṣayika.* Lines 10-15 record the grant of a village called Ardhākamaṇḍuka together with another locality called Candana-*vāṭaka,* both situated in the above-mentioned *viṣaya.* The reign-

5. Read संवद्धा.
6. A letter looking like ल before ल seems to have been rejected by the engraver owing to its damaged lower part.
7. लक्ष्मण seems to have been intended.
8. The sign for punctuation is indicated by a long horizontal stroke which is joined by the medial *i* sign of the last letter *ti* cursively.

ing king granted these localities in favour of a number of brāhmaṇas belonging to various *gōtras* and *caraṇas* along with *upādhyāya* Maṭusvāmin of Hōmvaka *agrahāra*. The brāhmaṇas are described as men of good conduct and learning. The grant was made on the occasion of the **uttarāyaṇa falling on the eleventh day of the dark fortnight of the month of Māgha**. The gift was made free from the obligation of paying any tax and from all obstacles and granted together with *uddēśa* (space above the ground) and *uparikara* (rent to be realized from temporary tenants). Lines 17-22 refer to three of the usual imprecatory and benedictory verses relating to land-grants. Lines 23-24 mention that the charter was written by Dāsuka of the *adhikaraṇa* and heated by Lakṣmaṇasvāmin.

NO. 22: KHANDIPADA-NUAPALLI PLATES OF ŚRĪ-CHARAMPARĀJA

Provenance	:	Khandipada-Ṅuapalli, Khallikote taluk, Ganjam district.
Reference	:	S.N. Rajaguru, *IO*, Vol. II (1960), pp. 323-29.
Language	:	Sanskrit, in prose, except the three verses at the end.
Metre	:	Verses 1-3 *anuṣṭubh*.
Script	:	Eastern variety of the north Indian alphabet of about the sixth century A.D.
Date	:	Not dated.

TEXT[1]

First Plate

1 ॐ स्वस्ति [।।*] [श्री] कप(पो)लकुमुदाकर[:*] शशिकला. . . व[2]
2 स्फुरद्भुजङ्ग भोगरत्नविकचारविन्दनेत्रजटाम-
3 . . .गमप्ररूढतरशौर्यःरालंकृत त्रिलोचनलोकेश्वरश्च
4 . . .शंतुवः सदामङ्गलः ।। विजयकोङ्गोदाद्भगव[ती]-
5 गिरिजानयनस्फुरितशिखशिखानलमसे(शे)श(ष)-
6 संतप्तजाह्नवीविमलसलिल भरितकपोल-
7 . . .[3] विपुलकुहरलीलायमानविविधरवतिमूल-
8 वातार्द्धविक्षिप्तनिपतदवनिमण्डलसलिल . . .[4]
9 . . .पतन . . . सकल[सुरासुर]-

Second Plate: First Side

10 किन्नरगन्द्धर्वमहोरगनमितबहुजन्मान्तरोपार्ज्जि-
11 तदुरितरहरहरचरणकमलानुध्यातः परममाहेश्वर-
12 समाकृष्टनिशितखड्गविमलकिरणच्छुरितांसु(शु)पीठनि[स]-

---

1. From the original. The charter is now preserved in the Orissa State Museum, Bhubaneswar.
2. The letters in the first line are very corroded.
3. Two letters appear to have been engraved but are not legible.
4. Two letters are damaged.

13 त्वव(ब)लवदरिगणस्वभुजव(ब)लोपार्जितभूमण्डलराज-
14 शब्दः **श्रीछरम्पराजः** कुशली [।।*] अस्मद्भूमण्डल(ले)श्री-
15 सामन्तमहासामन्तमहाराजराजनकराजपुत्त्रदण्ड-
16 नायककुमारामात्योपरिकतदायुक्तका[नन्यांश्च*] वर्त्तमान भवि-
17 ष्यतो व्यवहारिणः सकरणान्यथार्हं सर्व्वान्या(ना)दिशयति

Second Plate: Second Side

18 विदितमस्तु भवता[म्*] खिण्डिङ्गहारविषयसम्बद्ध-
19 एककटिकग्रामोस्मांभिः अकरीकृत्त्य बह्वृचगौत-
20 मसगोत्त्राय श्रीस्वामिचन्द्र १ दि(दी)क्षितदुर्गस्वामि २-
21 भट्टिस्वामि १ द्वितीय भट्टिस्वामि १ तृति(ती)यभट्टिस्वामि-
22 नामचन्द्रस्वामिः[5] स्वामिचन्द्रस्वामिभ्यो ब्राह्मणेभ्यो
23 मातापित्त्रोरात्मनश्च पुण्याभिवृद्धये सलिल[धारा]-
24 पुरस्सरेण विधिना प्रतिपादित[ः *।।] तथैव तेषां आ-
25 चन्द्रार्क्कक्षितिसमकालं भुंजानानां धर्म्मगौरवाच्च

Third Plate

26 द. . . . . .[6] ते वर्त्तितव्यः(व्यम्) [।। *] उक्तं च मानवे धर्म्मे [।*] [बहु][7]-
27 [भि]र्व्वसुधा दत्ता राजभिः सगरादिभिः[।*] [यस्य यस्य यदा भू]-
28 [मिः] तस्य तस्य तदा फलं(लम्) ।। [१*] स्वदत्ता(त्तां) परदत्ताम्वा(त्तां वा) [यो ह]-
29 रेत वसुन्द्धरां [।*] स विष्ठायां कृमिर्भूत्वा पितृभिः
30 सह पच्यते ।।[२*] दूतः श्रीस्वामिचन्द्रोत्त्रः(त्र) वा(धा)रदत्त
31 सुलेखकः [।*] खनकश्छन्नभोगी च सुवर्ण्णाख्यश्च
32 लाञ्छकः ।। [३*]

ABSTRACT

The charter begins with the expressions *oṃ* and *svasti*. Lines 1-4 contain a prose passage in praise of lord Trilōcana-Lōkēśvara (Śiva). Lines 4-14 have a long passage in prose, in which the reigning king **Śrī-Charamparāja** has been introduced as a devout worshipper at the feet of lord Śiva, and who earned the title of *rāja* by acquiring the earth on his own strength. He is represented in the next passage (lines 14-24), as making a grant of the

5. The *visarga* is redundant.
6. The letters are illegible due to corrosion.
7. The letters are illegible due to corrosion.

village of Ekakaṭika in the Khiṇḍiṅgahāra *viṣaya* of Kōṅgōda. The grant is stated to have been issued from the victorious Kōṅgōda. The village is said to have been granted by making it free from taxes and shared amongst the brāhmaṇas, namely, Śrī-Svāmicandra of the Bahvṛca *śākhā* and Gautama *gōtra* having one share, Dikṣita-Durgasvāmin, having two shares, Bhaṭṭisvāmin with one share, Dvitīya-Bhaṭṭisvāmin having one share and, among Tṛtīya Bhaṭṭisvāmin,[8] Nāmacandrasvāmin and Svāmicandrasvāmin, with the libation of water, for the increase of the merit of the donor's parents and himself. The grant was made permanent by means of the copper-plate charter. The royal order relating to the grant was addressed to *śrīsāmanta, mahāsāmanta, mahārāja, rājanaka, rājaputra, daṇḍanāyaka, uparika, tadāyuktaka*, and others, including the present and future *vyavahārins* and their *karaṇas*. This is followed by two verses in lines 26-30, said to have been quoted from *Mānava-Dharma*. Lines 30-32 refer to the *dūta* or the messenger Śrī-Svāmicandra, the executor of the grant, Dhāradatta, the writer, Channabhōgin, the engraver and Suvarṇa who are endorsed or marked by the seal.

---

8. The reference to three persons called Bhaṭṭisvāmin, two of whom are specifically styled second and third, is interesting.

NO. 23: RUSSELKONDA PLATES OF NEṬṬABHAÑJA, YEAR 26

Provenance	:	Banatumba, Ganjam district.
References	:	S.N. Rajaguru, *OHRJ*, Vol. I (1952), pp. 265-70; D.C. Sircar, *EI*, Vol. XXVIII (1949-50), pp. 258-63 and plates; and S. Tripathy, *IO*, Vol. VI (1974), pp. 244-49.
Language	:	Sanskrit, part prose and part verse.
Metre	:	Verse 1 *vaṁśasthavila*; verses 2, 3 *anuṣṭubh*; verse 4 *puṣpitāgrā*.
Script	:	North Indian variety influenced by the Kaliṅga type of script of about the eighth century A.D.
Date	:	26th regnal year.

TEXT[1]

First Plate: First Side

1[2]

1 सिद्धम्[3] स्वस्ति [।*]। जटाधरः खण्डशशाङ्कशेखरः कपालमाला(लः) सितभस्मधूसरः [।*]

2 स्फुरन्महापन्नगव(ब)द्धकंकनः(णः) सदा शिवम्वो(वं वो) विदधातु शङ्करः [।।*१] द्विरदवर-

3 तुरगपदातिपदोद्धतव(ब)हलधवलधूलीवितानीकृतं(त)नभस्तलात्

4 जाज्वल्यमानविविधरुचिरप्रहरणावरणात् देवोद्यानव-

5 नषण्डमण्डपोपशोभितात् हृष्टतुष्टप्रमुदितजनकोलाहलात्

6 कलिकलहडिम्व(म्ब)डंम(ब)रतस्करदुर्भिक्षरोगापगतात् प्रस्रवण-

---

1. From the original plates which are now preserved in the Orissa State Museum, Bhubaneswar.
2. This numerical figure indicates the serial number of the inscribed face and is incised in the left margin slightly below the beginning of the first line of the text.
3. Expressed by a symbol.

First Plate: Second Side

2[4]

7 जलगम्भीरकन्दरान्तरविनिसृत[5]विचित्र पुष्पफलपादोपेतात्
8 श्रीमद्वाराड्डावासितविजयस्कन्धावारात् कुलरुपश्रुतगुणवि-
9 स्तरप्रभावः स्वभुजव(ब)लपराक्रमाक्रान्तसकलारातिपक्षविक्षोभि-
10 ताप्रतिहतप्रभावप्रसरः द्रुमराजकुलसम्भूतः नवनवतिपु-
11 रुषान्तरप्रचूर्श[6]राज्यसन्ततिः प्रदानशूरऽ अनेक[7]शतसहस्रगोवदली[8]-
12 धनप्रदायी अनेकताम्रपट्टकाङ्कितद्विजकरसमर्पितभुवनतलः प[9]

Second Plate: First Side

3[10]

13 परलोकसंक्रामितधन[नि]चयः साक्षा[द्*]धर्म इव आचार्य्य इव शिष्य[11] [इव*]
14 कृतयुग इव विनय इव पितेव च अनुकम्पमान[:*] प्रजानामुपकारप्र-
15 वृत्तः पूर्णेन्दुवत्सौम्य[:*] तेजस्वी शरदर्कवत् सागर इव गम्भीर[:*] स्थिरधर्मा
16 सुमेरुवत् रघुनघु(हु)षमान्धात(तृ)कल्पः परमव्र(ब्र)ह्मण्यपरम-
17 माहेश्वरो मातापितृपादानुध्यातः प्रकटाभिधानः **श्रीनेट्टभञ्जदेवः**
18 कुशली [।*] काम्वेरालविषये श्रीसामन्तमहास(सा)मन्तराजराजनकराजपुत्रान्त-
19 रङ्गकुमारामात्योपरिकतदायुक्तकम्व(व)र्त्तमान भविष्यदधिकरणा[12]-

Second Plate: Second Side

4[13]

20 नन्यांश्च राजपादोपजीविकान्यथार्हं सत्कृत्य समाज्ञापयति विदि-

---

4. This numerical sign is engraved in the left margin below line 8, indicating the number of the inscribed face of the plate.
5. Read विनिःसृत.
6. The intended reading seems to be प्रच्युत.
7. Read शुरोऽनेक.
8. The intended reading is बलीवर्द.
9. The letter is superfluous; there is a circular sign below the letter indicating that the scribe deleted it.
10. This numerical symbol for 3 is incised in the left margin below line 13, indicating the number of the inscribed face of the plate.
11. There is a sign like a full stop, perhaps indicating the end of the line.
12. There is a mark like that indicating a stop at the end of the line.
13. This numerical symbol for 4 is incised in the left margin below line 20.

21 तमस्तु भवतां(ताम्) एतद्विषयसम्व(म्ब)ध(द्ध)वण्डूतुङ्गन्नाम[14]ग्राम:[15] चतु:-

22 सीमापरिक्षिप्त: करादानवर्जित: सर्वावा(बा)धपरिहृत: अकरीकृ-

23 त्य म(अ)स्माभि: कौशिकगोत्राय वाजसनेयचरणाय वासुदे-

24 वस्वामिने ३ गोलस्वामिने १ आदित्यदेव(वाय) १ यज्ञस्व(स्वा)मी(मिने) १ छरम्पस्व(स्वा)मि[ने*] १

25 शिव [स्वा] मि [ने] १ अपरछरम्पस्वामि[ने*] १ गोपेन्द्रस्वामि[ने*] २ कयारस्वामि [ने*] २

Third Plate: First Side

5[16]

26 कारायणस्वामि[17][ने*] १ भा[भो]यिस्वामि[ने*] १ जयस्वामि[ने*] १ अपर:(र)जयस्वा-

27 मि[ने*] १ रविचोणस्वामि[ने*] १ एभ्यो द्विजोत्तमेभ्य: नानागोत्त्रचरणेभ्य:

28 सलिलधारापुरस्सरेण विधिना । राज्ञी क्षत्त्रिदेवी कैवर्त्तदेवी

29 राजपुत्त्रि(त्त्री)मेघावलीदेवी आभ्यो नृपतिलव्ध(ब्ध)प्रसादानु-

30 ज्ञेभ्यो देव्य:[18] परलोकगमनपाथेयस्वस्वर्गगमनसोपान-

31 मालाधिगतये प्रतिपादित: [।*] तद्भवभु(द्भि:) तासामक्षयाय(यै) पुण्याभि-

32 वृद्धि(द्धये) ताम्रपट्टदर्शनात् यथाकालफल(लं) स्वीकृत्योप: (प)[19]-

Third Plate: Second Side

6[20]

33 [भु]ञ्जानेभ्य: नृपगौरवात् धर्मानुरोधाच्च चं(च)न्द्रार्कक्षिति-

34 समकालं:(लं) न कैश्चिद्विघात: करणीय[:] । ऊ(उ)क्तं च धर्मे(र्म)शास्त्रे [।*] मा भू-

35 दफलशङ्का व: परदत्तेति पार्थिवा: [।*] स्वदानात् फलमानन्त्यं प-

36 रदत्तानुपालने । [।*२] षष्टिम्ब(ष्टिं व)र्ष सह[21] सहस्राणि स्वगे(र्गे) मोदति भू-

37 मिद: [।*] आक्षेप्ता [चा*]नुमन्ता च तान्येव नरके वसेत् [।।*३] इति कमलदला-

---

14. D.C. Sircar reads चण्डूतुङ्ग, but the letter व is clear. The village may be identified with the present Banatumba, about four miles from the town of Russelkonda in Ganjam district.
15. The *visarga* sign has been indicated by two small horizontal strokes.
16. This numerical symbol for 5 is incised in the left margin, slightly above line 27.
17. The intended reading seems to be नारायणस्वामि[ने*].
18. Sircar suggests आसां नृपतिलब्धप्रसादानुज्ञानं देवीनाम्.
19. There is a horizontal line at the end.
20. This figure for 6 is slightly visible in the left margin near the beginning of the line.
21. These two letters are superfluous.

38 म्वु(म्बु)विन्द(न्दु)लोलां श्रियमनुचिन्त्य मनुष्यजीवितं च [।*] सकलमिदमु[दा*]हृतं च वु(बु)-

39 ध्वा(द्ध्वा) न हि पुरुषैः परकीर्तयो विलोप्या[:*] ॥ [४*] **संवत् षद्(ड्)विंशतिमे** राज्ये लिखित(तं)

40 वन्द्यदेव[22]भद्रेण [।*][23] उत्कीरित[24] धार भोगिकेन [॥*]

ABSTRACT

The charter begins with the symbol for *siddham* and the word *svasti.* This is followed by a verse in adoration of the god Śiva (lines 1-2). Lines 2-8 describe the victorious camp named *Vārāḍḍā* from where the charter was issued. The place is said to have been endowed with gardens and bowers attached to certain temples. The people of the locality have been described as totally contented and the place free from fights, thieves, famine and disease. The place is further described as beautified by trees watered by many springs which produced flowers and fruits of various kinds in great abundance. Lines 8-17 describe the reigning king, **Neṭṭabhañja**, who is compared to mighty epic kings like Raghu, Nahuṣa and Māndhātṛ. He is described as a devout worshipper of lord Śiva and who respected the brāhmaṇas. He is said to have been born into the family of Drumarāja and was the inheritor of the fortune of ninety-nine past generations of kings. Lines 18-20 refer to the king's order issued to the royal officers, to the present and future *adhikaraṇas* and other dependants present in the Kāmvērāla *viṣaya*. The officials and subordinates included the *sāmanta, mahāsāmanta, rājan, rājanaka, rājaputra, antaraṅga, kumārāmātya, uparika* and *tadāyuktaka*. Lines 20-22 refer to the grant of the village of Vaṇḍutuṅga, by the reigning king, as a free gift in favour of the following brāhmaṇas of the Kauśika *gōtra* and the Vājasanēya *caraṇa*, whose shares of the holding have been specified in lines 23-27: Vāsudēvasvāmin, 3 shares; Gōlasvāmin, 1; Ādityadēva, 1; Yajñasvāmin, 1; Charampasvāmin, 1; Śivasvāmin, 1; other Charampasvāmin, 1; Gōpēndrasvāmin, 2; Kayārasvāmin, 2; Nārāyaṇasvāmin, 1; Bhōyisvāmin, 1; Jayasvāmin, 1; other Jayasvāmin, 1; Ravicōṇasvāmin, 1. Lines 28-32 mention that the grant was actually made on behalf of the queens Kṣatridēvī and Kaivartadēvī, and the princess Mēghāvalīdēvī, for their easy access to heaven. This is followed by the usual entreaties (lines 32-39) to the future rulers for the preservation of the grant and the usual imprecatory and benedictory verses. The **date** of the charter is given in line 39 as the king's **26th regnal year**. Line 40 refers to the name of the writer as Vandya-Dēvabhadra and the engraver as Dhāra-*bhōgika*.

22. भ is written below the lines.
23. Some space has been left between the names of the writer and the engraver.
24. Read उत्कीर्ण्णं.

III

INSCRIPTIONS OF THE NALAS AND OTHER UNKNOWN ROYAL FAMILIES OF WEST AND SOUTH-WESTERN ORISSA

NO. 24: BARADIPADA COPPER-PLATE GRANT OF NANDARĀJADEVA, YEAR 3

Provenance : Baradipada, Kalahandi district.
Reference : A. Joshi, *New Light on the Cultural Heritage of Orissa*, pp. 34-36.
Language : Sanskrit, in prose.
Script : Eastern variety of the northern alphabet of about the sixth century A.D.
Date : 3rd regnal year, the ninth day.

TEXT[1]

First Plate

सिद्धम्[2] [।।*] स्वस्ति ।। प्रतिमत्तसूचिताभिनवम[ञ्ज]-
रिकुसुमोद्गमोद्धूषितशाखाप्रवालान्ता-
वलीलग्नमध्या समोद्घुदितम(मा)भा-
भि[:*] शिलिमुखैरलंकृत द्रुमान्तात्**पर्वत**-

Second Plate: First Side

द्वारात्पद[3](त)न्तसामन्तम(मु)कुटमणिमयूख-
द्युतिरुद्भासितचरणा[म्*]भोद्भवपी(वि)धो मा-
तापितृपादानुध्यात[:*] **श्रीनन्दराजदेव**[:*] कु-
शली ।। चिक्खलिकायां[4]त[त् *]प्रतिनिवासिनो

Second Plate: Second Side

जनपदां(दान्) समाज्ञापयति प्रज्ञातपद(द्र)-

---

1. From the original. The charter is now preserved in the Orissa State Museum, Bhubaneswar.
2. Expressed by a symbol.
3. The letter द looks like य, which is written variantly in this charter.
4. The locality may be the same as Cikhali of the Kanker plates of Pamparājadeva. This has been identified with its namesake, situated at a distance of 21 miles from Kanker in the Chhatisgarh division of Madhya Pradesh (*EI*, Vol. IX (1907-8), p. 168).

10 कवतां यथामेषां ब्राह्मणानं(नां) भानुश-
11 र्म्मशौरिशर्म्ममातृशर्म्मणां अ-
12 यं ग्रामो नानागोत्रचरणप(प्र)वरा[णा]-

Third Plate: First Side

13 माशशाङ्कादित्यसमकालं मातापित्रो-
14 रात्मनश्च पुण्योपचय(या)र्थं सलिलपू-
15 र्व्वकं प्रतिपादित(तं) [।*] [इ]त्य[व*]गम्य यथोचित
16 भागभोगादिकं[5]मुपनयन्त [:*] सुखं प्रतिव-
17 सत[:*] ।।

Third Plate: Second Side

18 **वि[ज]यराज्य संवत् ३ दिन नवमि(मी) ।।**

ABSTRACT

The charter begins with the symbol for *siddham* followed by the word *svasti.* Lines 1-5 describe the place of issue of the record, called **Parvatadvāra**. Lines 5-7 describe the reigning king **Śrī-Nandarājadeva**, whose feet were illuminated by the jewels of the crowns of his subordinate chiefs, and who was devoted at the feet of his parents. Line 8 mentions a place called Cikkhalikā where the royal order declaring the grant was addressed to its inhabitants. Lines 9-15 record that the locality called Prajñātapadraka[6] was granted to three brāhmaṇas named Bhānuśarman, Sauriśarman and Mātṛśarman, who belonged to various *gōtras, caraṇas* and *pravaras*. The grant was made permanent till the moon and the sun would endure, in order to acquire religious merit for the donor and his parents. The donees (or residents of the donated village) were then advised (lines 16-17) to pay the usual taxes, such as *bhāga* and *bhōga*, regularly. Line 18 records the **date** when the charter was issued, in the **regnal year of the king,** as **the 3rd year, the ninth day**.[7]

---

5. The *anusvāra* is superfluous.
6. The locality, presumably, was situated under the division of Cikkhalikā, which perhaps formed a *viṣaya* or district.
7. The number of days given seems to have been intended to indicate the days of a month, which has been omitted due to the inadvertence of the scribe.

NO. 25: TERASINGHA PLATES OF TUṢṬIKĀRA

Provenance	:	Terasingha, Kalahandi district.
References	:	S.N. Rajaguru, *JKHRS*, Vol. II, Nos. 2-3 (1947), pp. 107 ff. and plates; *idem*, *IO*, Vol. I, Pt. 2 (1958), pp. 81-85; and D.C. Sircar, *EI*, Vol. XXX (1954), pp. 274-78 and plate.
Language	:	Sanskrit, in prose, except six of the usual imprecatory and benedictory verses at the end.
Metre	:	Verses 1-6 *anuṣṭubh*.
Script	:	Kaliṅga variety of the southern alphabet of about the sixth century A.D. The obverse of the first plate is written in the 'box-headed' type of the central Indian alphabet.
Date	:	Not dated.

TEXT[1]

First Plate: First Side

1 स्वि(स्व)स्ति [।*][2] **पर्व्वतद्वारकाद्भग[3]वत्या** स्तस्भेनिर्य्या[4]पादभ[क्त]-
2 **श्रीसो(शो)भोङ्नाराजजनन्या कस्तुभसय्या[5]** दायज्वरोल[का]-
3 दि[6]भोगकक्षेत्र(त्रं) काश्यपस्यगात्र[7] ब्र(ब्रा)ह्मणद्रोणस्वा[मि]-
4 नस्य[8] आचन्द्रार्क्ककालाय दत्तयि(मि)ति ।।[9]

---

1. From the facsimile in *EI*, Vol. XXX (1954), pp. 276 and 277.
2. A letter looking like *pa*, originally engraved near *rvva*, had been erased and incised later near *sti*.
3. The letter *ga* has not been engraved properly. It resembles *ta*.
4. Read स्तम्भेश्वर्य्या:
5. Sircar suggests कौस्तुभेश्वर्य्या, which may be the intended reading.
6. Rajaguru reads देभोगक and takes it as the name of a locality. The expressions seem to indicate some tribal personal names.
7. Read सगोत्र.
8. Read द्रोणस्वामिने.
9. The first of the two *daṇḍas* is curved towards the left. A conch-shell has been incised after the *daṇḍas*.

First Plate: Second Side[10]

1 स्वस्ति [।*] **तरभ्रमरकात्** स्तम्भेश्वरीपादभक्तः मातापितृपादानुध्यातः **श्री[म]-**

2 **हाराजतुष्टिकारः** प्रस्तरवाटकवासिनः सर्व्वसमवेतान्कुटुम्बिनः स[मा]-

3 ज्ञापयति अस्त्येष वाटकोस्माभिः पुण्यायुर्ब्बलयशोविवृद्धये[11]

4 [आ]चन्द्रतारकार्क्कप्रतिष्ठमग्ग्रे[12](ग्र)हारं कृत्वा काश्यपसगोत्र(त्रा)य आर्य्यद्रोण-

Second Plate: First Side

5 शम्म(र्म्म)णे संप्रदत्तः [।*] तदेवं ज्ञात्वा भवद्भिः पूव्वो(र्व्वो)चितमर्य्यादोप[स्था]नं कत्त(र्त्त)व्य[म्] [।*]

6 अपि चात्र व्यासगीताः श्लोका भवन्ति ।।[13] भविष्यतश्च राज्ञो विज्ञापयति [।*] यस्य[14]

7 यस्य यस्य यदा भूमिस्तस्य [तस्य*] तदा फलम्[15] [।।*] स्वदत्तां परदत्तां वा यत्न(त्ना) द्र-

8 क्ष युधिष्ठिरः(र) [।*] मही[म्*]महिमतां श्रेष्ठ दानाच्छ्रेयोनुपालन[म्] [।।*१] षष्टिम्वष्ष[16]-

Second Plate: Second Side

9 सहस्त्राणि स्वर्ग्गे वसति [भूमिदः ।*] आच्छै(च्छे)त्ता चानुमन्ता च तान्येव नरके वसेत् [।।*२] स्वद-

10 त्ता(त्तां) परदत्ताम्वा(त्तां वा) यो हरेत वसुन्धरा[म्] [।*] स विष्ठायां कृमिर्भूत्वा पितृभिस्स-

11 ह पच्यते[17] [।।*३] व(ब)हुभिर्व्वसुधा दत्ता राजभिस्सगर(रा)दिभि(भिः) [।*] यस्य यस्य यदा भूमि-

12 स्तस्य तस्य तदा फलं(लम्) [।।*४] अग्निष्टोम्मस्थिभिय्यज्ञैः[18] वहुभिर्व्विपुलदक्षणेः[19] [।*]

Third Plate: First Side

13 यष्टो(ष्टा) भवति र(रा)जेन्द्रः य(यो) ददाति वसुन्धराम् [।।*५] आदित्यो वसा(स)वो रुद्राः

---

10. The text of the main charter granted by the reigning king begins from this reverse side of the plate.
11. Read भिवृद्धये.
12. The letter resembles च्र.
13. This punctuation mark is represented by two small horizontal strokes.
14. The word is redundant.
15. This is the second half of the verse. The same verse has been fully quoted below in lines 11 and 12.
16. Read षष्टिं वर्ष.
17. A small dot is incised here.
18. Read अग्निष्टोमादिभिर्यज्ञैः ; the letter ग्नि looks like त्रि.
19. Read बहुभिर्बहुदक्षिणैः

14 [हुताशन*] पुरोगमा [।*] शूलपाणिश्च भगवानभिनन्दन्ति भूमिदम् [।।*६] रहसि–
15 कसुबन्धोर्व्विदितं सद्गामकेन लिखितमिति।।[20] सुन्यघेत्त्लम्[21]
16 प्रस्थ(स्त)रक्षेत्लमू(मु)खं(खम्) [।*][22]

Third Plate: Second Side

17 सिद्धम् [।*] [स्वस्ति । पर्वतद्वारकाद्भगवत्या स्तम्भेश्वर्य्याः] . . .[23]

ABSTRACT

The first side of the first plate contains four lines of an endorsement, which states that it was issued from **Parvatadvāraka** by the mother of a king who was devoted to goddess Stambhēśvarī. The name of the queen-mother seems to be **Śobhōṅṅā-Kaustubhēśvarī**. It records the grant of a piece of land which was in the possession of some residents of the locality (named Dāya, Jvara and Ulākā) in favour of a brāhmaṇa named Droṇasvāmin of the Kāśyapa *gōtra*. The grant is stated to have been made a permanent holding as long as the sun and the moon would endure.

Another charter has been recorded on the second side of the first plate which continues till the end of the record on the obverse of the third plate. This charter is stated (lines 1-5) to have been issued from a place called **Tarabhramaraka** by **Mahārāja Tuṣṭikāra,** who was devoted to goddess Stambhēśvarī. The royal order relating to the grant of the locality called Prastara-*vāṭaka* was addressed to the agriculturist householders of the said village. It was granted as a permanent *agrahāra* to a brāhmaṇa named *ārya* Drōṇaśarman of the Kāśyapa *gōtra,* in order to acquire religious merit for the donor. Lines 5-6 refer to the donor's order to the inhabitants of the village to attend on the donee according to established custom. Lines 6-14 quote six of the usual imprecatory and benedictory verses. Lines 14-15 refer to the writer of the charter, named Subandhu, who was known as *sadgāmaka* and designated as a *rahasika*.[24] Lines 15-16 seem to indicate that a piece of fallow and rockey land was also granted along with the said village to the above donee. The reverse side of the third plate contains one line of writing, very faintly visible, which is same as the beginning of the first line engraved on the obverse side of the first plate.

---

20. The punctuation mark is represented by two small horizontal strokes.
21. The intended reading may be शून्यक्षेत्लम्.
22. The first half of this line is left blank.
23. The letters of this line are very faintly visible. The engraver had begun to incise the line which is found in first side of the first plate, but erased them after engraving one line.
24. This official designation seems to be the same as *rahasyādhikṛta* or the privy counsellor of many early medieval Indian inscriptions.

NO. 26: KESARIBEDA PLATES OF NALA ARTHAPATI-*BHAṬṬĀRAKA*, YEAR 7

Provenance	:	Kesaribeda, Koraput district, Orissa.
References	:	G. Ramadas, *JBORS*, Vol. XXXIV (1943), pp. 33-42; and D.C. Sircar, *EI*, Vol. XXVIII (1949-50), pp. 12-16 and plates.
Language	:	Sanskrit, in prose, except two of the usual imprecatory verse at the end.
Metre	:	Verses 1 and 2 *anuṣṭubh*.
Script	:	Southern variety of the 'box-headed' script of about the sixth century A.D.
Date	:	Year 7, the new moon day of the month of Mārgaśīrṣa.

TEXT[1]

First Plate

1 स्वस्ति [।।*] **पुष्कर्य्याः** महेश्वरमहासेनातिसृष्टराज्यविभ[व*]: त्रिपत(ता)-

2 काध्वजः नलनृपतिकुलान्वयः **श्रीमहाराजात्र्थपतिभट्टारकः**

3 केसलकग्रामे ब्राह्मर्नेत्तरा[2]न्कुटुम्बिनश्शीर्षकञ्चाज्ञापय[ति*]

Second Plate: First Side

4 यूयमस्माभि[:] कौत्ससगोत्राय दुर्ग्ग(र्ग्गा)र्य्याय रविरार्य्याय[3] रविदत्तार्य्याय[4] पू(पु)त्रपौत्रिक[म्*]

5 अर्त्थपतिभट(ट्टा)रकस्य(स्या)नुग्रहात्र्थ(र्थ)[म्*] उदकपूर्व्व[म्*] दत्त आचन्द्रतारकमभटप्रवेश[:*] सर्व्वकर-

6 विसर्ज्जितः अवहः [।*] न केनचि[त्] किञ्च(ञ्चि) द्वक्तव्याः [।*] यतः भवद्भि[श्च*]

---

1. From the facsimile in *EI*, Vol. XXVIII (1949-50), pp. 16 and 17.
2. ब्राह्मणोत्तरान्.
3. The third letter *rā* has a sign above it resembling the superscript *r* and along with it a sign for *ā*.
4. A letter resembling *ca* seems to have been erased after engraving.

Second Plate: Second Side

7 ध्रुवकर्म्मान्तारम्भे:(म्भै:) सुनिर्वृतविश्वस्तैर्व्वस्तव्य(व्यं) विषयोचितश्च शुश्रूशा(षा:)
8 कर्त्तव्या हिरण्यादयश्च प्रत्याय(या) देया: [।*] ततश्च भटा(ट्टा)रकराजस्य(स्या)-
9 प्यायन[म् ।*] अस्माभि: परितुष्ट(ष्टै)र्दत्त[:।*] य: कश्चित् व्यपेतधर्म्मा

Third Plate: First Side

10 रागा[द्*] द्रोहात्प्रला(लो)भाद्वा ग्रामे किञ्चित्प्रलोपयेत् [।*] स महापातक-
11 युक्त:[5] पञ्चभिन्न(र्न्न)रकं व्रजेत् [।।*१] उक्तञ्च [।*] षष्टी(ष्टिं) वर्षसहस्राणि
12 स(स्व)र्ग्गे नन्दति भूमिद: [।*] आक्षेप्ता च(चा)नुमन्ता च तान्येव नरके वसवति[6]

Third Plate: Second Side

13 **संव्व[7] ७ मार्ग्गशीर्षमास(सि) अमावास्याम् लिखित(तं) स्वमुहा[8]-**
14 ज्ञात्तेन रहस्याधिकृतेन चुल्लेन ।।[9]

ABSTRACT

The charter begins with the word *svasti*. Lines 1-6 record that the reigning king **Mahārāja Arthapati-bhaṭṭāraka** of the Nala family, who has been described as one who dedicated his kingdom and wealth to god Śiva and Mahāsēna[10] (Skanda) and who had the royal banner of *tri-patāka*, issued the order from **Puṣkarī** relating to the grant of village Kēśalaka in favour of the brāhmaṇas named Durgārya, Ravirārya and Ravidattārya of the Kautsa *gōtra*. The royal order was addressed to the agriculturist householders, headed by brāhmaṇas, as well as to the village headman. The donated village was exempted from the entrance of the *bhaṭas* and made permanent and free from all taxes. The donees are stated as not being disturbed by anybody. Lines 7-10 record that the villagers were asked to be careful about their obligations to the donees in accordance with the customs prevalent in the district and to regularly pay the usual *hiraṇya* (rent in metallic money) and other dues (share of the produce). The record further states that the fulfilment of these conditions would lead to the

---

5. Read पातकैर्युक्त: .
6. Read वसेत् [।।*२] इति.
7. Read संवत्.
8. Read स्वमुखा; it indicates the influence of the Prakrit dialect.
9. A horizontal line is incised after the punctuation indicating the end of the charter.
10. The expression *mahēśvara-mahāsēn-ātisṛṣṭa-rājya-vibhava* has also been explained as "to have obtained royal fortune through the grace of Mahēśvara (Śiva) and Mahāsēna" (Skanda-Kārttikeya).

satisfaction of *bhaṭṭāraka-rāja,* the reigning king. This is followed by two of the usual imprecatory verses. Line 13 states the **date** of the grant as **the 7th regnal year** of the donor and **the new moon day of the month of Mārgaśīrṣa**. Lines 13-14 state that the charter was drafted on the verbal order of the donor, by Culla, the **rahasyādhikṛta**.

NO. 27: RITHAPUR PLATES OF BHAVADATTAVARMAN, YEAR 11

Provenance	:	Rithapur, Amaraoti district, Maharashtra.
References	:	Y.R. Gupte, *EI*, Vol. XIX (1927-28), pp. 100-04 and plate; and S.N. Rajaguru, *IO*, Vol. I, Pt. 2 (1958), pp. 89-93.
Language	:	Sanskrit, in prose, except a verse in lines 20-21.
Metre	:	*Āryā*.
Script	:	Southern variety of the 'box-headed' type of the central Indian alphabet of about the sixth century A.D.
Date	:	11th regnal year, the seventh day of the dark fortnight of the month of Kārttika.

TEXT[1]

First Plate

1 सिद्ध[म्*] ।। स्वस्ति [।*] **नन्दिवर्द्धनात्** [।।*] महेश्वरमहासेनातिसृष्ट-
2 राज्यविभवः नलनृपवंशप्रसूतः त्रिपताकाध्वजः श्रीमहाराज-
3 **भवत्तवर्म्मा** कदम्बगिरिग्रामे ब्रा[2]ह्मणपुरोगान् समहर्त्त(त्त)र-
4 कुटुम्बी(म्बि)नः समाज्ञापयति यूयमस्माभिः भगवतः प्रजापतिः(तेः)
5 प्रसादसिद्धक्षेत्रे गङ्गायमुनयोस्संवै(वे)द्ये प्रयागस्थितैरुदकपूर्व्वकं

Seconı' Plate: First Side

6 मम चाचपी[3] भट्ट(ट्टा)रिकायाश्च दंम्पंत्य[4]स्यास्माकमनुग्रहार्त्थम्(र्त्थं) पराशरस-
7 गोत्राय मात्राढ्यार्य्याय पुत्राणां चास्याष्टानाम्(नां) यथा देवार्यस्यं
8 देवद[5]त्तार्यस्य कुमारदत्तार्य्यस्य वि(वी)रदत्तार्य्यस्य वसुद-
9 त्तार्य्यस्य गो(गौ)रिदत्तार्य्यस्य ध्रुवदत्तार्य्यस्य दुगर्गत्थार्य्यस्य[6] चेत्येवम्

1. From the photographs in *EI*, Vol. XIX (1927-28), pp. 102 and 103.
2. Originally, *pa* was written but was corrected later.
3. The intended reading may be अपि च.
4. Read दाम्पत्य.
5. द is written below the letter व.
6. Read दुर्ग्गदत्तार्य्यस्य.

10 आत्मनवमाय मात्राढ्यार्य्याय दत्ता(त्तो) यत एतेषाम् ब्राह्मणा[ना*]म् (ना) वि-

Second Plate: Second Side

11 षयोचिता: हिरण्यादय: सर्व्वप्रत्याया: दातव्या: शुश्रूषाच्च(च) कर्त्त-
12 व्या ।।[7] एष च ग्राम: आचन्द्रतारिकया स्थित्या सर्व्वकरविसर्ज्जित: आ(अ)भ-
13 टप्रवेश: अवह: अशुल्कै:(ल्क:) सर्व्ववादपरी(रि)हीन:[8] चिञ्चालप-
14 लाशपद्रकमर्य्यादया न कि[9]ञ्चिद्वक्तव्य: [।।*] यो वा कश्चिलो(ल्लो)भाद्रागाद्वा कर-
15 प्रवर्त्तनं भूमिलोप(पं) व्वा(वा) कुर्य्यात् स पञ्चभिर्म्महापातकैस्संयुक्तो भ-
16 वेत् [।*] अस्माभिश्च सदशनिवर्त्तनिक: सहल: सवाटक:

Third Plate: First Side

17 ग्रामोयम् दत्त: यत एतदर्थम्(र्थं) न क(के)नचित् किञ्चित् वक्तव्य: [।*] सि(सी)मा चास्य
18 ग्रामस्य उत्तरेण पर्व्वत: विषयसि(सी)मान्तिको कर्म्मन्तकेन सह मा-
19 लुकविरक: मधुकलतिका[10] पिण्डिरकवृक्षेण वकसामलकम्(कं) त्रिमन्दर-
20 श्च विरक: राज्यसि(सी)मेति [।।*] या[11]च(**चै**)**कादशेथ वर्षे कार्त्तिकमासस्य बहुल-**
21 **सप्तम्याम्** [।*] स्वमुखाज्ञया[12]भिलिखित:(ता) रहसि नियुक्तेण(न) चुल्लेन ।। [१*] **श्रीमहारा-**
22 **जार्थपतिभट्टारकेण** आत्मन: मातापित्रो:[13] पुण्यकीर्त्तिवर्द्धनधर्म्मस्थान(नं)

Third Plate: Second Side

23 [---][14] अष्टाणा[मा]चन्द्रार्कस्थितिका[लि]कमव[15](वि)चाल्यं भवत्विति आत्म-
24 न(ना) आर्य्यक[16]पादप्रसादानुगृहीतेन ताम्ब्र(म्र)शासनमेतत् कारितमि-
25 ति [।।*] स्वस्ति गोब्राह्मणप्रजाभ्य: ।।[17] सिद्धिरस्तु:(स्तु) ।।
26 पद्दोपाद्धयाय[18] पुत्रस्य पुत्रेण बोप्पदेवेण(ना)क्षतमिद[म्*।।]

---

7. The mark of punctuation is indicated by two horizontal strokes.
8. The intended reading seems to be हृत.
9. The letter कि is written below ञ्चि.
10. The letter का is written below ति between lines 19 and 20.
11. The letter या is written above च between lines 19-20.
12. The letter या is inserted below भि between lines 21-22. Y.R. Gupte reads this letter as सा.
13. The *visarga* is superfluous.
14. Gupte suggests पुत्राणां in this damaged portion.
15. Gupte reads as a sign xच for *upadhmānīya.*
16. Read आत्मनार्यक-
17. The punctuation is indicated by two horizontal strokes.
18. The intended reading seems to be पट्टोपाध्याय.

ABSTRACT

The charter begins with the words *siddham* and *svasti*. Lines 1-4 introduce the reigning king **Mahārāja Bhavattavarman** (or Bhavadattavarman), who was born in the Nala family, who had the banner of *tri-patāka* and who acquired the kingdom through the grace of the gods Mahēśvara (Śiva) and Mahāsēna (Kārttikēya). He issued the order from **Nandivardhana**, addressing the brāhmaṇas, the officers and the agricultural householders of the village named Kadambagiri. Lines 5-10 state that the king, while staying at Prayāga, the holy place at the confluence of the Gaṅgā and the Yamunā, declared the grant of the said village for blessing the matrimonial relationship of the king and the queen in favour of Mātrāḍḍhyārya of the Parāśara *gōtra* and his eight sons (namely, Devārya, Dēvadattārya, Kumāradattārya, Vīraḍattārya, Vasudattārya, Gaurīdattārya, Dhruvadattārya and Durgadattārya). Lines 11-14 record that the villagers were directed to pay all the taxes (including metallic money) and render all the customary services to the donees. The grant was made free from all taxes, tolls and customs duties and free from all disputes. Lines 14-17 record that whoever, out of covetousness or passion, levied taxes or confiscated the land would incur the five great sins. The grant is stated to have been granted along with the right to (acquire) ten *nivarttanas* of land, the right to plough and the right to use the village orchards and paths. Lines 18-20 specify the boundaries of the gift village. To the north of the village is the mountain up to the end of the boundary of the district, Māluka *viraka*,[19] with cultivated land, the Piṇḍiraka tree, the Madhuka (tree) with a creeper, the Vakasāmalaka tree and Trimandara *viraka*. Lines 20-21 refer to the **date** of the grant given in the **regnal year**, of the donor, as **year 11, the seventh day of the dark fortnight of the month of Kārttika**. Lines 21-26 record that the grant was written by the order of the king, by Culla, the **rāhasika**.[20] It was made and favoured by the illustrious Mahārāja Arthapati-*bhaṭṭāraka*, who was the *āryaka*,[21] so that the eight sons, the donees, would enjoy the gift enduring as long as the moon and the sun. The charter was engraved by Bōppadeva, who was Paddōpādhyāya's son's son.

---

19. The expression may denote a part or division of the locality.
20. This official designation is the same as privy counsellor or a private secretary.
21. The expression here seems to mean the father. Arthapati-*bhaṭṭāraka* seems to have been referred to as the father of Bhavadattavarman.

NO. 28: PODAGADH STONE INSCRIPTION OF SKANDAVARMAN, YEAR 12

Provenance : Podagadh, Koraput district, Orissa.
References : C.R. Krishnamacharlu, *EI*, Vol. XXI (1931-32), pp. 153-57 and plate; and S.N. Rajaguru, *IO*, Vol. I, Pt. 2 (1958), pp. 94-97.
Language : Sanskrit, in verse.
Metre : Verse 1 *āryā*, verses 2-8 and 10-13 *anuṣṭubh*; verse 9 *vaṁśasthāvila*.
Script : Southern variety of the alphabet of about the sixth century A.D.
Date : 12th regnal year, the twenty-seventh day of the month of Mādhava (Vaiśākha).

TEXT[1]

1 सिद्धम् ।। हरिणा जितं जयति जेष्यती[त्ये]षा गुणस्तुतिर्न्न[हि] [सा] [।*] ननु भगवा[नेव]
2 जयो जेतव्यं चाधिजेता [च] ।।[१*] श्रीनलान्वयमुक्ख्यस्य[2] विक्क्रमक्षपितद्विष: [।*]
3 नृपतेर्भवदत्तस्य सत्पुत्रेणाव्यवंस्थिताम्[3] ।। [२*] भ्रष्टामाकृष्य राजर्द्धिं
4 शून्यामावास्य पुष्करीम् [।*] पितु ≍ पितामहानाञ्च जनन्या ☓ क्रि (कृ)तिना [तत:] [।।*] [३*]
5 कृत्वा ध[र्म्मार्थ]नेभ्याशानि(मि)दमात्महितैषिणा [।*] पादमूलं कृतं विष्णो **[राज्ञा]श्री[स्कन्दव]–**
6 **र्म्मणा** ।। [४*] पूजार्त्थमस्य चैवेह सोदकम्भूरिदक्षिणम् [।*] पुरुषाय पुरं [द]. . .[4]
7 र्क्कतारका(क)[म्][4] ।।[५*] सत्रोपभोज्यं[5] विप्राणां यतीनाञ्च विशेषत[:] [।*] [दीनानाम]प्यनाथानां. . . .
8 च सर्व्वश: ।।[६*] अप्रवेश्यं भटैश्चेदं सदा करविसर्ज्जितम् । श्री[चक्रद्रो]णपुत्र(त्रा)य. . . .
9 यथोचित[म्*] ।।[७*] स्थितिश्चेयं पुरो बद्धा धर्म्या स्तम्भे निवे[शि]ता [।*] यश्चेमां

---

1. From the facsimile in *EI*, Vol. XXI (1931-32), pp. 156 and 157.
2. Read मुख्यस्य.
3. Read व्यवस्थिताम्.
4. The rest of the verse may be read as दत्तामचन्द्रार्कतारकम् ।।
5. H.N. Sastri suggests सत्वोपभोज्यं but the word सत्रो is clear.

हनापये[त्सं]स्थाम्महापा[त] . . . [6] ।। [८*]

10 व्यतिक्रमेद्यो हि महीपते[:*] स्थिति[म्] कुलाधम पार्त्थिवकिल्विषम्पिबे[त्*।]

11 समन्वियाद्यश्च [नरेन्द्र]सत्पथम् स वासुदेवाश्र[य]माप्नुयाच्चिर[म*] ।। [९*]

12 **द्वादशेब्दे** नरेन्द्रेण **माधवे मासि चोत्तमे [सप्तविंशे] दिने पुण्ये**

13 स्तम्भोयं [गा]हितस्स्वयम् ।।[१०*] स्थिति[7]र्भागवते [नैव]म् भर्तु≍प्रिय[चा]. . .

14 सेनापतिना कल्याणमालिने[8]हाल्पबुद्धिना ।। [११*]. . . .

15 लिखितं [चौ]लिसूनुना[9] भक्तया [जां]तुरदासेन [।।*१२]

16 [आ] जेन विश्वरुपेन(ण) निर्गुणेन गु[णैषिणा] [।।*१३]

ABSTRACT

The inscription begins with the word *svasti*, which is followed by a verse in lines 1-2 in adoration of Hari (Viṣṇu) in His aspect as the essence of victory. Verses 2-4 in lines 2-6 refer to the reigning king, whose name seems to be **Skandavarman**. He has been described as the son of Bhavadatta of the Nala family, who recovered the lost sovereignty of the family by restoring and repopulating the city of Puṣkarī. He is stated to have installed the footprints of Viṣṇu for worship. Verses 5-6 (lines 6-8) record that he granted (some land or a village) along with some money which was to be availed of, for a *satra* for feeding brāhmaṇas, ascetics and destitutes. Verse 7 records that the donated holding was made permanent and free of all taxes in the name of the Highest Being and non-interferable by royal officers. Verses 8-9 record the king's admonition of those who would be involved in the violation of the charity, and the promise of salvation through the grace of god Vāsudēva (Viṣṇu) to those who would follow the good path of kings and maintain the donation. Verse 10 records the date of the installation of the inscribed pillar under the personal supervision of the king, as **year 12, the twenty-seventh day of the month of Mādhava (Vaiśākha)**. Verse 11 refers to the general (*sēnāpati*), named Kalyāṇamālin, the composer of the record, who has been described as devoted to god Viṣṇu as well as to his master. Verse 12 refers to the writer of the record as Jānturadāsa, the son of Cauli. Part of a verse at the end seems to refer to a person named Viśvarūpa, son of Aja, who may have been the engraver of the inscription.

---

6. Krishnamacharlu suggests to reads it as महाशतकस्नुते.
7. The word स्थिति is clear in the facsimile. But Krishnamacharlu reads it as प्रीति.
8. Krishnamacharlu reads कल्पिता मालिनेहा...; Rajaguru and Krishnamacharlu read the name of the general as प्रीतिभागवत and that of the composer of the record as मालिन. But the name of the general is Kalyāṇamālin, who is also the composer of the record.
9. The person seems to be the same as चुल्ल, the writer of the charters of Arthapati-*bhaṭṭāraka* (No. 26) and Bhavadattavarman (No. 27).

NO. 29: RAJIM STONE INSCRIPTION OF THE NALA KING VILĀSATUṄGA

Provenance : Rajim, Raipur district, Madhya Pradesh.

References : D.R. Bhandarkar, *PRASWI*, for 1903-04, pp.24 ff.; A. Cunningham, *ASI* (*Reports*), Vol. VII (1869-70), pp. 148-56 and Vol. XVII (1881-82), pp. 6-20; V.V. Mirashi, *EI*, Vol. XXVI (1942), pp. 49-58 and plate; and S.N. Rajaguru *IO*, Vol. I, Pt. 2 (1958), pp. 98-102.

Language : Sanskrit, in verse.

Metre : Verse 1 *mandākrāntā*; verses 2, 5, 20, 21 *sragdharā*; verses 3, 4, 8, 12, 15, 22, 24-26 *śardūlavikrīḍita*; verses 6, 13 *āryā*; verse 7 *vasantatilakā*; verses 14, 18, 23 *upajāti*; verses 16, 19 *indravajrā*; verses 27, 29 *anuṣṭubh*; verse 28 *praharṣiṇī*.

Script : Eastern variety of the north Indian alphabet of about the seventh century A.D.

Date : Not dated.

TEXT[1]

1 . . . . [।*]— — — —◡◡◡◡◡ — —◡— —◡—
—, — — — — ◡◡◡◡◡— —◡— — चरित्र:। प्राप्तक्षीणानुप
◡◡◡ — —◡— —◡— —, — — — — ◡◡◡
◡◡ — —◡— —◡— —,— — — ◡ [।।*१]
2 — ◡— —◡◡◡◡◡— —◡—सारिचक्रं(क्रम्) । निर्म्मथ्य
क्षीरसिन्दुं(न्द्धुं) व्यदध(धा)दमरतां सम्प्रहृष्ट: सुराणाम्प्राप्तश्रीर्य्य: स
दिश्याच्छ्रियमनुपहतामायुरप्युर्ज्जितं [पन?]। [।*२] रम्ये धावनमेलह(?)
प्रविकसन्नीलो[त्पल*] —◡—, - हृद्यानुप[मां ◡—◡◡
3 [वराह?] —◡ सौख्योचिताम् । प्रोत्फुल्लामम्वु(म्बु)रुहस्थितद्विजवरां वि(बि)भ्रच्छ्रियं
सारसीं सन्तापप्रश्म(शम)क्षम: स जगत: शश्व[2][त्*] सुखायास्तु व: ।। [३*] कस्त्वं
देवि हरि: स्पृशस्यपसरक्रोडीकृत: कक्षया— — —निपुणा मुख[प्र]◡◡
4 — —न्नतिं सा क्षमा । हि (?) वाग्भिर्न्न तु कर्म्मणा प्रकटितं धिम्माञ्च का [मे] रति:

---

1. From the facsimile in *EI*, Vol. XXVI (1942), pp. 56 and 57.
2. This letter resembling श्व has been inserted below the line.

सत्यन्नः श्रियमित्यपास्तरभसां शिष्यन्प्रभुः पातु वः ।। [४*] शीर्य्यच्छैलेन्द्रशृङ्गप्रप-
तनरभसादुद्दम्भोधिवीचि[व्या]सङ्गा-सहेलोच्छलदति⏑⏑— —⏑— —
5 ⏑घोरम् । उच्चैर्य्योगीन्द्रलीलाविरचितवपुषो व्यस्तचन्द्रार्क्कतारं यस्याभूद्विश्वमध्यात्क्षय इव
स व(ब)लिश्रोनिहन्ता हरिर्व्वः ।। [५*] जयति प्रथितमहीभृत्तुङ्गशिरोनिहितनिजपादः ।
नित्योदितप्रतापो(पः) पूर्ण्णादित्यो. . . . .[।।*६]
6 [आ*]सीद्विलासिनिजरुपजितस्मरोपि शान्तात्मनाम्भुवि सदा स्पृहणीयवृत्तः । ख्यातो नृपो
नल इति प्रणतारिचक्रचूडामणिभ्रमरचुम्बितपादपद्मः ।। [७*] तस्याभून्नि[ज*]—⏑—
⏑⏑⏑— — —⏑—भूभृतो विन्ध्यस्ये[व*] नग[स्य*]
7 —⏑⏑⏑[रदृ]ष्टातिकान्तोन्नतेः । पृथ्वीराज इति क्रमोपचयनीं वि(बि)भ्रच्छ्रियं
निम्मलां सेव्यः सर्व्वजनस्य पापविगमाद्रेवाप्रवाहोपमः ।। [८*]— — —व जुगुप्सितः
सम[गुणै[ः ?]— —⏑— — ⏑—, — — —⏑⏑—
⏑⏑वधैर्योतस्म यो धि ⏑—।
8 [नि*]श्चिन्त्यातिकलिप्रपातमलिनामालोक्य लोकस्थितिं धात्रा सर्व्वगुणैः कृतः
क्षितिपति[र्म्मा]-[तृ] — —⏑ मः[3] ।। [९*] तस्योच्चै[ल्लपुधे]श्वरव्यतिक-
र[व्याप्तात्म]कार्य्यो ⏑—, मित्राणां⏑⏑—⏑—⏑⏑⏑— — —⏑—
—⏑—। [वि*]ख्यातो हिमवानिवा⏑⏑
9 ⏑ दः पुत्रः पतिर्भूभृतां धत्ते नाम विरुपराज इति यो दिग्वन्दिवृन्द[स्तुतम्] ।। [१०*]
[रु*]पेणाप्रतिमः [श्रु]तेन च-[4] सत्यान्वितस्त्या⏑—[5], [शैर्य्य]स्यायतन[म्भयं
परमि]ति——⏑— —⏑— ।— — —⏑⏑—⏑—⏑⏑⏑—
— —⏑— —[गु*]णैर्य्यस्योच्चै[र्मनु]—⏑—
10 ⏑ सकलं कीर्त्तिर्ज्जगद्भ्राम्यते ।।[११*] शत्रुघ्नोतिव(ब)लेन —⏑ [मद*]नो
दर्प्पेण कीर्त्या ⏑—, —न्त्यारामतनुर्व्व(र्ब्बु)धः पृथुरणे भीष्मः प्रतापेन च । — —
—⏑⏑—⏑—⏑⏑⏑— — —⏑— —⏑—, — — —
⏑⏑—⏑— —⏑⏑⏑— — —⏑—प्यः कृतः ।। [१२*] प्रति
[प*]—
11 [वों*]दयभाजः सवितुरि—द्गमोनुरागधरः । . . . .णपरा. . . . . .[।।*१३]
विलासिनस्तुङ्गतमा⏑— —, **विलासतुङ्गः** ⏑⏑—⏑— —।⏑—⏑—
—⏑⏑—⏑— —, ⏑—⏑— —⏑⏑—⏑— —
[।।*१४]— — [ख*]ङ्गलताभिघात⏑⏑
12 -[शङ्का]रिवृन्दाम्भुवं पश्येमान्न समोस्त्यनेन विजयाधी[शं?] स्तु[वं?] नेत्यतः । प—
—⏑⏑—⏑—⏑⏑⏑— — —⏑— —⏑—, मन्ये धीरपि—
⏑—⏑[वसु?]धां कालेन[ना] —⏑—[।।*१५] [म*]त्वा स्वदेहान्तरिते[न]
— —, — —⏑[वर्ण्ण]न्त्य[मु]धाखि[लानि ।*]
13 [अ*]न्तस्तमुद्दिश्य विधान[दृ]ष्टदाना(न)क्रियाभिर्न्नु सद्य एव ।। [१६*] यथो[च्चैर?]पि

3. V.V. Mirashi suggests the last seven letters of the verse as मान्धातृराजोपमः
4. The letter is not legible; Mirashi reads पां and suggests विमलः
5. Mirashi restores the letters as स्त्यागिनां.

—⏑⏑भूतलोके पु[ना]⏑— —⏑⏑मेव [राज्ञा]म् । युगस्य य —
⏑⏑—⏑— —, पूर्त्तम्प्र[पश्य*]न्ति परं स्मृतिज्ञाः ।। [१७*] ⏑ —
⏑—⏑⏑—⏑जे[भ्यः] चातुर्यशा[स्त्व?]⏑⏑—

14 ⏑ भावात् [।*] धर्म्मस्य मूलं च यशो वदन्ति ⏑ —⏑[त*]स्मात्तदुपार्जनीयम्
।। [१८*] मत्वा चलं जीवितमल्पसारं वु(बु)द्ध्वा क्वचित्कीर्त्तनमेव कायम् । कीर्त्तिः
स्थिरा यस्य स [जी]वलोके तत्पुण्यमूर्त्तिश्चि[रजीव] एव [।।*१९] — — — —
⏑ राज्ञा दशवदनभुजोत्क्षि[प्त]कै[लास*]-

15 [शृ*]श्रीहारि स्वेन धाम्ना स्फुरदमलसुधा[नि]त्यन[व्ये]न्दुनेद[म्] । देवस्याशेष-
दुःखप्रभवभयनुदः कारितं स्थानमुच्चैर्व्विष्णोः पुण्याभिवृद्धये [त्रि]दशजनसुख्यातिथ्यभाजः
सुतस्य ।। [२०*] प्रातर्व्वा(र्ब्बा)लार्क्करोचिर्व्यतिकरविलसच्चारुवामाधराभां वि(बि)भ्राणं
भूमिभाजां [सुवि*]-

16 श[द]ममलं दृश्यते दृष्टिरम्याम् । यद्दूरादेव सिद्धैरपरमतिमहद्भूषणं भूरिधाम्नः पुण्याधारं
सुमेरोः शिखरमिव [प]तल्लोलगङ्गाप्रवाहम् ।। [२१*] अग्रे तावदुपप्रमाण[कर*]णं
प्रख्यात— —⏑—, क्लेशप्राय[मिदं*] व्ययेन महता सम्भारसम्पा[दनम् ।*]

17 तत्सिद्धेरलम्मु[त्सु]खस्य पुनरप्या[भो]गचिन्ता परा लोके सर्व्वललामकीर्त्तनरकृतामायास
एवादितः ।। [२२*] कर्त्तुर्व्वरं पालयिता मतो मे पाल्यं निरायासमपे ⏑— —।
सर्व्वोतिलोभा⏑⏑—परं यत्सदर्शतां याति ⏑—पि राज्ञां(ज्ञाम्) ।।[२३*] विध्वस्तैः
प⏑—

18 ⏑ रेत्र च पराः पापात्मनां सम्पदः साधूनामपि पूर्व्वपुण्यविहिता दृश्यन्त एवोज्वलाः ।
तस्माद्धर्म्मफलप्रपञ्चरचितं दृष्ट्वा विचि[त्रं]⏑—, [त]त्त्वं पुरुषेण येन गुणिना—
—⏑वि[क्र]र्म्य(म्य)ते ।। [२४*] मत्वैवं स्वशरीरकञ्च कृतिभिर्व्विद्वद्भि [र*]-

19 [प्य*]स्थिरं लेलालोक ⏑—⏑—सुखमपि प्रत्यूहजालावृतम् । श्रुत्वा
शक्रपुरस्सरा[श्च] विभवैः पुण्यात्मभिः सेविताः कार्य्यः कीर्त्त[न*]दानपालनविधौ धर्म्मस्य
यत्नः [परः ।।*२५]— — —⏑विकासिनो मतिम[तां] भासन्ति भावो(वा) ⏑—,

20 — — —[यु]तदुग्धसि[क्त?]धवला— —[ति] वक्षः[स्थले] । यावद्वन्द्ववहो वि-
न्ति च जगत्तावत्प्रयत्नादिमाङ्कीर्त्तिम्पालयतः प्रिया [नर*]पतेन्यासास्थया सज्जनाः ।। [२६*]
भृत्यो मित्रमप[त्यं] ⏑ [अभू*]त्तस्यैव भूपतेः । दुर्ग्गगोल इति—⏑ [6],

21 ⏑⏑⏑⏑⏑ —⏑⏑ [।।*२७] — — —⏑⏑⏑⏑ [तो]-
न्यमार्ग्गमा[त्रं] विज्ञेया प्रविरचिता प्रशस्ति[रेषा] । राज्ञे —⏑⏑ वचना वि[जा]तभावा
सद्वृत्तेतिमहतादरेण मान्या ।। [२८*] जलह[स्ति]- [सु*]तेनेयं प्रशस्तिः शिल्पशालि[ना]
[।*]

22 उत्कीर्ण्णा सूत्रधारेण [साधुना] दुर्ग्गहस्तिना ।। [२९*]

---

6. Mirashi suggests reading प्राज्ञः

ABSTRACT

The inscription begins with verses[7] 1-6 in adoration of god Viṣṇu. Verse 4 is in the form of a dialogue between Hari (Viṣṇu) and goddess Lakṣmī and verse 5 is an invocation of the dwarf incarnation of Viṣṇu. Verse 6 seems to have been written in glorification of the royal family. Verse 7 describes the king Nala, who has been compared with the legendary king of that name glorified in the epic. Verses 8 and 9 describe the next king of the family named Pṛthvīrāja, who was like Māndhātṛ. Verses 10-12 are devoted to the glorification of Pṛthvīrāja's son Virūparāja. Verses 13-17 are apparently devoted to recording the glorious achievements of **Vilāsatuṅga**, presumably the son and successor of Virūparāja and the reigning king of the family. Verses 18-22 record that the king built an excellent and lofty temple for god Viṣṇu, for increasing the religious merit of his son. Verses 23-26 record the usual prayer to future rulers to preserve the religious monument, with the hope that it would last forever. Verses 27-28 record that the eulogy (*praśasti*) was composed by Durgagōla. Verse 29 records that it was incised by the *sūtradhāra* (artiṣan) Durgahastin, son of Jalahastin.

7. Verses 1 and 2 are almost completely damaged.

IV

MISCELLANEOUS INSCRIPTIONS OF NORTHERN ORISSA

NO. 30: ASANPAT NAṬARĀJA IMAGE INSCRIPTION OF ŚATRUBHAÑJA

Provenance	:	Asanpat, Keonjhar district, Orissa.
References	:	A. Das, *OHRJ*, Vol. XIII, No. 2 (1965), pp. 1 ff. and plate; S. Tripathy, *JOR*, Vol. I, No. 2 (1980), pp. 5-10; and D. C. Sircar, *EI*, Vol. XI (1973), pp. 121-26 and plate.
Language	:	Sanskrit, partly in prose and partly in verse.
Metre	:	Verse 1 *āryā*; verse 2 *āryāgīti*.
Script	:	Eastern variety of the north Indian alphabet of about the sixth century A.D.

TEXT[1]

1 स जयति नरेन्द्रचन्द्रः श्रीमान्ना(मन्ना)गान्वयो रणश्लाघी [।*] येन सपितुर्ग्गोत्तस्य च कृता
2 युगान्ताचला कीर्त्तिः [।।*१] स जयति पुनरेव देवपुत्त[:*] समरशतेषु अ(ष्व)खण्डितः[2] प्रतापः[।*]
3 महितलधनदो(द)गुणैकवृक्षः ससतुरङ्गः हृवै स तेज(जो)राशि[:*।।][२*] महाराजा(ज)श्रीमाण(न)भञ्जो(ञ्जा)–
4 त्मजेन महादेव्यां दमयन्त्यामुत्पन्ना(न्ने)[ना*]नेक समरसङ्घट्टविजयिना नागवङ्शो(वंशो)–
5 द्भवेन प्रभावोपह(न)तसर्व्वसामन्ताधिपतिना विन्ध्याटवीनाथेन स्वभुजोपार्ज्जित–
6 कीर्त्तिना पाटलीपुत्रगयाक्रिमिलः(ला)दला(?) [3]वर्द्धन[4]पुण्ड्रवर्द्धनवर्द्धमान गौक्ख–टिखद्रङ्गताम(म्र)लिप्ती–
7 उभय[5]तोसलीषु गवा(वां) लक्षप्रदेन नानादेशागतचातुर्व्वैद्यजाम्वारामीबृहस्पधु[6]
8 आहिच्छत्रकशङ्खकारमठ(ठे) याक्षेश्वरमणिभद्रमठे चान्येषु मठस्थानेषु

---

1. From the original and impressions. This inscribed slab bearing the image of Naṭarāja-Śiva is now preserved in the Orissa State Museum, Bhubaneswar.
2. The *visarga* is redundant. Read समरशप्तष्वखण्डितप्रतापः .
3. D.C. Sircar reads it doubtfully as लला.
4. A mark is given slightly over न to indicate the omission of the following name, which is written below.
5. Read लिप्त्युभय.
6. The meaning of this is not clear, Sircar suggests the intended reading to be ब्राह्मणेभ्यो–ग्रहारादिप्रदेन.

9 दत्तिसहस्रानेकहिरण्यलक्षप्रदेन ब्रह्मचारी(रि)चरकपरिव्राजक-

10 भिक्षुर्न्निग्र(र्न्निर्ग्र)न्थकवर्ण्णान्तका(रा)वसथविहारकारकेन(ण) पाषण्डभिक्षदेन

11 भारथ(त)पुराणेतिहासव्याकरणसमीक्षन्यायमीमान्सा(मांसा)च्छन्द[:*] श्र(श्रु)तिं-

12 बौद्धप्रकरणसांख्यज्ञेन विज्ञानराशिना सर्व्वकालाभिज्ञेन **महाराजश्री-**

13 **शत्नुभञ्जेन** देवायतनं कारितमिति [।।*]

ABSTRACT

The charter begins with two verses in lines 1-3 introducing the reigning king with a few epithets. He is described as having been born into Nāga family, the moon among the kings, the illustrious *raṇaślāghin* of his family, who made the fame of his family and his father last as long as the end of *kṛta-yuga* (*kali-yuga*). Further, he has been described as *dēvaputra*, whose valour remained unchecked in hundreds of battles, who was like the *kalpa-vṛkṣa*, having the quality of the god of wealth on earth and who was like the sun having a mass of splendour. Lines 3-13 contain a passage in prose, which records that the reigning king **Mahārāja Śatṛubhañja,** son of Mahārāja Mānabhañja, born of Mahādēvī Damayantī, who was born in the Nāga family and called the lord of Vindhyāṭavi, the forest kingdom in the Vindhyan region, made gifts of lakhs of cows at the holy places of Pāṭalīputra, Gayā, Kṛimila, Dalā (or Lalā)vardhana, Puṇḍravardhana, Gōkkhaṭi, Khadraṅga and Tāmralipti, and also in both the Tōsalis.[7] He made gifts of lakhs of *hiraṇya* or gold (coins) and made grants at various *maṭhas*, such as the *maṭha* called Śaṅkhakāra situated at Ahichatra and the Maṇibhadra *maṭha* at Yakṣēśvara. He built houses and monasteries for monks, who belonged to different religious communities, such as the brahmacārins, the *parivrājakas*, the *bhikṣus* and the *nirgranthakas*. He gave alms to the heretics. The king claims to have studied the *Bhārata*[8] (*Mahābhārata*), *Purāṇa, Itihāsa, Vyākaraṇa* (grammar), *Samīkṣā, Nyāya, Mīmāṁsā, Chandas* (metrical science), *Śruti* (*Vēda*), the scriptures of the Buddhists and *Sāṁkhya*. He has been described as the storehouse of superior knowledge and an expert in all the arts. He is stated at the end of the record to have built a temple for god (Śiva).

7. *Ubhaya* Tōsali is evidently the Uttara Tōsali and Dakṣiṇa Tōsali of the later Orissan epigraphs, comprising the region from Balasore district up to the northern part of Ganjam district in Orissa, up to Chilka lake, the river Mahanadi being the dividing line between the two Tōsalis.
8. The expression seems to have been intended to indicate both the epics, namely, the *Rāmāyaṇa* and the *Mahābhārata*.

NO. 31: SITABHINJI TEMPERA PAINTING INSCRIPTION OF DIŚĀBHAÑJA

Provenance	:	Sitabhinji, Keonjhar district, Orissa.
References	:	T.N. Ramachandran, *JAHRS*, Vol. XIX (1948-49), pp. 191 ff. and plate; D.C. Sircar, *EI*, Vol. XXXV (1963-64), pp. 47-49 and plate.
Language	:	Sanskrit.
Script	:	Eastern variety of the north Indian alphabet of about the seventh century A.D.

TEXT[1]

1 मा(म)हाराजश्रीदिशाभञ्ज[2]

1. From the photograph in *EI*, Vol. XXXV (1963-64), p. 47.
2. The king may have been connected with the Nāga family. He may possibly have been a descendant of the Nāga king Śatrubhañja (No. 30), who ruled the Keonjhar region during about the first part of the sixth century A. D. See Introduction, Section IV, in this volume.

NO. 32: JAYARAMPUR COPPER-PLATE GRANT OF THE TIME OF GŌPACANDRA, YEAR 1

Provenance	:	Jayarampur, Balasore district.
Reference	:	S.N. Rajaguru, *OHRJ*, Vol. XI, No. 4 (1963), pp. 206-29 and plate.
Language	:	Sanskrit, in prose, with the exception of the usual imprecatory and benedictory verses at the end.
Metre	:	Verses 1-12 *anuṣṭubh;* **verse** 13 *puṣpitāgrā.*
Script	:	Eastern variety of the northern class of alphabet of about the sixth century A.D.
Date	:	1st regnal year, the twentieth day of the month of Phālguna.

TEXT[1]

First Side

1 स्वस्ति [।*] चतुरुदधिसलिलसीमान्तायामानेकद्वीपनगरपत्तनाधिष्ठानाद्रिसरो[वर प्रवाह]-
सिद्धदेवतायतनश्रेष्ठमान्यां स्वध-

2 र्म्मकर्म्मनिरतचातुव(र्व)ण्र्या(ण्णा)श्रमप्रकृतिजनपदसमग्रायामनेकद्विजवरेश्व-
राग्निहोत्रहवन[2]हविर्धूमसुरभि(भी)कृ[त*] तपोवन-

3 अर्क्केन्दुमयूखेवभासितायामविरतवेदाध्ययना(न)न्यासध्वनिन्निरस्तदूरितायां तृ(त्रि)भू(भु)-
वनसाधारणानर्क्कविपन्नस(श)स्य स[र्व्व]-

4 त्ता(त्त)सुरभिस्वादुकुसुमफलभारे विविधतर(रु)[3]विटपलताप्रतानत्यां सुदृस्य(श्य)
सारसरुपगन्धगुणसम्पत्सि(त्स्थि)तायां पृथिव्यां चतुः

5 समुद्रातिक्रान्तयशसामुदारगुणसमुदयारुढ़गौरवाणामसंभारप्रमेयदानाव[ली. . .][4]
यदाचारपरो(रि)ग्रह-

6 प्रत्यन्ताशेस(ष)कलिदोसा(षा)च्छ्रीमतो धनचन्द्रात्सकलजनसाधारणधर्म्मप्रति-
लब्धाविग्रहा[त्सुक्ष]त्राय्र्या: श्रीगिरिदेव्या[द्*]व-

---

1. From the original; the charter is now preserved in the Orissa State Museum, Bhubaneswar.
2. Rajaguru reads ह(भ)वन.
3. Rajaguru reads तर.
4. Some letters are illegible due to corrosion in this portion of the plate.

7 ण्र्णाश्रमव्यवस्थाहेतुः साक्ष(क्षा)द्धर्म्म इवोपान्तजन्मा समस्ताभिकामिक-
गुणयश. . .मानसाभिर्म्मा(मा)नरिव प्र-

8 ज्ञाभिरारोपिताधिराज्यः शक्तित्रय(यो)पहतारात्रि(ति)पक्षेत्वन्तापकाराष्वपि [प्राणाद्ध. . . .]-
द्धरोत्सारितामर्शानुरक्ताप्र-

9 तिद्वेशासोपनताशेषराजमण्डलः परोपका[रेषु][अ]भिनिविष्टचेताः परममाहेश्वरो
महाराजाधिराजश्रीगोप-

10 **चन्द्रे** राज्यं प्रशासत **प्रवर्द्धमानविजयराज्य[संव]त्सरे प्रथमे फाल्गुनेमासे विंशतितमे**
दिवसे श्वेतवालिका-

11 वीथिसमुपगताव्द(द्व)र्त्तमानभविष्यत्कालोर्यत्कार्त्ताकृतिको[5][परिक]कुमारामात्यराजा(ज)
नकविजयवर्म्मविषयपतितदायुक्तकान्यांश्च राज-

12 पादप्रसादोपजीविनो यथार्हं मानयित्वा शिरोभिश्च प्रणम्यास्मदधिवासविंशत्या-
ग्रहारताम्रपट्टपटशासनहिरण्य[-]-

13 सामुदायिक[6] ग्रामवाटकेभ्यो महामहत्तरमहत्तरप्रधानसीतालअधिकरणञ्च विज्ञापयन्ति [।*]
अस्त्यवस्सम्विदितं प्रार्थिता

14 वयं **श्रीमहासामन्तमहाराजाच्युतेन** युष्मद्बोध्यां साधुभिरनेकैराचन्द्रार्क्क का-
[लीन]ताम्रपट्टपटशासनं स्थित्वा स(श)तामूल्ये[षु]

15 ग्रामक्षेत्रवास्तुनि युष्मत् क्रीत्वकृत्वा देवद्विजमठविहारावसथेभ्यो [ऽ*]भिसृष्टात्यतिसृज्य-
मानानि विथैव सम्यक्प्रति-

16 पाल्यमानान्येति [।।*] समाक्ष महताञ्च [।*] संसाराण्र्णवे सर्वप्राणिनाजलबुद्बुदावश्याय
प्रेषितो गजकलाभकण्ठाग्रभुजग जिह्वतडि-

17 त्सम्पत्चपलानि जीवितो त्याजवञ्चविभावञ्च दृष्ट्वा ममापि धर्म्मन(नि)मित्तमुत्सा[हो]
जातसोहमित्ररत्नचैत्योद्भवख्यापिताशेषत्रिभुवने प्रताप-

18 माहात्म्यातिशयभगवदार्य्यावलोकितेश्वराद्ध्यासितश्रीबोधिपद्रकमहाविहारे[7] विहारकरणाय
तस्मैश्च वलिचरुगन्द्धपुष्पप्रदीप्या(पा)-

19 दिक्रियाप्रवर्त्तनायार्य्यसंघाय च यथाकालं हविस(श्य)पिण्डपातशयनासनग्लानप्रत्यय
भैस(ष)ज्यपरिस्का(ष्का)रायाति स्र(सृ)ष्ट तदहनि

20 श्वेतवालिकाग्रामं क्रयेण दातुं ताम्रशासनीकृत्येति [।*] यतोस्माभिर्य्यु(र्यु)क्तमया प्रार्थयति
स च ग्राम समुद्र(द्रो)पसर्प्पितप्रत्यन्तत्वात्सह द[त्तम्] [।*]

21 गणाद्ध्यासन ते प्रतिभयानासुसञ्चितो (ता)र्थै [ऽ*]यर्थः कश्चाटतमदास(श)यितुं नदित्थं
भूतेन तस्तत[:*] को[ऽ*]र्थः अस्तिह सु(शु)द्धन्यासः [उ]-

22 त्पद्यमानात्यैकप्रयोजनेप्र(प्ये)तसम(मा)धान ग्रामक्षेत्त्रवास्तुनां च समस्तप्रवृत्त-
सुद्धायतामस्मैदी(र्द्दी)यम(मा)न पुनः [।*]

---

5. Rajaguru reads यत्कीर्त्तिकृतिकै; but the expression denotes an official designation, found also in other contemporary inscriptions. D.C. Sircar suggests that designation is "the superintendent or manager of state-affairs" [*Sel. Ins.*, Vol. I (1942), p. 360 and fn. 9].
6. Rajaguru reads सामुवायिक. This refers also to an official designation.
7. Rajaguru reads महाञ्वहारे.

23 धर्म्मसङ्गो(संघो) गोप च यो निर्देस(श)ये(य)ति यतः पुस्तपालभोगिभागमवधारणया इत्यवधृत्य दण्डभुक्त्याधिकृतः[8] महासामन्त [महाराजाच्युतेन]

24 [9]धर्म्मविनियुक्तकुमारामात्यराजानकविजयवर्म्माधिकृतश्वेतवालिकावी-थिव्यवहारिप्रासव्यम्परिबोध्य. . . . .[10]

25 श्वेतवालिकाग्रामस्सकलसमुदयः क्रयेन(ण) विषयाधिकरणमहामहत्तरगृहस्वाम्यादिभिः यत्नम. . . . . .[11]

Second Side

26 ....[12] महत्तर भवस्वामि....महत्तर धर्म्मस्वामि महत्तरदेवस्वामि महत्तरेन्दुस्वामि अशुनपद्रकीय[प्रधान] योगी......[13]

27 [प]द्रकीय तनुकप्रथा(धा)न [--द्रकी]य बौद्धस्वामि हुलवणजीय[14] वेत्तकर्म्मणिमुखीय प्रथा(धा)नसाहु श्वेतवालुकी[य---]

28 --भूषण धर्म्मप्राण प्रधानगोनाम कायत(स्थ)वरातवन्तीकश्च करणिक दत्तनन्दि करणिक अनुदत्तकरणिकादित्यदास पुस्तपाल[नाग----]

29 प्रभवेष्टभिः विक्रितेन निष्पन्नः क्रीत्वा मातापित्रोरात्मनश्च सर्व्वसत्वानां च पुण्याभिवृद्धये दक्ष(क्षि)णाय(या)दिशि स-धि बोधिपद्र[क]---[महा]यानिक(के)-

30 भ्यो भिक्षुसंघाय प्रतिपादितः यत्र श्रीभारोलाङ्गोलावैथेय पुस्तपालचन्द्रवर्म्मा करणिकाजताढ्य स्थाय(न)पाल [खगा]श्चेति[सर्व]दे-

31 यवर्ज्जितः प्रतिवर्षञ्चारिपिण्डकचुर्णिकाशतमेकं देयमित्यु[पनिवन्द्धच] **श्रीमहासामन्ताच्युतस्य** दत्तमस्य च ग्रामस्य सीमालिङ्गानि [।*]

32 उत्किरखाटिका पूर्व्वतः दक्षिणस्यां दिश्यप्रमेयद्युतिवेलाविभासिनिवोर्न(र्ण)नुपमा-चिन्त्यमृताद्ययापारमस्थिर--[प्रवल]-

33 माहतोद्धतक्षोभितजलतरं(र)ङ्गसंघट्टजनितकलकलारावफेणपुञ्जाट्टहासः करिम-करझसनक्रग्रा(ग्र)हादि विवि-

34 धविहगगणा(ण)विरुतोपगीतपुलिनस्सुरासुरमुनिगणसिद्धचारणमनुजमानुजेन्द्रादि-भिस्संस्तुतान्यान्यनिवेश(शो)ज्वितपुण्य-

35 सलिलकलिकलुसा(षा)पहरविविधरत्ननिचयो भगवाञ्जलनिधिः[।*] पश्चिमतो-डङ्ग्रामि(मी)यगुणदेवमण्डलवास्तु [।*] पश्चिमो(म)-

8. Rajaguru has overlooked this portion of the text in line 23. What he has read instead is actually written in line 24.
9. Rajaguru has overlooked this line of the text. He has read the twenty-fifth line as line 24 and as the last line of the obverse side of the charter.
10. The letters have been peeled off due to corrosion.
11. The letters have been peeled off due to corrosion.
12. The letters have been peeled off due to corrosion.
13. The letters have been peeled off due to corrosion.
14. Rajaguru reads it as हुलवलजेय and suggests reading हुणवलजेय. This seems to be the name of a locality, to which the person referred to in the subsequent reading of the text belonged.

36 त [:*] सृ(शृ)गालपद्रिकानामो द्दे(दे)शः [।*] ततोप्युत्तरतः गृहाधि(धी)क्षकादित्यदासस्य वृत्तिक्षेत्रं यावत(त्) ।।[15] ततः भगवतो गोविश्वरस्य मण्डलक्षेत्र[:]

37 पूर्व्वोत्तरस्यां दिशि वटवृक्षच्छरपोतद्वयमत्र पूर्व्वस्यां दिग्भागे ग्रामपुष्कि(ष्क)र(रि)ण्यः पूर्व्वादिरिति [।*] तदेतदुद्देशसमुदयञ्च प्रवि(ति)विभज्य [य]-

38 था शरीरमस्माभि[:*] वोढव्यं तद्यस्माभिरपि य[थोप]रिलिखितं यद्धर्म्मगो(गौ)रवा[त्*] विस(ष)याध (धि)करणं विज्ञाप्यान्यप्रतिपालनानुग्रहपरै[:*] ततो[हि]-

39 सस्माश्च भूमिदाने ये [ऽ*]स्मत्कुल्योन्यत[:*] मो -------त प्रेरितोन्यथा कुर्य्यात्स पञ्चमहापातकोपपातकादि संयुक्त[:*] स्या[दपि]-

40 चानुश्रुयते धर्म्मशास्त्रे ।। सस्टि[16] वर्षसहस्राणि स्वर्गे मोदति भूमिदः [।*] आक्षेसा चानुमन्ता च तान्येव नरक(के) वसे[त्*] ।। [१*] स्वदत्तां परदत्ताम्वा(त्तां वा)

41 यो हरेत वसुन्द्धरां [।*] स विष्ठाया(यां) कृमि[र्भूत्वा] पितृभिस्सह पच्यते ।। [२*] पूर्व्वदत्तां दिजातिभ्यो यत्नाद्रक्ष्य(क्ष) युधिष्ठिर [।*] महीम्महीमतां[17] श्रे-

42 ष्ठ दानाच्छ्रेयोनुपालनं ।।[18] [३*] बहुभिर्व्वसुधा [दत्ता राज]भिस्सगरादिभिः [।*] यस्य यस्य यदा भूमि[स्*]तस्य तस्य तदा [फलं ।।] [४*] आस्फोटस(य)न्ति

43 पितरः प्रवल्गन्ति पितामहाः [।*] भूमिदाता कुले जातः सोस्माद्वैत्तारयिष्यति ।। [५*] आदित्या(त्य)वसवो रुद्राः सोमोविष्णुर्हुतासनः [।*]

44 दण्डपाणिश्च[19] भगवानभिनन्दन्ति भूमि[दः।।] [६*] भूम्येवा ---- योगाश्रुतरस्याय दद्यात्सस्यवतीसती [।*] चावद्धते गृ(ग्र)हीतुश्च पुनोम्युभयत[म्]

45 शत[म्*] ।। [७*] आजन्मनि सहस्रेसु(षु) पापं यत्कृतवान्नर[:*।] अपि [गो]-चर्म्ममात्रेण भूमिदानेन शुध्यति ।। [८*] वृ[--ज]गतं यत्र गवन्तिष्ठत्ययं त्रित(तं) [।*]

46 बालवत्सप्रसूतानां गोचर्म्मं तदिति स्मृतं(तम्) ।। [९*]भूमिदानं याति लोकं सुराणां हत्सिर्य्युनुया[20] [।*] मा[---] मर्लोहकुम्भपक्वथनीलपूर्ण्ण-

47 हन्ताकरः क्षिप्यति कालदूतेर(रि)त्येवमनुचिन्त्य [।।*१०] ययीह दत्तानि पुरा नरेन्द्रैर्द्दानानि धर्म्मार्थयंशस्कराणि [।*]---- भिलाषान्नृपगौरवो(वा)च्च मया-

48 प्यनुज्ञात फलाणि(नि) तानि [।।*११] अपिच एताभिर्दारिद्रतया[21]न्मनुष्यैर्धनानी(नि)धर्म्मा-यतनीकृतानि [उत्सृष्टवान् प्रतिभाति] लोके कोसा(षा)वनी-

49 पः पुनरावनीतः [।।१२] क्षितितलजलचन्द्रलोला(लां) श्रियमनु[चि*]न्त्य मनुस्य(ष्य) धर्म्मभाव[:*।] निखिलमिदमुदाहृतं च वुध्वा---ध[र्म्म]यसो(शो)विलो-

---

15. The punctuation mark is indicated by two small horizontal strokes, slightly slanting. Rajaguru has taken them as a mark for the *visarga*.
16. Read षष्टिं.
17. Read महीं महीमतां.
18. The mark for punctuation is indicated by a sign resembling the letter ण.
19. The word शूलपाणि is usually seen in the early charters of Orissa.
20. This may be read as हरितयानया.
21. Rajaguru reads दारिद्र्यतया.

50 पनीया इति[22] [।।*१३] एतन्य[23] शासनं तापितं पुस्तपालभोगभट्टेन लिखितं कायस्थमानदत्तेनेति [।*] **संव्व(व)त्सर १ फाल्गुन दि २०** [।*]
51 खन्तं[24] चिल्लकेन [।।*]

ABSTRACT

The charter begins with the word *svasti.* This is followed by a passage in prose (lines 1-10) describing the kingdom of the reigning king **mahārājādhirāja Gōpacandra**, whose father was Dhanacandra and mother Śrī-Giridēvī. In lines 10-16, the passage records that during the **first regnal year** of *mahārājādhirāja* Gōpacandra, on **the twentieth day of the month of Phālguna,** the royal order relating to the grant of the village was addressed to the present and future royal officers assembled in the *vīthi* of **Śvētavālikā.** The officers mentioned are *kārttākṛtika* (whose name has been lost), Vijayavarman, designated as the *kumārāmātya-rājanaka,* the *viṣayapati* and his *adhikaraṇas,* the *mahāmahattara* and other officers who received royal favour, who were present at the time of royal declaration.

It is stated (lines 14-20) that **mahāsāmanta-mahārāja Acyuta,** the feudatory ruler of the area, obtained permission from his overlord to purchase and grant the village of Śvētavālikā[25] to the *ārya-saṁgha,* to build a *vihāra* at the *mahāvihāra* of Bōdhipadraka, where the deity *ārya*-Avalōkitēśvara had been installed. Further, the purpose of the grant included provisions for supplying *bali, caru,* and so on for the worship of the deity as well as for the maintenance of the *ārya-bhikṣu-saṃgha.* The gift village is stated to have been purchased and then donated, along with the tract of land formed by the sea after it receded, by **mahāsāmanta-mahārāja Acyuta,** by recording the grant on the copper-plate. Lines 21-25 mention the overlord's instructions relating to the usual share of the produce and other income to be paid to the *dharma-saṁgha,* through *mahārāja* Acyuta, who was in charge of Daṇḍabhukti. This was communicated to the officers of the subdivision of Śvētavālikā which was in the charge of *kumārāmātya-rājanaka* Vijayavarman. Lines 26-30 refer to the names of some officers who were associated with the transaction relating to the purchase of the locality which was donated to the *mahāyānika-bhikṣu-saṁgha* of Bōdhipadraka.

22. This word has been overlooked by Rajaguru.
23. This may be read as इदं.
24. Read खनितं.
25. The term *vīthi* often denoted a subdivision of a district and was sometimes also used in the sense of a district, forming part of a *bhukti* or province. Here it seems to have been used in the sense of a subdivision of Daṇḍabhukti, mentioned in line 23. Daṇḍabhukti seems to have been a province included in the dominions of Gōpacandra, and ruled by his feudatory *mahāsāmanta* Acyuta. The reference to Śvētavālikā as a village (line 31) indicates that the locality was named after the *vīthi* of the same name, constituting a part of it.

Lines 30-31 record that the grant was made by *mahāsāmanta* Acyuta, free from all taxes, but one hundred *aripiṇḍaka-curṇikā* was fixed, to be paid annually. Lines 31-38 specify the boundaries of the gift village. To the north of it and from the eastern side of the mouth of a river (*khāṭikā*), is the sea[26] to the west are situated the residential plots of land of Guṇadēva-*maṇḍala* belonging to Ōḍaṅga-*grāma*, again on the west is the locality called Śṛgālapadraka. To its north is the land (granted in lieu of service) of Ādityadāsa, the *gṛhādhīkṣaka* and the endowed land of Bhagavat-Gōviśvara (god Śiva?), to its north-east is the big banyan tree, and to its east is the village tank. Lines 35-39 record the donor's instruction to the officers of the district relating to the grant and the usual entreaties. Lines 40-50 contain the usual imprecatory and benedictory verses quoted from the *Dharmaśāstra*. Lines 50-51 record that the copper-plate charter was heated by Bhōgabhaṭṭa, the *pustapāla*. It was written by the *kāyastha* Mānadatta. In line 50, the **date** of the grant is again mentioned in numerical symbols as **samvat 1, the twentieth day of the month of Phālguna.** Line 51 refers to Cillaka who engraved the charter.

26. This evidently refers to the Bay of Bengal.

NO. 33: ERBANG PLATE OF ŚAMBHUYAŚAS, YEAR 235

Provenance	:	Erbang, Puri district.
Reference	:	S.N. Rajaguru, *OHRJ*, Vol. XII, No. 3 (1964), pp. 113-22 and plate.
Language	:	Sanskrit, in prose, with the exception of an imprecatory verse in lines 13-14.
Metre	:	*Anuṣṭubh*.
Script	:	Eastern variety of the northern alphabet of about the sixth century A.D.
Date	:	*Samvat* 235, the eighteenth day of Jyēṣṭha.

TEXT[1]

First Side

1 सिद्धम्[2] स्वस्ति [। *]जयस्कन्धावारात् **हान्दकवासकाच्छुत**नयविनयविभु(भू)षणप्रण-

2 यी(यि)जनयथेष्टभोग्यविभव[:*] सर्व्वदिक्परिसरप्रतिष्ठितानन्त[3] पुण्यकीर्त्तिरापन्नभय-

3 मन्त्वदीक्षितो निजभुजपराक्रम(मा)क्रान्तशत्रुपक्ष[:*] प्रजापालनदक्षिणो मुद्ग-

4 [लकु]लाम्व(म्ब)रेन्दुपरमदैवतव(ब)प्पपादानुध्यातो **महाराजश्रीशम्भुयश**[:](शा:)

5 [कुश]ली [।*] दक्षिणतोसल्यां वर्त्तमानभविष्यन्महासामन्तमहाराजराज-

6 [पु]त्रकुमारामात्योपरिकविषयपतित[4]दायुक्तकदाण्डवा(पा)सिकस्थाना-

7 [न्तरि]कानन्यांश्च राजपादोपजि(जी)विनश्चाटभटवल्लभजाति(ती)यां(यान्)
अ[न्तरकुला][5]-

8 कोणविषये च महामहत्तरकूटकोलसा[द्या*]धिक[र*]णं पु(पू)जयति मानयत्यादिश-

9 ति चास्तु वो विदितं यथैतद्विषयसंम्व(संब)द्धः कन्निर्धकग्रामस्स(सो)परिक-

---

1. From the facsimile in *OHRJ*, Vol. XII (1964), pp. 122 and 123.
2. Expressed by a symbol.
3. Rajaguru reads प्रतिष्ठानन्त.
4. The त has been inserted below the line.
5. Rajaguru suggests अन्नरकुद्दाकोण or अस्तरकुद्दकोण as the name of the *viṣaya*. There is a locality called अन्तरकुल situated under Gop Police Station of Puri district which is on the bank of a small river called Kandhāriā-*nadī*, a tributary of the river Kuśabhadrā. The locality is situated near Erbang, the findspot of the charter.

Second Side

10 रसोद्देस(श)सर्व्वपीडारही(हि)त आचन्द्राक(र्क)काल मातापित्रो[रात्मन:*] पु-
11 ण्याभिवृद्धये वत्ससगोत्रव(ब)ह्वृचचरणभट्टशर्व्वकुण्डदत्ताय दत्त-
12 स्तदेषास्मद्दत्तिद्धधर्म्म[गौरवाश्च(च्च)] प्रतिपालनीयेति ।। उक्तञ्च धर्म्मशास्त्रे ।।
13 बहुभिर्व्वसुधा दत्ता राजभि: सगरादिभि: [।*] यस्य यस्य यदा भू-
14 मिस्तस्य तस्य तदा फलं(लम्) ।।[१*] लिखितं महासन्धिविग्रहिकोद्योत[कु]-
15 ण्ड [ता*]पिता पेडापालकगुहस्वामिना ।। **सम्वत् २००. ३०. ५**
16 **ज्येष्ठ १०.८**[6] [।।]

ABSTRACT

The charter begins with the symbol for *siddham* and the word *svasti*. Lines 1-5 introduce the reigning king **Mahārāja Śambhuyaśas** of the Mudgala family. He has been described as *paramadaivata* and devoted to the feet of his father. He is stated to have issued the order relating to the grant of land from the **victorious camp at Hāndaka**. Lines 5-11 refer to the royal order addressed to the present and future *mahāsāmanta, mahārāja, rājaputra, kumārāmātya, uparika, viṣayapati, tadāyuktaka, daṇḍapāśika, sthānāntarika* and other royal officers, the *cāṭas* and *bhaṭas* of the kingdom, along with the officers of the district of Antarakulākoṇa, such as, *mahattara, kūṭakōla* and their *adhikaraṇas* (assistants). The village named Kannirdhaka, situated in the above-mentioned district, was granted in favour of the brāhmaṇa Śarvvakuṇḍadatta of the Vatsa *gōtra* and Bahvṛca *caraṇa* by making it free from all obstructions. Lines 13-14 contain a customary verse. Lines 14-15 refer to the writer of the record as Udyōtakuṇḍa, designated as *mahāsandhivigrahin*. The charter was heated by Guhasvāmin, the *pēḍāpālaka*, referred to in line 15. The **date** of the grant is given at the end as **samvat 235, the eighteenth day of the month of Jyēṣṭha.**

6. The portion with the date in the facsimile is illegible. The original plate is not available for a verification of the numerical symbols. Rajaguru also suggests reading the last numerical symbol of the year as 9 and thus the *samvat* as 200. 30. 9.

NO. 34: SORO PLATE OF MAHĀRĀJA ŚAMBHUYAŚAS, YEAR 260

Provenance	:	Badkhuri, near Soro, Balasore district, Orissa.
References	:	N.G. Majumdar, *EI*, Vol. XXIII (1935-36), pp. 199-202 and plate; and S.N. Rajaguru, *IO*, Vol. I, Pt. 2 (1958), pp. 117-19.
Language	:	Sanskrit, in prose, except the usual imprecatory and benedictory verses at the end.
Metre	:	Verse 1 *anuṣṭubh*.
Script	:	Eastern variety of the northern alphabet of about the sixth century A.D.
Date	:	*Samvat* 260, the thirtieth day of the month of Kārttika.

TEXT[1]

First Side

1 सिद्धम्[2] [।*] जयस्कन्धावारात्**तम्परवङ्मवासका**च्छुतविनयविभू-
2 षणः प्रणयिजनयथेष्टभोग्यविभवः सर्व्वदिक्परिसर-
3 प्रतिष्ठितानन्तपुण्यकीर्त्तिरापन्नाभयमन्त्रदीक्षितो निज-
4 भुजपराक्रम(मा)क्रान्तशत्रुपक्षः प्रजापालनदक्षिणो मुद्गल-
5 कुलाम्व(म्ब)रेन्दुश्रीचूड़ामणिः परमदैवतव(ब)प्पपादानुध्यातो महा-
6 **राजश्रीशम्भुयशाः** कुशली [।*] उत्तरतोसल्यां वर्त्तमानभवि-
7 ष्यन्महासामन्तमहाराजराजपुत्त्रकुमारामात्योपरिक-
8 विषयपतितदायुक्तकदाण्डवा[पा]सिकस्थानान्तरिकानन्या(न्यां)-
9 श्च वल्लभजातीयान्सरेफ(फा)हारविषयमहामहत्तर-
10 [कू]टकोलसाद्यधिकरणं मानयति विदितमस्तु वो यथै-

Second Side

11 तद्विषयसम्बद्ध[3]सरेफासङ्ग्रामे घण्टाकर्ण्णक्षेत्रे तिम्पिरा-

---

1. From the original and facsimile in *EI*, Vol. XXIII (1935-36), pp. 200-1. The charter is now preserved in the Orissa State Museum, Bhubaneswar.
2. Expressed by a symbol.
3. The word सम्वद्ध is inserted below the line in smaller letters.

12 ष्टौ स(श)स्यसहिता वास्तुहस्तशतद्वयसमेता: सोपरिकरा:
13 सोद्देशा[:] सर्व्वपीडावर्ज्जिता आचन्द्रार्क्कसमकालं मातापित्रो-
14 रात्मनश्च पुण्याभिवृद्धये भारद्वाजसगोत्रकाण्वेय-
15 भरणस्वामिने प्रतिपादितास्तदेषास्मद्दत्तिः प्रतिपाल-
16 यितव्येत्याज्ञा स्वयं । उक्तञ्च धर्म्मशास्त्रे [।*] बहुभिर्व्वसुधा दत्ता
17 राजभि[:*] सगरादिभि[:* ।] यस्य यस्य यदा भूमिः तस्य[4] तस्य तदा
18 फलं(लम्) । [।*१] लिखितं(तं) महासान्धिविग्रहिक नारायणेन
19 तापित्तं(तं) महत्तरविदे[श]स्वामिन(ना) । **संव्व(व)त् २००.६० कार्त्ति[क*] दि ३०** [।।*]

ABSTRACT

The charter begins with a symbol for *siddham*, followed by a passage in prose in lines 1-6, which describe the reigning king **Mahārāja Śambhuyaśas** of the Mudgala family. He has been called *paramadaivata* and one who meditated on the feet of his father. He issued the order from the **victorious camp at Tamparavaḍama**. Lines 6-16 refer to the royal order relating to the grant of eight *ṭimpiras* of arable land along with the homestead land measuring two hundred *hasta*, situated at Ghaṇṭākarṇa-*kṣētra* in the village of Sarēphāsaṅga included in the district (*viṣaya*) of Sarēphāhāra of Uttara Tōsali. The order was addressed to the present and future *mahāsāmanta, mahārāja, rājaputra, kumārāmātya, uparika, viṣayapati, tadāyuktaka, dāṇḍapāśika, sthānāntarikas* and others of the province, as well as the officers of the district, such as, the *mahāmahattara* and *kūṭakōla* along with their subordinate officers. The grant was made in favour of the brāhmaṇa Bharaṇasvāmin, who belonged to the Bharadvāja *gōtra* and the Kāṇva (*śākhā*) of the Yajurvēda, in order to obtain religious merit for the king and his parents. It was made a permanent deed and free from all obstructions. Lines 16-18 contain a customary verse. Line 18 refers to the writer of the grant, Nārāyaṇa, the *mahāsandhivigrahika*. It was heated by Vidēśasvāmin, the *mahattara*, mentioned in line 19. The **date** of the grant is mentioned at the end of the same line as **samvat 260, the thirtieth day of the month of Kārttika.**

4. Read भूमिस्तस्य.

NO. 35: KANAS PLATE OF LŌKAVIGRAHA, YEAR 280

Provenance	:	Kanas, Puri district, Orissa.
References	:	S.N. Rajaguru, *JKHRS*, Vol. III, Nos. 1-3 (1950), pp. 261-66; *idem*, *IO*, Vol. I, Pt. 2 (1958), pp. 120 ff. and plates; and D.C. Sircar, *EI*, Vol. XXVIII (1949-50), pp. 329 ff. and plate.
Language	:	Sanskrit, in prose, except the two imprecatory verses at the end.
Metre	:	Verses 1-2 *anuṣṭubh*.
Script	:	Eastern variety of the north Indian alphabet of about the sixth century A.D.
Date	:	Gupta year 280, the fifth day of the month of Phālguna.

TEXT[1]

First Side

1 सिद्धम्[2] स्वस्ति [।।*] चतु[रु*]दधिसलिलवि(वी)ची(चि)[मेखलानिली]नायां सद्वीप[गिरिप]–

2 त्तनवत्यां वसुन्धरायां **प्रवर्त्तमाने गुप्त[का]लसम्व(संव)त्त्सरे अ[शी]-त्यु[त्त]रशत[द्व*]–**

3 ये तो[स]ल्यां साष्टादशा[ट्ट](ट)वीराज्यं परमदेव[ता]धिदैवत **श्रीलोकवि–**

4 **ग्रहभट्टारके**[प्र]शासति [द]क्षि[णतो]सल्यामुटि[3]दविषयात् विनि[यु]–

5 [क्त]का[:*][4] सवैश्वासिकविषयपत्यं [स]वृ(बृ)हद्द्रोगिकाधिकर[णा] वर्त्तमान–

6 भविष्यन्महासामन्तम[हा]राजराजपुत्रकुमा[रा]मात्योपरिकतदायु–

7 क्तक[वैश्वासिक]विषयप[त्यंस]वृ(बृ)हद्द्रोगिकाधिकरणानन्यांश्च [भाग]भुजो

8 य[था]र्हं [सं]पूज्य विज्ञा[प]यन्ति [।*] विदितमस्तु भो भवतां यथास्मद्विषय–

9 सम्व(म्ब)द्ध ऊ[र्द्ध्व]शृङ्गग्रा[म:] चि[रखिलशू]न्यमनेकगुणमित्यवधृत्य

10 प[रमदे]वताधि[दैवत] श्रीप[रमभट्टार]कपा[दानुज्ञ]यास्माभि: धर्म्मार्थकाम–

---

1. From the original and facsimile in *EI*, Vol. XXVIII (1949-50), pp. 330-31.
2. Expressed by a symbol.
3. D.C. Sircar suggest reading ल्यां मुटिद; Rajaguru reads सटिद.
4. Rajaguru reads ततिच्छपत्तने.

11 विनिष्पत्त[ये] [आचन्द्रार्क्क]सम[कालीयाक्षयनी]वीधर्म्मेण च[तुः]–

Second Side

12 सीमालिङ्गानि संस्थाप्य चैकाम्व(म्ब)कीय श्रीम[णि]नागेश्वरभट्टारकम[ठी]–
13 यव(ब)लिचरुसत्त्रप्रवर्त्तनाय नानागोत्त्रमैत्त्रायणीयछात्रव्रा(ब्रा)ह्म–
14 णानां स्थि[त]ये ताम्रप[ट्टी]कृत्य प्रतिपादित[:] [।*] तदेवं विदित्य(त्वा) धर्म्माभिला–
15 षादनु[पा]लयि[तुमर्ह]थेति ।। **सम्व(संव)त् २००.८० फाल्गुण(न) दि ५** [।।*]
16 [अ]नु[सृ]तं सूर्य्य ......[5] लिभटै[:।][6] वैश्वासिकभवनाग । विषय–
17 पति[श्रीदत्त ।] .....जिरोदां[स]वृ(बृ)हद्भोगिक सुडुमाक । करणि–
18 कनागदत्त [। द्रङ्गपाल][7] ......कैश्चेति ।। व(ब)हुभिर्व्वसुधा दत्ता राजभिः
19 सगरादिभि[:] [।*] यस्य यस्य यदा भूमिस्तस्य तस्य त[दा*] फलं(लम्) ।। [१*]
20 षष्टिं वर्षसहस्राणि स्वर्ग्गे तिष्ठति भूमिदः [।*] आक्षेप्ता चानुमन्ता च
21 तान्येव नरके वसेत ।। 0 ।।[8] [२*]

ABSTRACT

The inscription begins with the symbol for *siddham* and the word *svasti* followed by a passage in prose. Lines 1-14 record that in the **Gupta year 280,** when **Śrī-Lōkavigraha-bhaṭṭāraka**, described as *paramȧ-dēvat-ādhidaivata,* was ruling in Tōsali comprising eighteen forest states, the grant of the village Ūrddhvaśṛṅga[9] was made by the royal officers of Uṭida *viṣaya* in Dakṣiṇa Tōsali. The royal officers included the *vaiśvāsika, viṣayapati* and *aṁśa-bṛhadbhōgika*. The declaration regarding the grant was addressed to the present and future enjoyers of the share of the produce, such as the *mahāsāmanta, mahārāja, rājaputra, kumārāmātya, uparika, tadāyuktaka, vaiśvāsika, viṣayapati* and *aṁśa-bṛhadbhōgika*. The officers, having ascertained that the gift village had no land uncultivated for a long time and that its land possessed many qualities, granted it with a view to gain *dharma, artha* and *kāma*, with the permission of the reigning king who has been described as the *parama-dēvat-ādhidaivata-Śrī-*

---

5. This part of the plate is very corroded and the letters have peeled off.
6. The *daṇda* is redundant.
7. The designation seems to be same as (द्राङ्गिक) of some inscriptions of other parts of India.
8. A floral design is engraved between the two sets of double *daṇḍas, EI,* Vol. XXVIII (1949-50), p. 331 shows another similar mark, though it is found neither in the facsimile facing the same page nor in the original plate.
9. The village may be identified with the present Olasingh in Puri district, the findspot of a copper-plate charter of Bhānudatta (No. 37). This locality seems to be the place of issue of the said charter.

paramabhaṭṭāraka. The grant was made permanent, to last as long as the moon and the sun would endure, with the determination of four boundaries. The purpose of the grant has been stated to provide the *bali, caru*, and *sattra* at the *maṭha* of the illustrious Maṇināgeśvara-*bhaṭṭāraka* of Ēkāmbaka and the maintenance of the brāhmaṇas of different *gōtras*, who were students of the Maitrāyaṇīya school, associated with the said *maṭha*. The **date** of the grant is again stated in line 15 in numerical figures as **samvat 280, the fifth day of the month of Phālguna.** The grant is stated (lines 16-18) to have been endorsed, among others, by the *vaiśvāsika* Bhavanāga, *viṣayapati* Śrīdatta, *aṁśa-bṛhadbhōgika* Suḍumāka and *karaṇika* Nāgadatta. The inscription ends with two of the usual imprecatory and benedictory verses (lines 18-21).

NO. 36: PATIAKELLA GRANT OF MAHĀRĀJA ŚIVARĀJA, YEAR 283

Provenance	:	Patiakella, Puri district (previously in Cuttack district), Orissa.
References	:	R.D. Banerji, *EI*, Vol. IX (1907-08), pp. 285-88 and plate; and S.N. Rajaguru, *IO*, Vol. I, Pt. 2 (1958), pp. 124-27.
Language	:	Sanskrit, in prose, with the exception of the two imprecatory verses at the end.
Metre	:	Verses 1-2 *anuṣṭubh*.
Script	:	Eastern variety of the north Indian alphabet of about the sixth century A.D.
Date	:	*Samvat* 283.

TEXT[1]

First Side

1 सिद्धम्[2] स्वस्ति [।*] सलिलनिधिवेला[यित]चलतरङ्गाभरणरुचिरमङ्गुर. . . .[3]

2 पत्तनवत्या(त्यां) वसुमत्या(त्यां) **प्रवर्त्तमानमाणवङ्श(वंश)राज्यकाले त्र्यधिकाशीत्युत्त[र].** . . . .[4]

3 मौद्गलामलकुले गगनतलशीतदीधितिनिवाते सितचरिते परममाहेश्वर **श्रीशम्भुयय्यन**[5]

4 शासति दक्षिणतोसल्या(ल्यां) **वोर्त्तनोकात्परमदेवताधिदै**वतश्रीपरमभट्टारक चरणकमलामलक्षौ-

5 णिहाराधिगमप्रतिहत:[6] कलियुगागतदुरितनिचय:(यो) **महाराजशिवराज:** कुशली अस्मिन्नेव

6 विषये समुपगता भविष्यत्सामन्तराजराजस्थानीयोपरिककुमारामात्यतदायुक्तकमहामहत्तर-

7 व(बृ)हद्भौगिकाधिकरणान्येव राजपादोजीवी यथार्ह(र्हं) श्रावयति मानयति च विदितमस्तु भवतां य[था]-

---

1. From the facsimiles in *EI*, Vol. IX (1907-8), pp. 286 and 287.
2. Expressed by a symbol.
3. A portion from the right corner of the plate is broken and lost, carrying away about eight letters from both sides of the plate.
4. A portion from the right corner of the plate is broken and lost, carrying away about eight letters from both sides of the plate.
5. Sten Konow suggests शम्भुयय्येनु; R.D. Banerji reads शग्गुयय्यने; the intended reading is perhaps शम्भुयश सि.
6. The *visarga* is superfluous.

8 च्च विषयें सम्व(म्ब)द्धतण्डुल्वलुग्राम(मो) वोर्त्तनोके चावासात्तस्माभि[:*] मातापित्रोरात्मनश्च पुण्या-

9 भिवृद्धये सलिलधारापूर्व्वकेणाचन्द्रार्कसमकालियाक्षय[7]निवि(नीवि)धर्म्मेण नानागोत्त्र-

Second Side

10 चरणेभ्य अनिरुद्ध[8]स्वामिगोमिदेवस्वामिवो(बो)प्पस्वामिपितृस्वामि-

11 हरुङ्गस्वामिचन्द्रस्वामिभद्रस्वामिछेदिस्वामिपुष्यस्वामिकरस्वामिरोहिणीस्वामि-

12 वु(बु)द्धस्वामिमहासेणस्वामिविष्णुस्वामियदुस्वामिमातङ्स्वामिनागस्वामिभोगस्वामि-

13 अन[न्त]स्वामिप्रभाकरस्वामिनाव. . .रस्वामिदीपिस्वामियम्वुस्वामिगोमिस्वामिव(ब)-लस्वामि-

14 ज्येष्ठस्वामि अदर्शनदेव धनदेवकुमारस्वामिज्येष्ठस्वामिरेवतिस्वामिप्रायस्वामि-

15 पुष्यस्वामिछेडिस्वामिव(ब)प्पस्वामिश्रवस्वामिगोपालस्वामिगोमिस्वामि एभ्यस्ताम्र-

16 पट्टीकृत्य संप्रदत्तः [।*] पूर्व्वराजकृतो धर्म्मोनुपालनीयैति[9] मत्वा भवद्भिः [। *] धर्म्मशास्त्ते-ष्वपि श्रु(श्रू)यते [।*]

17 व(ब)हुभिर्व्वसुधा दत्ता राजभिः सगरादिभिः [।*] यस्य यस्य यदा भूमिस्तस्य तस्य [तदा फलम्][।।*१] [षष्टिं] वर्ष-

18 सहस्राणि स्वर्ग्गे तिष्ठति भूमिदः [।*] आक्षेप्ता चानुमन्ता च तान्येव नरके वसेत् [।।*२] **सम्वत् २००. . . .**[10]

ABSTRACT

The charter begins with the symbol for *siddham* and the word *svasti.* Lines 1-5 state that, in **the year 283 of the rule of the Māṇa family,** when **Śambhuyaśas** of the Mudgala family, a devout worshipper of Mahēśvara, was ruling the earth, Mahārāja Śivarāja, a devotee at the feet of his overlord, being in good health, made a proclamation from his residence at **Vōrttanōka** of Dakṣiṇa Tōsali. Lines 6-9 refer to the royal order addressed to all the present and future feudatory chiefs, *rājasthānīyas, uparikas, kumārāmātyas, tadāyuktakas, mahāmahattara, bṛhadbhōgikas* and their *adhikaraṇas* and other dependants of the king present in the said *viṣaya,* which relate to the grant of the village Taṇḍralvalu, situated in the *viṣaya* of Vōrttanōka. The grant was made a permanent endowment, so as to last as long as the sun and the moon would endure, and for the increase of the merit of the king and his parents. Lines 10-15 refer to the names of the donees of different *gōtras* and *caraṇas* to whom the grant was issued and include Aniruddhasvāmin, Gōmisvāmin, Surasvāmin, Bōppasvāmin, Pitṛsvāmin, Hāruṅgasvāmin, Candrasvāmin, Bhadrasvāmin, Chēdisvāmin,

7. Read कालमक्षय-.
8. R.D. Banerji reads अनुरुद्ध.
9. Read पालनीय इति.
10. This portion with the reference to the day and month is broken and lost.

Puṣyasvāmin, . . . Karasvāmin, Rōhiṇīsvāmin, Buddhasvāmin, Mahāsēṇasvāmin, Viṣṇusvāmin, Yadusvāmin, Mātraḍasvāmin, Nāgasvāmin, Bhōgasvāmin, Anantasvāmin, Prabhākarasvāmin, Nāva . . . rasvāmin, Dīpisvāmin, Jamvusvāmin, Gōmisvāmin, Balasvāmin, Jyēṣṭhasvāmin, Adarśanadēva, Dhanadēva, Kumārasvāmin, Jyēṣṭhasvāmin Rēvatīsvāmin, Prāyasvāmin, Puṣyasvāmin, Chēḍisvāmin, Bappasvāmin, Śravasvāmin, Gōpālasvāmin and Gōmisvāmin. Line 16 refers to the king's instruction to observe the law laid down by the former kings relating to land-grants. Lines 17-18 contain two of the usual benedictory verses. The **date** of the grant has been mentioned again in numerical symbols at the end of the charter in line 18, but only the first symbol reading **200** is visible.

NO. 37: OLASING PLATE OF BHĀNUDATTA, YEAR 5

Provenance	:	Olasing, Puri district.
References	:	S. N. Rajaguru, *OHRJ*, Vol. II, No. 1 (1953-54), pp. 31-46; *idem*, *IO*, Vol. I, Pt. 2 (1958), pp. 133-35; and D.C. Sircar, *EI*, Vol. XXVIII (1949-50), pp. 332-34 and plate.
Language	:	Sanskrit, in prose, except two of the usual imprecatory verses at the end.
Metre	:	Verses 1-2 *anuṣṭubh*.
Script	:	Eastern variety of the northern alphabet of about the sixth century A.D.
Date	:	5th regnal year, the twenty-fourth day of the month of Āśvina.

TEXT[1]

First Side

1 सिद्धम्[2] [।। *] स्वस्ति [।। *] **अन्द्धसृङ्गे** स्थित:[3] परम[दै]वतश्रीपरम[भट्टारकपादा]-
2 नुध्यातो महा[प्र]ति[हा]रम[हा]रा[जम]हासामन्त**श्रीभानु[दत्त:]**
3 कुशली [।*] उ[त्त]मा[लो]कविषये[4]समुपागतान्वर्तमान[भविष्य]-
4 न्महा[साम]न्तमहाराज[राज]पुत्र[कु]मारामात्योप[रिक]-
5 विषयपतितदायुक्तकदाण्डवा(पा)सिकस्थानान्तरिकानन्यांश्च
6 चाट भटादिन[धिक]रणांश्च पूजयति । अस्तु व: [स]म्वि[संवि]दित(तं)[5]
7 यथा[स्मा]भिरेतद्विषयसम्व(म्ब)द्धचिर[खिल]शून्यकु-
8 म्वुकीरिक्षिलाकग्राम:[6] श्रीपरमभट्टा[रक]पादा[ना]-

---

1. From the original and the facsimile in *EI*, Vol. XXVIII (1949-50), pp. 334-35.
2. Expressed by a symbol which is very faintly visible.
3. Rajaguru reads अन्द्धमुनिसुत: ; D.C. Sircar suggests अन्द्धसुभिक्षत: ; it seems to be the name of the locality from where the charter was issued. It may be the same as उर्द्धवशृङ्ग, the gift village mentioned in the charter of Lōkavigraha (No. 35) and may be identified with the present Olasing in Puri district, the findspot of the charter.
4. Rajaguru reads उड्डामलोक विषय.
5. Rajaguru reads दत्तिम्विदित.
6. Rajaguru reads कुम्वकंशुङ्खलाक ग्राम: ; letters ग्रा and म seem to have been engraved but erased later on by the engraver.

9 म्पुण्याभिवृद्धये ताम्रपट्टेनाचन्द्रा[र्क्क]समकाल(लं) [चै]-
10 काम्व(म्ब)कामणिनागभट्टारकाय[7] मैत्त्राय[णी]यच्छात्रमढव्रा(ब्रा)-
11 [ह्म]णानाम्प्रतिप(पा)दितस्तदमीषामुचितं ताम्रप[ट्टदानं]

Second Side

12 दत्वा भुञ्जानानाम्वा(म्बा)धा[8] न केनचित्कार्या श्रीपरमभट्टा[र*]कपा[9]-
13 दीयधर्मगौरवाच्च दत्तिरेषा परिपालयितव्येति ।।
14 **सम्व(संव)त् ५[10] आश्व दि २०.४** [।।*] उक्तञ्च धर्म्मशास्त्रे [।*]
व(ब)हु[भि]र्व्वसु[धा]-
15 दत्ता राजभिः सगरादिभिः [।*] यस्य यस्य यदा भूमि[स्तस्य] त-
16 स्य तदा [फ]लं(लम्) ।। [१*] स्वदत्ताम्परदत्ताम्वा(त्तां वा) यो हरेत वसुद्ध(न्ध)रा(राम्)
[।*] [स वि]-
17 ष्ठायां कृमिर्भूत्वा पितृभिः सह प[च्यते] [।।*२] लिखितं सा[न्धि]-
18 विग्रहिकगोविन्दे[न] [।*] तापितं पेडापाल प्रतिष्ठितेन [।*]
19 उत्कीर्ण्णं शिवनन्दनेति ।। =[11] ।।

ABSTRACT

The charter begins with the symbol for *siddham* and the word *svasti*. It records (lines 1-6) that **Mahārāja Bhānudatta,** designated as *mahāsāmanta* and *mahāpratihāra*, who was devoted at the feet of his overlord, issued the royal order while he was staying at **Andhaśṛṅga**. The order was addressed to the present and future *mahāsāmanta, mahārāja, rājaputra, kumārāmātya, uparika, viṣayapati, tadāyuktaka, dāṇḍapāśika, sthānāntarika* and other officers like the *cāṭas* and *bhaṭas* who would be associated with the district of Uttamālōka. Lines 7-13 record the grant of the village Kumvukirikṣilāka, situated in the said *viṣaya*, by the reigning king, for the increase of the religious merit of his overlord, and made it permanent so as to last as long as the moon and the sun would endure. The lands in the gift village are stated to have remained previously uncultivated. The grant was made in favour of the deity Maṇināgēśvara-*bhaṭṭāraka* of Ēkāmbaka and the brāhmaṇa students of the Maitrāyaṇīya school of *Yajurvēda* who resided in the *maṭha* of the said deity. It was made by recording in a copper-

7. Rajaguru reads अम्विका मणिनागेश्वर भट्टारकाय; the Kanas plates (No. 35) read चेकाम्वकीय मणिनागेश्वर भट्टारकमठीय.
8. Rajaguru reads स्ववर्ण्णनानाम्वाधा.
9. Rajaguru reads परमवन्दित.
10. Rajaguru reads the numerical symbol as 7, but the symbol for 5 is clear in the original plate.
11. Two slanting strokes are engraved between two sets of double *daṇḍas*.

plate and people were requested not to stand in the way of the donees in enjoying the grant but to protect in showing respect for the religious merit of the donor's overlord. Line 14 records the **date** of the charter as **the 5th regnal year** of the donor, **the twenty-fourth day of the month of Āśva (Āśvina)**. Lines 14-17 contain two of the customary verses quoted from the *Dharmaśāstra.* Lines 17-19 record that the charter was written by the *sandhivigrahika* Gōvinda, the plate was heated by the *pēḍāpāla* Pratiṣṭhita and engraved by Śivanandana.

NO. 38: BALASORE COPPER-PLATE GRANT OF ŚRĪ-BHĀNU, YEAR 5

Provenance	:	Near Balasore town, Balasore district, Orissa.
References	:	Haridas Mitra, *IHQ*, Vol. XI (1935), pp. 611-26 and plate; R.K. Ghoshal, *EI*, Vol. XXVI (1942), pp. 239 ff.; S.N. Rajaguru, *IO*, Vol. I, Pt. 2 (1958), pp. 128-30.
Language	:	Sanskrit, in prose, with the exception of four of the imprecatory and benedictory verses at the end.
Metre	:	Verses 1-4 *anuṣṭubh*.
Script	:	Eastern variety of the north Indian alphabet of about the seventh century A.D.
Date	:	5th regnal year, the fourth day of the month of Mārgaśīrṣa.

TEXT[1]

First Side

1 सिद्धम्[2] स्वस्ति [।।*] **सगढा[3]वासका**न्महाप्रतीहारमहाराजमहासामन्त**श्रीभानुः**
2 कुशली [।*] सगढाहारविषये समुपगतान्वर्त्तमानभविष्यन्महासा-
3 मन्तमहाराजराजपुत्रकुमारामात्योपरिकविषयपतितदा-
4 युक्तकदाण्डवासिक[4]स्थानान्तरिकानन्यांश्च चाट भटादि(दी)न्महामहत्तरवृ(बृ)हत्-
5 भोगिकाद्यधिकरणञ्च यथार्हम्पूजयति वो(बो)धयति चास्तु वो विदित-
6 मेतद्विषयसम्व(म्ब)द्ध चिरंखिलशुन्य[5] वन्दीरक[6]ग्रामोस्माभिः श्रीपरम-
7 भट्टारकपादानामाचन्द्रार्कसमकालम्पुण्याभिवृद्धये वत्ससगोत्र-
8 वाजसनेयचरणेभ्यः महामहत्तरप्रियमित्रस्वामिवाटमित्र-
9 स्वामिध्रुवमित्रस्वामि आरुहमित्र[7]स्वामिनामा(म)ग्रहारीकृत्य प्रतिपादितः [।*]
10 तदेषां समुचितराजदत्तिदानन्दत्वा भुञ्जानानां न केनचिद्बा(द्बा)धा करणीया [।*]

---

1. From the facsimile in *IHQ*, Vol. XI (1935), pp. 611 and 612.
2. Expressed by a symbol.
3. R.K. Ghoshal suggests सरेफ, but the letter फ is quite different from ढ in this charter written in lines 13 and 14.
4. Read दाण्डपाशिक.
5. Mitra reads चिरंखिल जोन्यवन्दीरकग्राम and interprets it as "the village the other minor (plots of land) (अन्यवन्दीरक) which was long fallow".
6. R.K. Ghoshal suggests the name of the village as नन्दीरट.
7. This may also be read as आरुङ्गमित्र as suggested by Ghoshal.

Second Side

11 श्रीपरमभट्टारकपादानां गौरवाच्चैषा दत्तिः परिपालयितव्येति [।*]

12 **सम्वत् ५ मार्ग्ग दि ४** ।। उक्तञ्च धर्म्मशास्त्रे [।*] व(ब)हुभिर्व्वसुधा दत्ता

13 राजभिः सगरादिभिः [।*] यस्य यस्य यदा भूमिः तस्य तस्य तदा फलं(लम्) ।। [१*] मा भू-

14 दफलशङ्का वः [पर]दत्तेति पार्थिवाः [।*] स्वदानात्फलमानन्त्यम्परदाना-

15 नुपालनं (नम्) ।। [२*] षष्टिम्व[8]र्षसहस्राणि स्वर्ग्गे मोदति भूमि[दः *।]

16 आक्षेप्ता चानुमन्ता च तान्येव नरकं(के) वसेत् ।। [३*] पूर्व्वदत्तां द्विजातिभ्यः

17 यत्नाद्रक्ष युधिष्ठिरः[9] [।*] महीं महीव(म)तां श्रेष्ठ दानाच्छ्रेयोनुपालनं(नम्) ।। [४*]

18 लिखितन्सान्धि[10]विग्रहिकेनारुणदत्तेन तापितं पेडापालक[11]प्रतिष्ठितचन्द्रेणेति[12] [।।]

ABSTRACT

The charter begins with the symbol for *siddham* and the word *svasti*. Line 1 states that the reigning king **Śrī-Bhānu**, who had the titles of *mahāpratihāra*, *mahārāja* and *mahāsāmanta*, issued the order from his residence at **Sagaḍhā.** Lines 2-9 record that the royal order was addressed to the present and future rulers and officers. These included *mahāsāmanta, mahārāja, rājaputra, kumārāmātya, uparika, viṣayapati, tadāyuktaka, dāṇḍapāśikà, sthānāntarika* and other officers such as the *cāṭas* and *bhaṭas, mahāmahattara* and *bṛhadbhōgin* and their assistants, assembled in the village of Vandīraka, situated in the *viṣaya* of Sagaḍhāhāra. The said village, which remained previously uncultivated, was granted to four brāhmaṇas, by the reigning king, after obtaining permission from his overlord. The gift village was made a permanent *agrahāra*. The names of the four brāhmaṇas are the *mahattara* Priyamitrasvāmin, Vāṭamitrasvāmin, Dhruvamitrasvāmin and Āruhamitrasvāmin (or Āruṅgamitrasvāmin). The purpose of the grant was to obtain religious merit. Lines 10-11 refer to the donor's instruction to the donees to pay the usual royal dues and enjoy the gift. Line 12 states the date of the grant mentioned in the regnal year of the king as samvat 5, the fourth day of the month of Mārgaśīrṣa. Lines 12-17 quote four of the usual imprecatory and benedictory verses. Line 18 refers to the writer of the charter Aruṇadatta, the *sandhivigrahin* and Pratiṣṭhitacandra, the *pēḍāpālaka*, who heated the plate.

8. Read षष्टिं वर्ष.
9. The *visarga* is superfluous.
10. Read लिखितं सान्धि-
11. Mitra reads पीडापालक and interprets it as an apprentice. This is the official designation of the "keeper of the records" and found in many of the early medieval copper-plate records of Orissa.
12. Mitra takes the name to be of two different persons—प्रतिष्ठित and चन्द्र.

NO. 39: SORO PLATE OF MAHĀRĀJA BHĀNUDATTA, YEAR 5

Provenance	:	Badkhuri, near Soro, Balasore district, Orissa.
References	:	N.G. Majumdar, *EI*, Vol. XXIII (1935-36), pp. 203 ff. and plate; and S.N. Rajaguru, *IO*, Vol. I, Pt. 2 (1958), pp. 131-35.
Language	:	Sanskrit, in prose, except three of the imprecatory verses at the end.
Metre	:	Verses 1-3 *anuṣṭubh*.
Script	:	Eastern variety of the north Indian alphabet of about the seventh century A.D.
Date	:	5th regnal year, the seventeenth day of the month of Phālguna.

TEXT[1]

First Side

1 सिद्धम्[2] स्वस्ति [।।*] **विरञ्जावासका**न्महाप्रतिहार**महाराजभानुदत्तः** कुशली [।*]
2 सरेफाहारविषये समुपगतान्वर्त्तमान भविष्यन्महासा-
3 मन्तमहाराजराजपुत्रकुमारामात्योपरिकविषयपति-
4 तदायुक्तकदाण्डवा(पा)सिक स्थानान्तरिकानन्यांश्च चाटभटजाती-
5 यान्तद्विषय[3]विनियुक्तकांश्च समहामहत्तरवृ(बृ)हद्भोगिक-
6 कूटकोलसाद्यधिकरणान्यथार्हम्पूजयति मानयति चास्तु
7 वो विदितमेतद्विषयसम्व(म्ब)द्धचिरखिला(ल)शून्य व(ब)हि[र्व्वा]टक-
8 ग्रामोस्माभिः श्रीपरमभट्टारकपादानामाचन्द्रार्कसम-
9 कालं पुण्याभिवृद्धये वत्ससगोत्रवाजसनेयचरणेभ्यः
10 महामहत्तरप्रियमित्रस्वामिवाटमित्रस्वामिधृवमित्रस्वामि-
11 आरुरङ्गमित्रस्वामिनाम्प्र[4]तिपादितः सर्व्वपीडावर्जितः [।*]

---

1. From the original and facsimile in *EI*, Vol. XXIII (1935-36), p. 203. The plate is now preserved in the Orissa State Museum, Bhubaneswar.
2. Expressed by a symbol.
3. Read यांस्तद्विषय-
4. Read स्वामिभ्यः प्रति-.

Second Side

12 तदेषां समुचितताम्रपट्टदानं दत्वा भुञ्जानानां न केनचित्
13 वा(बा)धा करणीया श्रीपरमभट्टारकपादानाङ्गौरवाच्चैषा दत्तिः
14 परिपालयितव्येति **सम्वत् ५ फल्गु दि १०.७** ।। उक्तञ्च धर्म्म-
15 शास्त्रे[।*] । व(ब)हुभिर्व्वसुधा दत्ता राजभिः सगरादिभिः [।*] यस्य
16 यस्य यदा भूमिः तस्य तस्य तदा फलं(लम्) ।। [१*] मा भूदफलष(श)-
17 ङ्का वः परदत्तेति पार्थिवाः[।*] स्वदानात्फलमानन्त्यं परदाना-
18 नुपालनं(नम्) ।। [२*] स्वदत्तां परदत्ताम्वा(त्तां वा)यो हरेत वसुन्द्धराम् [।*]
19 स विष्ठायां कृमिर्भूत्वा पितृभिः सह पच्यतेति[5] ।। [३*] लिखितं
20 सान्द्धिविग्रहिकारुणदत्तेन तापितं पेडापालकप्रति-
21 ष्ठितचन्द्रेणेति ।।

ABSTRACT

The inscription, after the symbol for *siddham* and the word *svasti,* introduces (line 1) the reigning king **mahārāja-mahāpratihāra Bhānudatta,** stated to have issued the order from his residence at **Virañjā (Virajā)**. Lines 2-11 state that the declaration of the royal order relating to the grant of a land, which remained previously uncultivated, was made at the *viṣaya* of Sarēphāhāra before the assembly of the present and future *mahārāja, mahāsāmanta, rājaputra, kumārāmātya, uparika, viṣayapati, tadāyuktaka, dāṇḍapāsika, sthānāntarika* and other officers of the district such as the *cāṭa,* the *bhaṭa, mahāmahattara, bṛhadbhōgika, kūṭakōla* and their *adhikaraṇas.* The land, situated in the village of Vahirvāṭaka under the said district, was granted by means of a copper-plate grant to the *mahāmahattaras,* namely, Priyamitrasvāmin, Vāṭamitrasvāmin, Dhruva-mitrasvāmin and Āruṅgamitrasvāmin who belonged to the Vatsa *gōtra* and Vājasaneya *caraṇa,* with permission from the donor's overlord. The purpose of the grant was to increase religious merit. It was made free from all obstructions. Line 14 refers to the **date** of the charter in the **regnal year** of the king as **samvat 5, the seventeenth day of the month of Phālguna.** Lines 15-19 contain three of the imprecatory verses, stated to have been quoted from the *Dharmaśāstra*. The record is stated (lines 20-21) to have been written by Aruṇadatta the *sandhivigrahin,* and heated by the *pēḍāpālaka* Pratiṣṭhitacandra.

---

5. Read पच्यते ।। [३*] इति.

NO. 40: SORO PLATE OF SŌMADATTA, YEAR 15

Provenance	:	Badkhuri near Soro, Balasore district.
References	:	N.G. Majumdar, *EI*, Vol. XXIII (1935-36), pp. 202 ff. and plate; and S.N. Rajaguru, *IO*, Vol. I, Pt. 2 (1958), pp. 138-40.
Language	:	Sanskrit, in prose, with the exception of four of the usual benedictory and imprecatory verses at the end.
Metre	:	Verses 1-4 *anuṣṭubh*.
Script	:	Eastern variety of the north Indian alphabet of about the seventh century A.D.
Date	:	15th regnal year, the thirteenth day of Vaiśākha.

TEXT[1]

First Side

1 सिद्धम्[2] स्वस्ति [।*] **जयस्कन्धावारादाम्रतक्षकवासकात्परमदैवताधिदैवतश्री-**
2 पर[म]भट्टारकपादानुध्यातो **महाव(ब)लाधिकृतान्तरङ्गमहासान्धि-**
3 **विग्रहिकसोमदत्तः** कुशली [।*] ओड्रविषये उत्तरतोसल्यां सरेफा-
4 हारविषये वर्त्तमानभविष्यन्महासामन्तमहाराजराजपुत्रकुमारा-
5 मात्योपरिकविषयपतितदायुक्तकदाण्डवा(पा)सिकस्थानान्तरिकान-
6 न्यांश्च चाटभटवल्लभजातीयान्विषयमहामहत्तरकूटकोलस-
7 पुस्तपालाद्यधिकरणञ्च यथार्हम्पूजयत्यवगमयति च विदित-
8 मस्तु भवतां यथास्माभिरेतद्विषयसम्व(म्ब)द्धअडयारग्रामो(मः) श्रीपरम-
9 [भ]ट्टारकपादानामाचन्द्रार्कसमकालम्पुण्यभिवृद्धये राजदत्ति-
10 ताम्रपट्टस्थित्या वात्स्यसगोत्रवाजसनेयध्रुवमित्र स्वाम्यारुङ्ग-
11 स्वाम्यादीनाम्प्रतिपादितस्तदेषां समुचितताम्रपट्टदा[न*]न्दत्वा
12 भुञ्जानानां न केनचिदन्यथा करणीया एषा च दत्तिः परमदैवत-

Second Side

13 श्रीपरमभट्टारकपादानां धर्म्मस्य च गौरवात्प्रतिपालयितव्या ।।

---

1. From the original plate and the facsimiles in *EI*, Vol. XXIII (1935-36), pp. 200 and 201.
2. Expressed by a symbol.

14 उक्तञ्च धर्म्मशास्त्रे [।*] व(ब)हुभिर्व्वसुधा दत्ता राजभिः सगरादिभिः [।*]

15 यस्य यस्य यदा भूमिस्तस्य तस्य तदा फलं(लम्) । [।*१] स्वदत्ताम्परदत्ताम्वा[3]

16 यो हरेत वसुन्द्धरां(राम्)[।*] स विष्ठायां कृमिर्भूत्वा पितृभिः सह पच्यते ।। [२*]

17 मा भूदफलशङ्का वः परदत्तेति पार्थिवाः[। *] स्वदानात्फलमानन्त्यं

18 परदानानुपालनं(नम्) ।। [३*] षष्टिम्वर्ष[4]सहस्राणि स्वर्गे मोदति

19 भूमिदः [। *] आक्षेप्ता चानुमन्ता च तान्येव नरकम्वसेदिति[5] ।। [४*]

20 **सम्वत् १०.५ वैशाख दि १०.३** लिखितं सान्धिविग्रहिक-

21 केशवेन तापितं महत्तरकसूर्यदेवेन ।।

ABSTRACT

The charter begins with the symbol for *siddham* and the word *svasti.* Lines 1-3 introduce the reigning king **Sōmadatta**, who issued order relating to the grant from the victorious camp of **Āmratakṣaka**. He has been designated as the *mahābalādhikṛta, antaraṅga* and *mahāsandhivigrahika* and as devoted to his overlord, who has been described as the *parama-daivat-ādhi-daivata* and *paramabhaṭṭāraka*. Lines 3-7 record that the royal declaration was addressed to the present and future *mahāsāmanta, mahārāja, rājaputra, kumārāmātya, uparika, viṣayapati, tadāyuktaka, dāṇḍapāśika* and other officers such as the *cāṭas, bhaṭas, mahāmahattara, kūṭakōla, pustapāla* and their *adhikaraṇas,* in the district of Sarēphāhāra, situated in Ōḍra-*viṣaya*[6] of the province of Uttara Tōsali. Lines 8-13 record the grant of the village named Aḍayāra, situated in the said district (Sarēphāhāra), in favour of Dhruvamitrasvāmin, Āruṅgasvāmin and others who belonged to the Vatsa *gōtra* and Vājasanēya (*caraṇa*), for the purpose of increasing the religious merit of the overlord. The grant, by means of a copper-plate charter, was made by the king with the permission of his overlord. This is followed by a reference to the donor's instruction to all-not to cause obstruction in the enjoyment of the gift by the donees. Lines 14-19 contain four of the usual imprecatory and benedictory verses quoted from the *Dharmaśāstra*. Line 20 refers to the **date** of the record given in the **regnal year** of the donor as **the year 15, the thirteenth day of the month of Vaiśākha**. The record is stated (lines 20-21) to have been written by Kēśava, the *sandhivigrahin*, and heated by Sūryadēva, the *mahattara*.

---

3. Read स्वदत्तां परदत्तां वा.
4. Read षष्टिं वर्ष.
5. Read नरकं वसेदिति.
6. Ōḍra-*viṣaya* here seems to indicate a territorial division, larger than a district.

NO. 41: SORO PLATE OF SŌMADATTA, YEAR 15

Provenance	:	Badkhuri near Soro, Balasore district.
References	:	N.G. Majumdar, *EI*, Vol. XXIII (1935-36), pp. 202-03 and plate; and S.N. Rajaguru, *IO*, Vol. I, Pt. 2 (1958), pp. 136-37.
Language	:	Sanskrit, in prose, with the exception of the imprecatory verses in lines 12-16.
Metre	:	Verses 1-3 *anuṣṭubh*.
Script	:	Eastern variety of the north Indian alphabet of about the seventh century A.D.
Date	:	15th regnal year, the twenty-fourth day of the month of Māgha.

TEXT[1]

First Side

1 सिद्धम[2] स्वस्ति [।।*] **शाञ्चाटकात्**परमदैवतश्रीपरमभट्टारकपादानुध्यातो **महा**
2 **व(ब)लाधिकृतान्तरङ्गमहासान्धिविग्रहिकसोमदत्तः** कुशली [।*] सरेफाहार-
3 सम्व(म्ब)द्धवरुकोण[3] विषये वर्त्तमानभविष्यन्महासामन्तमहाराजराज-
4 पुत्रकुमारामात्योपरिकविषयपतितदायुक्तकदाण्डवा(पा)सिकस्थानान्तरिका-
5 नन्यांश्य चाटभटवल्लभजातीयान्विषयमहामहत्तरकूटकोलस-
6 पुस्तपालाद्यधिकरणं च यथार्हम्पूजयत्यवगमयति च विदितमस्तु भव-
7 तामेतद्विषयसम्व(म्ब)द्धचिरखिल[शू]न्यव(ब)हिर्व्वाटक ग्रामः परमदैवत-
8 श्रीपरमभट(ट्टा)रकप(पा)दानामाचन्द्रार्क्कसमकालं पुण्याभिवृद्धये वत्स्य(त्स)सगो-
9 त्रवाजसनेयचरणध्रुवमित्रस्वाम्यारुङ्गस्वामिभ्यां राजताम्रपट्टस्थित्या
10 प्रतिपादितस्तदनयोस्समुचितराजदत्तिताम्रपट्टदानं दत्त्वा भुञ्जानयोर्न
11 कैनचिद्वा(द्वा)धा कार्या एषा च दत्तिः परमदैवतश्रीपरमभट्टारकपादानां

---

1. From the original and facsimile in *EI*, Vol. XXIII (1935-36), pp. 201 and 202; this plate and also No. 40 are now preserved in the Orissa State Museum, Bhubaneswar.
2. Expressed by a symbol.
3. Majumdar reads वरुकाण and Rajaguru वरुकण.

Second Side

12 धर्म्मस्य च गौरवात्प्रतिपालयितव्या । उक्तं च धर्म्मशास्त्रे [।*] व(ब)हुभिर्व्वसु-
13 धा दत्ता राजभिस्सगरादिभिः [। *] यस्य यस्य यदा भूमिस्तस्य तस्य तदा
14 फलं(लम्) ।। [१*] मा भूदफलशङ्का वः परदत्तेति पार्थिवाः [।*] स्वदानात्फल-
15 मानन्त्यं परदानानुपालनं(नम्) ।। [२*] षष्टिं वर्ष सहस्राणि स्वर्ग्गे ति-
16 ष्ठति भूमिदः [।*] आक्षेप्ता चानुमन्ता च तान्येव नरके वसेदिति ।। [३*]
17 **सम्वत् १०.५ माघ दि २०.४** लिखितं शुभसिंहेन ।
18 तापितं पेडापालकदिवाकरेण । उत्कीर्ण्णं नारायणेन ।।

ABSTRACT

The charter begins with the symbol for *siddham* and the word *svasti.* Line 1 refers to the name of the locality, *Śāñcāṭaka,* from where the charter was issued. Lines 1-2 introduce the reigning king *Sōmadatta,* who has been described as one who is devoted at the feet of his overlord, described as *paramadaivata* and *paramabhaṭṭāraka.* He has been designated as *mahābalādhikṛta, antaraṅga* and *mahāsandhivigrahika.* This is followed by the issue of the royal order (lines 3-6) from Varukōṇa *viṣaya,* included in Sarēphāhāra, addressed to the future and present *mahāsāmanta, mahārāja, rājaputra, kumārāmātya, uparika, viṣayapati, tadāyuktaka, dāṇḍapāśika, sthānāntarika* and others such as the *cāṭas,* the *bhaṭas,* the *mahāmahattara, kūṭakōla* and *pustapāla.* Lines 7-12 record the grant of a piece of land in the village of Vahirvāṭaka, situated in the said *viṣaya,* which long remained uncultivated. The grant was made a permanent gift and the purpose was to increase the religious merit of the overlord of the donor. The royal order, by means of a copper-plate grant, was issued in favour of Dhruvamitrasvāmin and Āruṅgamitrasvāmin who belonged to the Vatsa *gōtra* and Vājasanēya *caraṇa,* with the permission of the overlord. This is followed by three of the imprecatory verses in lines 12-16. Line 17 refers to the **date** of the grant in the **regnal year** of the donor as **samvat 15, the twenty-fourth day of the month of Māgha.** Lines 17-18 refer to the persons associated with the execution of the royal order, who are Śubhasiṁha, the writer of the charter, Divākara, who heated the plate (designated as the *pēḍāpālakaṇ*), and Nārāyaṇa, the engraver of the charter.

NO. 42: MIDNAPORE PLATE OF SŌMADATTA, YEAR 19

Provenance	:	Midnapore, Midnapore district, West Bengal.
References	:	R.C. Majumdar, *JASB* (*Letters*), Vol. XI (1945), pp. 3-8 and plate; and S.N. Rajaguru, *IO*, Vol. I, Pt. 2 (1958), pp. 141 ff.
Language	:	Sanskrit, in verse, except a portion in the first line.
Metre	:	Verses 1-11 *anuṣṭubh*.
Script	:	Eastern variety of the northern alphabet of about the seventh century A.D.
Date	:	19th year, the nineteenth day of the month of Bhādra.

TEXT[1]

1 **[स*]म्वत् १०.९ भाद्र दि १०.९** [।।*] विष्णोः पोत्त्राग्रविक्षेपक्षणभा[वितसाध्वसां ।
शेषा*]–[2]

2 शेषशिरोमध्यमध्यासीन महातनुं ।। [१*] कामारातिशिरोभ्रष्ट[गङ्गौघध्वस्त*]-

3 कल्मषां [।*] **श्रीशशाङ्के** महीं पाति चतुर्जलधि मेखलां(लाम्) ।। [२*] तस्य पादन-
[खज्योत्स्ना*]-

4 विभूषितशिरोमणौ [।*] **श्रीसामन्तमहाराजसोम**दत्ते गुणाधिके ।। [३*] सा. . .

5 गमोत्सन्नकालेयध्वान्तसंहतौ [।*] सहितामुत्कलदेशेन दण्डभुक्तिं प्रशा[सति ।।*४]

6 सत्यशौर्यकृतास्त्रत्वरुपविद्यादयः पृथक [।*] पाण्डवेषु स्थिताः सन्ति य[स्मि]-

7 न्नेकत्त्रे ते गुणाः ।। [५*] अमात्यो यस्य गुणवान्प्रकीर्ण्णदास इति श्रुतः [।*] साधुकारि-

8 तया नित्यं यः पूज्यैः पूज्यते द्विजैः ।। [६*] आगामिनो नृपान्सर्व्वान् ज्ञापयित्वा

9 प्रणम्य च [।*] प्राह ताविरकं सर्व्वं करणं लोकसङ्गतं ।। [७*] भूमेर्गोचर्ममात्त्रा[याः]

10 दाने स्वर्गः फलं स्मृतं [।*] पराशरसुतस्योच्चैर्व्वाचं श्रुत्वेति भासितां(ताम्) ।। [८*]
तेने[दं च]

11 समाम्नात(तं)मनुशास्त्रानुवर्त्तिना [।*] श्रीसामन्तेन कृतिना सोमदत्ते[न]

12 धीमता ।। [९*] भट्टेश्वराय गुणिने काश्यपाध्वर्यवे [।*] मुहा[3]कुम्भारपद्रको-

---

1. From the facsimile in *JASB* (*Letters*), Vol. XI (1945) and plate I.
2. A portion of the upper and lower right corners of the plate is broken affecting the first six lines in the upper right corner and lines 13 to 15.
3. Read this as महा-

13 दत्तः सर्व्वमण्डलवर्ज्जित[:*] ।। [१०*] तद्योच्चास्मत्कुले जातो मोहादन्योपि वा [नरः ।*]

14 पापं प्रकुरुते लोभान्महापातकवान्भवेत् ।। [११*] सुखानामन्व××××

15 ××स्यात्यल्पधीमतः [।*] द्विजदेवस्य भाहेतोः श्लोकाः ××××सहिता××

ABSTRACT

The charter begins with the **date** of issue, mentioned in the regnal year of the reigning king as **samvat 19, the nineteenth day of the month of Bhādrapada.** Lines 1-3 describe the illustrious monarch **Śaśāṅka**, the protector of the earth bounded by the four oceans. Lines 4-9 record that during his rule, his illustrious feudatory **sāmanta mahārāja Sōmadatta** ruled Daṇḍabhukti along with Utkala, whose excellent minister was Prakīrṇṇadāsa and who, having saluted the brāhmaṇas and informed all the future kings, addressed all the officers of **Tāviraka**[4] as well as the people associated with the grant. Lines 9-10 record the prevalent popular belief that the gift of even a *gōcarma*[5] measure of land would lead to the attainment of heaven, which is loudly proclaimed by the son of Parāśara. Lines 11-15 record that the illustrious feudatory, who was a keen follower of the Law code of Manu, declared the grant of the village Mahā Kumbhārapadraka, by making it detached from all territorial divisions, in favour of the meritorious Bhaṭṭēśvara of Kāśyapa (*gōtra*). Lines 14-15 contain the usual imprecatory verses, but the lines are greatly corroded.

---

4. This seems to indicate the office of *kāyasthas* situated at Tāviraka, which was under the minister for war and peace (*sandhivigrahin*). The seal attached to the plate contains the legend *tāvirādhikaraṇasya* (of the officer of Tāvira). The expression seems to indicate that the office was often held by the feudatory rulers, who sometimes acted as ministers of a sovereign.
5. This land-measure is generally taken to be equal to 150 cubit-square.

NO. 43: MIDNAPORE PLATE OF ŚUBHAKĪRTTI, YEAR 8

Provenance : Midnapore, Midnapore district, West Bengal.
References : R.C. Majumdar, *JASB* (*Letters*), Vol. XI (1945), pp. 9 ff. and plate; and S.N. Rajaguru, *IO*, Vol. I, Part 2 (1958), pp. 144 ff.
Language : Sanskrit, in verse, except a portion in line 1.
Metre : Verses 1-9 *anuṣṭubh*.
Script : Eastern variety of the northern alphabet of about the seventh century A.D.
Date : 8th regnal year, the twelfth day of the month of Puṣya (Pauṣa).

TEXT[1]

First Side

1 **[सम्व]त् ८ पौष दि** १०.२ अस्मिन्दिवसमाससम्वत्सरे ।। विष्णो: पोत्राग्रविक्षे-
2 पक्षणभावितसाध्वसां [।*] शेषाशेषशिरोमध्यमध्यासीनमहातनुं ।। [१ *] कामारा-
3 तिशिरोभ्रष्टगङ्गौघध्व[स्त*]कल्मषां [।*] **श्रीशशाङ्के** महीम्पाति चतुर्ज्जलधिमेखलां(लाम्) [।।*२]
4 यस्य गाम्भीर्यलावण्यव(ब)हुरत्नतयानया [।*] न समः क्षारकालुष्यं व्यालोपय[2]-
5 तयोदधि[:*] ।। [३ *] तस्य पादनखज्योत्स्नाविभूषितशिरोमणौ [।*] **श्रीमान्महाप्रति-(ती)**
6 **हारे शुभकीर्त्तौ** विचक्षणे:[3] ।। [४*] दण्डभुक्तिमिमां पाति पितृवत्पापवर्जिते [।*]
7 धर्मशास्त्रानुरोधेन न्यायान्यायं विचेतरि ।। [५ *] अस्यां **ताविर**करणं विप्रप्र-
8 धानसङ्गतं [।*] भविष्यद्वर्त्तमानाधीन्वि(दीन वि)ज्ञापयति सू(शु)नृतं ।। [६ *] कृत्वास्मत्तो
9 यथान्यायं शुभकीर्त्तिरियं[4] वु(बु)धः [।*] चत्वारिङ्स(रिंश)द्ददौ द्रोणान् द्रोणवापं च
10 वास्तुनः ।। [७ *] केतकपद्रिद्देशे[5] ग्रामे कुम्भारपद्रके [*] । भारद्वाजसगोत्रा-

---

1. From the facsimile in *JASB* (*Letters*), Vol. XI (1945), plate II.
2. A letter seems to be missing here.
3. The *visarga* is redundant.
4. Read. . .रिमं.
5. Read देशे; the locality seems to denote a district in which the village कुम्भारपद्रक was situated.

11 य माध्यन्दिनाय धीमते [।।८*] दाम्यस्वामिन एतस्मै पित्रो[:*] पुण्याभिवृद्धये [।।*९][6]

12 तद्यो वास्मत्कुले जातो मोहादन्योपि वा नरः [।*] पापं प्रकुरुते मोहान्महा

Second Side[7]

13 [पा*]तकवान्भवेत् ।। [१०*]

ABSTRACT

The charter begins with the **date** of the grant as **samvat 8, the twelfth day of the month of Pauṣa.** This is followed by three verses (lines 1-5), describing the illustrious monarch *Śaśāṅka,* who was the protector of the earth bounded by the four oceans. Verses 4 to 9 in lines 5-11 record that during Śaśāṅka's rule, his feudatory, **mahāpratihāra Śubhakīrtti** was in charge of the division of Daṇḍabhukti. His administrative office at **Tāvira** was full of eminent brāhmaṇas. The royal order relating to the grant was issued from this office, which was addressed to the future and present officers and associates. Śubhakīrtti, having purchased forty *drōṇas* of land and one *drōṇavāpa* of homestead in the village of Kumbhārapadraka situated in the division of Kētakapadraka, donated in favour of Dāmyasvāmin of the Bhāradvāja *gōtra* and Mādhyandina (*śākhā*) in order to increase the religious merit of his parents. Lines 12 and 13 contain one imprecatory verse.

6. The first half of the verse is not given.
7. A photograph of the reverse side of the plate is not given.

NO. 44: STONE INSCRIPTIONS FROM THE TEMPLES OF PARAŚURĀMEŚVARA AND ŚATRUGHNEŚVARA

Provenance	:	Bhubaneswar, Puri district, Orissa.
Reference	:	K.C. Panigrahi, *JRASB* (*Letters*), Vol. XV (1949), pp. 109-18 and plates.
Language	:	Sanskrit.
Script	:	Eastern variety of the northern alphabet of about the seventh century A.D.

TEXT[1]

The Paraśurāmeśvara Temple Inscriptions

No. 1 आद्य(दि)त्य

No. 2 सोम

No. 3 अंगारक

No. 4 वु(बु)ध

No. 5 व्रि(बृ)हस्पति

No. 6 शुक्र

No. 7 सणिश्छर (शनिश्चर)

No. 8 राहु

TEXT[2]

The Śatrughneśvara Temple Inscriptions

No. 1 सोम

No. 2 वु(बु)ध[3]

No. 3 वृ(बृ)हस्पति

No. 4 शुक्र

---

1. From the photographs in *JRASB* (*Letters*), Vol. XV (1949), plates XII-XV. The inscriptions are found on the door of the sanctum of the said temple.
2. From the photographs in *JRASB* (*Letters*), Vol. XV (1949), plates XVI and XVII. A slab containing images of eight planets, with inscribed names, has now been shifted to the Orissa State Museum, Bhubaneswar, from the said temple premises.
3. K.C. Panigrahi reads बुद्ध.

V

INSCRIPTIONS OF THE ŚAILŌDBHAVAS DYNASTY

NO. 45: GANJAM PLATES OF MĀDHAVARĀJA, GUPTA *SAMVAT* 300

Provenance	:	Ganjam district.
References	:	E. Hultzsch, *EI*, Vol. VI (1900-1), pp. 144-46 and plate; and S.N. Rajaguru, *IO*, Vol. I, Pt. 2 (1958), pp. 157-61.
Language	:	Sanskrit, in prose, except the customary verses at the end.
Metre	:	Verses 1-4 *anuṣṭubh*.
Script	:	Eastern variety of the northern class of the post-Gupta Brāhmī alphabet of about the seventh century A.D.
Date	:	Gupta year 300; on the occasion of a solar eclipse.

TEXT[1]

First Plate

1 सिद्धम्[2] स्वस्ति ।[3] चतुरूदधिसलिलवीचिमेखलानिलीनायां सद्वीपा(प)-
2 गर(गिरि)पत्तनवत्या(त्यां) **गौप्ताव्दे(ब्दे) वर्षशतत्त्रये वर्त्तमाने**
3 महाराजाधिराजा(ज)श्श्री(श्री)शशाङ्कराज्ये[4] शासति गग!ण(न)तल-
4 विनि[:*]सृतभगीरथावतारिताया हिमवद्गिरि(रे)रुपरि
5 पतना[द*]नेकशिलासंहा(संघा)तविभिन्नव(ब)हि ≍ पातालात्तर्ज्जलौधे[5]
6 सुरसरित इव विविधतरुवरकुसुमसञ्च्छन्नोभयतटा-

Second Plate: First Side

7 न्तविनिपतितजलाशयाया: शालिमासरित: कुला(कूलो)पकण्ठा-
8 द्वे(द्वि)जयकोङ्गदात्म(न्म)हाराजमहासामन्तश्रीमाधवराजस्य प्रियतनयो
9 महाराजा(ज)यशोभीतस्तस्यापि प्रियसूनु: स्वगुणमरीचिनिकर-
10 प्रवो(बो)धितशिलोद्भवकुलकमलो विकोशनीलोत्पल-
11 प्रतिस्पर्द्धिनीखड्ग धारानिशितनिश्शेषप्रतिहतरिपु[6]-

---

1. From the facsimile in *EI*, Vol. VI (1900-1), p. 144.
2. Expressed by a symbol.
3. The punctuation is indicated by a short horizontal stroke.
4. Read महाराजाधिराजश्रीशशाङ्कराजे.
5. Hultzsch suggests वहिष्पातितान्तर्जलौधाया: (?).
6. The line should be read प्रतिस्पर्द्धिनिशितखड्गधाराप्रतिहतनि:शेषरिपु-.

12 व(ब)लो दीनानाथकृपणवनीपकोपभुज्यमानविभवः स्वभु-
13 जपरिघयुगलोपार्ज्जितनृपश्री[:*] कमलविमलरुथ(चि)र-

Second Plate: Second Side

14 तनुर्ज्जगन्म(ण्ड)लमण्डनश्रुतशौर्यधैर्यगुणान्वितो महावृषभपर्यङ्क-
15 ककुधो(दो)पधानविन्यस्तवा(बा)होर्व्वा(र्बा)लचन्द्रो[द्*]द्योतितजटाकलापैकदे-
16 शस्य भगवतस्स्थित्युत्पत्तिप्रलयसृष्टिसङ्हा(संहा)रकारणस्य
17 नृ(त्रि)भुवनगुरोः पादभक्तः परमव्र(ब्र)ह्मण्यो **महाराजमहासा-**
18 **मन्तश्रीमाधवराजः** कुशली कृष्णगिरिविषयसंव(ब)द्धच्छवल-
19 क्खयग्रामे वर्त्तमानभविष्यक्कु(त्कु)मारामात्योपरिकतदायुक्तकानन्या(न्यां)श्च
20 यथार्ह(र्हं) पूजयति मानयति च [।*] विदितमस्तु भवतामयं ग्रामो-

Third Plate: First Side

21 स्माभिरर्द्धेण[7] मातापित्रोरात्मनश्च पुण्याभिवृद्धये सलिलधारापुर-
22 स्सरेणाचन्द्रार्क्कसमकालीनाक्षयनीये[8] भरद्वाजसगोत्त्रायाङ्गि-
23 रसवा(बा)र्हस्पत्यप्रवराय छरम्पस्वामिने सूर्य्योपरागे प्रतिपादित[:*] ।।
24 उक्तञ्च स्मृतिशास्त्रे ।[9] व(ब)हुभिर्व्वसुधा दत्ता राजभिस्सगरादिभिः [।*]
25 यस्य यस्य यदा भूमि[स्*]तस्य तस्य तदा फलं(लम्) ।। [१*] षष्टिं वर्षसहस्रा-
26 णि स्वर्गे मोदति भूमिदः [।*] आज्ञेप्ता चानुमन्ता च तान्येव नरके
27 वसे[त्*] ।। [2*] स्वदत्ता(त्तां) परदत्ताम्वा(त्तां वा) ।[10] यो हरेत वसुन्द्धरा[म्*।] स विष्ठायां

Third Plate: Second Side

28 [कृमि]र्भूत्वा पितृभिस्सह पच्यते ।। [३*] मा भुत(भूद)फलशङ्का व[:] परदत्ते-
29 [ति] पार्थिव(वाः) ।। (।)स्वदाना[त्*] फलमानन्त्यं ।।[11] परद[त्तानुपालने] । [४*]
30 . . . .[12]
31 [प्रय]च्छति ।।

---

7. Hultzsch suggests. . . र्थे-; but the intended reading seems to mean half of the said village.
8. Hultzsch suggests. . . लीनोक्षयणीयो ; but the record seems to indicate the expression अक्षयनीवि, that is, a permanent endowment, which is found in several early medieval epigraphs of Orissa.
9. The punctuation is indicated by a small horizontal stroke.
10. The punctuation is redundant.
11. The punctuation is redundant.
12. The line is illegible.

ABSTRACT

The charter opens with a symbol for *siddham* and the word *svasti.* It records (lines 1-4) that in the **current Gupta year 300**, the glorious **mahārājādhirāja Śaśāṅkarāja** was ruling over the earth surrounded by the waters of the four oceans, together with the islands, mountains and cities. Lines 4-8 record the description of the chief city of the kingdom which was situated near the bank of the river Śālimā, resembling the holy Gaṅgā. Lines 8-18 introduce the reigning king, the glorious **mahārāja-mahāsāmanta Śrī-Mādhavarāja**, the son of *mahārāja* Yaśōbhīta and the grandson of the glorious *mahārāja-mahāsāmanta* Śrī-Mādhavarāja I. He has been described as a devotee of the god Brahman. From the victorious Kōṅgēda (Kōṅgōda),[13] he caused the prosperity of the Śailōdbhava (*Śilōdbhava*) family to which he belonged, by his own arms. He was also devoted to the feet of the blessed lord of the three worlds. Lines 18-23 record that the royal order in respect of the grant was addressed to the present and future officials, such as *kumārāmātya, uparika* and *tadāyuktaka,* and others at the village named Cchavalakkhaya, situated in the district of Kṛṣṇagiri. The officers were informed that half of the said village was granted, with the libation of water, to Charampasvāmin of the Bharadvāja *gōtra* and Āṅgirasa-Bārhaspatya *pravara.* The grant was made on the occasion of a solar eclipse, to increase religious merit of the donor and his parents. It was made a permanent endowment according to the system of *akṣaya-nīvi*, for the enjoyment of the donee, and to last as long as the sun and the moon would exist. Lines 24-31 record four of the imprecatory and benedictory verses stated to have been quoted from the *Smṛti-śāstra.*

---

13. Kōṅgōda here seems to indicate the chief city of the kingdom of the same name.

NO. 46: KHURDA PLATES OF ŚRĪ-MĀDHAVARĀJA, *ALIAS* ŚRĪ-SAINYABHĪTA

Provenance : Uttar-Mundamohana near Khurda, Puri district.
References : G.M. Laskar, *JASB*, Vol. LXXIII, Pt.1 (1904), pp. 282 ff. and plate; and S.N. Rajaguru, *IO*, Vol. I, Part 2 (1958), pp. 162 ff.
Language : Sanskrit, in prose, except the customary verses at the end.
Metre : Verses 1-3 *anuṣṭubh.*
Script : Eastern variety of the northern alphabet of about the seventh century A.D.

TEXT[1]

First Plate

1 स्वस्ति [।*] जयस्कन्द्धावारात्**कोङ्गोदवासका**त्सकलक्षमा(क्ष्मा)तलो-
2 पलक्षितक्षमानयविनयविक्क्रमस्य प्रतापवारितारिस्यै(सै)न्य-
3 स्य श्रीसैन्यभीतस्य पैत्त्र(पौत्र)प्रसृतविपुलामलयशस:
4 सततमयशोभीतस्य श्रीमतो यशोभीतस्यात्मजो-
5 भगवंम(भगवन्म)ह(हे)श्वरचरणयुगले(लै)कशरण्य:(ण:)शैशव एव विद्याचतुष्ट-
6 याभ्यासोन्मीलितसहजप्रज्ञातिशयावगतसमस्ता-
7 र्थतत्व:(त्त:) स्वमतविरचितात्यदद्भू(द्भु)तकाव्यार्थवो(बो)धनैककार्य्यसङ्ग(सगृ)हि(ही)-

Second Plate: First Side

8 तविद्वद्विदग्धजनसमूहो निजभूजव(ब)लावलेपावमि-. . .[2]
9 स्तपर्य्यन्तसामन्तशिरोमणिमरीचिसंमूर्छितचरण. . . .
10 छिन्नान्तरेतरारातिवर्ग्गो यथाक्रमप्रवृत्तसमनुरञ्जित. . .
11 महानिपानमिव सर्व्वसत्वैर्यथेवृमुपभुज्यमान. . .

---

1. From the original and photographs in *JASB*, Vol. LXXIII, Pt 1 (1904). The charter is now preserved in the Orissa State Museum, Bhubaneswar.
2. The plate is broken here, damaging a few letters from the right hand side of the writing.

12 वभोगसारसत्वसारप्रकर्षप्रकाशितशैलोद्भवान्ववाय. . .

13 नतसकलकलिङ्गाधिपत्यः सकलकलावासकौमूर्त्त[3]

14 व जगता प्रमदः प्रवृत्तचक्रश्चक्रधर इव भगवान्माधवः

Second Plate: Second Side

15 **श्रीमाधवराजः** कुशली [।]थोरणविषये[4] श्रीसामन्तमहासाम-

16 न्तमहाराजराजपुत्रदण्ड[5]दण्डनायककुमारामात्योपरिकवि[ष]-

17 यपतितदायुक्तकादीन्राजप्रसादोपजीविनः सकर[णां] [व-]

18 र्त्तमान भविष्यतो यथार्हं सत्कृत्योपदर्शयति भवति. . . .[भव]-

19 तां विदितमेतद्विषयसंव(ब)द्धारहण्णग्रामे कुम्भारच्छे. . . .

20 द्वयं वत्ससगोत्रवाजसनेयिकाण्वप्रजापतिस्वामिने [मातापि]-

21 त्रोरात्मनश्च पुण्याभिवृद्धये ताम्र[6]पट्टस्थित्य. . . .

Third Plate

22 तदस्याचन्द्रार्क्ककालं यथास्थितिभुञ्जानस्य धर्म्मगौरवान(न्न)केन-

23 चि[द्]विद्वि[7]घात[:*] कार्य्य[:।] उक्तञ्च ऋषिभिः[।*] व(ब)हुभिर्व्वसुधा दत्ता व(ब)हू(हु)भिश्चा-

24 नू(नु)पालिता [।*] यस्य यस्य यदा भूमि[:*] तस्य तस्य तदा फलं(लम्) [।।*१]

25 मा भूदफलशङ्का व[:*] परदत्तेति पार्थिवा[:*।] स्वदानात्फलमान-

26 न्त्यं परदानानुपालनं । [।*२] स्वदत्तां परदत्तां वा यो हरेत वसुन्धरां [।*] स

27 विष्ठायां क्रि(कृ)मिर्भूत्वा पितृभिस्सह पच्यते [।।*३]

ABSTRACT

The chapter begins with the word *svasti*. Lines 1-15 record that it was issued from the victorious residence of **Kōṅgōda**. The reigning king is then introduced as **Śrī-Mādhavarāja**, who was the grandson of Śrī-Sainyabhīta and son of Śrī-Yaśōbhīta, and who was a devout worshipper at the feet of god Mahēśvara (Śiva). He is stated to have subdued the enemies and acquired the sovereignty of the whole of Kaliṅga country. Lines 15 to 22 record the grant of a locality called Kumbhāracchēda comprising the village Arahaṇṇa, situated in the *viṣaya* of Thōraṇa, by the king. The royal order regarding the grant was addressed to *śrīsāmanta, mahāsāmanta,*

3. Read कौमुद इव.
4. This may be the locality around the present village Sorana near Banpur in Puri district.
5. The first दण्ड is superfluous.
6. The editor of the grant reads ताम्त्र and corrects it as ताम्र.
7. The second द्वि is superfluous.

mahārāja, rājaputra, daṇḍanāyaka, kumārāmātya, uparika, viṣayapati, tadāyuktaka and other royal dependants, along with their assistants, the present and future officials and subordinates, who belonged to the said *viṣaya*. The grant was made by means of a copper-plate charter, in favour of Prajāpatisvāmin of the Vatsa *gōtra* and a student of the Kāṇva branch of the Vājasanēyī texts, for the increase of religious merit of the donor and his parents.This is followed by the entreaty of the donor against any obstruction in the donee's lawful enjoyment of the gift land. Lines 23-27 contain the usual imprecatory and benedictory verses, stated to have been said by the sages.

NO. 47: BUGUDA PLATES OF MĀDHAVAVARMAN

Provenance	:	Buguda, Ganjam district.
References	:	F. Kielhorn, *EI*, Vol. III (1894-95), pp. 41 ff.; *idem*, Vol. VII (1902-3), pp. 100 ff. and plate; and S.N. Rajaguru, *IO*, Vol. I, Pt. 2 (1958), pp. 166-72.
Language	:	Sanskrit, in verse, with the exception of the grant portion in prose.
Metre	:	Verses 1, 4 *śārdūlavikrīḍita*; verses 2, 11 *sragdharā*; verses 3, 6-7, 9-10, and 13 *vasantatilakā*; verses 5, 14-19 *anuṣṭubh* (*ślōka*); verse 8 *indravajrā*; verse 12 *āryā*.
Script	:	Eastern variety of the north Indian alphabet of about the tenth century A.D.

TEXT[1]

First Plate

1 सिद्धम्[2] स्वस्ति [।।*] इन्दोर्द्धौतमृणालतन्तुभिरिव श्लिष्टाः करैः कोमलैर्व्व(र्ब)द्धाहेर-
2 [रु]णै स्फुरत्फण(णि)मर्णैं(णे)र्द्दिग्धप्रभासोङ्शु(सोंशु)भिः[।*] पार्व्वत्याः सकचग्रहव्यति-
3 करव्यावृत्तव(ब)न्धश्लथा गङ्गाम्भः प्लुतिभिन्नभस्मकणिकाः शम्भो-
4 र्ज्जटाः पान्तु वः ।। [१*] श्रीमानुच्चे(च्चै)र्न्नभस्तो गुरुरचलपतेः क्षोभजिद्यः क्ष-
5 माया गम्भीरस्तोयराशेरथ दिवसकराङ्भा(रांभा)स्वदालोककारि(री)[।*]आ[3]-
6 ह्लादो(दी) सर्व्वस्य चेन्दोस्तृ(स्ति)भुवनभवनप्रेरकश्चापि वायो राजे-
7 न्द्रः स्थाणुमूर्त्तिज्ज(र्ज्ज)यति कलिमलक्षालनो **माधवेन्द्रः** ।। [2*] प्राङ्शु(प्रांशु)र्म्म-
8 हेभकरिपि(पी)वरचारुवा(बा)हु[:*] कृष्णाश्मसञ्चयविभेदविशालवक्षा[:* ।]
9 राजीवकोमलदलायतलोचनान्तः ख्यातः कलिङ्गजनतासु पु-
10 लिन्दसेनः ।। [३*] तेनेत्थं गुणिनापि सत्व(त्त्व)महता नेष्टं भुवो मण्डलं श-
11 (क्तो) यः परिपालनाय जगतः को नाम स स्यादिति [।*] प्रत्यादि-

1. From the facsimile in *EI*, Vol. VII (1902-3), pp. 100-1. The charter is now preserved in the Government Museum, Madras.
2. Expressed by a symbol.
3. The letter should be omitted to suit the metre.

Second Plate: First Side

12 ष्टवि[भू]त्सवेन भगवानाराधितः शाश्वतस्तच्चित्तानुगुणं विधित्सु-
13 रदिशद्वारदिशवाञ्च्छा[4] स्वयम्भूरपि ।। [४*] स शिलाशकलोद्भेदी
14 तेनाप्यालोक्य धीमत(ता) [।*] परिकल्पितसद्वङ्श(द्वंशः) प्रभुः शौ(शे)लोद्भवः
15 कृतः [।।*] [५*] शैलोद्भवस्य कुलजोरणभीत आसीद्य(द्ये)नासकृत् कृतभियां
16 द्विषदङ्गनानां [।*] ज्योत्स्नाप्रवो(बो)धसमये स्वधियैव सार्द्धमाकम्पितो
17 नयनपक्ष्मजलेषु चन्द्रः ।। [६*] तस्याभवद्विवु(बु)धपालसमस्य सू-
18 नुः श्रीसैन्यभीत इति भूमिपतिर्ग्गरि(री)यान् [।*] यं प्राप्य ने(नै)कशत(वै)-
19 रिघटाविघट्टि(ट्ट)लव्ध(ब्ध)प्रसादविजय(यं) मुमुदे धारित्री [।।*७] तस्यापि वङ्शे(वंशे)-
20 थ यथ(था)र्थनामा जातो यशोभीत इति क्षितीशः [।*] येन प्ररुढो-
21 पि शुभैश्चरित्रैर्मृष्टः कलङ्क[:*] कलिदर्प्पणस्य ।। [८*] जातः स तस्य

Second Plate: Second Side

22 तनयः सुकृती समस्तसीमन्तिनीनयनषट्पदपुण्डरीकः [।*]
23 **श्रीसैन्यभीत** इति भूमिपतिम्महेभकुम्भस्थलीदलनदुर्ल्ल-
24 लितासिधारः ।। [९*] जातेन येन कमलाकरवत् स्वगोत्रमुन्मीलि-
25 तं दिनकृतेव महोदयेन [।*] संक्षिप्तमण्डलरुचश्च गताः प्रणाशमा-
26 शु द्विषो ग्रह[ग*]णा इव यस्य दीप्त्या ।। [१०*] कालेयैर्भूतधात्रीपतिभिरु-
27 पचितानेकपापावतारैर्न्नीता येषां कथापि प्रलयमभिमता की-
28 र्त्तिपाले(लै)रजस्रं [।*] यज्ञैस्तैरश्वमेधप्रभृतिभिरमरा लम्भितास्तृप्तिमुर्व्वी-
29 मुद्बसारातिपक्ष[क्ष*]यकृतिपटुना **श्रीनिवासेन** येन [।।*११] कै(को)ङ्गोदकृत-
30 निकेतः शरन्निशाकरमरीचिसितकीर्त्तिः [।*] स **श्रीमाधव[व*]र्म्मा** रिपु-
31 मानविघट्टनः कुशली ।। [१२*] गुड्डविषये श्रीसामन्तमह(हा)सा-

Third Plate: First Side

32 [म*]न्तमहाराजराज(जा)नकराजपुत्रदण्डनायकान्तरङ्गकुमा-
33 [रा*]मात्योपरिकतदायुक्तकविषयपतिवैश्वासिकपत्त-
34 लकादी[न्*] ब्रा(ब्रा)ह्मणपूर्व्वाञ्जनपदमन्यांश्च वर्त्तमानभविष्यतो
35 व्यवहारिणाः(णः) स(सा)धारणान्यथार्हं दतेत्योपदर्शयति ।। विदि-
36 तमस्तु भवतामेतद्विषयसम्व(म्बः)न्द्ध(द्ध)खदिरपाट्टक(के) पुइपिणो
37 ग्रामः [स्व]पित्रोरात्मनश्च पुण्याभिवृद्धये **सूर्यग्रहपरागेण**[5] तै-
38 त्तरि(त्तिरीय)चरणाय हरितकगोत्रः त्रयार्षेय आंङ्गिरसंवर्हषयौवनाश्वे-[6]

4. रदिशद्वारदिशद्वा is engraved twice. Read वाञ्च्छां स्व-.
5. The letter ण is superfluous.
6. The line should be read तैत्तिरीयचरणाय हारितगोत्रायाङ्गिरसाम्बरीषयौवनाश्वेति त्रिप्रवराय.

39 [ति?] ।। [7]युवनश्ववदम्वर्षवदङ्गिरोवत् वामणस्य नप्ता आदित्यदेवस्य
40 सूनु भट्टवामण सलिलधारापुर:सरेण अकरीकृत्य प्रतिपादि-
41 तस्तदेषाम(मा)चन्द्रार्क्ककालमुपभुञ्ज(ञ्जा)नानां धर्म्मगो(गौ)रवान्न केनचिद्व्घा-
42 [ते] वर्त्तितव्यं [।।*] अपि च [।*] विद्युद्विलासतरलामवगम्य स-

Third Plate: Second Side

43 म्यक् लोकस्थितिं (सम्यग्लोकस्थितिं) यशसि रसक्तमनोभिरुच्चै: [।*] नित्यं परोप-
44 कृतिमात्ररतैर्भवद्भिर्द्धर्म्माभिराधनंपरैरनुमोदितव्यं [।।*१३] उक्तञ्च मान-
45 वे धर्म्मे [।*] व(ब)हुभिर्व्वसुधा दत्ता राजभि: सगरादिभि: [।*] यस्य यस्य यदा भूमि-
46 स्तस्य तस्य तदा फलं ।। [१४*] स्वदत्तां परदत्ताम्वा(त्तां वा) यो हरै(रे)त वसुन्धरां
[।*] स विष्टा(ष्ठा)(यां)
47 कृमिर्भूत्वा पितृभि: सह पच्यते ।। [१५*] मा भूदफलशङ्का व: परदते(त्ते)ति(पि)
48 पार्थि(वा:) [।*] स्वदानात् फलमानन्त्यं परदत्तानु पालनं [।।*१६] षर्ष्टि(ष्टिं) वर्षसह-
49 स्राणि स्वर्ग्गे मोदति भूमिद: । आक्षेप्ता चानुमन्ता च तान्येव नरके वसे(त्) ।। [१७*]
लि-
50 खितोपेन्द्रसिङ्घोत्र[8] तनय: कुण्डभोगिनो(न:) [।*] लाञ्छितं जयसिङ्घेन(सिंहेन) उकीर्ण्णं
51 [द]ड्डिभोगिना ।। [१८*] सम्यगाराधितस्वामिप्रसाद: [श्रे]ष्ट(ष्ठ)दूतको(क:) [।*]
गङ्गभद्रो-
52 . . . . . . प्रातिहार्ये व्यवस्थित: ।। [१९*]

ABSTRACT

The inscription begins with the symbol for *siddham* and the word *svasti*. Verse 1 invokes the protection of god Śambhu (Śiva). Verse 2 is in glorification of the donor, the reigning king, who is called **rājēndra Mādhavēndra**. Verses 3-12 give the genealogy of the donor. Pulindasēna, the first personage of the family, has been described as 'famous amongst the people of Kaliṅga'. Although he possessed many excellent qualities and a great personality, he did not covet sovereignty for himself. Rather, he worshipped Brahman so that the god might create a fit ruler of the land. Verse 5 states that his wish was fulfilled by Brahman who created, out of rock, the lord Śailōdbhava, stated to be the founder of a distinguished family. In that family was born Raṇabhīta or Araṇabhīta whose son, Sainyabhīta, was the lord of the earth. In his family Yaśōbhīta or Ayaśobhīta was born, whose son again was Sainyabhīta. Sainyabhīta was the powerful and pious prince **Mādhavavarman** ruling the kingdom of Kōṅgōda.

---

7. The punctuation is superfluous.
8. Read लेखिता उपेन्द्रसिंहोत्र.

The formal part of the grant follows in lines 30-42. The illustrious **Mādhavavarman**, from his residence at **Kaiṅgōḍa (Kōngōda)**, issued the order informing the officials, the brāhmaṇas and inhabitants of the *viṣaya* of Guḍḍa[9] on the occasion of a **solar eclipse,** that he granted a village named Puipiṇa, situated within Khadira-**pāṭaka**[10] under the said district, in favour of Bhaṭṭa Vāmana, son of Ādityadēva and grandson of Vāmana, who was a student of the Taittirīya *caraṇa,* of the Hārita *gōtra* and with the threefold *pravara* of Āṅgirasa, Ambarīṣa and Yauvanāśva, in order to increase his religious merit and that of his parents. The royal order regarding the grant was addressed to *sāmanta-mahārāja, rājanaka, rājaputra, daṇḍanāyaka, antaraṅga, kumārāmātya, uparika, tadāyuktaka, viṣayapati, vaiśvāsika, pattalaka* and others. Lines 41-42 mention the usual admonition not to disturb the donee in the enjoyment of the land granted to him. This is followed by the customary benedictive and imprecatory verses, here stated to be quotations from the *Mānava-Dharmaśāstra.* Lines 50-52, containing two verses, inform us that the grant was written by Upēndrasiṁha, son of Kuṇḍabhōgin, marked (sealed) by Jayasiṁha and engraved by Daḍḍibhōgin. The inscription ends with the statement that the *dūtaka* (executor) of the grant was Gaṅgabhadra, designated as the *pratihāra*.

9. This may be the area around the present Buguda in Ganjam district, Orissa.
10. This may be identified with the present Khairapati, situated under the Buguda Police Station, 5 miles to the north of Buguda in Ganjam district.

NO. 48: PURUSHOTTAMPUR PLATES OF MĀDHAVAVARMAN, YEAR 13

Provenance	:	Purushottampur, Ganjam district.
References	:	S.N. Rajaguru, *OHRJ*, Vol. II, Nos. 3 and 4 (1953-54), pp. 6-22; *idem*, *IO*, Vol. I, Pt. 2 (1958), pp. 173-77; and D.C. Sircar, *EI*, Vol. XXX (1954), pp. 264-68 and plate.
Language	:	Sanskrit, in verse, except the grant portion in prose.
Metre	:	Verses 1 and 4 *śārdūlavikrīḍita*; verses 2 and 11 *sragdharā*; verses 3, 6, 7, 9 and 10 *vasantatilakā*; verses 5, 13-17 *anuṣṭubh*; verse 8 *indravajrā* and verse 12 *āryā*.
Script	:	Eastern variety of the north Indian alphabet of about the eighth century A.D.
Date	:	13th regnal year.

TEXT[1]

First Plate

1 सिद्धम[2] स्वस्ति [।।*]इन्दोर्द्ध(र्द्धौ)तमृणालतन्त(न्तु)भिरिवा(व) श्ली(श्लि)ष्टाः करै[:*] कोमलैव(र्ब)द्धा-

2 हेररुणै[:] स्फुरत्फणिमणि(णे)दि(र्दि)[ग्ध]प्रभाङ्शु(सोंशु)भि[:* ।] पार्व्वत्या[:*] सकचग्र-

3 हव्यतिकरव्यावृत्तव(ब)न्द्धस्ल(श्ल)था गङ्गाम्भा(म्भः)प्लुति[भिन्न]भस्मकणिका[:*] श[म्भो]-

4 र्ज्जटो(टाः)पान्तु व[:] ।। [१*] श्रीमानु(च्चै)न(र्न)भस्त(स्तो) गुरुर[मर]पते[:*] क्षोभि(भ)ज(जि)द्य[:*] [क्ष*]माया

5 गम्भीरस्तोयराशेरथ दिव[स*]कर(राद्) भास्वद(दा)लोककारी [।*] आह्लादी[3] सव्व(र्व्व)-

6 स्य चेन्दोस्तृ(स्त्रि)भुवन भु(भ)वनप्रेरकश्चापि वायो राजा स स्थाणु[मू]-

1. From the original. The charter is now preserved in the Orissa State Museum, Bhubaneswar.
2. Expressed by a symbol. The letters in the charter are greatly damaged at places. The reading of the damaged letters has been restored with the help of other extant charters of the same king containing the same verses.
3. The letter आ may be deleted to suit the metre.

7 र्त्तिज्ज(र्ज्ज)यति कल(लि)मलक्षालनो **माधव(वे)न्द्रः** ।। [2*] प्राङ्शु(प्रांशु)-म्म(र्म्म)हेभक[र]-
8 पीवरचारुवा(बा)हु[:*] कृष्णाश्मसञ्चयविभेदविषा(शा)लवक्षो(क्षा:) [।*] राजीव-
9 कोमलदलायतलोचनान्ता(न्त:) ख्यातः कलिङ्गजनतासु पुलिन्द-
10 सेन[:] ।। [३*] तेनेत्थं गुणिनापि सत्व(त्त्व)महता नेष्टं भुवो म्म(म)ण्डलं [शक्तो]-
11 य[:*] परिपालनाय जगतः को नाम स स्यादिति [।*] [प्रत्यादिष्ट विभू]-
12 त्सवेन भगवां(वा)नाराधित[:] सा(शा)श्वत[स्*]तच्चिता(त्ता)नुगुणं [विधित्सुर]-

Second Plate: First Side

13 [दि]शद्वाञ्छा(ञ्छां) स्वयम्भूरपि ।। [४*] स शिलास(श)कलोद्भेदी ते[नाप्यालोक्य]
14 [धी]मता [।*] [परिक]ल्पित[स]द्वङ्श(द्वंशः) प्रभु[:*] शैलोद्ध[व][:*] कृतः [।।*५] शैलोद्भवस्य [कुलजो र]-
15 णभीत आसीद्येनासकृत्कृतभिया द्विषदङ्गनाना(म्*।) ज्यो[त्स्ना]-
16 त्स्ना[4] प्रवो(बो)धसमये स्वा(स्व)धिये(यै)व सार्द्धमाकम्पितो नयनप(क्ष्म)पक्ष्म[5]
17 जलेषु चन्द्रः ।। [६*] तस्य(स्या)द्भ(भ)वद्विवु(बु)धपालसमस्य सूनु[:] श्रीसैन्यभी-
18 त इति भु(भू)मिपतिग्ग(र्ग)रि(री)यां(यान्) [।*] यं प्राप्य नैकशतनागघट्टा(टा)-विघट्टलब्ध(ब्ध)-
19 प्रसादविजयं मुमुदे धारित्री [।।*७] तस्यापि वङ्शे[6] यथार्थना[मा जा]-
20 तोयशोभीत इति क्षिति(ती)शः [।] येन प्ररुढोपि शुभैश्चरि-
21 त्रैर्मृष्ट[:*] कलङ्क[:*] कलिदर्प्पणस्य [।।*८] जातस्य तस्य तनयक[7] [सु-]
22 कृति(ती) समस्तसीमन्तिनीनयनषट्पदपुण्डरीकः । **श्रीसेन्यभी-**
23 **त** इति भु(भू)मिपतिर्म्महेभकुम्भ[स्थली] [दलन*] दुर्ल्ललो(लि)तासिधारः [।।*९] जाते-
24 न येन कमलाकरवत्स(त्स्व)गो[त्रमु]न्मीलितं दिनकृतेव म-

Second Plate: Second Side

25 होदयेन [।*] संक्षिप्तमण्डलरुचश्रु(श्च) गता[:*] प्रणाशु(श)माशु द्विषो ग्र-
26 हगणा इव यस्य दीप्त्या ।। [१०*] का[लेयै]र्भूतधात्री ।[8] पति[भि*]रुपचिता-
27 नेकपापावतार(रै)नि(र्नी)ता येषां कथापि प्रलयमभिमता की-
28 र्त्तिमा(पा)लैरजस्र[म्*] । [य]ज्ञैस्तैरश्वमेधप्रभृतिभिरमरा लम्भिता[स्*]तृ-
29 प्ति[मु]र्व्वीमु[द*] दृप्तारातिपक्षक्षयकृतिपटुना **श्रीनिवासेन** येन [।।*११] **[कोङ्गो]**-

4. This letter may be deleted.
5. The second पक्ष्म is superfluous.
6. Read वंशेथ.
7. Read जातः तस्य तनयः .
8. The punctuation is superfluous.

30 दकृतनिकेत[:*] श(शा)रदनिशाकरमरीचिसितकीर्त्ति[:*।] स **श्रीमाधव-**

31 **वर्म्मा** रि[पु*]मानवि[घट्ट*]नकुशली ।। [१२*] अस्मिं(स्मिन्) [कोङ्गा]दमण्डले शारे[9]-

32 साम[न्त]महासामन्तमहाराजराजपुत्र(त्रा)न्तरङ्गदण्डपासि(शि)[कोप-]

33 री(रि)क ।[10] विषयपतितदानियुक्तक[11] वर्त्तमान भविष्यव्यवहारी(रि)ण[:*]

34 सकरण(णान्) यथार्ह(र्हं) पु(पू)जय[ति*] मानयति [च*] विदितमस्तु भवतां(ताम्) ।। देव-

35 ग्रामविषयसम्व(म्ब)द्धः अम्व(म्ब)ग्रामोयं चातु[:*] सीमोपलक्षितः ।[12]

36 मुद्गल्यसगोत्रअंकाश भ्रमानुप्रवर[13] छन्दोग[चर]णाय [भ]ट्टना-

37 [रा]य[णा][य*] दत(त्तः) म(अ)स्मत्मा(न्मा)तापित्रोरात्मन[श्च] पुण्याव(भि)वृद्धये सलिलधा[रा]-

Third Plate

38 [पुरः]सरेणा[च]न्द्रार्कक्षिती(ति)समकालं प्रतिपाति(दि)तो यत[श्च] [ताम्र]-

39 पट्टकदर्शना[त्*] धर्मगौरवा[त्*] च काले[14] कालान्तराध(द)पि न कैश्च(श्चित्) परि[प]-

40 न्थिना(भिः) भवितव्यमिति । उक्तञ्च मानवे धर्म्मशास्त्रे [।*] व(ब)हुभि[र्व]सुधा [भु]-

41 [क्ता] राजभि[:*] सगरादिभिः [।*] यस्य [यस्य*] यदा भु(भू)[स्]तस्य तस्य तदा फल[म्] । [।*१३]

42 मा भू[दफल] शङ्का व[:*] परदत्तेति पार्थिव(वाः) [।*] स्वदानात्फ[लमा]नन्त्य(न्त्यं) प[र]-

43 [द]त्तानुपालने । [।*१४] स्वदत्ताम्परदत्ताम्वा(त्तां वा) यो हरेति(त) व[सु]न्धरा[म्*] [।*]स वि-

44 [ष्ठायां कृ]मिर्भूत्वा पितृभि[:*] सह पच्यते । [।*१५] लिखितोपेन्द्रसि(सिं)[हे]-

45 न तनयः[15] कुण्डभोगिना(नः) [।*] लिञ्छित[16] जयसि(सिं)[हे]न उत्कीर्ण्ण[17] च्छेड्डि[भो]-[18]

46 गि[ना] [।।१६] दूतक(को) ग(गं)ग भद्र[स्तु*] प्रातिहाये(र्ये) व्यवस्थितः । [*१७] **सम्वत (त्) १०.३** । [।*]

---

9. Read श्री.
10. The mark of punctuation is redundant.
11. This should be तद्विनियुक्तक.
12. The punctuation is superfluous.
13. This intended reading seems to be आङ्गिरसप्रवर भार्म्याश्वानुप्रवर.
14. Sircar overlooks this word.
15. Read सुतेन.
16. Read लाञ्छितं.
17. Read चोत्कीर्ण्णं.
18. Rajaguru reads उत्कीर्ण्णञ्चाक्षशालिना.

ABSTRACT

The charter up to line 29 is the same as the Buguda plates of Mādhavavarman-Sainyabhīta (No. 47), who is also the donor of the present grant. In lines 29-30, the name of **Mādhavavarman** occurs as **Śrīnivāsa,** who issued the charter from **Kōṅgōda**. The formal part of the grant then follows from line 31 and records that the illustrious **Mādhavavarman** issued the order relating to the grant, addressed to his subordinates and officials, such as *śrī-sāmanta, mahāsāmanta, mahārāja, rājaputra, antaraṅga, daṇḍapāśika, uparika, viṣayapati, viniyuktaka* and all the present and future recipients of royal favour. The royal order was in respect of the grant of the village Āmba-*grāma,* attached to the Dēvagrāma *viṣaya,* in favour of a brāhmaṇa named *bhaṭṭa* Nārāyaṇa of Maudgalya *gōtra,* Āṅgirasa *pravara,* Bhārmyāśva *anupravara* and Chandōga *caraṇa,* with the libation of water so as to last as long as the moon, the sun and the earth would endure. The purpose of the grant was to increase the religious merit of the donor and his parents. Lines 39 to 40 mention the usual admonition not to disturb the donee in the enjoyment of the granted village. Verses 13-15 are three benedictory and imprecatory verses, quoted from the *Mānava-Dharmaśāstra*. Lines 44-46 contain two verses recording that the charter was written by Upēndrasiṁha, son of Kuṇḍabhōgin. It was endowed with a seal by Jayasiṁha and engraved by Cheḍḍibhōgin. It was executed by the *dūtaka* Gaṅgabhadra, who was employed in the post of *pratihāra*. The **date** of the grant is given at the end in the **regnal year** of the reigning king as **samvat 13**.

NO. 49: PURI PLATES OF MĀDHAVAVARMAN, YEAR 13

Provenance	:	Biroboi, Puri district, Orissa.
References	:	R.G. Basak, *EI*, Vol. XXIII (1935-36), pp. 122-31 and plate; and S.N. Rajaguru, *IO*, Vol. I, Pt. 2 (1958), pp. 178-85.
Language	:	Sanskrit, in verse, except the grant portion.
Metre	:	Verses 1 and 3 *śārdūlavikrīḍita*; verses 2, 5, 6, 8 and 9 *vasantatilakā*; verses 4 and 12-17 *anuṣṭubh*; verse 7 *indravajrā;* verse 10 *sragdharā*; verse 11 *āryā*.
Script	:	Eastern variety of the northern alphabet of about the eighth century A.D.
Date	:	13th regnal year.

TEXT[1]

First Plate

1 सिद्धम्[2] स्वस्ति [।।*] [इ]न्दो[र्द्धौ]तमृणालतन्तुभिरिव शिलष्टा[:*] करै[:*] कौमलैव(र्ब)द्धाहेररु-

2 णै[:*] स्फुरत्फणिमणै(णे)र्दी(र्दि)ग्धप्रभासोङ्शु(सोंशु)भि[:*।] पार्व्वत्या[:*] स[कच*] ग्रहव्यतिकरव्यावृत(त्त)व(ब)-

3 न्धश्लथा गङ्गाम्भ[:*] प्लुतिभिन्नभस्मकणिका[:*] शम्भोर्जटा[:*] पान्तु वः । [।*१] प्राङ्शु(प्रांशु)र्महेभक-

4 रपीवरचारुव(बा)हु[:*]कृष्णाश्मसञ्चयविभेदविषा(शा)लवक्षा[:*] [।*] राजीवकोमलदलाय-

5 [त]लोचनान्ता(न्तः) श्या(ख्या)त[:*] कलिङ्गजनतासु पुली(लि)न्दसेन [:*] [।।*2] तेनेत्थं गुणिनापि सत्व(त्त्व)महता

6 नेष्ठं(ष्टं) भुवो मण्डल(लं)शक्तो य[:*] परिपालनाय जगत[:*] को नाम स स्यादिति [।*] प्रत्या-

7 दिष्टविभूत्सवेन भगवानारा[धि]त[:*] शाश्वत[:*] तचि(च्चि)ता(त्ता)नुगुणं विदित्सु-

8 रदिशद्वाञ्छा(ञ्छां) स्वयम्भो(म्भू)रपि ।। [३*] स शिलास(श)कलोद्भेदी तेनाप्यालोक्य-धि(धी)म-

1. From the facsimile in *EI*, Vol. XXIII (1935-36).
2. Expressed by a symbol.

9 ता [।*] परिकल्पितसद्वङ्शे(द्वंशः) प्रभु[:*] शैलोद्भ[व:*] कृतः [।।*४] शैलोद्भवस्य कुलजो[ऽ*]रण-
10 भीत आसीद्येनासकृत्कृतभियां द्विषदङ्गनानां[।*] ज्योति(त्)स्नाप्रवो(बो)धसम-
11 ये स्वधिय(यै)व साद्ध(र्द्ध)माकम्पितो नयनपक्ष्मजलेषु चन्द्रः। [।*५] तस्याभ-
12 वद्विवु(बु)धपालसमस्य सु(सू)नुः श्रीसइ[सै]न्यभीत इति भूमिपतिर्ग[री]-

Second Plate: First Side

13 यां(यान्) [।*] यं प्रा[प्य*] नैकशतनागघटाविघट्टलव्ध(ब्ध)प्रसादविज[यं] मुमुदे
14 धरित्री [।।*६] तस्या[3] तस्यापि वङ्शे(वंशे)[थ*] यथार्थनामा जातोयशोभीत इति क्षि-
15 ति(ती)शः [।*] येन प्ररु(रू)ढोपि शुभ[4] शुभैश्चरित्रैर्म्मृष्ट[:*] कलङ्क [:*] कली(लि)दर्प्पणस्य [।।*७]
16 [जातोऽथ*] तस्य तनयस्सुकृति(ती) समस्तस(सी)मन्तिनीनयनषट्पदपुण्डरीक[:*] ।। (।)**श्री**-
17 **सैन्यभीत** इति भूमिपतिर्महेभकुम्भस्थलीदलनदुर्ललितासि-
18 धार [:*] [।।*८] जातेन येन कमलाकरवत्स्वगोत्रम् उन्मीलितं[5] दिनकृतेव
19 महोदयेन [।*] संक्षिप्तमण्डलरुचश्च गता[:*] प्रणाशमाशु द्विषो ग्रहग-
20 णा इव यस्य दीप्त्या [।।*९] कालेयैर्भूतधात्रीपतिभिरुपचितानेकपापा-
21 वतारैनी(र्नी)ता येषां कथापि प्रलयमभिमता कीर्त्तिमा(पा)लैरजस्त्रम् [।*]
22 यज्ञैस्तैरश्वमेधप्रभृतिभिरमरा लम्भिता[स्*]तृप्तिमुर्व्वीमुद्दप्तारा ति-
23 पक्षक्षयकृतिपटुना **श्रीनिवासेन** येन ।। [१०*] कोङ्गोदकृतनिकेतः

Second Plate: Second Side

24 शारदनिशाकर[6] मरि(री)चिसिति(त)कीर्त्ति[:*।] स **श्रीमाधव[व*]र्म्मा** रिपुमा-
25 नविघट्टन[:*] कुशली [।।*११] आस्मिं (अस्मिन्) भूम्म(म)ण्डले श्रीसामन्तमहासाम-
26 न्तमहाराजराजनकराजपुत्रात(न्त)रङ्गदण्डनायक दण्डपाशि-
27 नोपरिकर[7] विषयपतितदानियु[क्त*] काम्व(कान् व)र्त्तमानभविष्यतो व्य-
28 वहारिण[:*] सकरणां(णान्) व्रा(ब्रा)ह्मणपुरोगादी[न्*] जानपदांश्चाट्ट(ट)भटवल्लभ-
29 जातीयां (यान्) यथाहं(र्हं) पूं(पू)जयति मानयति [।*] विदितमस्तु भवतां(ताम्)
30 थोरणविषयसम्वन्द्ध(म्बद्ध) सालग्राम[:*] ......[8] कौशिक-
31 गोत्राय अउ(औ)तथ्यप्रवराय.....नाना(आनु)प्रवराय छन्दोगचरणा-

---

3. This word is redundant.
4. This शुभ is superfluous.
5. Read गोत्रमुन्मीलीतं.
6. The Buguda plates (No. 47). Read शरन्निशाकर.
7. Read कोपरिकर.
8. R.G. Basak reads the missing five letters as विनिर्गताय; but the missing word seems to have been related to the gift village सालग्राम.

32 य कौथुमशाखाय भट्टवित्तदेवस्य (देवाय) मातापित्रोरात्मनश्च पुण्या-
33 भिवृद्धये सलिलधारापुर[:*] सरेणाकरत्वेन मा(आ)चन्द्रार्क्कक्षिती(ति)सम-
34 कालं प्रतिपादितोस्माभि[:*।] यतश्च ताम्व्र(म्र)पट्टकं(क)दर्शना[द्*] धर्म्मगौर-

Third Plate

35 वा[त्*] कल्पकल्पान्तरेणापि न कैश्च (केनचित्)परिपन्थिना भवितव्यमिति ।
36 उक्तञ्च मानवे धर्म्मशास्त्रे [।*] व(ब)हुभिर्व्वसुधा दत्ता राजभि [स्*]सगरादि-
37 भि: [।*] यस्य यस्य यदा भूमि[स्]तस्य तस्य तदा फलं(लम्) ।। [१२*] मा भूव(द)फलश-
38 ङ्का व: परदत्तेति पाथि(र्थि)व:(वा:) [।*] स्वदानात्फलमानन्त्यं परदत्तानुपाल-
39 नं(ने) ।[।*१३] स्वदत्तां परदत्ताम्वा(त्तां वा) यो हरेति(त) वसुन्द्धरा[म्*।] स विष्ठायां कृमिर्भूत्वा
40 पितृभि[:*] सह पच्चते ।। [१४*] षष्टिं वर्षसहस्त्राणि स्वर्ग्गे मोदति भू-
41 मिद:[।*] आक्षेप्ता चानुमन्ता च तान्येव नरकम्व(के व)सेत् ।। [१५*] ला(ले)खितो-
42 पेन्द्रसिङ्घेनत्र(सिंहोत्र) तनया(य:) कुण्डभोगिना(न:) [।*] लाञ्छितं जयसिङ्घे(सिंहे)न उत्की-
43 र्ण्णं च्छड्डिभोगिनो(ना) [।।*१६] सम्यगाराधितस्वामिप्रसादश्लिष्टमानस: [।*] दूत-
44 [को] गङ्गभद्रो[त्र*] प्रातिहाय(र्य्ये) व्यवस्थित: ।। [१७*] **सम्वत् १०.३**[9] ।।

ABSTRACT

The charter begins with the symbol for *siddham* and the word *svasti.* The inscription up to line 25 is the same as the other records of the donor **Mādhavavarman-Sainyabhīta** containing the invocation to god Śiva and then describing the genealogy of the donor and the royal achievements. The formal part of the grant begins from line 25, recording that the reigning king's order, addressing the officers of his kingdom, all the *sāmantas, mahāsāmantas, mahārāja, rājaputra, antaraṅga, daṇḍanāyaka, daṇḍapāśika, uparika, viṣayapati, tadāyuktakas* and all the present and future recipients of the royal favour, and having duly honoured the brāhmaṇas, that he granted the village Sāla-*grāma,* situated under the *viṣaya* of Thōraṇa, to bhaṭṭa Vittadeva of the Kauśika *gōtra,* Autathya *pravara* and Chandōga *caraṇa* and Kauthuma *śākhā*. Lines 33-35 deal with the usual admonition not to interfere with the donee, relating to the grant in the lawful enjoyment of the gift village. Lines 36-41 record four of the usual imprecatory

9. Basak reads the numerical symbols as 20 and 3; but the first symbol closely resembles the numeral 10 of the Purushottampur plates. It seems this grant was also issued in the same 13th regnal year of the donor.

9 शक्तो यः परिपालनाय जगतः को नाम स स्य(स्या)दिति [।*] प्रत्यादिष्टविभुत्सवेन भगवा-

10 नारागि(धि)तः शाश्वतः तच्चित्तानुगुणं विधित्सुरदिशद्वाञ्च्छां स्वयम्भूरपि ॥ [४*] लोकप्रतीति-

11 वा(बा)ह्यः शकलशिलासम्पुटात्प्रसूत इव [।*] देवकुमारान्यतमो हरनिर्माणात्ततो दृष्टः ॥ [५*]

12 सोप्याश्चर्य्यमनोभुवाधिपतिना शम्भोः प्रसादात्क्षणं भीतोद्भ्रान्तसविस्म[य]स्थिति-

Second Plate: First Side

13 मता सम्भाव्य सौम्यं वपुः [।*] भूतानन्दकरः कृतश्च विजयी शैलोद्भवः क्ष्मापतिः शास्ता दुष्पथ-

14 गामिनां सुकृतिनां रुपीव धर्म्मः स्वयं(म्) ॥ [६*] शैलोद्भव इति ख्यातस्ततो वङ्शः(वंशः) शुभः क्षितौ [।*] उत्सवा-

15 तिशयस्थानमद्धुतानामिवाद्धुतं(तम्) ॥ [७*] शैलोद्भवस्य कुलजोरणभीत आसीद्य(द्ये)-नासकृत्कृतभियां

16 द्विषदङ्गनानां [।*] ज्योत्स्नाप्रवो(बो)धसमये स्वधियैव सार्द्धमाकम्पितो नयनपक्ष्मजलेषु

17 चन्द्रः ॥ [८*] तस्याभवद्विवु(बु)धपालसमस्य सूनुः श्रीसैन्यभीत इति भूमिपतिर्गरीयान् [।*]

18 यम्प्राप्य नैकशतनागघटाविघट्टलव्ध(ब्ध)प्रसादविजयं मुमुदे धरित्री ॥ [९*] तस्यापि

19 वङ्शे(वंशे)थ यथार्थनामा जातोयशोभीत इति क्षितीशः [।*] येन प्ररुढोपि शुभैश्चरित्रै-

20 र्मृष्टः कलङ्कः कलिदर्प्पणस्य ॥ [१०*] जातस्स तस्य तनयस्सुकृती समस्तसीमा(म)न्ति-

21 नीनयनषट्पदपुण्डरीकः [।*] **श्रीसैन्यभीत** इति भूमिपतिर्म्महेभकुम्भस्थलीदलनदुर्ल्ललि-

22 तासिधारः ॥ [११*] जातेन येन कमलाकरवत्स्वगोत्रमुन्मीलितं दिनकृतेव महोदयेन [।*] संक्षिप्त-

23 मण्डलरुचश्च गताः प्रणाशमाशु द्विषो ग्रहगणा इव यस्य दीप्त्या ॥ [१२*] कालेयैर्भूतधात्री-

24 पतिभिरुपचितानेकपापावतारैर्येषां नीता कथापि प्रलयमभिमता कीर्त्ति-

25 मा(पा)लैरज[स्त्रं] [।*] यज्ञैस्तैरश्वमेधप्रभृतिभिरसकृत्म(त्स)म्यगिष्टैरकारि स्फीतां तृप्तिं सुरो(रौ)घ [:*]

Second Plate: Second Side

26 प्रतिहतव(ब)लच्छद्म(चु)पक्षेण येन ॥ [१३*]**माधवपुर** विहितस्थितिरम्वु(म्बु)-दनिर्मुक्तचन्द्रसितकीर्त्तिः [।*]

27 स **श्रीमाधववर्म्मा** रिपुमानविघट्टनः कुशली ॥ [१४*] विषयेस्मिं(स्मिन्) जयपुरे वर्त्तमान भविष्यत[:*]

28 द्विजातिपूर्व्वान्नृपतीन्राजस्थानीयसंयुतान् ॥ [१५*] कुमारामात्यमायुक्तात्(न्) करणोपरिकानपि [।*]

29 तथा जनपदं सर्व्वमर्हयत्यानुपूर्व्य(र्व्व)तः ॥ [१६*] विदितमस्तु भवतामेतद्विज(ष)-
यसम्व(म्ब)द्ध व्याघ्रपुर-
30 भुक्तौ तमतडाग्रामश्चतुः सीम्ना त्र(त्र)योविङ्श (विंश)तितिम्पीरपरिमाणः स्कन्दादित्यस्वामि
रुद्र-
31 स्वामि दद्दस्वामि वेदस्वामि महेन्द्रस्वामि खदिरादित्यस्वामि प्रद्युम्नस्वामि पाण्डरमाच्चु(तृ)-
32 स्वाम्यादित्यस्वामि यज्ञस्वाम्यग्रस्वामिछरम्पस्वामिकायवरस्वामिशर्व्वस्वामिमातृ-
33 चन्द्रस्वामिवोन्तेल्वादित्यस्वामि गोलस्वामिम(मा)धवस्वामिमातृचन्द्रस्वामिं दत्तस्वामि-
34 धर्म्मस्वामिव(बा)मदेवस्वामिश्रीस्वामिस्वामिचन्द्रस्वामिभ्यो द्विजातिभ्यो मातापित्रोरात्मनश्च
35 पुण्याभिवृद्धये प्रतिपादितः तदेतच्छासनदर्शनादेषां यथोचितं ताम्व्र(म्र)पट्टदानं
36 दत्वा भुञ्जनानां धर्म्मगौरवान्न केनचिद्विघातै(ते) वर्त्तितव्यमपि च ॥ विद्युद्विलास-
37 तरलामवगम्य सम्यग्लोकस्थितिं यशसि म(स)क्तमनोभिरुरच्चैः [।*] एष द्विजा(जो)
पकृति-

Third Plate

38 मान्नारतैर्भवद्भिर्द्धर्म्मानुरोधानुपरैरनुमोदितव्यः ॥ [१७*] उक्तं च मानवे धर्म्मशास्त्रे ॥
39 व(ब)हुभिर्व्वसुधा दत्ता व(ब)हुभिश्चानुपालिता [।*] यस्य यस्य यदा भूमिस्तस्य तस्य
तदा फलं(लम्) ॥ [१८*]
40 अपि च । मा भूदफलशङ्का वः परदत्तेति पार्थिवाः [।*] स्वदानात्फलमानन्त्यं परदानानुपा-
41 लनें(ने) ॥ [१९*] अभूद्त्विगुपाद्ध्याय(यो) गुहचन्द्रोत्र दूतकः [।*] लेखितो-
42 पेन्द्रसिड्ह(सिंह)श्च तनयः कुण्डभोगिनः ॥ [२०*] उत्कीर्ण्णस्ताम्र-
43 पट्टोयं दुरितप्रतिघातकृत् [।*] स्कन्दभोगिणा(ना) सम्यक्
44 जयसिड्हे(सिंहे)न तापितः ॥ [२१*] जयति जयन्तप्रतिमः प्रसभसमाकृष्ट-
45 रिपुनृपश्रीकः[।*] श्रीवरमोरः[4] क्षितिपो वरदीकृतलोकनांथ-
46 सखः ॥ [२२*] **सम्वत् ५० श्रावण दिन २०.४** [॥*]

ABSTRACT

The record opens with the symbol for *siddham* and the word *svasti*, followed by a verse in adoration of god Śiva in communion with Pārvatī. Verse 2 mentions Mahēndra mountain and the ocean. Verse 3 refers to Pulindasēna, an inhabitant of Kaliṅga country, who worshipped the god Svayambhū (verse 4), as a result of which was born out of rock (verse 5) the victorious king Śailōdbhava (verse 6). Verses 7-10 record that in his family was born Raṇabhīta or Araṇabhīta, whose son was Sainyabhīta. In the latter's lineage was born king Yaśōbhīta or Ayaśobhīta. Yaśōbhīta's son **Sainyabhīta II** issued the present grant. Verses 11-13 give an account of

4. N.G. Majumdar reads श्रीधरपो(पौ)रः ।

the royal donor eulogistically. Verse 14 states that he was also called **Mādhavavarman** and that he resided in the city of **Mādhavapura.** Verses 15-16 record the royal order addressed to the officers, brāhmaṇas and others of the Jayapura *viṣaya.*

In lines 29-36 the formal part of the grant begins in prose. In the village of Tamataḍā, situated in the Vyāghrapura *bhukti* of the said *viṣaya*, a plot of land measuring twenty-three *ṭimpiras* was granted by means of the charter to the following brāhmaṇas: Skandādityasvāmin, Rudrasvāmin, Daḍḍasvāmin, Vēdasvāmin, Mahēndrasvāmin, Khadirādityasvāmin, Pradyumnasvāmin, Paṇḍaramātṛsvāmin, Ādityasvāmin, Yajñasvāmin, Agrasvāmin, Charampasvāmin, Kāyavarasvāmin, Śarvvasvāmin, Mātṛcandrasvāmin, Vōntēlvādityasvāmin, Gōlasvāmin, Mādhavasvāmin, Dattasvāmin, Dharmmasvāmin, Vāmadēvasvāmin, Śrīsvāmin, and Svāmicandrasvāmin. This is followed by three of the customary verses. Verse 20 records that Guhacandra, a *ṛtvik* and *upādhyāya,* served as the *dūtaka* or the executor of the grant and Upēndrasiṁha, son of Kuṇḍabhōgin, acted as the writer of the record . Verse 21 speaks of the charter as having been engraved by Skandabhōgin and heated by Jayasiṁha. Verse 22 of the record states that the king showed favour to his feudatory (?) Śrivaramōra and had been graciously disposed towards him. The king has been called Lōkanātha in this verse. The **date** of the grant is given at the end of the record in the **regnal year** of the king as **samvat 50, the twenty-fourth day of the month of Śrāvaṇa.**

NO. 51: BANPUR GRANT OF MADHYAMARĀJA

Provenance : Banpur, Puri district, Orissa.

References : S.N. Rajaguru, *JKHRS*, Vol. II (1947), pp. 59-65; *idem*, *IO*, Vol. I, Pt. 2 (1958), pp. 191 ff.; and D.C. Sircar, *EI*, Vol. XXIX, (1951-52), pp. 33-38 and plate.

Language : Sanskrit, in verse, with the exception of the last line.

Metre : Verses 1, 3, 5, 14, 15, 17-19 *śārdūlavikrīḍita*; verses 2, 12, 13, 16, *sragdharā*; verses 4, 7, 8, 10, 11, 20 *vasantatilakā*; verse 6 *anuṣṭubh.*; verse 9 *indravajrā*.

Script : Eastern variety of the northern alphabet of about the eighth century A.D.

TEXT[1]

First Plate

1 सिद्धम[2] स्वस्ति [।।*] विजय**कोङ्गोदवास**कात् [।*] इन्दोत्द्धौतमृणालत[न्*]तुभिरिव

2 श्लिष्टाः करै[:*] कोमलै ।[3] व्वं(र्ब)द्धाहेररुणै[:*] स्फुरत्फण(णि)मणेर्द्दिग्ध[:]-(ग्ध)प्रभासोड्शु(सोंशु)भिः [।*]

3 पार्व्वत्या[:*] सकचग्रहव्यतिकरव्यावृत्तव(ब)न्द्धश्लथा गङ्गाम्भ[:*]प्लुतिभिन्नभस्मक-[णि]का[:*] शम्भो-

4 ज(र्ज)टा[:*] पात्तु(न्तु)वः ।। [१*]श्रीमानुच्चैर्न्नभस्तो गुरुरमरपते[:*][4] क्षोभजिद्य [:*] क्ष[माया] गम्भी-

5 रस्तोयराशेरथ दिवसकराद्भास्वदालोककारी [।] ह्लादी सर्व्वस्य चेन्दोस्त्रिभुवनभ-

6 वनपे(प्रे)रकश्चापि वा यो ।[5] राजा स्स(स) स्थाणुमूर्त्तिज(र्ज)यति कलिमलक्षालनो **माधवेन्द्र**[: ।।* 2]

7 प्राच्याम्भोनिधिरुच(द्ध)सान्द्र(नु)रतुल[:*] पुष्प[6]द्रुमालीर्वृ(वृ)तः स्यन्दंनि(न्दन्नि)र्झरवारि-

---

1. From the facsimile in *EI*, Vol. XXIX (1951-52), pp. 36 and 37.
2. Expressed by a symbol.
3. The punctuation is superfluous.
4. The Parikud (No. 52) and Nivina (No. 54) plates read अचलपतेः .
5. The punctuation is superfluous.
6. The Cuttack Museum plates (No. 50) read पुष्प.

8 दारितदरीफेनस्खलनि(न्रि)स(स्व)[:* ।] स्वानन्तस्तपतन्निवल्गुविरुतैरापू-

9 रितान्तर्गुं(र्गु)हः श्रीमा[न्*] मेरु[रिवोद्गतः कु]लगिरिः ख्यातो महेन्द्र[:*] क्षितौः(तौ) ।। [३*]

10 प्राङ्शु (प्रांशु)र्महेभकरपीवरच्चा(चा)रुवा(बा)हु[:*] कृष्णाश्मसंचयविभेदविशालवक्षाः [।*]

11 आ(रा)जीवकोमलदलायतलोचनान्तः ख्यातः कलिङ्गजनतासु पुलिन्दसेन[: ।। *४]

12 तेनेत्थं गुणिनापि सत्व(त्त्व)महता नेष्टं भुवो मण्डलं ।[7] शक्तो य[:*] परिपालनाय जग-

13 तः को नाम स स्यादिति । प्रत्यादिष्टविभु(भू)त्सवेन भगवां(वा)नाराधित[:*] शाश्वतस्तच्चित्ता-

14 णु(नु)गुण(णं) विधिस्सु(त्सु)रदिशद्वाञ्चछां स्वयम्भो(म्भू)रपिः(पि) [।।*५] स शिलास(श)कलोद्भेदी तेनाप्या-

15 लोक्य धि(धी)मता । परिकल्पितसद्वङ्श(द्वंशः) प्रभुः शैलोद्भव[:*] कृतः[।।*6] शैलोद्भवस्य कुल-

16 जोरणभीत आसीद्येनासकृत्क(त्कृ)तभिया(यां) द्विषदङ्गनानां(नाम्) । ज्योत्स्नाप्रवो(बो)धसमये स्वधियै-

17 व सार्द्धमाकम्पितो नयनपक्ष्मजलेषु चन्द्रः ।। [७*][8]

Second Plate: First Side

18 तस्याभवद्विवु(बु)धपालसमस्य सूनुः श्रीसैन्यभीत इति भूमिपतिर्ग्ग-

19 रीयान् । यं प्राप्या(प्य) ने(नै)कशतनागघटाविघट्टलव्ध(ब्ध)प्रसादविजये(यं) मुमुदे धरि-

20 त्त्रीः(त्री) [।।८*] तस्यापि वङ् शे(वंशे)थ यथार्थनामा जातो यशोभीत इति क्षितीशः [।*] येना(न) प्ररु(रू)-

21 ढोपि शुभैश्चरित्त्रैः मृ(त्त्रैर्मृ)ष्टः कलङ्क[:*] कलिदर्प्पणस्यः (स्य) ।। [९*] जातस्य(स्स) तस्य न(त)नयः

22 सुकृती समस्तसीमन्तिनीनयनषर्प(द्प)दपुण्डरीकः [।*] श्रीसैन्यभीत इति भूमि-

23 पतिर्म्महेभकुम्भस्थलीदलनदुर्ल्ललि(लि)तासी(सि)धारः [।।*१०] जातेन येन कमलाकर-

24 वत्स्वगोत्त्रमुन्मीलितो(तं) दिनकृतेव महोदयेनः(नः)[।*] संक्षिप्तमण्डलरुचश्च-

25 गता[:*] प्रना(णा)शमाशु द्विषो ग्रहगणा इव यस्य दीप्त्याः(प्तया) ।। [११*] कालेयैर्भूतधा-

26 त्त्रीपतिभिरुपचितानेकपापावतारैर्न्नीता(तां) कथापि प्रल-

27 यमभिमता कीर्त्ति(र्त्ति)मा(पा)लैरजस्त्रं(स्त्रम्)। यज्ञैस्तैरश्वमेधप्रभृतिभिरमरा-

28 लम्भितास्तृप्तिमू(मु)र्व्वि(र्व्वी)मुर्द्र(द्ध)प्तारातिपक्षक्षयकृतिपटुना श्रीनिवासेन येनः(न)।। [१२*]

29 तस्योत्खाताखिलारेम(र्म)रुदिव जननाद्भास्वदुष्णांशुतेजा ।[9] जातो[10] मानी दयालुर्न्न-

---

7. The punctuation is superfluous.
8. The rest of the line is left blank.
9. The punctuation is superfluous.
10. Other records of the family read शूरो.

30 रपतिर**यशोभीतदेव**स्तनू(नु)ज[:*] मातङ्गान्योतितुङ्गाम(ङ्गान्) व(ब)हलमदमुचा (च)श्चारुव-

31 क्त्रा[न्*] प्रचण्डा:(ण्डान्) व(ब)द्ध्वाकर्षत्यखिन्न: पुनरपि दयते यत्नत: स्स(स)प्रगल्भ: ।। [१३*] केचिद्वन्य-

32 मृगेण सार्द्धमचरंस्तां तां स्थितिं लीलया ।[11] केचिच्चोद्ध(द्धर्व)मुखा[:*] सहस्रकिरण:(ण) ज्वा-

33 लावलीप्रेक्षिण[:।*] केचिद्वल्कलिनस्थ(स्त)थाजिनधरा: केचिर्ज(ज्ज)टाधारिण(णो) ।[12] नानारु(रू)प-

Second Plate: Second Side

34 धरास्तपन्ति मुनयो दिव्याष्प(स्प)दाकांक्षिण: ।। [१४*] केचिच्छैलगुहोदरेषु नियता धू-

35 मावलीपायिन:[13] अन्ये वायुफलाम्वु(म्बु)भक्षनियता[:*] केचिन्निराहारका(का:) ।। (।) इत्थं

36 योगयु(जु)षो विहाय वसति(तिं) ध्यायन्ति दिव्यं पदं ।[14] चित्रं **मध्यमराजदेव**गुणधृ-

37 द्राज्यो(ज्ये)पि तत्प्राप्तवां: (वान्) ।। [१५*] यस्याह्वानास्स(त्स)मीयु: सुरभवनगता दिव्यसत्वा(त्त्वा:) प्रग-

38 ल्भा: तै(ल्भास्तै:) सार्द्धं नित्यकालं सुकृतगुणकथालापहृद्य(द्यान्) प्रकुर्व्व:(र्व्वन्) [।*] शम्भोस्तस्यानु-

39 कारी पदममरमजं शाश्वतं शान्तरूपं लव्धो(ब्धो)त्साहस्स वीर: क्षिति[त]ल-

40 वसते(ति)र्न्निर्ज्जितारातिपक्ष: ।। [१६*] स्थित्युत्पत्ति विनाशकारणपरं यन्ज्यो(ज्ज्यो)-तिरव्याहतं।[15]

41 व्यक्ताव्यक्तमनन्तशक्तिनियतं देवातिदेवो महा:(हान्) तस्यानुग्रहकारिवि-

42 क्रमधन(नु)श्चेष्टा: करोत्यद्भुता: स श्रीमानतुल[:*] शशाङ्कधवल: क्षोणीय-

43 श[:*]ख्यापित: ।।[१७*] आकर्ण्णादतुलं विकृष्य तरसा चापद्वय(यं) लीलया:(या)[16]

44 अष्टाभि[:*] कवचैवि(र्वि)वेष्ट्य फलकानारादू(दु)भाभ्यामपि । पाणिभ्यां चतुर: शिलीमु-

45 खमुखैर्भिन्त(त्त्वा) सुतीक्ष्णैभृ(र्भृ)श:(श)ञ्जातो द्दि(दि)व्यगति[:*] पृथासुतसमं(म:) कोङ्गोदरत्न(त्नं) क्षितो:(तौ) ।। [१८*]

46 वर्म्मभ्यां सकलं शरीरमसकृत्स(त्सं)वेष्ट्य लीलान्वित: पि(पी)नौ द्वै(द्वौ) पुरुषो(षौ) निधाय युग-

47 प[त्*] स्कन्द्धद्वये लीलया । सद्य[:*] शातकृपाण भासुरकरो धावत्यखिन्नो भृश(शं)

48 भूपालो हनुमत्पराक्रम इति ख्यात[:*] क्षमामण्डलै:(ले) ।। [१९*] जातेन शुभ्रव-

49 पुषा शशिनेव येन सम्व(संव)र्द्धितं कुमुदषण्डमिव स्वगोत्रं(त्रम्) । सङ्कोचित-

---

11. The punctuation mark is superfluous.
12. The punctuation mark is superfluous.
13. The rule of *sandhi* has not been observed here for the sake of the metre.
14. The punctuation mark is superfluous.
15. The punctuation mark is superfluous.
16. The rule of *sandhi* has not been observed here for the sake of the metre.

50 ञ्च रिपुपङ्कजवृन्दमारास्सो(त्सो)यं नि(नृ)पो जयति लव्ध(ब्ध)जयप्रतापः ।। [२०*]

Third Plate

51 अस्मिं(स्मिन्) कोङ्गोदमण्डले महासामन्तश्री[17]

ABSTRACT

This incomplete charter begins as usual with the symbol for *siddham* and the word *svasti* followed by twenty verses. Verse 1 is in adoration of Śiva as is usually found in all the extent charters of the Śailōdbhava kings. Verse 2 introduces the king Mādhavēndra, which is also found in other Śailōdbhava grants. Verse 3 introduces mount Mahēndra. Verse 4 to 5 describe Pulindasēna who was a devotee of lord Svayambhū (Śiva) and famous among the people of Kaliṅga. Verses 6 to 10 describe the genealogy of Mādhavavarman starting from the anonymous king Śailōdbhava, his descendant Raṇabhīta (or Araṇabhīta), whose son was Mādhavavarman I, his descendant Yaśōbhīta (or Ayaśōbhīta) and his son Mādhavavarman II *alias* Sainyabhīta. Verse 11 refers to the achievements of Mādhavavarman-Sainyabhīta. Verse 12 calls the same king Śrīnivāsa, who has been credited with the performance of number of sacrifices including the *aśvamēdha*. Verses 13 to 20 describe the reigning king **Madhyamarāja-Ayaśōbhīta** and his achievements. Lines 29-50 deal with the eulogies of the reigning king, who is also the donor of the present grant. He has been compared with god Śambhu and said to have had discourses with the departed saints coming from heaven at his call. He was as fair as the moon and his fame pervaded the earth. He was an expert at archery, comparable to Pṛthā (i.e., Arjuna) and also had enormous physical strength, capable of carrying two stout persons on his shoulders, like that of Hanumat, the famous monkey-hero of the Rāmāyaṇa. After verse 20 the charter abruptly ends in line 50, just at the beginning of the royal order relating to the grant.

---

17. The record ends here abruptly.

NO. 52: PARIKUD PLATES OF MADHYAMARĀJA, YEAR 26

Provenance	:	Parikud, Puri district, Orissa.
References	:	*Vaṅgīya-Sāhitya-Pariṣad-Patrikā,* (1911-12) Vol. XVI, p. 193; R.D. Banerji, *EI*, Vol. XI, (1911-12), pp. 281 ff. and plate; and S.N. Rajaguru, *IO*, Vol. I, Pt. 2 (1958), pp. 199 ff.
Language	:	Sanskrit, in verse, except the grant portion.
Metre	:	Verses 1, 2, 4, 12, 13, 15, 16 and 17 *śārdūlavikrīḍita;* verses 3, 6, 7, 9, 18 and 24 *vasantatilakā;* verses 5, 19-22 *anuṣṭubh;* verse 8 *indravajrā;* verses 10, 11 and 14 *sragdharā;* verse 23 *puṣpitāgrā.*
Script	:	Eastern variety of the northern alphabet of about the eighth century A.D.
Date	:	26th regnal year.

TEXT[1]

First Plate

1 सिद्धम्[2] स्वस्ति [।।*] इन्दोर्द्धौतमृणालतन्तुभिरिव श्लिष्टाः करै[:*] कोमलै[र्व]-(र्ब)द्धाहेररुणै[:*] स्फुरत्फ-

2 णिमणेर्दिग्धप्रभाशो(सो)ङ्शु(सोंशु)भि[:][।*] पार्व्वत्या[स्*]सकचग्रहव्यतिकरव्यावृ[त् ।*]तव(ब)न्द्धश्लथा गङ्गाम्भ[:*] प्लुति-

3 भि[न्*]नभस्मकणिका[:*]शम्भोर्जटा[:*] पान्तु व[:*] । [।*१]श्रीमानुचै(च्चै)र्नभस्तो गुरुरचलपते[:*] क्षोभजिद्य[:*]

4 क्षमाया गम्भीरा(रो)म्भीयराशेरथ[3] दिवसकरा[द्] भास्वदालोककारी [।*] ह्लादी सर्व्वस्य चेन्दोस्त्रि-

5 भुवनभवनप्रेरकश्चापि वायो राजा स स्थान(णु)मु(मू)र्त्तिज(र्ज)यति कलिमलक्षालनो माध-

6 वेन्द्र[:*] । [।*२]प्राङ्शु(प्रांशु)र्म्महेभकरपीवरचारुवा(बा)हु[:*] कृष्णाश्म-संचयविभेदविशालवक्षा[:] [।*] राजीव-

---

1. From the facsimile in *EI*, Vol. XI (1911-12), pp. 284 and 285.
2. Expressed by a symbol.
3. The Banpur plates (No. 51) read तोयराशेरथ.

7 क(को)मलदलायतलोचनान्त[:*]ख्यात[:*] कलिङ्गजनतासु पुलिन्दसेन[:*] । [।*३] तेने[त्*]थं

8 गुणिनापि सत्व(त्त्व)महता न्येष्टं[4] भू(भु)वो म्म(म)ण्डलं शक्तो यः परिपालनाय जगत[:*] को ना-

9 म स स्यादिति । प्रत्यादिष्टविभुत्सवेन भगवानाराधित[श्*] शाश्वतं ।[5] स्त [च्*]चि-[त्*]तानुगुणं

10 विधित्सुरदिशा(श)द्वाञ्चछा(ञ्च्छां) स्वयम्भूरपि । [।*४] स शिलास(श)कलोद्भेदी तेनाप्यालोक्य धि(धी)म-

11 त(ता)। परिकल्पितसद्वङ्शै(द्वंशः) प्रभु[श्] ।[6] शैलोद्भव[:*] कृत[:*] ।।[५*] शैलोद्भवस्य कुलजो रण-

12 भीत आसीद्य(द्ये)नासकृ[त्*] कृतभिया(यां) द्विषदङ्गनानां [।*]ज्योत्स्नाप्रवो(बो)धसम-

Second Plate: First Side

13 ये स्वधिये(यै)व सार्धमार्कम्पितो नयनपक्ष्मजलेषु चन्द्र[:*] [।।*६] तस्य(स्या) भवद्विवु(बु)धपालसमस्य [सू]-

14 [नु][:*] श्रीसैन्यभीत इति भूमिपतिर्ग्गरीया[न्*।] यं प्राप्य नैकशतनागघटाविघ[ट्ट] लद्ध(ब्ध)प्रसाद-

15 विजय(यं) मुमुदे धरित्रि (त्री)[।।*७] तस्यापि वङ्शे(वंशे)थ यथा[र्थनामा] जाता (तो) यशोभीत इति क्षिति(ती)श[:*।] येन प्ररू-

16 ढोपि शुभैश्चरित्तैर्मृष्ट[:*] कलंक[:*] कलिदर्प्पणस्य । [।*८] जातोथ तस्य तनय[स्*]सुकृति(ती) समस्तसीमन्ती(न्ति)-

17 नीनयनषट्पदपुण्डरीक[:*।] श्रीसैन्यभीत इति भूमी(मि)पतिर्म्महेम्कुम्भस्त-(स्थ) लीदलनद(दु)-

18 र्ल्लली(लि)तासिधार[:*][।।*९] कालेयैर्भूतधातृ(त्री)पतिभिरुपचितानै(ने)-कपापावतारैनि(र्नी)त(ता) येशा(षां) क[था]पि प्र-

19 लयमभिमता कीत्ति(र्त्ति)सा(पा)लैरजश्र(श्रं)। यज्ञैस्तैरश्मेधप्रभृतिभिरमरा लम्भितास्त्रि(स्तृ)प्तिमु-

20 र्व्वि(र्वी) [मुद्व]सारातिपक्षक्षयकृतिपटुना श्रीनिवासेन येन । [।*१०] तस्योत्खाताखिलारेम्म-(र्म्म)रुदिव ज-

21 नना[7]द्भास्वदुष्णाङ्शु(ष्णांशु)तेजा[श्*]शी[शू]रो मानी दयालुन(र्न)रपति[8] **यशोभीतदेवस्तनू(नु)ज[:*]** । मातङ्गान्योती(ति)तु-

---

4. Read नेष्टं.
5. The punctuation mark is superfluous.
6. The punctuation mark is superfluous.
7. R.D. Banerji reads अवनो (?).
8. R.D. Banerji reads [षु*].

22 ङ्गा[न्] व(ब)ह[ल*]मदमुचश्चारुवक्त्रप्रचण्डः व(ब)द्वा(द्ध्वा)कर्षत्यश्वेन[9] पुनरपि तपते[10] यत्नत[स्*]स प्रगल्भ[:।।*११]

23 केचिद्वह्न्य(न्य)मृगेण सार्द्धमचि(च)रंस्तास्ता स्थितिं लि(ली)लया केचि[च्*]-चोद्दर्ध(द्ध्र्व)मुखास्सहस्त्रकिरणज्वाला-

24 वलिप्रेक्षण(णा)[:।*] केचिद्वष्क(ल्क)लिनस्तथाजिनधरा[:*] केचिर्ज्ज(ज्ज)टाधारिणा-(णो) नानारु(रू)पधरास्तपन्ति मुन-

25 यो[11] दिव्यास्पदाकाङ्क्षिण[:*] [।।*१२] केचिद्सै(च्छै)लगुहोदरेषु नियता धूमावलीपायिन [:*] अन्ये वायुफला-

26 म्वु(म्बु)भक्षनिरताः केचिन्निराहारका[:*।] इथ[12] योगयु(जु)गो(षो) विहाय वसती ध्यायन्ति दिव्यं पदं चित्रं

27 **मध्यमराजदेव**गुणधृद्राज्येपि तत्प्राप्तवा[न्*][13]। [।*१३] यस्याह्व(ह्वा)नान्म(त्स)-म(मी)यु[:*] सुरभवनग-

Second Plate: Second Side

28 ता दिव्यसत्वा(त्त्वा)[:*] प्रगल्भा[स्*] ।[14] तै[स्*]सार्द्ध[म्*] नित्यकालं स(सु)कृ[त*] गुणकथालापहृद्य(द्या)[:*] प्रकुर्व्व[न्*][।*] शम्भो[स्*]सं-

29 स्थानकारी[15] पदममरजव[:*] शाश्वत(तं) शान्तरूपं लव्धो(ब्धो)त्साह [स्*]स वीर[:*] क्षितितलवसती(तिं) निर्ज्जितारा-

30 तिपक्ष[:*][।।*१४] स्थित्युत्त(प्त)ति(त्ति)विनाशकारणपरमं(रं) ज्यो- [16] व्याहत(तं) व्यक्ताव्यक्तमनन्तशक्ति नियतं देवाति-

31 देवो महा[न्*।] तस्यानुग्रहकारिविक्रमधनु[श्*]चेष्टा(ष्टां) करोत्यद्भुता(तां) स श्रीमानतुल-[श्*]शशाङ्का(ङ्क)धवलक्षो-

32 नि(णी)यश[:*]ख्यापिता(तां) [।।*१५] आकर्ण्णादतुल(लं) विकृश्य(ष्य)तर[सा*] चापद्वयैर्लीलया ।।[17] अष्टाभि[:*] कप(व)चैर्व्विवेष्ट्य

33 फलकी(का)नारादुभाभ्यामपि[।*] पाणिभ्या(भ्यां)श्चतुरः शिलि(ली)मुखै(ख)मुखै[:*] . . . .[18] सुति(ती)क्ष्णैभृ(र्भृ)शः(शं) जातो दी(दि)व्यगति[:*] पृ-

34 थातुशतसम[:*][19] कोङ्गोदरत्न(त्नं) क्षितो(तौ)[।।*१६] वर्म्मा(र्म)भ्यां सकल(लं) शरीरमसकृत्संव्ये(वे)ष्ट्य लीलान्वितं पीने(नौ)

---

9. Banpur plates of Madhyamarāja (No. 51) reads कर्षत्यखिन्नः which is better.
10. The Banpur plates (No. 51) read दयते.
11. Banerji reads यतिपा-.
12. Read इत्थं.
13. Banerji reads राज्य(ज्यं) पितु[:*] प्राप्तवा[न्*].
14. The punctuation mark is superfluous.
15. The Banpur plates (No. 51) read स्तस्यानुकारी.
16. The Banpur charter (No. 51) has यज्ज्योतिरव्याहतं.
17. The *daṇḍas* are superfluous.
18. Read the missing syllables as भित्वा, as in the Banpur plates (No. 51).
19. Read पृथासुतसमः as in the Banpur plates.

35 द्वो(द्वौ) पुरुषो(षौ) निधाय य(यु)गवत्(पत्) स्कन्धद्वये लीलया[।*] सद्य[:*] शातकृपाणभासुरकरो धावत्य-

36 खि[न्*]नो भृश(शं) भूपालो हनुम[त्*] पराक्रम इति ख्यात[:*] क्षमामण्डले ।[।१७*] जातेन येन वपुषा शशि-

37 नेव येन संवर्द्धितङ्कुमुदश(ष)ण्डमिवात्मगोत्र (त्रं)[।*] संकोचितं च रिपुपङ्कजवृन्दमाराधात्[20] कोपेन

38 [यो] जयति लब्ध(ब्ध)जयप्रताप[:*] कटात्[21] श्रीशैलोद्भवकुलतिलको महामखवाजपेयाश्व-

39 मेधावभृथस्नाननिर्व्वि(र्व)र्त्तितप्रख्यातकीर्त्तिक्रम[:*] परममाहेश्वरा(रो) मातापितृपादानुध्यात[:*]

40 **श्रीमध्यमराजदेव**[:*] कुशली[।*] अस्मिं(न्) कोङ्गोदमण्डले श्रीसामन्तमहासा[म*] न्तमहाराजरा-

41 ज(जा)नकराजपुत्रा[न्त]रङ्गदण्डनाना[22]यकोपरिकविषयपति[त*]दायुक्तकवर्त्तमान-भविष्यद्व्यव-

42 हारिण[:] सकारण्यं व्रा(ब्रा)ह्मणपुरोगादि[23] जनपदाञ्च यथार्ह(र्हं) मानयति [बोध]य[ति आ]-

Third Plate: First Side

43 ज्ञापयति च विदितमस्तु भवता(तां) श्रीकटकभुक्तिविष[य*] सम्व(म्ब)द्ध पूर्व्वखण्ड....

44 [मो] द्वादशतिम्पिर[24] प्रमाण[स्]सर्व्वपीडावर्जितश्चाटभटाप्रवेश्यो न किनचिदनप[रिग्रा*][25]

45 ह्य[:*] **षड्विंशतिमे सम्वत्सरे विजयवर्द्धमानराज्ये** मातापित्रोरात्मनश्च पुण्याभि[वृ*]-

46 ध(द्ध)ये सलिलधारापुर[स्*]सरेण(णा)चन्द्रार्कक्षितिसमकालमस्माभिना(र्ना)नागोत्रप्रवर-

47 चरणाय व्रा(ब्रा)ह्मण गोलस्वामि[26] गोवर्द्धनस्वामि वन्द्धुस्वामि कवडिस्वामि नारायण-

48 स्वामि माधवस्वामि भरणिस्वामि दुर्ग्गस्वामि आदित्यस्वामि रुद्रस्वामि शिवस्वामि-

49 सुखस्वामिने विश्रके[27] प्रतिपादित[:*] यतो ह्यस्य यथाकालमुपयुज्यतो न केनश्चि-(चि)द्विघाता[:*] कर-

50 णि(णी)य[:*] । उक्तञ्च धर्म्मशास्त्रे[।।*] व(ब)हुभिर्व्वसुधा दत(त्ता) राजभि-[स्*]सगरादिभि[:*।] यस्य यस्य यदा भु(भू)मि[स्*]-

---

20. Read आरात्.
21. R.D. Banerji suggests कटकाच्छ्री.
22. One ना is redundant.
23. Read सकरणान् ब्राह्मणपुरोगान्.
24. Banerji reads तिम्मिर, but तिम्पिर is quite clear in the photolitho print. This is a unit of land-measure.
25. Read केनचित् परिग्राह्य.
26. Banerji reads शीलस्वामि.
27. The reading is doubtful.

51 तस्य तस्य तद(दा) फलं(लम्) [।।*१९] मा भु(भू)दफलशङ्का व[:*] परद[त्*]तेति
पाथि(र्थि)वा[:*।] स्वदानात्फलमानन्त्य(न्त्यं) परदत्ता-
52 नुपालन(ने) [।।*२०] स्वदता(त्तां) परदता(त्ता)म्वा(त्तां वा) यो हरेति(त) वसुन्धरां[।*]
स्व(स) विष्ठाया(यां) कृमिर्भु(र्भू)त्ता(त्वा) ।[28] पितृभि[स्*]सह
53 पच्यते [।।*२१] हरते हारयते भु(भू)मि(मिं) मन्दवु(बु)द्धि[स्*]तमोवृत[:*।] स
व(ब)द्धो वारुणै[:*] पासै(शैः) ती(ति)र्य[ग्*] योनिष(षु) जा-
54 यति(ते)[।।*२२] इति कमलदलाम्वु(म्बु)वि(बि)न्दुलोलां श्री(श्रि)यमनुचिन्त्य
मनुष्यजीवितञ्च[।*] सकलमिदमु-
55 दाहृतञ्च वु(बु)द्ध्वा न ही(हि) पुरुषै[:*] परकीर्त्तयो विलोप्या[:*।।][२३*]
विद्युद्विलासतरलामवगम्य स[म्य*]क्(ग्)लोक-
56 स्थितिं यस(श)शि(सि) श(स)त्तमनोभिरुचै(च्चै)[:*।] नित्य(त्यं) परो[पकृति*]
मात्त्ररतै[र्भवद्भि*]ध(र्ध)र्म्माभिराधनपरैरनुमोदि[त]-

Third Plate: Second Side

57 [व्यं][।।*२४] ....लिखित सान्धिविग्रहिक-
58 ....देवेन[।*] लाञ्चि(ञ्छि)तं.........
59 दृढ्ढेन ।। **स[म्वत्]**..............[29] **कार्त्तिक शुक्ल**......

ABSTRACT

The inscription begins as usual with the symbol for *siddham* and the word *svasti.* All the eighteen verses, excepting the imprecatory and benedictory ones at the end of the charter, are found in most of the Śailōdbhava copper-plate grants. Verse 1 is in adoration to god Śambhū (Śiva). Verse 2 introduces the king named Mādhavēndra. Verse 3 introduces Pulindasēna, the famous hero among the people of Kaliṅga and a devotee of Svayambhū (Śiva). Verse 4 records the genealogy of the Śailōdbhava family from the very beginning. Verse 5 describes the birth of the first historical king of the family from a rock. Verses 6 to 9 record that in the family of Śailōdbhava, there was a king named Raṇabhīta, his son was Mādhavavarman-Sainyabhīta, his descendant was Yaśōbhīta, whose son was Mādhavavarman-Sainyabhīta II. Verse 10 calls Mādhavavarman as Śrīnivāsa, who is credited with performing a number of holy sacrifices. Verses 11 to 18 describe the reigning king **Madhyamarāja-Yaśōbhīta** and his achievements. Lines 38-50 deal with the grant of land and credit Madhyamarāja with the performance of the **vājapēya** and **aśvamēdha** sacrifices, who assumed the title of *paramamāhēśvara,* and who was an ornament of the family of

28. The punctuation mark is superfluous.
29. Two illegible numerical symbols have been read by R.D. Banerji as 88; but the regnal year of the king seems to have been written here as 20.6.

Śailōdbhava. He made a declaration from his capital addressing the royal officials of Kōṅgōdamaṇḍala, such as *śrīsāmanta, mahāsāmanta, mahārāja, rājanaka, rājaputra, antaraṅga, daṇḍanāyaka, viṣayapati, tadāyuktaka* as well as the present and future *vyavahārins,* the brāhmaṇas and other citizens. Lines 43-49 deal with the grant of twelve *timpiras* of land by the reigning king, which was divided among a group of brāhmanas belonging to different *gōtras* and *pravaras,* in the victorious **26th regnal year**. The names of the brāhmaṇas are mentioned in these lines as Gōlasvāmin, Gōvarbhanasvāmin, Bandhusvāmin, Kavaḍisvāmin, Nārāyaṇasvāmin, Mādhavasvāmin, Bharaṇisvāmin, Durgasvāmin, Ādityasvāmin, Rudrasvāmin and Śivasvāmin. The gift land is stated to have been situated in the Kaṭakabhukti *viṣaya.* But the village comprising the land cannot be determined due to the damaged condition of the plate. The land was granted after making it free from all obstructions for the increase of the religious merit of the donor and his parents. This is followed by six of the usual imprecatory and benedictory verses quoted from the *Dharmaśāstra.* The last line refers to the **date** of the issue of the grant which is now lost due to corrosion. Only the name of the month with the **lunar tithi** has been restored as **Kārttika śukla.**

NO. 53: RANPUR PLATES OF DHARMARĀJA, YEAR 3

Provenance	:	Ranpur, Puri district, Orissa.
Reference	:	S.N. Rajaguru, *IO*, Vol. I, Pt. 2 (1958), pp. 218-22.
Language	:	Sanskrit, in verse, except the grant portion.
Metre	:	Verses 1, 3, 12, 15, 19 *śārdūlavikrīḍita;* verses 2, 5, 6, 8, 9, 13 *vasantatilakā;* verses 4, 14, 17, 20, 21 *anuṣṭubh;* verse 7 *indravajrā;* verses 10, 11, 16 *sragdharā;* verse 18 *nardaṭaka;* verse 22 *puṣpitāgrā.*
Script	:	Eastern variety of the northern class of alphabet of about the eighth century A.D.
Date	:	3rd regnal year, the fifth day of the bright fortnight in the month of Jyēṣṭha.

TEXT[1]

First Plate

1 सिद्धम्[2] स्वस्ति [।। *] [इ]न्दोर्द्धौतमृणालतन्तुभिरिव:[3] श्लिष्टाः करैः कोमलैर्व(र्ब) द्धाहे[रु]-

2 णै[:] स्फुरत्फणिमणैर्द्दिग्धप्रभासोङ्शु(सोंशु)भि:[।*] पार्वत्या[स्*] सकचग्रह-व्यतिकरव्या-

3 [वृत्त]व(ब)न्द्धश्लथा गङ्गाम्भः प्लुतिभिन्नभस्मकणिका[:*] शम्भोर्जटाः पान्तु वः।। [१*] प्राङ् शु(प्रांशु)र्महे-

4 भकरपीवरचारुवा(बा)हु[:*] कृष्णाश्मसंचयविभेदविशालवक्षाः[।*] राजीवकोमलदलाय-

5 तलोचनान्तः ख्यातः कलिङ्गजनतासु पुलिन्दसेन[:*]।।[२*] तेनेत्थं गुणिनापि सत्व(त्त्व)-महता

6 ने[ष्टं] भुवो मण्डलं शक्तो यः परिपालनाय जगतः को नाम स स्यादिति ।। (।) प्रत्यादि-

---

1. From the original plates; the charter is now preserved in the Orissa State Museum, Bhubaneswar.
2. Expressed by a symbol.
3. *Visarga* is redundant.

7 [4][ष्टवि]भूत्सवेन भगवानाराधितः शाश्वा(श्व)तस्तच्चिन्तानुगुणं विधित्सुरदिशद्वाञ्च्छा(ञ्च्छां)

8 [स्वयम्भू]रपि ।।[३*] स शिलाशकलोद्भेदि(दी) तेनाप्य(प्या)लोक्य धि(धी)मता [।*] परिकल्पित स-

9 [द्वंशैः] [प्रभुः शै]लोद्भवः कृतः ।।[४*] शैलोद्भवस्य कुलजो रणभीत आसीद्येनासकृत्क्र-

10 [तभियां द्विषद]ङ्गनानां[।*] ज्योत्स्नाप्रवो(बो)धसमये स्वधियैव सार्धमाकम्पितो नयन-

11 [पक्ष्मजलेषु च]न्द्र[:*] ।। [५*] तस्याभवद्विवु(बु)धपालसमस्य सूनु[:*] श्रीसैन्यभीत इति भूमि-

12 [पतिर्गरीयान् [।] [यं] प्राप्य नैकशतनागघटाविघट्टलव्ध(ब्ध)प्रसादविजयं मुमुदे धरि-

13 [त्री ।। [६*] तस्यापि व]ङ् शे(वंशे)थ यथार्थनामा जातो यशोभीत इति क्षितिशः [।*] येन प्ररूढोपि

14 [शु भैश्चरित्रैर्मृ]ष्टः कलङ्क[:*] कलिदर्पणस्य ।। [७] जातस्य तस्य तनयः सुकृती समस्त-

Second Plate: First Side

15 सीमन्तिनीनयनषट्पदपुण्डरीकः [।*] श्रीसैन्यभीत इति भूमिपतिर्महेभकुम्भ[स्थ]-

16 लीदलनदुर्ललितासिधार[:*] ।। [८*] जातेन येन कमलाकरवत्स्वगोत्रमुन्मीलित(तं) दिनकृ-

17 तेव महोदयेन[5] [।*] संक्षिप्तमण्डलरुचश्च गताः प्रणाशमाशु द्विषो ग्रहगणा [इ]-

18 व यस्य दीप्त्या ।।[९*] कालेयैर्भूतधात्रीपतिभिरुपचितानेकपापावतारैर्न्नीता येषा(षां)

19 कथापि प्रलयमभिमता कीर्त्तिमा(पा)लैरजस्रं(स्रम्)[।*] यज्ञैस्तैरश्वमेधप्रभृतिभिरमरा-

20 लम्भितास्तृप्तिमुर्व्वीमुद्वृत्तारातिपक्षक्षयकृतिपटुना श्रीनिवासेन येन ।।[१०*] तस्योत्खा-

21 ताखिलारेर्मरुदिव जननाद्भास्वदुष्णाङ् शु(ष्णांशु)तेजा[6] शूरो मानी दयालुर्नरपति-

22 रयशोभीतदेवस्तनू(नु)जः [।*] मातङ्गान्योतितुङ्गाद्बहल[7]मदमुचश्चारुवक्त्रां(क्त्रान्)

23 प्रचण्डां(ण्डान्) व(ब)द्ध्वाकर्षत्यखिन्नः पुनरपि तय(प)ते[8] यत्नतः स प्रगल्भः ।। [११*] केचिच्छै-

24 लगुहोदरेषु नियता धूमावलीपायिनः अन्ये वायुफलाम्वु(म्बु)भक्षनिरता[:*] केचिन्नि-

25 राहारका[:*] ।[9] इत्थं योगजुषो विहाय वसतिं ध्यायन्ती(न्ति) दिव्यं पदं चित्रं मध्यमराजदेवगुण-

---

4. This line, and the following lines up to the end of the plate, are damaged affecting some letters at the beginning of the lines. The plate is broken in this portion and lost. The reading of the missing letters has been restored from the introductory part of the other Śailōdbhava grants.
5. Rajaguru reads सहोदयेन.
6. There is a small horizontal line, intended perhaps for a mark of punctuation. But the punctuation is not necessary here.
7. Read तुङ्गान् बहल-.
8. Rajaguru reads दयते.
9. There is a small dot-like sign intended perhaps for punctuation.

26 धृद्राज्येपि[10] तत्प्राप्तवां(वान्) ।।[१२*] तस्याभवत्सकलश(शा)स्त्रविशेषवेदी **श्रीधर्म्मराज** इति सूनुरधी-

27 तशास्त्र[:*।] यस्यातिनिर्मलयश: परिवर्द्धमानं पादौ हरेरिव न मायित[11]मातृ(त्रि)लोक्या[:*] ।।[१३*] नि-

28 राश्रयैः प्रयत्नेन गुणैः स परिवारितः वैमुख्यादीर्ष्य(र्ष)या चैवः[12] सर्वदोषैर्विवर्जि-

29 त[:*][13] ।। [१४*] काले हन्ति[14] रिपून्महारणशतव्यापारलव्धोन्नंती[15] काल(ले) स(भ)क्तिमुपैति शुभ्रचरि [तैः]

Second Plate: Second Side

30 शम्भोः कथाविस्तरैः [।*] काले धर्म्मविवेचनाय निरतैर्ब्रा(ब्रा)ह्मण्यमध्य(ध्ये) स्थितः क्रौञ्चारेरि-

31 व यस्य चेष्टितमलं लोक:(कैः) समालोक(क्य)ते ।। [१५*] राज्य(ज्यं) लव्धै(ब्धै)व दर्पादविगणिततया मा-

32 धवो ज्येष्ठभावां(वान्) देशादस्मादपात्रं कृतविषममतिर्विग्रहे फासिकायां(याम्)[।*] युद्धक्षोभेण

33 भग्नो नृपतिपरमसौ संशृ(श्रि)तस्तीवराख्यं पश्चात्तेमापि सार्धं(र्द्धं) पुनरपि विजितो विन्द्ध्यपादे-

34 षु जीर्ण्णः ।। [१६*] शौर्यं श्रीर्यौवनं राज्यमेकैकं मदकारकं(कम्)[।*] सर्वं **श्रीमान भीतस्य** निर्विकारमुप-

35 स्थितं(तम्) ।।[१७*] तुरगखुराभिघातविदलद्धरणीतलजं जयगजकर्ण्णचामरविधूननविस्फु-

36 रितं(तम्)[।*] सुभटफरप्रसर्पणनिरुद्धककुद्गगनं व(ब)लरज एव यस्य जयति द्विष-

37 तां ध्वजिनीं(नीम्) ।।[१८*] आरच्य प्रसभं घटा गजगणैरश्वीयपादातकैजि(र्जि)-त्वान्याम्व(न्यान्ब)लशा-

38 लिना(नो) नृपवरानागत्य दृष्टेर्भुवं(वम्) [।*] युद्धे भीमपराक्रमेण विजिता निवृत्पदं प्रापिता दृ-

39 श्यन्ते भवनाङ्गणे प्रतिदिनं प्रातः प्रणामार्थिनः ।। [१६*] विजयमातृचन्द्रपाटकाद्ध्री-

40 शैलोद्भवकुलतिलको महामखवाजपेयाश्वमेघावभृथस्नाननिर्वर्त्तितसूनो-

41 स्तनयो वहुविविध[16]मत्तवारणवरतुरगपदातिशस्त्रसंपा(सम्पा)तस(सं)कुलो(ल)व(ब)ह्वा ह-

42 वविनिहतशत्रुरन(ने)कविक्रमाक्रान्तसकलभूमण्डलप्रथितयशश्चातुर्दन्तसं-

43 ग्रामादसकृल्लव्ध(ब्ध)प्रतापः परममाहेश्वरो मातापितृपादानुध्यातः **श्रीध-**

---

10. Rajaguru reads ग्राज्येपि.
11. The Nivina grant reads मायति.
12. The *visarga* is superfluous.
13. Rajaguru reads तैः
14. Rajaguru reads कालैर्हन्ति.
15. Read लब्धोन्नतीन्.
16. Read बहुविध.

44 **र्म्मराजदेवः** कुशली ।। अस्मिं(स्मिन्) कोङ्गोदमण्डले श्रीसामंत(मन्त)महासामन्त-

Third Plate: First Side

45 महाराजराजनकराजपुत्रान्तरङ्गदा(द)ण्डनायकदाण्डपासि(शि)कोपरिकस्तद्विनि-
46 युक्तकव्यवहारिणः सकरणानन्यांश्च व्रा(ब्रा)ह्मणपुरोगादिवैषयिकजनपदान्यथा-
47 र्हं पूजयति मानयत्याज्ञापयति च विदितमस्तु भवता[म्*।] तनेकण्ड्राविषयस-
48 म्व(म्ब)द्धउसवाटक ग्राम(मे) क्षेत्रटिम्पीर पञ्च अकरीकृत्य आत्रेयसगोत्त्रा(त्रा)य
49 अत्रीणात्रेयार्च्चनानसः श्यवाश्च[17] भट्टतृ(ति)लोच्च(च)नस्वामिने मातापित्रोरात्मन-
50 श्च पुण्याभिवृद्धये सलिलधारापुरःसरेण प्रतिपादितस्तदेषामाचन्द्रार्कका-
51 लं मु(उ)पभुञ्जानस्य धर्म्मगौरवान्न केनचित्परिपन्थिना भवितव्यमिति ।।
52 उक्तञ्च मानवे धर्म्मे[।*] व(ब)हुभिर्व्वसुधा दत्ता राजभिः सगरादि-
53 भिः [।*] यस्य यस्य यदा भूमिस्तस्य तस्य तदा फलं(लम्) ।। [२०*] स्वदत्तां पर-
54 दतम्वा(त्तां वा) यो हरेत वसुन्द्धरां(राम्)[।*] स विष्ठाया(यां) कृमिर्भूत्वा पितृभिः सह पच्य-
55 ते ।।[२१*] इति कमलदलाम्वु(म्बु) वि(बि)न्दुलोला(लों) श्रियमनुचिन्त्य मनुष्यजीवितञ्च
56 सकलमिदमुदाहृतञ्च वु(बु)ध्वा न हि पुरुषैः परकीर्त्तयो विलोप्या(प्याः) ।।[२२*] दूतको-
57 त्त्रा(त्रा)कृत श्रीणण्ण लिखितं वृ(बृ)हद्भोगिना धृ(ध्रु)वदत्तेन लाञ्छितं पेटा-
58 पालोद्योतसिङ्हे(सिंहे)न उत्कीर्ण्णं स्थविरवृद्धेनेति । **सम्वत् ३ ज्येष्ठ शुदि ५** [।।*]

ABSTRACT

The charter begins with the symbol for *siddham* and the word *svasti*. Verses 1-12 are found in the copper-plate grants of the Śailōdbhava kings (Nos. 47-52). Verses 13 to 19 introduce the reigning king, **Dharmarāja**, who had also the secondary name **Śrī-Mānabhīta**. He is stated to be the son of Madhyamarāja. While describing the noble qualities and the military achievements of **Dharmarāja**, the verses mention the event that he defeated his elder brother Mādhava twice, first at the battlefield of Phāsikā and then finally defeated him along with Tīvara in a battle fought at the foot of the Vindhyas. This is followed by a prose passage (lines 39-51) referring to the grant. Dharmarāja, a devout worshipper of god Śiva and a devotee at the feet of his parents, issued a declaration regarding the grant of land from the victorious camp at **Mātṛcandra-pāṭaka**, addressed to the feudatories and officials of Kōṅgōda-*maṇḍala*, such as the *śrīsāmanta, mahāsāmanta, mahārāja, rājanaka, rājaputra, antaraṅga, daṇḍanāyaka, dāṇḍapāśika, uparika* and other inhabitants of the kingdom. He granted five *ṭimpiras* of

17. The *gōtra* is actually Dattātreya which has three *pravaras*, namely, Ātrēya, Arcanānasa and Śāvāśva.

land in a locality called Usavāṭaka in Tanekaṇḍrā *viṣaya,* in favour of *bhaṭṭa* Trilōcanasvāmin of the Ātrēya *gōtra* with the three *pravaras,* namely, Ātrēya, Arcanānasa and Śāvāśva, with libations of water, in order to increase the religious merit of the donor and his parents. The grant was made free from taxes. The inhabitants were directed not to make any kind of obstruction in the donee's enjoyment of the gift land. Lines 52-56 record three of the usual imprecatory and benedictory verses. Lines 57 and 58 contain the names of the officers responsible for the execution of the grant and the date of the issue of the charter. Śri-Ṇaṇṇa acted as the *dūtaka* or the executor of the grant. Dhruvadatta was the writer of the grant, whose designation was· **bṛhadbhōgin**. Udyōtasiṁha, the *pēṭāpāla* (or the keeper of the records) endowed the charter with a seal and it was engraved by Sthavira-Vṛddha. The **date** of the grant is given in the **rẹgnal year** of the king as **the year 3, the fifth day of the bright fortnight of the month of Jyēṣṭha**.

NO. 54: NIVINA COPPER-PLATE GRANT OF DHARMARĀJA, YEAR 9(?)

Provenance : Nimmina, Ganjam district, Orissa.

References : N.P. Chakravarti, *EI*, Vol. XXI (1931-32), pp. 34 ff. and plate; and S.N. Rajaguru, *IO*, Vol. I, Pt. 2 (1958), pp. 206 ff.

Language : Sanskrit, in verse, except the grant portion.

Metre : Verses 1, 4, 12 *śārdulavikrīḍita;* verses 2, 10, 11, 14 *sragdharā;* verses 3, 6, 7, 9, 13 *vasantatilakā;* verses 5, 15, 16, 17 *anuṣṭubh;* verse 8 *indravajrā.*

Script : Eastern variety of the northern alphabet of about the eighth century A.D.

Date : 9th regnal year (?), Vaiśākha *su di prathama-pakṣa dvitīyā.*

TEXT[1]

First Plate

1 सिद्धम्[2] स्वस्ति ।। इन्द्रो(न्दो)र्द्धौतमृणाल[तन्तुभि]रिव:[3] शिलष्टा: करै[:*] कोमलै-

2 व(र्ब)द्धाहेररुण(णै:) स्फुरत्फणिमणै(णे)[र्दिग्ध]प्रभा[सों]शुभि:[।*] [पार्व्व]त्या[:*] सकच-

3 ग्रहव्यतिकर:(र)व्यात्रृत्तव(ब)न्द्धश्लथा गङ्गाम्भ[:प्लुतिभिन्नभस्मकणि]का[:*] शम्भोर्ज्जटा[:*]

4 पान्तु व: ।।[१*] श्रीमांभिन(श्रीमानुच्चै)र्ण्ण(न्नं)भस्ते(स्तो)गुरुरचलपति(ते:) क्षो[भजिद्य:] क्षमा[या] गम्भीरस्तोयरा-

5 शेरथ दिवसकरा[द*]भस्म(भास्व)दालोककारि(री)। ह्लादी सर्व्वस्य चेन्दोस्तृ(स्त्रि) भुवनभवनप्रेकश्चि(श्चा)पि

6 वायो राजा स्व(स) स्थाणुमूर्त्तिर्ज्जयति कलिमलक्षालनो माधवेन्द्र:[।।][२*] प्राङ्शु(प्रांशु)र्म्महिभक-

1. From the facsimile in *EI*, Vol. XXI (1931-32).
2. Expressed by a symbol.
3. The *visarga* is superfluous.

राजीव[कोमलद]लायतलो-

8 चनान्तः ।[6] ख्यातः कलिङ्गजनि(न)त(ता)स(सु) पुलिन्दसेनः ।।[३*] तेनेत्थं गुणि[नापि] स[त्*]त्वमहतो(ता) न(ने)-

9 षृ(ष्टं) भुव्वोर्म्मण्डलं[7] ।[8] शक्तोयं परिपालनाया(य) जगतः को नाम[स*] स्यादि[ति] प्रत्यादिष्टवि-

10 भुत्सवेन भगवां[9]नाराधित(तः) स्वा(शा)श्वतं(तस्)तच्चि[त्तानु] गुणं वि[धित्सुर]दिश[द्*] वाञ्छा(ञ्छां) श्व(स्व)-

11 यम्भो(म्भू)[र]पिः[10] ।।[४*] स शिलास(श)कलो[द्भे]दे(दी) तेना[प्यालोक्य] धीमता [।*] [प] रिकल्पितः[11] (त)-

Second Plate: First Side

12 [सद्वंशः*] प्रभु[:*] शैलोद्भव[:*] कृतः [।।*५] शैलोद्भवस्य कुल[जो] रणभीत आसीद्येनासकृ-

13 त्कृतभियां वि(द्वि)षदंगनानां । ज्योत्स्न्या(त्स्ना)प्रव(बो)ह(ध)समये स्वधी(धि)ये(यै)व सार्द्धमाकम्पितो नय-

14 नपक्ष(क्ष्म)जलेषु चन्द्रः ।।[६*] तस्याभवद्विवु(बु)धपालसमस्य सानुं[12] श्रीसैन्य[भीत] इति भूमि-

15 पतिर्ग्गरीया[न्*] यं प्राप्य नागघटाघट[13] लव्ध(ब्ध)प्रसादविजय(यं) मुमु[दे*] धरितृ(त्री)। [।*७] तस्यापि वंशे-

16 षु(थ) यथाथ(र्थ)नामो(मा) जातोयशोभीत इति [क्षिती*]षः(शः)। [ये*]न पु(प्र)रु(रू)ढो[पि*] शुभे(भै)श्चरित्रे(त्रै)मृ(र्मृ)ष्टः कलंक[:*] कलिनदल-

17 न स्यात्[14] ।[।*८] जातो[थ*] तस्य तनय[:] [सुकृती*] [समस्त*] सीमन्तिनि(नी)नयनषट्पदपुरीण्डरिकः[15] [।*] श्री[सै]न्यभीत इ-

18 ति भूमिपतिर्म्महेभकुम्भस्थलि(ली)दलनदुल(र्ल)लितासिधारा(रः)[।।*९] कलयै(कालेयै)-भूत धातृ(त्री)पतिभिरु[16]

---

4. Read सञ्चयविभेदविशालवक्षाः
5. The punctuation mark is superfluous.
6. The punctuation mark is superfluous.
7. Read भुवो मण्डलम्.
8. The punctuation mark is superfluous.
9. The *anusvāra* is superfluous.
10. The *visarga* is superfluous.
11. The *visarga* is superfluous.
12. Read सूनुः .
13. Read नैकशतनागघटाविघट्ट.
14. Read कलिदर्पणस्य.
15. Read पुण्डरीकः .
16. There is a sign of punctuation or a letter before प.

19 पचितान्यै(ने)कपापावतारैः ।। नीता[17] येषां कथाभि(पि) प्रलयमभिमता कीर्तिमा(पा)लैर [ज*]स्रं[।*]

20 यज्ञ(ज्ञै)स्तैरश्वमेधप्रभृतिभिरमरा लम्वि(म्भि)त(ता)स्तृप्तिमु[र्व्वी] मुदृ(द्दृ)प्तारात्रि(ति)पक्ष-क्षयकृतिपटु-

21 ना श्रीनिवासेनि(न) येनः[18] । [।*१०] तस्योत्खाताखिलारेर्म्मरुरि(दि)व [ज]ननोद्भास्वतु(दु)ष्णांशुतेजाः ।।[19] शूरो मा-

22 नि(नी) दयालुर्नरपतिरयशोभीतदेवस्तनूजः । मातङ्गान्योतितु[ङ्ग][20] व(ब)हलमदमु-

Second Plate: Second Side

23 चा(च)श्चारुवक्त्रां(क्त्रान्) प्रचण्डां(ण्डान्) व(ब)द्धाकर्षतिखिनं[21] पुनरपि नवते यत्कृतं(तः) सम्प्रगल्भा(ल्भः) [।।*११]

24 केचिद्व(द्व)न्यमृगेण सार्द्ध(र्द्धं) रमते(न्ते) ततां(था)[22] स्थितिलीलयः(या) ।[23] केचित्(च्)चोर्द्ध(द्ध्व)मुखामयूख[24]-

25 किरणज्वालावलिप्रेक्षणः(णाः) [।*] केचित् शैलगुहोदरेषु निरता[25] धूमावलि(ली)पाइ(यि)न[:*] अ-

26 ने(न्ये) वायुफलां(ला)वु(म्बु)भक्षनिरता[:*] केचि[न्*]नी(नि)राहारकाः । इ[त्*]थं योगजुषो विहाय वसति(तिं)

27 ध्यायंति(न्ति) दिव्यं पदं[26] चित्रन्म(म्म)ध्यमराजदेवतृ[27] गुणां(ण)ध्रि(धृ)द्राज्यंपि[28] तत्प्राप्तवां(वान्) ।। [१२*] तस्याभ-

28 वत्सकलशास्त्रविशेषवेदी ।[29] **श्रीधर्म्मराज** इति सुनुरधीति(त)शास्त्रः ।।(।)तस्या-

29 तिनी(नि)र्म्मलयशः परिवर्द्धमान(नं) पादौ हरेरिउ(रिव) न मायति मर्त्ति(र्त्त)लोक्याः (कः) ।।[१३*] राज्यं लव्धा(ब्द्धवा) प्र-

30 दर्पादविगणिततयो(या) माधवो जे(ज्ये)ष्ठभावां(वान्) ।[29] तस्या तस्मादपस्त्त्वं[30] कृतविषममतिवि(र्वि)ग्र-

---

17. Read पापावतारैर्नीता and the punctuation mark is redundant.
18. The *visarga* is superfluous.
19. The *daṇḍas* are redundant.
20. Read तुङ्गान्.
21. Read बद्धवाकर्षत्यखिन्नः
22. The Parikud grant has सार्द्धमाचरंस्तथा.
23. The punctuation mark is superfluous.
24. The Parikud grant has मुखास्सहस्र.
25. The Parikud (No. 52) and Kondedda grant (No. 58) read नियता.
26. The punctuation is superfluous.
27. The letter तृ should be omitted.
28. Read राज्येपि.
29. The punctuation mark is superfluous.
30. Read देशादस्मादपास्तुं as in the Kondedda grant (No. 58).

31 हे फासिकायां । युद्धक्षोभेन(ण) ल(भ)ग्नो नृपतिपरमसौ संशृ(श्रि)तस्त्रि(स्ती)[व]राख्य: ।[31] प–

32 श्चां(श्चात्)तेनापि सार्द्धं पुनरपि विजिता(तो) विन्ध्यधपादेषु जीर्ण्णात्(र्ण्ण:) ।।[१४*] शोर्य्यं श्रीर्यौवनं

33 राज्यमेकैक्यं(कं) मदमा(का)रकं । सर्वं **श्रीमानभीतस्य** नि[र्वि]कारमुपस्थित:(तं) ।।[१५*] **अल**–

Third Plate: First Side

34 **तालङ्गपुरकोटात्** । परममाहेश्वरो मातापितृपादानुध्यातो(त:) प–

35 रमभट(ट्टा)रको महारा[जा*]धिराज[32]परमेश्वर[:*] **श्री[म*]द्धर्म्मर(रा)जदेव**[:*] कुशली ।। अस्मी(स्मि)त्को)(न्को)ङ्गो–

36 दमण्डले श्रीसामन्तमा(म)हासामन्तमा(म)हाराजनकराजक[33]राजपुत्रा:(त्रा)[न्तर*]ङ्गदण्डना–

37 यक[दण्ड*]पाशिकोपरिकस्तकद्विनि[34]युक्तकसकरणव्यवहारिण(णो)[35]नान्यांश्च ब्रा(ब्रा)ह्मण–

38 पुरोगादिवे(वै)षइ(यि)कजनपदां(दान्) यथार्ह(र्हं) मानय[ति*] वो(बो)धयति ज्ञापयति विदितमस्तु

39 भवतां(ताम्) खिण्डिङ्गहारविष[य*]संमंध[36] निविनाग्रामात्(म:) ।[37] सवरिदेवदिखिद(दीक्षित) ।[38]

40 भट्ट(ट्टाय) वच्छ(त्स)गोत्राय पञ्चरिषप्रवरअनुप्रवराय[39] कौथुक(म)शाखाय छ(छा)न्दो[ग्य*]चरणाय

41 मातापित्रोरात्मनश्च पुन्या(ण्या)भिवृध(द्ध)यो(ये) सलिलधारापुर[:*]सरेण(णा)चन्द्रार्क– क्षितिसमकाल[म्*] अ–

42 करि(री)कृत्य ताम्ब्र(म्र)शाश(स)त्वे(ने)न प्रतिप्रा(पा)दित(तो)स्मात्(भि)न(र्न)कोचित् (केनचित्) विघातित[व्य*]मिति ।। ग्रामस्य शी(सी)मा कत(कृता)

43 पश्चिमदिशहि(दिशि) तृ(त्रि)कुट जोडपापदिवणराइ वाल्मिक वंङ्क(वङ्क)सिलवणराइ [।*] उत(त्त)रदिशहि(दिशि)

44 तृ(त्रि)कुट । पाणिसिलसाखतरिमणि वाढैवणि[40] [।*] उत्तरदिसहि(दिशि) दिघसिल [।*] पूवेहि(पूर्वस्यां) जोडवणराइ

---

31. The punctuation is superfluous.
32. ज is written in smaller letters and inserted between रा and प.
33. Read महाराजराजनक–.
34. It should be स्तद्विनियुक्तक–.
35. Delete ना.
36. Read संबद्ध.
37. The punctuation mark is superfluous.
38. The punctuation mark is superfluous.
39. Read पञ्चर्षिप्रवरानुप्रवराय.
40. This part of the record specifying the boundaries of the gift village is full of errors due to the inadvertance of the scribe and the engraver. The meanings of the expressions are not clear.

45 वड [।*] पूवउतरकोणेहि सोमणि तृकुट । पूर्वदखिण(णे)हि से...म तृकुट । पूवदिसहि खो-

46 ल्लाड[।*] पूवदखिणकोणहि वाघगुहु(हा) तृकुट [।*] दखिणदिश पवदिसिल गाडि सवति: ।।

Third Plate: Second Side

47 –पर [41] द्वौ टिम्पिर: ।। **सम्वत्[42] [वै]शाख सु(शु)दि प्रथम पक्ष द्विती[या*]**

48 उक्तञ्च धर्म्मशास्त्वे[।*] व(ब)हुभि: [वसु]धा[43] दताम्[दत्ता] राजा(ज)भि: सगरादिभि:[।*]

49 र्यस्य (यस्य) यस्य यदा भूमि[स् *]।[44] तस्य तस्य [तदा फलं] ।।[१६*] स्वद[त्*]तां परद[त्*]ताम्वा(त्तां वा) यो ह-

50 रेति(त) वसुन्द्धरां[।*] स विष्ठायां कृमि[र्भूत्वा] पितृ[भि:*] सह पच्यते: (ते) ।।[१७*] इतिको(दूतको)-

51 च्र महाक्षपट[ल] . . . .देवो(व:) प्रधानतन[य*?] [45] लाञ्छितं जयसिंहेन

52 उत्कीर्णं च्चा(छ)ड्डिभयेन:[46] म्मिति:[47] ।।

ABSTRACT

The charter begins with the symbol for *siddham* and the word *svasti.* The following twelve verses in lines 1-27 contain the eulogistic description of the Śailōdbhava family and the achievements of the individual rulers copied from the charters of the reigning monarch. Verses 13-15 in lines 28-33 describe the achievements of the reigning king **Dharmarāja**, who was well-versed in all the sacred scriptures and was the son of Madhyamarāja-Ayaśōbhīta. He is stated to have had an elder brother named Mādhava, who turned out to be an enemy as soon as Dharmarāja ascended the throne. But Dharmarāja defeated him in a battle fought at Phāsikā. Mādhava then took shelter under a king named Tivara. However, both Mādhava and Tivara were defeated by Dharmarāja in a battle fought at the foot of the Vindhyas. He is stated to have assumed the secondary name Mānabhīta.

---

41. The first letter at the commencement is not clear in the facsimile.
42. The editor of the grant reads the final *t* of the word *samvat* to be the numerical figure for 9. But there seems to be no numerical figure after the word *samvat*. The close similarity between the numerical figure 9 and the final *t* has induced the editor to suggest this.
43. Read बहुभिर्वसुधा.
44. The punctuation mark is superfluous.
45. The editor of the grant suggests प्रधानतम: (?).
46. The editor of the grant suggests च्चाहिभयेन; this should be छड्डिभोगिन.
47. Read इति.

A prose passage (lines 34-37) records that the charter was issued from **Alatālaṅghapura-kōṭa**. Dharmarāja is stated in this passage to have assumed the titles of *paramamāheśvara, paramabhaṭṭāraka, mahārājādhirāja, parameśvara* and is said to have been devoted to his parents. Lines 37-42 record the grant of the village Nivinā, situated in the district of Khiṇḍiṅgahāra of Kōṅgōda-*maṇḍala,* by the reigning king in favour of Savaridēvadīkṣita-bhaṭṭa of the Vatsa *gōtra,* Pañcārṣēya *pravara,* Kauthuma *śākhā* and Chandōga *caraṇa,* for the increase of religious merit of the donor and his parents. The royal order conveying the grant was addressed to the officers and feudatories of Kōṅgōda-*maṇḍala* such as *śrīsāmanta, mahāsāmanta, rājanaka, rājaputra, antaraṅga, daṇḍanāyaka, daṇḍapāśika, uparika, viniyuktaka,* the *karaṇas* and the *vyavahārins* and the brāhmaṇas. The grant was made free from all taxes. Lines 43-46 describe the boundaries of the gift village. The demarcation is enumerated as follows: to the west of the gift village were the *trikuṭa* (a hillock), Jōḍāpāpadi-*vaṇarai* (?); an ant-hill, Vaṅkaśilā-*vaṇarai;* to the north, the *trikuṭa,* Sākhātarīmaṇi-*Vāḍhaivaṇi* (?); to the north again, the *dighasilā;* to the east, Jōḍā-*vaṇarai-vāḍa;* to the north-east, Sōmaṇi-*trikuṭa;* to the south-east (See. . .ma) *trikuṭa* (the name of a *trikuṭa,* the letters are illegible, possibly denoting a hillock); to the east again, the village of Khōllaḍa; to the south-east again, the Vāgha-*guhā* (a cave)-*trikuṭa;* to the south again the Pavadisilā-*gādi* (the name of a tank). Line 47 refers to two *ṭimpiras* of land (possibly an additional plot of land), perhaps granted either to the same donee or to some other person within the above boundaries of the gift village. In the same line the **date** of the grant is stated, in which the reading of the year is uncertain. After the word **samvat,** there is no space left for the numerical symbol for the year. The grant is stated to have been issued in **the month of Vaiśākha**, on **the second day of the first or the bright fortnight**. Lines 48-50 contain two imprecatory and benedictory verses quoted from the *Dharmaśāstra*. Lines 50-52 contain the names of the officers associated with the execution of the grant. The *dūtaka* or the executor of the charter was the *mahākṣapaṭala* (the name is lost, only the suffix *dēva* is visible). The document was registered or endowed with a seal by Jayasiṁha and engraved by Chaḍḍi-*bhōgin.*

NO. 55: BANPUR GRANT OF DHARMARĀJA *ALIAS* MĀNABHITA

Provenance	:	Banpur, Puri district.
References	:	D.C. Sircar, *EI*, Vol. XXIX (1951-52), pp. 38-43 and plate; and S.N. Rajaguru, *IO*, Vol. I, Pt. 2 (1958), pp. 223-28.
Language	:	Sanskrit, in verse, except the grant portion.
Metre	:	Verses 1, 3, 11, 14, 18 *śārdūlavikrīḍita;* verses 2, 5, 6, 8, 12, and 22 *vasantatilakā*; verses 4, 13, 16, 19-21 *anuṣṭubh;* verse 7 *indravajrā*; verses 9, 10, 15 *sragdharā*; verse 17 *nardaṭaka*; verse 23 *puṣpitāgra.*
Script	:	Eastern variety of the northern alphabet of about the eighth century A.D.
Date	:	*Samvat* 1 (?), the month of Phālguna.

TEXT[1]

First Plate

1 सिद्धम्[2] स्वस्ति:(स्ति) [।।*] इन्दोर्द्धू(र्द्धौ)तमृणालतन्तुभिरिव श्लिष्टा[:] करै: कोमलै: व(र्ब)द्धाहेररुणै[:*] स्फु-

2 रत्फणिमणेर्दिग्धप्रभाशोड्शु(सोंशु)भि: [।*]पार्व्वत्या[:*]सकचग्रहव्यतिकरव्यावृत्त-व(ब)न्धश्लथा ।[3] गङ्गा-

3 म्वु(म्बु)प्लुतिभिन्नभस्मकणिका[:*] शम्भोर्जटा ऽपान्त(न्तु) व: । [।*१] प्राङ् शु(प्रांशु)र्महेभकरपीवरचारुवा(बा)हु[:*] कृष्णाश्म-

4 सण्च(ञ्च)[य*]विभेदविशाला(ल)वक्षा[:*।] राजीवकोमलदलायतलोचनान्त: ख्यात: कलिङ्गजनतासु

5 पुलिन्दसेन[:*] । [।*२] तेनेन्थं(त्थं) गुणिनो(ना)पि सत्व(त्त्व)महता नेष्टं भुवोर्म(म)ण्डलं।[4] शक्तो य: परी(रि)पालना-

1. From the facsimile in *EI*, Vol. XXIX (1951-52), pp. 39 and 41.
2. Expressed by a symbol.
3. The punctuation mark is superfluous.
4. The punctuation mark is superfluous.

6 य जगत: को नाम स स्यादिति । प्रत्यादिष्टविभुर्भ(त्स)वेन भग[5]वानाराधित[:*] शाश्वत: तञ्चित्तानु[6]-

7 गुणं विधिस्सु(त्सु)रदिशद्वाञ्च्छां स्वस(य)म्भो(म्भू)रपि ।। [३*] स शिलाशकलोद्भेदी तेनाप्यालोक्या(क्य) धीम-

8 ता [।*] परी(रि)कल्पितसद्वङ्श(वंश:) प्रभु: शैलोद्भव: कृत: [।।*४] शैलोद्भवस्य कुलजोरणभीत आसीत्ये(द्ये)-

9 नासकृत्कृता(त)भिया(यां) द्विषदङ्गनानां(नाम्) । ज्योत्स्नाप्रवो(बो)धसमये स्वधियैव सार्धमाकं(क)म्पितो

10 नयनपक्ष्मजलेषु चन्द्र[:*] ।। [५*] तस्याभवद्विवु(बु)धपालरमस्य सूनु: श्रीसैन्यभीत इ-

11 ति भूमिपतिग(र्ग)रीयान् [।*] यं प्राप्य नैकशतनागघटाविघट्टलव्ध(ब्ध)प्रतापविजयं म(मु)मुदे

12 धरी(रि)त्री ।। [६*] तस्यापि वङ्शे(वंशे)थ यथार्थनामा जातोयशोभीत इति क्षितीश: [।*]येन प्र-

Second Plate: First Side

13 रु(रू)ढोपि शुभैश्चरित्रै:मृ(र्मृ)ष्ट: कलङ्क: कलिदर्प्पणस्य ।। [७*] जातोथ [तस्य तनय] स्सुकृ-

14 ती समस्तसीमन्त(न्ति)नीनयनषड्प(ट्प)दपुण्डरीक[:*] श्रीसैन्यभीत [इति भूमि] पतिर्म्महे-

15 भकुम्भस्थलीदलनदुर्ललितासिधार: ।। [८*] कालेयैर्भूतधात्रिपतिभिरुपचितानेकपा-

16 पावतारैर्नीता येषां कथापि प्रलयमभिमता कीर्त्तिमा(पा)लैरजस्त्रं(स्त्रम्) [।*] यज्ञैस्तैरश्वमेध-

17 प्रभि(भृ)तिभिरमरा लम्भितातृ(स्तृ)प्तिमुर्व्वीमुदु(द्व)ष्टारातिपक्षक्षयकृतिपटुना श्रीनिवासेन

18 येन ।। [९*] तस्योत्खाताखिलारि(रे)र्म्मरुदिव जनितो भास्वदुष्णाङ्शु(ष्णांशु)तेजा[:*] शूरो मानी दया-

19 लुर्नरपतिरयशोभीतदेवस्तनूज[:*] । मातङ्गान्योतितुङ्गान्व(न्ब)हलमदमुच-

20 श्चारुवक्त्राप्प्र(न्प्र)चण्डान् व(ब)द्ध्वाकर्षत्यखिन्न: पुनरपि दयते यत्नत: सम्प्रगल्भ: ।। [१०*] केचि-

21 श्छै(च्छै)लगुहोदरेषु निरता धूमावलीपायिन:[7] अन्ये वायुफलाम्वु(म्बु)भक्षनिरता[:*] केच्चि(चि)न्ति(न्नि)रा-

22 द्वारका[:*] । इत्थं योगजुषो विहाय वसतीं(तिं) धा(ध्या)यंन्ति(यन्ति) दिव्यां(व्य)म्पदं चिन्न(न्नं) मध्यमराजदेव-

23 गुणधृद्राज्येपि तत्प्रासवान् ।। [११*] तस्याभवत्सकलशास्त्रविशेषवेदी **श्री धर्म्मराज**

24 इति सूनुरधी[त*]शास्त्र: । यस्यातिनिर्मलयश: परिवर्द्धमान(नं) पादौ हरे-

---

5. ग is engraved in a small form above the line.
6. Read तस्तच्चित्तानु-.
7. The rule of *sandhi* has not been observed here for the sake of the metre.

Second Plate: Second Side

25 रिव न मायितमा तृ(त्रि)लोक्या:[।।*१२] निराश्रयै[:*] प्रयत्नेन गुणैस्स परिवारित: वैमुख्यादी-

26 र्षया चैव सर्व्वदोषैर्व्विवर्ज्जित: ।।[१३*] काले हन्ति रिपु(पू)न्मा(न्म)हारणशतव्यापारलव्धो-(ब्धो)न्नतीन(न्)[8]

27 काले धर्म्मविवेचनाय न(नि)रतो व्रा(ब्रा)ह्मण्यमध्ये स्थित: क्रौञ्चारेरिव यस्य चेष्टितमलं लोक(कै:)

28 समालोक्यते ।। [१४*] राज्यं लव्धै(ब्ध्वै)व दर्प्पादविगणिततयो(या) माधवो ज्येष्ठभावात्(न्) देशां(शा)दस्माद-

29 पास्तु [ड्कृ]तव(वि)षममतिर्व्विग्रहे फासिकायां ।।(याम् ।) युद्धक्षोभेण भग्नो नृपतिवरमसौ संश्रित-

30 स्तीवर(रा)ख्यं पश्चात्तेनापि सार्द्धं पुनरपि विजितो विन्ध्यपादेषु जीर्ण्ण: [।। *१५] शौर्यं श्री[र्यौ]-

31 वनं राज्यमेकैकं मदकारकं(कम्) [।*] सर्व्व(र्व्वं)**श्रीमानभीत**स्य निर्व्विकारमुपस्थितं(तम्) ।।[१६*] तुरग-

32 खुराभिघातविदलद्धरणीतलजं जयगजकर्ण्ण:(र्ण्ण)चामरविधूननविस्फुरितं(तम्)। सुभ-

33 टफरप्रसर्प्पणनिरुद्धककू(कु)द्गगनं व(ब)लरज एव यस्य जयति द्विषतां ध्वजिनीं(नीम्) ।। [१७*] आ-

34 रच्य प्रसभं घटा गजगणैरश्वीयप(पा)दातकै: [कै]जि(र्जि)त्वान्यां(न्या)म्व(न्ब)लशालिनो नृपवरानागत्य

35 दृष्टेर्भुवं(वम्) [।*] युद्धे भीमप[रा*]क्रमेण विजिता निवृत्पदं प्रापिता:(ता) दृश्यन्ते भवनाङ्गणे प्रतिदिनं

36 प्रात: प्रणामार्थिन: [।।*१८] विजयासिलिद[9] वासकात् श्रीशैलोद्भवकुलतिलकमहाम-

Third Plate: First Side

37 खवाजपेयाश्वमेधावभृथ[10]स्त्रा(स्ना)ना(न)निर्व्वर्त्तितसूनोस्तनयो व(ब)हुविविध[11] मत्तवारणवर-

38 तुरगम(प)दातिशस्त्रसं(स)म्पातसङ्कुलो(ल)व(ब)ह्वाहवविनिहतशत्रुरनेकविक्रमा-क्रान्तसकल भू-

39 मण्डलो सु(भु)जव(ब)लातुलप्रथितयश(शा)ञ्चा(श्च)तुर्दन्तसङ्ग्रा(संग्रा)मदसकृल्ल-व्ध(ब्ध)प्रताप: परममाहेश्व-

---

8. The second *pāda* of the stanza has been engraved at the end of the charter in lines 54-55.

9. Sircar suggests सिलिड or असिलिड.

10. Read मेधावभृथ.

11. Read बहुविध.

40 रो मातापितृपादानुध्यातः **श्रीधर्म्मराजदेवः** कुशली । थोरणविषये ।।[12] महासामन्त-

41 श्रीसामन्त ।[13] महार(रा)ज ।[14] राजनक ।[15] राजपुत्रान्तरङ्ग ।[16] दा(द)ण्डनायक ।[17] दाण्डवा(पा)-शिकौपरि[क*]स्त(त)द्विनि-

42 युक्तकव्यवहारिणस्सकरणानन्याङ्श्च(न्यांश्च) व्रा(ब्रा)ह्मणपुरोगादिवैषयिकजनपद(दां)श्चाट भट-

43 वल्लभजातीयान्यथार्हम्पूजयति मानयत्याज्ञापयति च ।।[18] विदितमस्तु भवताम् [।*] एतद्विष-

44 यसम्व(म्ब)द्ध[19]-

44(a) दर्हता(दा)चार्य्य नासिचन्द्र ।।[20] तद्शि(च्छि)ष्य एकशाटप्रवु(बु)द्धचन्द्र ।[21] याव[त*] जीवति ।[22] व(ब) लिश(स)त्रचरुप्रवर्त्तनाय ।[23] भग[व]ती श्रीराज्ञी-

44(b) श्रीकल्याणदेवी ।[24] थोरणविषयसम्व(संब)द्ध ।[25] सुवर्ण्णरलोण्डी टिम्पीर त्रि(त्री)-णि । ३ । राण्डसीमसम्व(संब)द्ध मधुवाटकग्राम ।[26] टिम्पी-

44(c) रद्वयं 2 पादा(दः) १

45 तदनुमोदितोस्माभि [:*][27] यतस्ताम्व्र(म्र)पट(ट्ट)कदर्शनात् यथाकालसमुचितफलमुप-भुञ्जानो(न)[स्य*] धर्म्म-

46 गौरवात् केनचित्परिपथ्थि(न्थि)ना [न*] भवितव्यमिति । उक्तञ्च धर्म्मशास्त्रे ।।[28] व(ब)हुभिर्वसुधा दत्ता राजभिस्सग-

47 रादिभि[:*।] र्य(य)स्य यस्य यदा भूमित(स्त)स्य तस्य तदा फल[म्*] । [*१९] स्वदा(द)न्ता(त्तां)म्पर(पर)दत्ताम्वा(त्तां वा) यो हरेत वसुन्द्धरां(राम्) [।*]

48 स विष्ठायां कृमिर्भूत्वा पितृभिस्सह पच्यते । [।*२०] मा भूदफलशङ्का वः परदत्तेति पार्थिवाः स्व-

---

12. The punctuation mark is superfluous.
13. The punctuation mark is superfluous.
14. The punctuation mark is superfluous.
15. The punctuation mark is superfluous.
16. The punctuation mark is superfluous.
17. The punctuation mark is superfluous.
18. The punctuation mark is superfluous.
19. After these letters, two and half lines of writing in smaller characters have been inserted between lines 43 and 45. Only the important words of the omitted passage have been inserted in this small space. These lines may be read as 44(a), 44(b) and 44(c). This omission and correction are due to the carelessness of the scribe.
20. The punctuation mark is superfluous.
21. The punctuation mark is superfluous.
22. The punctuation mark is superfluous.
23. The punctuation mark is superfluous.
24. The punctuation mark is superfluous.
25. The punctuation mark is superfluous.
26. The punctuation mark is superfluous.
27. It may be तद्दानमनुमोदितमस्माभिः
28. The mark of punctuation is in the form of two horizontal strokes instead of the usual vertical ones.

Third Plate: Second Side

49 दानात्फलमानन्त्यं परदत्तानुपालनं(ने) । [।*२१] विद्युद्विलासतरलामवगम्य सम्य[ग्*]लोक-
स्थितं(तिं)

50 यशसि [सक्त*] मनोभिरुच्चैः [।*] नित्यं [प]रोपकृतिमात्ररतैर्भवद्भिः ध(द्धिर्ध)-
र्म्माभिराधनपरैरनुमोदि-

51 तव्या । [।*२२] इति कमलदलाम्वु(म्बु)वि(बि)न्दुलो[ला]ञ्च्छ्र(लां श्रि)यमनुचिन्त्य
मनुष्यजीवितं (त)ञ्च । सकलमिद-

52 मुदाहृतं(त)ञ्चः(ञ्च) वु(बु)द्धवा न हि पुरुषैः परकीर्त्तयो व्वि(वि)लोप्या[:* ।।] [२३*]
[दूतकोत्र] पञ्चकरणोपरि[क*] वै-

53 श्वासिकवृ(बृ)हद्भोगी [सामन्त] उत्कीर्ण्णा अ[क्षशालिकेन] आदित्यदेवेन लाञ्छि-

54 तं पेटापाला(ल)व(ब)लवर्म्म[णा] । **[सं*] वत् १. . . .ल्गु**[29] . . . .[।।*] काले
स(भ)[क्ति*]मुपैति शु-

55 भ्रचरितैः शम्भोः कथाविस्तरैः ।। . . . . . .पृथा. . . . इति ।

ABSTRACT

The introductory part of the charter containing eighteen verses is found in the other records of the issuer of the present one. These verses deal with the career and achievements of the donor and his predecessors. A prose passage in lines 36-46 refers to the place of issue of the charter as the victorious Āsilida. **Dharmarāja**, the reigning king and the donor of the grant, is described here as a devout worshipper of Mahesvara (Śiva) and as devoted to his parents. He is also described as an ornament of the family of Śailōdbhava and as the son's son of one who took an *avabhṛtha* bath after the *aśvamēdha* sacrifice.

The passage recording the grant, though defective due to the omission of some words carelessly by the scribe, refers to the queen Kalyāṇadēvī (perhaps the queen-mother), who seems to be the real donor of the grant which was endorsed by the king. A plot of land measuring three *ṭimpiras*, situated in a locality called Suvarnaralōṇḍi in the district of Thōraṇa and another plot of land measuring two and one-fourth *ṭimpiras* at the village of Madhuvāṭaka, attached to the Rāṇḍa-sīma, were granted in favour of *ēka-śāṭa* Prabuddhacandra, who was a disciple of the *arhadācārya* Nāsicandra. The grant was made, possibly for the maintenance of a religious establishment, with *bali, caru* and *satra* and was in the charge of Prabuddhacandra. It is stated in the grant that the donee would enjoy the gift till his death. Then follows the usual mandate not to create any obstruction in the enjoyment by the donee of this religious deed made by the

29. The numeral 1 for the year is only legible. The name of the month may be फाल्गुन.

donor. This is followed by five of the imprecatory and benedictory verses. Lines 52-54 mention the names of officers associated with the grant. The executor or the *dūtaka* is stated to be Sāmanta designated as the *bṛhadbhōgin*, *pañcakaraṇōparika* and *vaiśvāsika.* It is stated to have been engraved by the *akṣaśālika* or the goldsmith, named Ādityadēva, and endowed or registered with a seal by the *pēṭāpāla* or the keeper of the royal documents named Balavarman. The **date** of the grant is mentioned in line 54, which has been doubtfully read as **samvat 1**, the second symbol being lost, and the name of the **month** seems to be **Phālguna**. The omitted part of the verse 14 is inserted in line 55.

NO. 56: PURI COPPER-PLATE GRANT OF DHARMARĀJA, YEAR 12

Provenance	:	Uttaraparsva *math* in Puri, Puri district.
References	:	S.N. Rajaguru, *JBORS*, Vol. XVI (1930), pp. 176 ff. and plate; and *idem*, *IO*, Vol. I, Pt. 2 (1958), pp. 229 ff.
Language	:	Sanskrit, in verse, except the grant portion.
Metre	:	Verses 1, 3, 12, 15, 19 *śārdūlavikrīḍita;* verses 2, 5, 6, 8, 9, 13 *vasantatilakā;* verses 4, 14, 17, 20, 21 *anuṣṭubh;* verse 7 *indravajrā;* verses 10, 11, 16 *sragdharā;* verse 18 *nardaṭaka;* verse 22 *puṣpitāgrā.*
Script	:	Eastern variety of the northern alphabet of about the eighth century A.D.
Date	:	12th regnal year, the eighth day of the bright fortnight of the month of Vaiśākha.

TEXT[1]

First Plate

1 सिद्धम्[2] स्वस्ति [।।*] इन्दोर्द्धौतमृणालतन्तुभिरिव:[3] शिलष्टा: करै: कोमलैर्व(र्ब)द्धाहेररुणै[:]

2 स्फुरत्फणिमणेर्दिग्धप्रभासोङ्शु(सोंशु)भि:[।*] पार्व्वत्या[:*] सकचग्रहव्यति-
करव्यावृत्तव(ब)-

3 न्धश्लथा गङ्गाम्भ:प्लुतिभिन्नभस्मकणिका[:*] शम्भोर्जटा[:] पान्तु व: ।। [१*]
प्राङ्शु(प्रांशु)र्महेभ-

4 करपीवरचारुवा(बा)हु[:*] कृष्णाश्मसंचयविभेद विशालवक्षा[:*।] राजीव-
कोमलदलायतलो-

5 चनान्त: ख्यात: कलिङ्गजनतासु पुलिन्दसेन[:*] ।। [२*] तेनेत्थं गुणिनापि सत्व(त्त्व)महता
नेष्टं भु-

6 वो मण्डलं शक्तो य: परिपालनाय जगत: को नाम स स्यादिति [।*]प्रत्यादिष्टविभुत्सवे-

7 न भगवानाराधित: शश्वतस्तच्चित्तानुगुणं विधित्सुरदिशद्राञ्छां स्वयम्भूरपि [।।] [३*]

---

1. From the facsimile in *JBORS*, Vol. XVI (1930).
2. Expressed by a symbol.
3. The *visarga* is superfluous.

8 स शिला[शक]लोद्भेदी तेनाप्यालोक्य धीमता [।*] परिकल्पितसद्वङ्श:(द्वंश:)[4] प्रभु: शै-

9 लोद्भव[:*] कृ[त: ।।] [४*] [शै]लोद्भवस्य कुलजोरणभीत आसीद्येनासकृत्कृतभियां द्विषदङ्गना-

10 नां(नाम्) [।*] ज्योत्स्नाप्रवो(बो)धसमये स्वधियैव सार्द्धमाकम्पितो नयनपक्ष्मजलेषु चन्द्र: ।।[५*] तस्याभ-

11 वद्विवु(बु)धपालसमस्य[5] सूनु[: *] श्रीसैन्यभीत इति भूमिपतिर्गरीयां(यान्) [। *] यं प्राप्य नै-

12 कशतनागघटाविघट्टलव्ध(ब्ध)प्रसादविजय(यं) मुमुदे धरित्री ।। [६*] तस्यापि वङ्शे-(वंशे)-

13 थ यथार्थनामा जातोयशोभीत इति क्षितीश: [।*] येन प्ररूढोपि शुभैश्चरि-

14 त्रैर्मृष्ट: कलङ्क[:*] कलिदर्पणस्य [।।*७] जातोथ तस्य तनय: सुकृती समस्तसी-

Second Plate: First Side

15 मन्तिनीनयनषट्पदपुण्डरीक[:*] श्रीसैन्यभीत इति भूमिपतिर्महेभकुम्भस्थली-

16 दलनदुर्ल्ललितासिधार[:*] ।।[८*] जातेन येन कमलाकरवत्स्वगोत्रमुन्मीलित(तं) दिनकृते-

17 व स(म)होदयेन [।*] संक्षिप्तमण्डलरुचश्च गता: प्रणाशमाशु द्विषो ग्रहगणा इव

18 यस्य दीप्त्या ।। [९*] कालेयैर्भूतधात्रीपतिभिरुपचितानेकपापावतारैर्नीता येषां क-

19 थापि प्रलयमभिमता कीर्त्तिमा(पा)लैरजस्त्रं(स्रम्) यज्ञैस्तैरश्वमेधप्रभृतिभिरमरा ल-

20 म्भितास्तृ[प्ति]मुर्व्वीमुद्वृत्तारातिपक्षक्षयकृतिपटुना श्रीनिवासेन येन ।। [१०*] तस्यो-

21 त्खाता[6]खिलारेर्मरुदिव जननाद्भास्वदुष्णाङ्शु(ष्णांशु)तेजा शूरो मानी दयालु-

22 र्नरपतिरयशोभीतदेवस्तनुज: [।*] मातङ्गान्योतितुङ्गाद्व(न्ब)हलमदमु-

23 चश्चारुव [क्त्रान्] प्रचण्डां(ण्डान्) व(ब)ध्वाकर्षत्यखिन्न: पुनरपि तयते[7] यत्नत: सप्रगल्भ: ।।[११*]

24 केचिच्छैलगुहोदरेषु नियता[8] धूमावलीपायिन: अन्ये वायुफलाम्वु(म्बु)भक्षनिरता:

25 केचिन्निराहारका[:*।] इत्थं योगजुषो विहाय वसति(तिं) ध्यायन्ति दिव्यं पदं चित्रं मध्यम-

26 राजदेवगुणधृद्राज्येपि तत्प्रासवां(वान्) ।।[१२*] तस्याभवत्सकलशास्त्रविशेषवेदी श्रीधर्म्मरा-

27 ज इति सूनुरधीतशास्त्र: [।*] यस्यातिनिर्मलयश: परिवर्द्धमान(नं) पादौ हरेरिव न मा-

28 यितमातृ(त्रि)लोक्या[:*] ।। [१३*] निराश्रयै: प्रयत्नेन गुणै: स परिवारित: [।*] वैमुख्यादीर्षया

---

4. Rajaguru reads तद्वंश: .
5. Rajaguru reads सखस्य.
6. Rajaguru reads तस्योज्जि(ज्ञे)ता.
7. The Banpur charter has दयते.
8. The Banpur charter has निरता.

Second Plate: Second Side[9]

29 चैव:(व) सर्व्वदोषैर्व्विवर्ज्जित: ।। [१४*] काले हन्ति रिपून्महारणशतव्यापारि(र)लव्धो(ब्धो)न्नत: (तीन्)

30 काले स(भ)क्तिमुपैति शुभ्र(भ्र)चरितै: शम्भो: कथाविस्तरै[:*] [।*] काले धर्म्मविवेचनाय नि-

31 रतो व्रा(ब्रा)ह्मण्यमध्ये स्थित: क्रौञ्चारेरिव यस्य चेष्टितमलें लोक:(कै:) समालोक्यते ।। [१५*]

32 राज्यं लब्धै(ब्ध्वै)व दर्पादविगणिततयो[10](या)माधवो ज्येष्ठभावादेशा(वान् देशा) दस्मादपास्तु(स्तुं) कृ-

33 तविषममतिर्व्विग्रहे फासिकायां(याम्) [।*] युद्धक्षोभेण भग्नो नृपतिपरमसौ संशृ(श्रि)तस्ती-

34 वराख्यं पश्चात्तेनापि सार्द्धं पुनरपि विजितो विन्द्ध्यपादेषु जीर्ण्ण: ।। [१६*] शोर्य्यं श्रीर्यौव-

35 नं राज्यमेकैकं मदकारकं(कम्) [।*] सर्व्वं **श्रीमानभीतस्य** निर्व्विकारमुपस्थितं(तम्) ।। [१७*] तुर-

36 गखुराभिघातविदलद्धरणीतलजं जयगजकर्ण्णचामरविधूननविस्फु-

37 रितं(तम्) [।*] सुभटफरप्रसर्प्पणनिरुद्धककुद्गगनं व(ब)लरज एव यस्य[11] जयति द्विषतां

38 ध्वजिनीं(नीम्)[12] ।। [१८*] आरच्य प्रसभं घटा गजगणैरश्वीयपादातकै:-जि(कैर्जि)त्वान्यां(न्या)व(न्ब)लशालिना(नो)

39 नृपवर(रा)नागत्य दृष्टेर्भुवं(वम्) [।*] युद्धे भीमपराक्रमेण विजिता निर्वि(वृ)त्पदं प्रापिता

40 दृश्यन्ते भवनाङ्गणे प्रतिदिनं प्रात: प्रणामार्थिन: ।। [१९*] विजयमातृचन्द्रपाटका-

41 च्छ्रीशैलोद्भवकुलतिलको महामखवाजपेयाश्वमेधावभृथस्नाननिर्व्व-

42 र्त्तितसूनोस्तनयो वहु[13]विविधमत्तवारणवरतुरगपदातिशस्त्रसम्पात-

Third Plate: First Side

43 संकुलोव(ब)ह्वाहवविनिहतशत्रुरनेकविक्रमाक्रान्तसकलभूमण्डलो प्र[14]-

44 थितयश(शा)श्चातुर्द्दन्तसंग्रामादसकृल्लव्ध(ब्ध)प्रताप: परममाहेश्वरो मा-

45 तापितृपादानुध्यात: **श्रीधर्म्मराजदेव:** कुशली ।। अस्मिन्कोङ्गोदमण्डले श्रीसा-

---

9. The facsimile of this side of the charter is illegible at several places due mainly to the defective method of applying ink while copying the inscription. The reading of the illegible portions has been restored with the help of the other records of the family.
10. Rajaguru reads विगणितनयो.
11. Rajaguru reads सुभटवेरप्रसर्पणनिरुद्धककुपगगनं वलमददूरतो यस्य.
12. Rajaguru reads वृजिनीम्.
13. Rajaguru reads वङ्ग; read बहुविध.
14. The Banpur charter of Dharmarāja reads भुजवलातुलप्रथित-.

46 मन्तमहासामन्तमहाराजराजनक[15] राजपुत्त्रान्तरङ्गदा(द)ण्डनायकदाण्डपासि(शि)कको[16]–
47 परिकस्तद्विनियुक्तकव्यवहारिणः सकरणानन्यांश्च व्रा(ब्रा)ह्मणपुरोगादिवैष–
48 यिकजनपदान्यथार्हं पूजयति मानयत्याज्ञापयति च विदितमस्तु भवतां(ताम्) [।*] वर्त्तनिवि–
49 षये दोङ्गीग्रामसम्वद्ध[17] मत्सिनीपरिभृतेन किणियाच्छेदक्षेत्रटिम्पीरद्व–
50 यमेकैकदुकग्रामे[18] पूर्व्वेण ग्रामरथ्या दक्षिणेन वृक्षपंक्ति[:*] पश्चिमेन तटाक[:*]
51 उत्तरेण पथस्सीमान्तेण कांसकारभिट्टाकवास्तुसमेतेन जातो(तु)कर्ण्णसगोत्त्राय
52 वासिष्ठात्रेयजातो(तु)कर्ण्णप्रवराय वाजसनेयचरणाय काण्व[19]शाखामासिकाख्य
53 गोलस्वामिनस्य[20] अकरीकृत्य मातापित्रोरात्मनश्च पुण्याभिवृद्धये सलिलधारा–
54 पुरः सरेण प्रतिपादितस्तदेषामाचन्द्रार्ककाल[म्*] समुपभुञ्जानस्य धर्म्मगौरवा[त्*]
55 न केनचिद्विघात(तं) वर्त्तितव्यमिति ।। उक्तं च मानवधर्म्मशास्त्रे । व(ब)हुभिर्व्वसुधा दत्ता
56 राजभिः सगरादिभिः [।*] यस्य यस्य यदा भूमिस्तस्य तस्य तदा फलं(लम्) ।। [२०*]
स्वदत्तां प–

Third Plate: Second Side

57 रदत्ताम्वा[21] यो हरेत वसुन्द्धरां [। *] स विष्ठायां कृमिर्भूत्वा पितृभिः सह पच्यते ।।
[२१*]
58 इति कमलदलाम्वु(म्बु)वि(बि)न्दुलोलां श्रियमनुचिन्त्य मनुष्यजीवितञ्च [।*] सकल–
59 मिदमुदाहृतं च वु(बु)ध्वा न हि पुरुषैः परकीर्त्तयो विलोप्या[:*] ।। [२२*] दूतकोत्र
म–
60 हासामन्तगोषा(पा?)लदेव वृ(बृ)हद्द्रोगी सामन्तेन लिखितं लाञ्छितं[22] पेटापाल–
61 व(ब)लवर्म्मेण उत्कीर्ण्णं स्थविरवृद्धेन(ने)ति ।। **सम्वत् १०.२ (?)[23] वैशाख शुदि**
८ [।।*]

ABSTRACT

The nineteen verses forming the introductory part of the charter describe the achievements of the predecessors of the reigning king as well as himself. Lines

---

15. Rajaguru overlooks राजनक.
16. Read दण्डपाशिको–
17. The reading of the name of the village is doubtful. Read सम्बद्ध.
18. The name of the village has been read by Rajaguru as कैकदुकग्रामे.
19. Rajaguru reads काण्य.
20. Read स्वामिने.
21. Read दत्तां वा.
22. Rajaguru overlooks this word.
23. The date of the grant has been doubtfully read by S.N. Rajaguru as सम्वत् 512 वैशाख शुदि 8. The letters and the symbols in this part of the facsimile are illegible and cannot be compared properly. The two numerical symbols after the word सम्वत् most probably read 10.2 (12), indicating the regnal year of the reigning king.

40-55 contain a prose passage which records that the charter was issued from the victorious **Mātṛcandra-pāṭaka** by the reigning king **Dharmarāja**, who was also known as Mānabhīta, described as the best of all in the family of Śailōdbhava and the son's son of one who performed the *vājapēya* and *aśvamēdha* sacrifices. He was a devout worshipper of god Mahēśvara and a devotee at the feet of his parents. The royal order relating to the grant was addressed to the officers and feudatories of Kōṅgōda-*maṇḍala*. The grant consisted of two *ṭimpiras* of land situated in the area called Kiṇiyā-*chēda* in the village named Dōṅgi-*grāma* in the district of Varttani, and one (*ṭimpira*) of land in the village of Duka-*grāma*, apparently situated in the same *viṣaya*, which were issued in favour of the brāhmaṇa Āsika-Gōlasvāmin of the Jātukarṇa *gōtra*, Vāsiṣṭha-Ātrēya-Jātukarṇa *pravara*, Kāṇva *śākhā* and Vājasanēya *caraṇa*. The boundaries of the gift lands have been specified in lines 50-51 as follows: to the east of lands was Grāma-rathyā (?), to the south were rows of trees, to the west was the tank and to north up to the house of a bronze-smith at the end of the road. The lands were made free from paying taxes and made permanent till the existence of the sun and the moon. The purpose of the grant was to increase the religious merit of the donor and his parents. Lines 55-59 contain three of the usual imprecatory and benedictory verses. Lines 59-61 mention the names and designations of the officers connected with the execution of the grant. Gōṣāladēva, the *mahāsāmanta*, acted as the *dūtaka* or the executor of the grant. *Sāmanta*, the *Bṛhadbhōgin*, was the writer of the charter. Balavarman, the *pēṭapāla* or the keeper of the records, endowed the charter with a seal and Sthaviravṛddha was the engraver of the charter. The **date** of the charter is given at the end of line 61, but the reading is very doubtful due to the unsatisfactory preservation of the plate and also due to the illegible facsimile printed along with the text. The numerals for the year may be read as **12**, presumably the **regnal year of the reigning king**. The day and the month may be read as **the eighth day of the bright fortnight of the month of Vaiśākha**.

NO. 57: CHANDEŚWAR PLATES OF DHARMARĀJA, YEAR 18

Provenance	:	Chandeswar, under Tangi Police Station, Puri district.
References	:	S.N. Rajaguru, *JKHRS*, Vol. II, No. 1 (1947), pp. 65 ff.; *idem*, *IO*, Vol. I, Pt. 2 (1958), pp. 213 ff.; and D.C. Sircar, *EI*, Vol. XXX (1954), pp. 269-73.
Language	:	Sanskrit, in verse, except the grant portion.
Metre	:	Verses 1, 9, 11, 12 *anuṣṭubh*; verses 2, 3, 5, 8, 14 *vasantatilakā*; verse 4 *indravajrā*; verses 6, 7, 10 *sragdharā*; verse 13 *puṣpitāgrā*.
Script	:	Eastern variety of the northern class of alphabet of about the eighth century A.D.
Date	:	Samvat 18 (?), Caitra, *amāvasyā*.

TEXT[1]

Second Plate[2]: First Side

1 ङ्श(वंश) प्रभुः शैलोद्भव [:*] कृतः[3] [।।*१] शैलोद्भवस्य [कुल]जो रणभीत आसीद्येनासकृत्

2 कृतभिया (यां) द्विश(ष)दङ्गनानां(नाम्) [।*] ज्योत्स्नाप्रवो(बो)धसमये स्वधे(धि)यैव [सार्द्ध]माकम्पितो नय-

3 नपक्ष्मजलेषु चन्द्रः [।।*२] तस्याभवद्वि[व](बु)धपा[लस]मस्य सूनु[:*] श्रीसैन्यभीत इति

4 भूमिपतिर्ग्गरि(री)यां(यान्) । यं प्राप्य नैक[शत]ना[ग]घटाविघट(ट्ट)लद्ध(ब्ध)-प्र[4]सादवि-

5 जयं मुमुदे धरित्तिः(त्री) [।।*३] तस्यापि वग्शे(वंशे)[थ*] यथार्थनाम(मा)जाता(तो) यशोभीत इति क्षिति(ती)श[:*]

---

1. From the original plates. The charter is now preserved in the Orissa State Museum, Bhubaneswar.
2. The first plate is lost.
3. This is a continuation from the first plate which obviously contained one side of writing. This verse is known from the other extant records of Dharmarāja-Mānabhīta in its complete form [cf. *EI*, Vol. XXIX (1951-52), p. 41].
4. Space for one letter has been left blank after प्र only the top *mātrā* of the letter seems to have been engraved.

6 [येन] प्र[रू]ढोपि शुभैश्चरित्रैमृ(र्मृ)ष्ट[:*] कलङ्क[:*] कलिदर्प्पणस्य:(स्य) [।।*४] जातोथ तस्य त–

7 [नय][:*] सुकृति(ती) समस्तसीमन्तिनीनयनषड्प(ट्प)दपुण्डरि(री)क[: *।] श्रीसैन्यभीत इति भु(भू)[मि]–

8 पतिम(र्म)हेभकुम्भस्थलीदलनदुर्ललो(लि)तासिधारा:(र:) [।।*५] कालेयैर्भूतधात्रि(त्री)–पतिभी(भि)

9 रुपचितानैकपापावतारैनि(र्नी)ता येषां कथापि प्रलयमभिमता कीर्त्तिमा(पा)लैरज–

10 श्रं(स्रम्) [।*] यज्ञैस्तैरश्वमेधप्रभृतिभिरमरा लम्भितास्तृप्तिमुर्व्वि(र्व्वी)मुद्रि(द्ध)तारातिपक्षक्ष–[य]

11 कृतिपु(प)टुना श्रीनिवासेन येन । [।*६] तस्योत्खाताखिलारेर्म्मरुदिव जननो[द्*]भा–

Second Plate: Second Side

12 स्वदुष्णांड्शु(ष्णांशु)तेजा[:*] शु(शू)रा(रो) मानी दयालुर्ण्ण(र्न)रपति[र*]यश(शो)–भीतदेवस्तनु(नू)ज[:*] । त्मा(मा)तङ्गान्योति[तुङ्गान्व](न्ब)–

13 हलमदमुचश्चारुवक्त्ना[न्*] प्रचण्डा[न्*] व(ब)द्ध्वाकर्षत्यखि[न्*]न[:*] पुनरपि तयते यत्नत[5][:*] सप्रग[ल्भ][:* ।।] [७*] त–

14 स्या भवत्स[क*]लशि(शा)स्त्रविशेस(ष)व(वे)दि(दी) श्रीधर्म्मराजदेव[6] इतिसु–(सू)नुरधीतशास्त्र: [।*] यस्यातिनिर्म्म–

15 लयश[: *]परिवर्द्धमान(नं) पादा हरेरिव न माइ(यि)तमा त्रिलोक्या[:* ।।] [८*] निराश्रयै[:*] प्रयत्न(त्ने)न गुणै[:*]

16 स परिवारित:[।*] वैमुख्यादीर्षया चैव सर्व्वदो[7]षैर्व्विवर्ज्ज(र्ज्जि)त: [।। *९] राज्यं लब्ध–(ब्ध्वै)व दर्प्पादवि–

17 गणितत[या] माधव(वो) जे(ज्ये)ष्ठभावा:(वान्) तेषादस्मादपात्नं[8] कृतविषय(म)मति ।[9] वि(र्वि)ग्रहे फा–

18 सिकां(का)यां(याम्) [।*] युद्धक्षोभे[ण] भग्न:(ग्रा) नृपतिप(व)रमवशौ:[10] स(सं)श्री(श्रि)तस्ति(स्ती)वराख्यं(ख्यम्) ।[। *१०][11] शौय(र्यं) श्री–

19 यो(र्यौ)वनं राज्यमेकैकं प(म)दक(का)रकं(कम्) । सर्व्व(र्व्वं) **श्रीमानभीतस्य**[निर्व्वि]–कारमुपस्थितं[तम्] । [।*११] तुरगखु–

20 राभिघातविदल[द्*]धरणि(णी)तलजं [ज*]यगज[कर्ण्ण*] चामरविधु(धू)ननविस्फुरि–[तम्*] सुभट[फर*]प्रर्प्परसनि–[12]

5. The Nivina charter reads नवते यत्कृत:

6. देव may be omitted to suit the metre.

7. दी was originally engraved.

8. Read देशादस्मादपास्तुं as in other records.

9. The punctuation is superfluous.

10. Read असौ.

11. The last foot of the verse has been omitted due to the inadvertance of the scribe.

12. Read प्रसर्प्पण.

21 रुध(द्ध)क[कु*] द्र[13] **कोन्तलयिवासकात्**[14] श्रीशैलोद्भवकुलतिलको महामखवाजप(पे)-याश्व

22 मेघावभृ[थ]स्नाननिर्व्वर्त्ति[त]प्रखा(ख्या)तकीर्त्तिक्रमपरमम(मा)हेश्वरा(रो) मातापितृपादानुध्यात[:*] श्रि(श्री)

23 **धर्म्मराजे(ज) [दे]व**[:*] कुशली अस्मिं(स्मिन्) कोङ्गोदमण्डले श्रीसामन्तमह(हा)-सामन्तमहाराजराजन-

Third Plate: First Side

24 [करा]जपुत्रा[न्*]तरङ्ग[15] दण्डनाना[16]यकदण्डपासि(शि)कोपरिक[स्तद्वि]नियुक्त[क]-व्यवहा-

25 रिण[:*] सकरणां(णान्) व्रा(ब्रा)ह्मणपुरोगादिजनपदाञ्च[17] श्चा(चा)टभटवल्लभजाति-(ती)यां(यान्)

26 यथार्ह(र्हं) पू[ज*]यत्याज्ञापयति च विदितमस्तु भवता[म्*।] किराततलक[18] विषयस-

27 म्वद्ध(म्बद्ध)शिवाविवास[19]ग्रामोयं चतु[: *]सीमोपलक्षित[: *] कौण्डिण्य(न्य)सगोत्राय

28 वाजसनेयचरणाय भट(ट्ट)शुभदेवस्य(देवाय)मातापित्रोरात्मनस्य(श्च)पुण्याभिवृ-

29 द्धये सलिलधारापुर[:*]सरेण चन्द्रार्कक्षितिसमकालमकरीकृत्य ग्रहोपरागे

30 प्रतिपादितोस्माभि: [।*] मु(उ)पभुञ्जानो(ञ्जतो) धर्म्मगौ[र*]वाय कालान्तरेना(णा)-पि न

31 कश्चिं[20] परिपन्थिना भवितव्यमिति । उक्तञ्च धर्म्मशास्त्रे [।*] व(ब)हुभिर्व्वसुधा दता(त्ता)राजभि[:*]

32 सगरादिभि:[। *] यस्य यस्य यद(दा)भूमि[स्*]तस्य तस्य तदा फलं(लम्) । [।*१२] मा भु(भू)दफलशङ्का व[:*]

33 परदते(त्ते)ति पार्थिव(वा:) [।*] स्वदाना[त्*] फलमानन्त्यं परदता(त्ता)नुपालन(ने) [।।*१३] स्वदता(त्तां) परदताम्वा(त्तां वा) यो हरे-

34 ति(त) वसुन्द्ध(न्ध)रा[म्*।] सु(स्व)विष्ठाय(यां)[21] कृमिर्भु(र्भू) त्रि(त्वा) पित्रि(तृ)भि [:*] सह पच्यते । [।*१४] इति कमलदला

35 म्वु(म्बु)वि(बि)न्द(न्दु)लोलां श्री(श्रि)यमनुचिन्त्य मनुष्यजीवितं(त)ञ्च [।*] सकलमिदमुदाहृतञ्च वु(बु)द्धा(द्ध्वा)

13. The Banpur grant of Dharmarāja reads the rest of the verse as द्रगनं बलरज एव यस्य जयति द्विषतां ध्वजिनीं(नीम्) ।।.

14. Rajaguru reads कनकोन्तलवासकात्.

15. The inscription has a mark here resembling the *anusvāra* above the letter र.

16. One ना is redundant.

17. Read पदांश्च.

18. Rajaguru reads राजतिलक.

19. D.C. Sircar reads शिवा[धि]वास.

20. Read केनचित्.

21. These letters appear to have been written over some previously engraved letters.

Third Plate: Second Side

36 न हि पुरुषै[:*] परकीर्त्तयो वी(वि)लोप्या: [।।*१५] विद्युद्विलासतरलमवग-

37 म्य स[म्यग्*] लोकस्थिति:(तिं)यशसी(सि) शक्तमनोभिरुचै(च्चै:)[22] [।*] नित्यं परो [पकृति*]मात्ररतै[र्भवद्भि*]ध(र्ध)र्मा-

38 भिराधन[23]परैरनुमोदितव्यं(व्यम्) [।।[24] *१६] दूत्त(त)कोच्च [स]चि[व][25] धर्म्मचन्द्र- [:* ।] लिखितं सा-

39 न्धिविग्रहिकं(क) भोगी(गि)सामन्त(न्तेन) [।।*] लाञ्छितं पेटापालजे(ज्ये)ष्ठसिङ्घे- (सिंहे)न [।*] उ-

40 त्क(त्की)र्ण्णं [थ]विरवृद्धेनेति । **चैच्च(त्र)वदि अमृ(मा)वास्यी[26] स्ससन्द्धा[27]** १०. ०.

41 । १० . ० . ८ ।[28]

ABSTRACT

Line 1 contains a fragmentary verse which is continued from the previous plate. Lines 1-21 contain eleven verses which are also found in the other extant records of the reigning king **Dharmarāja-Mānabhīta,** the donor of the present grant. The verses describe the achievements of the king and his predecessors. Lines 17-18 contain an incomplete verse which informs that Dharmarāja had an elder brother, Mādhava by name; whom he defeated on the battlefield of Phāsikā. Mādhava took shelter with a king named Tivara. Lines 21 to 23 record that Dharmarāja-Mānabhīta, a devotee of god Mahēśvara, who was the son's son of the performer of the *aśvamēdha* and *vājapēya* sacrifices and who was an ornament of Śailōdbhava family, issued an order from the residence at **Kōntalayi**, addressed to the officers and feudatories and others of Kōṅgōda-maṇḍala, relating to the grant of the village Śivāvivāsa, situated in the district of Kirātatalaka along with its four boundaries. The village was granted in favour of Bhaṭṭa Śubhadēva of the Kauṇḍinya *gōtra* and Vājasanēya *caraṇa,* with libations of water, on the occasion of a solar eclipse, for the increase of religious merit of the donor and his parents. The grant was made permanent so as to exist till the sun, the moon and the earth would endure. It was issued by making

22. Rajaguru reads मनोभिकारै.
23. Rajaguru reads परोदयरतैभि.
24. A *visarga* sign is seen instead of the punctuation mark.
25. Rajaguru reads दूतकोच्चूचित.
26. Read अमावस्या.
27. Read सम्वत्; Rajaguru reads स्वस्ति सम्वत् and omits the numerical symbols following this word. There are some indistinct marks, which appear to have been erased by the engraver perhaps to incise them in the following line.
28. Rajaguru reads the symbols as 10.0.5; Sircar suggests that the intended reading may be 10.8, i.e., 18 which would indicate the regnal year of the reigning king.

it a rent-free holding for the enjoyment of the donee. Lines 30 and 31 record the usual mandate to others not to make any obstruction in the donee's enjoyment of the grant. Lines 31-38 record five of the usual imprecatory and benedictory verses stated to have been quoted from the *Dharmąśāstra,* related to the merits of donating land and the consequences of confiscating one's land. The officers responsible for the preparation and execution of the charter have been mentioned in lines 38-40. The minister (*saciva*) named Dharmacandra acted as the *dūtaka* or the executor of the grant. The *sandhivigrahika* (or the minister for war and peace), whose name was Sāmanta and who was also designated as a *bhōgin,* endowed the charter with a seal. The person named Tha(Stha)vira-vṛddha engraved the charter. Lines 40-41 contain the **date** of the issue of the charter, though the reading is very much doubtful due to unsatisfactory preservation of the letters. It is stated to have been issued in **the year 10, 0, 8 (?) in the month of Caitra,** on **the day of amāvasyā during the dark fortnight**. The year may be the **18th regnal year** of the donor.

NO. 58: KONDEDDA GRANT OF DHARMARĀJA, YEAR 30

Provenance : Not known.
References : Y.R. Gupte, *EI*, Vol. XIX (1927-28), pp. 265 ff. and plate; and S.N. Rajaguru, *IO*, Vol. I, Pt. 2 (1958), pp. 235 ff.
Language : Sanskrit, in verse, except the grant portion.
Metre : Verses 1, 3, 11, 14, 18 *śārdūlavikrīḍita;* verses 2, 5, 6, 8, 12 *vasantatilakā;* verses 4, 13, 16, 19-21 *anuṣṭubh;* verse 7 *indravajrā;* verses 9, 10, 15 *sragdharā;* verse 17 *nardaṭaka.*
Script : Eastern variety of the northern class of alphabet of about the eighth century A.D.
Date : 30th regnal year (?), the eighth day of the bright fortnight in the month of Vaiśākha.

TEXT[1]

First Plate

1 सिद्धम्[2] स्वस्ति [।।*] इन्दोर्द्धौतमृणालतन्तुभिरिवः[3] श्लिष्टाः करैः कोमलैर्व(र्ब)द्धाहेररुणै[ः]
2 त्स्फु(स्फु)रत्फणिमणेर्द्दिग्धः(ग्ध)प्रभासोङ् शु(सोंशु)भिः[4][।*]पार्वत्या[ः*]-
सकचग्रहव्यतिकरव्यावृत्तव(ब)-
3 न्धश्लथा गङ्गाम्भः प्लुतिभिन्नभस्मकणिका[ः*] शम्भोर्जटा[ः*] पान्तु वः ।। [१*]
प्राङ् शु(प्रांशु)र्महेभकर-
4 पीवरचारुव(बा)हु[ः*] कृष्णाश्मसंचयविभेदविशालवक्षा[ः* ।] राजीवकोमलदलाय-
5 [त]लोचनान्तः ख्यातः कलिङ्गजनतासु पुलिन्दसेन : ।। [२*] तेनेत्थं गुणिनापि सत्व(त्त्व)-
6 [म]हता नेष्टं भुवो मण्डलं शक्तो यः परिपालनाय जगतः को नाम स स्यादिति [।*]
7 प्रत्यादिष्टविभु(भू)त्सवेन भगवानाराधितः शाश्वतस्तच्चित्तानुगुणं विधित्सु-
8 रदिशद्वाञ्छां स्वयम्भूरपि ।। [३*] स शिलाशकलोद्भेदी तेनाप्यालोक्य धी-
9 मता [।*] परिकल्पितसद्वङ्शः(द्वंशः) प्रभुः शैलोद्भवः कृतः ।। [४*] शैलोद्भवस्य

1. From the facsimile in *EI*, Vol. XIX (1927-28).
2. Expressed by a symbol.
3. The *visarga* is superfluous.
4. Gupte reads प्रभासाङ्शु(सांशु)भिः .

10 कुलजोर[ण]भीत आसीद्येनासकृत्कृतभियां द्विषदङ्गनानां~[5] [। *] ज्योत्स्नाप्रवो(बो)-
11 धसमये स्वधियैव सार्धमाकम्पितो नयनपक्ष्मजलेषु चन्द्रः ।। [५*] तस्याभव-
12 द्विवु(बु)धपालसमस्य सूनु[:*] श्रीसैन्यभीत इति भूमिपतिर्गरीयां(यान्) [।*] यं प्राप्य
13 ने(नै)कशतनागघट्टाविघट्टलव्ध(ब्ध)प्रसादविजयं मुमुद(दे) धरित्री ।। [६*]तस्यापि
14 वङ्शे(वंशे)थ यथार्थनामा जातोयशोभीत इति क्षितीशः [।*] येन प्ररूढोपि
15 शुभैश्चरित्रैर्मृष्टः कलङ्क[:*] कलिदर्पणस्य ।।[७*] जातोथ तस्य तनयः

Second Plate: First Side

16 [सु]कृती समस्तसीमन्तिनीनयनषट्पदपुण्डरीकः[।*] श्रीसैन्यभीत इति भूमिप-
17 तिम्म(र्म्म)हेभकुम्भस्थलीदलनदुर्ललिती(ता)सिधारा(रः) ।। [८*] कालेयैर्भूतधात्रीपति-
18 भि[रुप]चितानेकपापावतारैर्न्नीतां(ता) येषां कथापि प्रलयमभिमत(ता) की-
19 [र्त्ति]मा(पा)लैरजस्त्रं [।*] यज्ञैस्तैरश्वमेधप्रभृतिभिरमरालम्भितास्तृप्तिमुर्व्वी-
20 मुद्दृप्तारातिपक्षक्षयकृतिपटुना श्रीनिवासेन येन ।। [९*] तस्योत्खाताखिला-
21 रेर्मरुदिव जननोद्भ्रास्वदुष्णाङ्शु(ष्णांशु) तेजा[:*] शु(शू)रो मानी दयालुर्नरप-
22 तिरयशोभीतदेवस्तनूजः[।*] मातङ्गान्योतितुङ्गाद्व(न्ब) हलमदमुच-
23 श्चारुवक्त्रां(क्त्रान्) प्रचण्डां(ण्डान्) व(ब)द्ध्वाकर्षत्यखिन्नः पुनरपि तयते[6] यत्नत[:] सप्र-
24 गल्भः ।। [१०*] केचिच्छैलगुहोदरेषु नियता धूमावलीपायिनः अन्ये वायुफला-
25 म्वु(म्बु)भक्षनिरता[:*] केचिन्निराहारका[:]~[7] [।*] इत्थं योगजुषो विहाय वसतिं ध्यायन्ति [दिव्यं]
26 पदं चित्रन्म(त्रं म)ध्यमराजदेवगुणधृद्राज्येपि तत्प्राप्तवां(वान्) ।। [११*] तस्याभवत्सकल-[शा]-
27 स्त्रविशेषवेदी **श्रीधर्म्मराज** इति सूनुरधीतशास्त्र[:*।] तस्यातिनिर्मलय[शः]
28 परिवर्द्धमान(नं) पादा हरेरिव न मायितमात्रि(त्रि)लोक्या[:] ।। [१२*] निराश्रयैः प्रयत्नेन
29 गुणैः स परिवारितः [।*] वैमुख्यादीर्षया चैवः[8] सर्व्वदोषैर्व्विवर्जित[:] ।। [१३*]

Second Plate: Second Side

30 काले हन्ति रिपून्महारणशतव्यापारलव्धो(ब्धो)न्नतीः(तीन्) काले स(भ)क्तिमुपैति शुभ्र(भ्र)-
31 चवि(रि)तैः शम्भोः कथाविस्तरैः [।*] काले धर्म्मविवेचनाय निरतो व्रा(ब्रा)ह्मण्यमध्ये

5. There is a small horizontal stroke perhaps, indicating a punctuation mark.
6. This word has been read differently in the Śailōdbhava grants. The Banpur plates of Madhyamarāja read दयते, whereas the Parikud plates of the same king has तयते; the Nivina charter of his son Dharmarāja reads नवते and the Chandeswar plates of Dharmarāja read तयते.
7. A small horizontal stroke is found here, perhaps indicating a punctuation mark.
8. The *visarga* is superfluous.

32 स्थितः क्रोञ्चारेरिव यस्य चेष्टितमलं लोकः(कैः) समालोक्यते ।। [१४*] राज्यं लव्धा(ब्ध्वै)व
33 दर्प्पादविगणिततयो(या) माघवोज्येष्ठ भावां(वान्) देशादस्मादपास्तुं कृतविषममति-
34 र्विग्रहे फासिकायां [।*] युद्धक्षोभेण भग्नो नृपतिप(व)रमसौ संशृ(श्रि)तस्त्री(स्ती)वराख्य-(ख्यं)-
35 पश्चात्तेनापि सार्द्धं पुनरपि विजितो विन्द्ध्यपादेषु जीर्ण्णः ।। [१५*] शौर्यं श्रीर्यौव-
36 नं राज्यमेकैकं मदकारकं [।*] सर्व्वन्(र्व्वं) **श्रीमानभीतस्य** निर्व्विकारमुपस्थि-
37 त[म्*] ।। [१६*] तुरगखुराभिघातविदलद्धरणीतलजं जयगजकर्ण्णचाम-
38 रविधूत(न)नविस्फुरितं [।*] सुभटफरप्रसर्प्पणनिरुद्धककुव्ग(द्व)गनं व(ब)-
39 लरज एव यस्य जयति द्विषतां ध्वजिनीं(नीम्) ।। [१७*] आरच्य प्रसभं घटा गजगणै-रश्वी-
40 यपादातकैः जित्वात्या(न्या)न्व(न्ब)लशालिनो नृपवरानागत्य दृष्टेर्भुवं(वम्) [।*] युद्धे भीमप-
41 राक्रमेण विजिता निर्वृ(वृ)त्पदं प्रापिताः दृश्यन्ते भवनाङ्गणे प्रतिदिनं प्रातः
42 प्रणामार्थिन[:*] ।। [१८*] विजय**सौम्यपुरवासका**च्छ्रीशैलोद्भवकुलतिलको
43 महामखवाजपेयाश्वमेधावभृथस्नाननिर्व्वर्त्तितसूनोस्तनयो व(ब)हुवि-
44 धमत्तवारणवरतुरगपदातिशस्त्रसंपातसंकुलो व(ब)ह्वाहव-

Third Plate: First Side

45 विनिहतशत्रुरनेकविक्रमाक्रान्तसकलभूमण्डलप्रथितयश(शा)श्चा(श्च)तुर्द्दन्त[9]-
46 संग्रामादसकृत(ल्)लव्ध(ब्ध)प्रताप[:*] परममाहेश्वरो मातापितृपाद(दा)नुध्यातः **श्रीध-**
47 **र्म्मराजदेवः** कुशली ।। अस्मिं(स्मिन्) कोङ्गोदमण्डले श्रीसामन्तमहासामन्तम-
48 हाराजराज(जा)नकराजपुत्रान्तरङ्गदा(द)ण्डनायकदाण्डपाशिकोपरिक(का)स्तद्विनि-
49 युक्तकव्यवहारि[ण]: सकरणानन्यांश्च व्रा(ब्रा)ह्मणपुरोगादिवैषयिकजन-
50 पदान्यथार्हन्पू(र्हं पू)जयति मानयत्याज्ञापयति च विदितमस्तु भवता(तां) खि-
51 ड्डिङ्गहारविषयसम्व(म्ब)द्धकोण्डेड्डुग्रामार्द्धोयं अकरीकृत्य-
52 [कौ]शिकसगोत्राय वाजसनेयचरणाय औदलवत् देवरात-
53 विश्वामित्त्र(त्र)प्रवराय अग्निहोत्त्री(त्री) भट्टगोणदेवस्वामिने मातापित्रोरात्मनश्च-
54 पुण्यभिवृद्धये सलिलधारापुरस्सरेणाचन्द्रार्कं[10] कालमुपभुञ्जानस्य ध-
55 र्म्मगौरवान्न केनचिद्विघाते वर्त्तितव्यमिति ।। उक्तञ्च धर्म्मशास्त्रे [।*] व(ब)हुभिर्व्व-
56 सुधा दत्ता राजभिः सगरादिभिः [।*] यस्य यस्य यदा भूमिस्तस्य तस्य तदा फ-
57 लं(लम्) ।। [१९*] स्वदत्तां परदत्तां म्वा(वा) यो हरेत वसुन्द्धरां [।*] स्वविष्टायां कृमिर्भूत्वा पितृभि[:*]
58 सह पच्यते ।। [२०*] मा भूदफलशङ्का वः परदत्तेति पार्थिवा[:*] स्वदानात्फलमा-

---

9. Gupte reads श्चानुद्दन्तिः .
10. Some words like दत्तः, यथा ....have been left out by the scribe inadvertently.

59 नन्त्यं परदत्तानुपालनं ।। [२१*] दूतकोत्राधिकृतचरम्पदेव(वो)लिखितं

Third Plate: Second Side

60 [सु ?] दामोदरेण लाञ्छितं [पे]टपाल. . . .[11]
61 उत्कीर्ण्णं स्थविरा(र)वृद्धेनेति [।।] **सम्वत् ३० वैशाख शुदि ८** (?)[12] [।।*]

ABSTRACT

The contents of the text up to line 41 are the same as those of the other known records of the reigning king **Dharmarāja-Mānabhīta**, who was the illustrious son of Madhyamarāja of the Śailōdbhava dynasty. Lines 42-55 record that the present charter was issued from the victorious camp at **Saumyapura** by the king. The royal order relating to the grant was addressed to the royal officers and the residents of the locality informing that the king granted half of the village Kōṇḍēḍḍē situated in the district of Khiḍḍiṅgahāra, by making it a tax-free endowment, to the brāhmaṇa named Bhaṭṭa Gōṇadēvasvāmin of the Kauśika *gōtra,* Vājasanēya *caraṇa* and Audala, Dēvarāta and Viśvāmitra *pravaras,* who maintained the sacrificial fire. The donee was to enjoy the grant as long as the sun and the moon would endure and without obstruction from anybody. Lines 56-59 contain three of the usual imprecatory and benedictory verses. The *dūtaka* (or the executor of the charter) was Carampadeva. Lines 60-61 record that the charter was written by Dāmōdara, endowed or registered with a seal by a person designated as *pēṭāpāla* (or keeper of the records) and engraved by Sthaviravṛddha. The **date** of issue of the charter is given at the end, as **the eighth day of the bright fortnight of the month of Vaiśākha,** in the **30th regnal year** of the reigning king.

11. The facsimile is illegible here due to the corroded nature of the plate. Gupte reads the designation of पेटापाल (keeper of records) as टापल and takes it as the name of the person who endowed the charter with a seal.
12. The second half of this line, particularly the portion mentioning the date, is greatly damaged and the reading of the numerical symbols is doubtful.

NO. 59: TEKKALI PLATES OF MADHYAMARĀJA III

Provenance : Tekkali, Srikakulam district, Andhra Pradesh.

References : H.P. Shastri, *JBORS*, Vol. IV, Pt. 1 (1918), pp. 162-67 and plate; S.N. Rajaguru and Gopavandhu-Vidyabhusan, *Praci*, Vol. III, Pt. 2 (1933), pp. 79-91; *ArEP* of 1935-36, p. 64; Bhandarkar's *List*, No. 1676; and S.N. Rajaguru, *IO*, Vol. I, Pt. 2 (1958), pp. 241-47.

Language : Sanskrit, in verse.

Metre : Verses 1, 11, *śārdūlavikrīḍita*; verses 2, 10, 12 *vasantatilakā*; verses 3, 4-8 *anuṣṭubh*; verse 9 *indravajrā*; verse 13 *sragdharā*.

Script : Eastern variety of the northern alphabet of about the eighth century A.D.

TEXT[1]

First Side

1 [अन्ये*] वायुफ[ला*]म्वु(म्बु)भक्षनिरता:[2] केचिन्निराहारका: । इ[3] इत्थं योगजुषो
2 विहाय व[स*]न्ति(ती) ध्यायन्ति दिव्यं पदं वि[4]चित्रं मध्यमराजदेवगुण-
3 धृद्राज्येपि तत्प्रासवान्[5] ।। [१*] तस्याभवत्सकलशास्त्रविशेषवेदि(दी) श्रीधर्म-
4 राज इति सूनुरधि(धी)तशास्त्र: । यस्यातिनिर्म्मलयश: परिवर्द्धमानपा-
5 दौ हरेरिव न मायिन (त)म(मा)र्त्त्य(त्रि)लोके(क्या:) ।। [२*] निराश्रयै: प्रयत्नेन गुणै: स परिवा-
6 रित:[।*]वैमुख्यादिरिषया(दीर्षया) चैवसर्व्वदोषै[:*] विवर्ज्जित: ।। [३*] शौर्यं श्रीर्यौवनं रा-

---

1. From the facsimile in *JBORS*, Vol. IV, Pt. 1 (1918). This is the middle plate of a set of three, the first and the third plates of the set being lost. Some known verses of the Śailōdbhava grants and the known kings of this family mentioned in this plate enable us to assume that the plate belonged to the Śailōdbhava dynasty.
2. Shastri reads भक्षणरता: .
3. The letter is superfluous.
4. The letter वि is redundant.
5. Shastri reads धृद्राज्यं पितु:(त)प्रासवन् ।। .

7 [ज्यमे]कैकं मदकारण(कम्) [। *] सर्व्वं[6] श्रीमानभि(भी)तस्य निर्विकारमु[प*]स्थितं-
(तम्)[7] ।। [४*]

8 [सक]लगुणार्ज्जितकि(की)र्ति(र्त्ति)स्तस्याभूदौरसस्तु यः सूनुः । श्री[मान्*] मध्यम-

9 राजो नृपतिमणिम(मु)क्तालि(ली)ढपादय(यु)ग्मः[8] ।। [५*] क्षि(क्षी)रोदान्मधुसुदनं गतव-

10 ति(ती) तस्या(स्मा)द्रघूणां कुलं याता या शशी(शि)नस्ततोपि[9] व(ब)हुधा मर्त्येश्वरा-

11 णामपि [।*] मत्वैव(वं) कुलदैत्यल(लं) नरपतिः(तेः) सामान्य भोग्या पुरा [।*]
[सा*] लक्ष्मि(क्ष्मी)[ः*] कृतवत्य[10]

12 स्तनुर[भू*]च्छ्री(च्छ्री)मानभीतात्मजः ।। [६*] स्फारोत्खातः कृपाणनिर्म्मलकर [ः*]
श्रीमानतुङ्गोद्ध-

13 तान्[11] वालेनैव[हताश्च*] येनरिद(प)वः प्राप्तं महि(ही)मण्डलं । स्वर्याते पितरि प्रतापविभवे
ध-

14 र्म्मे कनिष्ठः सदा श्रीमान्य(नय)शोभयात्परिगतः[12] ख्यातिं क्षितौ प्राप्तवान् ।। [७*]

15 अरातिकरिकुम्भानां यस्यास्ति[13] भिदुरः करः । श्रीरणक्षोभ सज्ञानं ततो

Second Side

16 लोकोप्यचि(ची)करत् ।। [८*] तस्मिन्नरातितिमिरं प्रसरं विभिद्य कृत्वा जनस्य

17 सफलामुदयेन चेष्टां(ष्टाम्) । अस्तं समस्तजगदेकमहाप्रदि(दी)पे भूमे-

18 र्गते दिनकृति(ती)व विधेर्नियोगात् ।। [९*] भ्राता तस्य नसुन्दपर्वतशिरो रत्न(त्ना)धिता-

19 पि द्युताः पैतृव्योल्लपराजः इत्यवनिपो जात[ः स शक्रोपमः] । को-

20 पाकृष्ट कृपाणमात्रक स्फुटः संख्ये विजित्य द्विषः राजाश्वं (?) पुनरा(रु)त्तर(रा)-

21 ङ्गतमपि प्रापामलं यो यशः ।। [१०*] पक्षच्छेदभयात्तु भूभृदपरव्यापार-

22 [लव्धो(ब्धो)] न्नते[14]र्गम्भि(म्भी)रा दुरुस्व(स)त्वयोगमहिमा लव्ध्वा(ब्ध्वा) पृथ(थि)व्यां
ततः । तस्य-

23 [श्री]र्युवराजतैल्लपनिभात्य[ः*] प्राप्त[15] जन्मोदयो भूयो **मध्यमराज**[वंश]य-

24 [शसा] वा(बा)ल्ये [ऽ*] भवद्भूपतिः ।। [११*] दर्पोद्धतं(तान्) व(ब)ली(लि)रिपू-
[न्*] समरादु[दस्य] संयम्य पै(पौ)रुषधन[ः*]

25 निजविक्रमेण[16] । लव्ध्वा(ब्ध्वा) जयश्रियमदभ्र रिपुप्रतापा[त्*] नारायणायितमिह-

---

6. Shastri reads सर्व्वैः.
7. Shastri reads निर्विकारं म[नः] स्थितम् ।.
8. Shastri reads नियतिमणिमक्त(मुक्ता)ली(लि)ढ पादयशः ।।.
9. Shastri reads सुतेपि.
10. Rajaguru reads रुद्रव[ल][सुत].
11. Shastri reads पूयमाङ्कतुङ्गोद्धता.
12. Shastri reads श्रीमानयुधाभयात्परिगतः
13. Shastri reads यस्यास्ति.
14. Shastri reads लोकन्नते.
15. Shastri reads निभात् स(यम्)प्राप्य.
16. Shastri reads स यम्यमेरुजधनं न्यजयिक्रमेण.

26 क्षितिपेन येन ।। [१२*] लोकालोक(कं) विलंघ्य[न्*] स्फुरदम[ल*]-
करोद्दामरश्मिप्रतापान् शोभाप्रा-
27 सा प्रकाशभ्रमदुरुवितमः संघभि(र्वि)च्छिन्नमु(मू)र्त्तेः । भूमेरालोकहेतोरिपु-
28 जलधिमा(म)हामेखलाभूतवह्नेः कृत्स्न्यां(त्स्नं) व्याप्य(स)प्रयातं हररा(रु)[चि*]हसित
यद्यशः (यशशो) व-
29 न्द(न्द्य)विस्वं(श्वम्)[17] ।।[१३*]

ABSTRACT

Of the twelve and a half verses in this stray copper-plate grant, three and half at the beginning are found in other published Śailōdbhava grants. The remaining nine verses are known for the first time. Verses 5 and 6 describe the career and achievements of Madhyamarāja, son of Śrī-Mānabhīta. He has been described as the one who obtained boon from goddess Lakṣmī. He is mentioned in verse 7 as having gained the sovereignty of the earth by vanquishing his foes during his very childhood after the demise of his father and having acquired fame on the earth. In verse 8, he is described as a powerful king whom people named *raṇakṣōbha* Verses 9-11 record that on the death of this king, his cousin Allaparāja got himself crowned as the king for some time and he also earned great name and fame. He was succeeded by **Madhyamarāja III**, born of prince Tailapanibha. After getting himself duly coronated, his fame spread over all parts of the earth. Verses 12-13 are written in praise of the reigning king, **Madhyamarāja III**, who has been compared to god Nārāyaṇa, whose strength shone like fire amidst his enemies and whose fame spread all over his kingdom.

17. The reading of this line is very doubtful. Shastri reads the rest of the line as स्था स्थानादास यशर्स्यादित वि(भि)षय यशोभीरु(र)[वा]ध । भि सूक्तेः त. . . .

NO. 60: TWO INCOMPLETE PALIMPSESTS FROM DHARAKOTE

Provenance : Dharakote, Ganjam district, Orissa.
Reference : S.N. Rajaguru, *IO*, Vol. I, Pt. 2 (1958), pp. 248-53.
Language : Sanskrit, in verse.
Metre : Verses 1, 3, 5, 6, 7, 9 *śārdūlavikrīḍita*; verse 2 *vasantatilakā*; verse 4 *anuṣṭubh*.

TEXT[1]

First Plate[2]

1 सिद्धम्[3] स्वस्ति [।।*] इन्द(न्दो)र्द्धे(र्द्धौ)तमृणालतन्तुभिरिव श्लिष्टा[:*] करैः कोमलैर्व्व-(र्ब्ब)द्धा-

2 हे[र*]रुणै : स्फुरत्फणिमणौ(णे)र्दिग्धप्रभाशोङ्शु(सोंशु)भि: [।*] पार्व्वत्या[:*]सक-

3 चग्रहव्यतिकरव्याव्रि(वृ)त्तव(ब)न्द्धश्लथा गङ्गाम्भ:प्लुतिभिन्नभस्मकंणि-

4 का: शम्भोर्जटा[:*] पान्तु वः ।। [१ *] प्राङ्शु (प्रांशु)र्म्महेभकरपि(पी)वरचारुवा(बा)-हुः कृष्णा-

5 ष्म(श्म)सञ्चयविभेदविशालवक्षाः । राजीवकोमलदलायतलो-

6 चा(च)नान्तः ख्यातः कलिङ्गजनतासु पुलिन्दसेनः [।।*२] तेनेत्थं गुणिना-

7 पि सत्व(त्त्व)महता नि(ने)ष्टं भुवो मण्डल:(लं) शक्तो यः परिपालनाय ज-

8 गतः को नाम स स्यादिति [।*] प्रत्यादिति(ष्ट)विभुच्छवेन भगवानाराधितः सा(शा)-

9 श्वतः तमता[4] ।। [३ *] परिकल्प(ल्पि)तसद्व(द्वं)शःत्प्र(प्र)भु[: *] शैलोद्भवः कृतः-[।।*४][5] शै-

1. From the original; the plates are now preserved in the Orissa State Museum, Bhubaneswar.
2. This is the first side of the first plate, its reverse being incised with the introductory part of a Bhañja copper-plate grant of Khiñjali-*maṇḍala* (*c.* tenth century A.D.). The middle plate of this set of three, the ring and the royal seal attached to the set are lost.
3. Expressed by a symbol.
4. These three letters are superfluous; the verse is incomplete.
5. The first foot of the verse is omitted.

10 लोद्भवस्य कुलजे(जो)रणभि(भी)ता(त) [आ*]सि(सी)त ।[6] गोत्रमुन्मीलितं दिनकृतेव मं-

Second Plate: First Side

11 होदयेन[8] [। *] संक्षिप्तमण्डलरुचश्च गता: प्रणाशमाशु द्विषो ग्रहगणा
12 इव यस्य दि(दी)प्त्या [।।*५] कालेयैर्भूत्त(त)द्धा(धा)त्रीपतिभिरुपचितान्रे(ने)कपापावतारै:[9]
13 सीतमासकृत् कृतभिया(यां)[10] द्विषदङ्गना[नां*] [। *] ज्योत्स्नाप्रवो(बो)द्ध(ध)-[समये*] स्वधियैव
14 साद्ध(र्द्ध)माकम्पितो नयनपक्ष्मजले[षु*] चन्द्र [: *।।] [६*] तस्य(स्या)भवद्विवु(बु)द्ध-(ध)पालसे(स)स(म)स्यसु(सू)-
15 नु[:*] श्रीसैन्यभीत इति भूमिपतिग्ग(र्ग)रि(री)या[न्*] य:(यं) प्राप्य नैकशतनाग-
16 घटाविघट्टलव्द्ध(ब्ध)प्रसादविजयं मु[मुदे][11] धरी(रि)तृ(त्री) [।। *७] [त*]स्यापि वङ्शे(वंशे)-
17 थ य[था*]र्थनाम(मा) जायो(तो)यशोभि(भी)त इति क्षिति(ती)स(श:)[।*] येन प्र[रू]ढोपि शुभै-
18 श्चरित्रे(त्रै)मृ(र्मृ)ष्ट[:*] कलङ्क[:*] कलिदपु(र्प)णस्य [।।*८] जातोथ [तस्य*] तनय[: *] सुकृति(ती)
19 समस्तसि(सी)मन्तिनि(नी)म(न)यनषट्पददु(पु)ण्डरि(री)क[:*।] श्रीसन्यत[12] इति भूमि-
20 पदहभ्रि कुम्भस्थलरि[13]दलम(न)द(दु)ल्ल(र्ल्ल)ली(लि)त(ता)सिध(धा)रा(र) [।।*९] जलय भूतधिराज[14]-

ABSTRACT

The charter begins with the symbol for *siddham* and the word *svasti.* Nine verses written on one side each of the two plates follow. These verses are found in the other charters issued by the kings of the Śailōdbhava family. But the verses from 3 to 6 are fragmentary in nature. The first verse is in praise of lord Śiva. The rest of the verses describe the career and achieve-

6. The punctuation is superfluous; the verse is left incomplete here, but is continued again in line 13, in the second plate.
7. The verse begins with जातेन येन कमलाकरवत्स्वगोत्र which is inadvertently omitted here. This is the tenth verse of the Buguda Plates of Mādhavavarman (No. 47).
8. Rajaguru reads सहोदयेन.
9. The verse is left incomplete.
10. This verse begins with शैलोद्भवस्य कुलजोरणभीत आसीद्येनासकृत्कृतभियां in other Śailodbhava grants.
11. Two letters are not legible due to corrosion.
12. This may be श्रीसैन्यभीत as in the other Śailōdbhava grants.
13. Read पतिर्महिभकुम्भस्थली.
14. The stanza abruptly ends here; the intended reading seems to be कालेयैर्भूतधात्रीपति. . . .

ments of the Śailōdbhava kings beginning from the legendary figures of Pulindasēna and Śailōdbhava, the founder of the dynasty. Into this dynasty was born the king named Araṇabhīta or Raṇabhīta. His son was Śrī-Sainyabhīta and into his lineage was born the king named Ayaśōbhīta or Yaśobhīta. His son was Śrī-Sainyabhīta II. The inscription abruptly ends here and the description of the achievements of this king remains incomplete as the third plate containing the rest of the grant is missing (the missing plate forms the middle or the second plate of the Bhañja charter which is engraved on the reverse sides of these plates).

BIBLIOGRAPHY

Beal, S., tr., 1884. *Buddhist Records of the Western World* (2 vols.) (London).

———, 1911. *The Life of Hiuen-Tsang* (London).

Behera, S.C., 1982. *Rise and Fall of the Sailodbhavas* (Calcutta, Punthi Pustak).

Fleet, J.F., ed., 1888. *Corpus Inscriptionum Indicarum (Gupta Inscriptions)* Vol. III (Calcutta Government Pub.).

Ganguly, G.K., 1975. *Historical Geography and Dynastic History of Orissa* (Calcutta, Punthi Pustak).

Joshi, A., 1979. *New Light on the Cultural Heritage of Orissa* (Cuttack, Banisree).

Majumdar, B.C., 1925. *Orissa in the Making* (Calcutta).

Majumdar, R.C., ed., 1954. *History and Culture of the Indian People.* "The Classical Age", Vol. III (Bombay, Bharatiya Vidya Bhavan).

———, ed., 1964. *History and Culture of the Indian People (The Age of Imperial Unity)*, Vol. IV (Bombay, Bharatiya Vidya Bhavan).

Maltby, T.J., 1918. *Ganjam District Manual* (Madras).

Misra, B., 1934. *Orissa under the Bhauma Kings* (Calcutta).

Ojha, G.H., 1959. *Bharatiya Pracina Lipimala* (Hindi) (Delhi, Munshiram Manoharlal).

Rajaguru, S.N., ed., 1958. *Inscriptions of Orissa,* Vol. I, Pt. 2 (Bhubaneswar, State Museum Pub.).

———, ed., 1960. *Inscriptions of Orissa,* Vol. II (Bhubaneswar, State Museum Pub.).

———, ed., 1961. *Inscriptions of Orissa,* Vol. III, Pt. 2 (Bhubaneswar, Orissa Sahitya Academy Pub.).

Rao, B.V. Krishna, 1942. *A History of Early Dynasties of Andhradesa* (Madras).

Row, N. Mukunda., ed., 1982. *Three Grants from Ragolu.* (Epigraphical Series No. 18 of the Archaeology & Museums, Andhra Pradesh) (Hyderabad).

Sircar, D.C., 1939. *The Successors of the Satavahanas in Lower Deccan* (Calcutta, University of Calcutta).

———, ed., 1942. *Select Inscriptions, Bearing on Indian History and Civilization,* Vol. I (Calcutta, University of Calcutta).

———, 1965. *Indian Epigraphy* (Delhi, Banaras, Patna, Motilal Banarsidass).

———, 1960. *Studies in the Geography of Ancient and Medieval India* (Delhi, Banaras, Patna, Motilal Banarsidass).

Tripathy, S., ed., 1974. *Inscriptions of Orissa,* Vol. VI (Bhubaneswar, State Museum Pub.).

———, 1986. *Early and Medieval Coins and Currency System of Orissa* (Calcutta, Punthi Pustak).
Watters, T., 1904-5. *On Yuan Chwang's Travels in India* (2 vols.) (London).

Periodicals and Reports

Banerji, R.D., 1907-8. "Patiakella Grant of Maharaja Sivaraja, (Gupta) Samvat 283', pp. 285 ff. (Calcutta).
———, 1910-11. "Grant of Madhyamaraja", *Vangiya-Sahitya-Parishad-Patrika*, Vol. XVI (Calcutta), pp. 193 ff.
———, 1911-12. "Parikud Plates of Madhyamaraja", *EI*, Vol. XI, Pt. 4 (Calcutta), pp. 281 ff.
Basak, R.G., 1935-36. "The Puri Plates of Madhavavarman-Sainyabhita", *EI*, Vol. XXIII (Delhi), pp. 122-31.
Behera, S.C., 1964. "Origin of the Mathara Dynasty of Kalinga", *OHRJ*, Vol. XXII, No. 2 (Bhubaneswar) pp. 57-59.
———, 1957. "Two Sets of Copper Plate Grants from Baranga", *OHRJ* Vol. VI, Nos. 2, 3. (Bhubaneswar), pp. 106-14.
Bhandarkar, D.R., 1903-4. "Rajim Stone Inscription" in Cousens' *PRASWI* (Bombay), p. 48.
Bhanumurty, V., 1905-52. "Duha Copper Plate Grant of Sri-Satrudamana of Devagiri (*c*.340 A.D.)", *JAHRS*, Vol. XXI (Rajahmundry), pp. 159-60.
Bhattacharya, D.C., 1930. "A Newly Discovered Copper Plate From Tippera", *IHQ*, Vol. VI, No.1 (Calcutta), pp. 45-60.
Chakravarti, N.P., 1931-32. "Nivina Copper Plate Grants of Dharmarajadeva", *EI*, Vol. XXI, Pt. 1 (Calcutta), pp. 34-41.
Das, A., 1965. "Asanapat", *OHRJ*, Vol. XIII, No. 2 (Bhubaneswar), pp. 1-8.
De, S.C., 1963-64. "Gallavalli Plates of Prthivimaharaja: Year 49" *EI*, Vol. XXXV, (Delhi), pp. 221-23.
Fleet, J. F., 1884. "Sanskrit and Old Canarese Inscriptions", *IA*, Vol. XIII (Bombay, Feb.), pp. 48-50.
———, 1884. "Sanskrit and Old Canarese Inscriptions", *IA*, Vol. XIII (Bombay, April), pp. 120-23.
Gai, G.S., 1968. "Temburu Plates of Umavarman, Year 40", *EI*, Vol. XXXVII, Pt. 7 (Delhi), pp. 337-40.
Ghoshal, R.K., 1940. "Santabommali Plates of Indravarman", *EI*, Vol. XXV (Delhi), pp. 194-98.
———, 1940. "Jirjingi Plates of Ganga Indravarman, the year 39", *EI*, Vol. XXV (Delhi), pp. 281-88.
———, 1942. "Dhavalapeta Plates of Maharaja Umavarman", *EI*, Vol. XXVI (Delhi), pp. 132-35.
———, 1942. "A Note on the Balasore Plate of Bhanu(datta), *EI*, Vol. XXVI (Delhi), pp. 209 ff.

———, 1947-48. "Bobbili Plates of Candavarman, Year 4", *EI*, Vol. XXVII, Pt. 1, pp. 33-36.

Gupte, Y.R., 1927-28. "Rithapur Plates of Bhavattavarman", *EI*, Vol. XIX (Delhi), pp. 100-4.

———, 1927-28. "Kondedda Grant of Dharmaraja", *EI*, Vol. XIX (Delhi), pp. 265-71.

Hultzsch, 1894-95. "Achyutapuram Plates of Indravarman", *EI*, Vol. III (Calcutta), pp. 127-30.

———, 1896-97. "Komarti Plates of Candavarman", *EI*, Vol. IV, Pt. 2 (Calcutta), pp. 142-45.

———, 1900-1. "Copper Plates of the Time of Sasankaraja, Gupta Samvat 300", *EI*, Vol. VI (Calcutta), pp. 143 ff.

———, 1908. "Timmapuram Plates of Visnuvardhana I Visamasiddhi", *EI*, Vol. IX (Calcutta), pp. 317 ff.

———, 1913-14. "Brhatprostha Grant of Umavarman", *EI*, Vol. XII, Pt. 1 (Calcutta), pp. 4-6.

———, 1913-14. "Ragolu Plates of Saktivarman", *EI*, Vol. XII, Pt. 1 (Calcutta), pp. 1-3.

———, 1923-24. "Urlam Plates of Hastivarman, the year 80", *EI*, Vol. XVII (Calcutta), pp. 330-34.

Jagadev, G.H., 1931-32. "A New Grant of Umavarman", *JAHRS*, Vol. VI, Pt. 1 (Rajahmudry), pp. 53-56.

Kielhorn, F., 1894-95. "Buguda Plates of Madhavavarman", *EI*, Vol. III (Calcutta), pp. 41-46.

———, 1900-1. "Aihole Inscription of Pulakesin II", *EI*, Vol. VI (Calcutta), pp. 1 ff.

———, 1900-1. "Two Grants of Dandimahadevi", *EI*, Vol. VI (Calcutta), pp. 133-42.

———, 1902-3. "A Note on the Buguda Plates of Madhavavarman", *EI*, Vol. VII, Pt. 2 (Calcutta), pp. 100-2.

Krishnamacharlu, C.R., 1931-32. "The Nala Inscription at Podagadh, 12th Year", *EI*, XXI (Delhi), pp. 153-57.

———, 1937-38. "Jurada Grant of Nettabhanja", *EI*, Vol. XXIV, Pt. 1 (Delhi), pp. 15-20.

Lal, Hira, 1907-8. "Kanker Copper Plates of Pamparajadeva, (Kalacuri Samvat 965 and 966)", *EI*, Vol. IX (Calcutta), pp. 166-70.

———, 1907-8. "Ragholi Plates of Jayavardhana II", *EI*, Vol. IX, Pt. 1 (Calcutta), pp. 41-46.

———, 1925-26. "Four Bhanja Copper Plate Grants", *EI*, Vol. XVIII (Calcutta), pp. 287-300.

Laskar, G.M., 1904. "The Khurda Copper Plate Grant of Madhava, King of Kalinga", *JASB*, Vol. LXXIII, Pt. 1 (Calcutta), pp. 282 ff.

Majumdar, B.C., 1935-36. "Maranjamura Charter of Yayati II", *JBORS*, Vol. II, Pt. 1 (Patna), pp. 53 ff.

Majumdar, N.G., 1935-36. "Mallasarul Copper Plate Inscription of Vijayasena of the Time of Gopacandra/Regnal Year 3", *EI,* Vol. XXIII (Delhi), pp. 159 ff.

———, 1935-36. "Four Copper Plates From Soro", *EI,* Vol. XXIII (Delhi), pp. 202 ff.

———, 1937-38. "Cuttack Museum Plates of Madhavavarman", *EI,* Vol. XXIV, Pt. 2 (Delhi), pp. 148-53.

Majumdar, R.C., 1935-36. "Narasimhapalli Plates of Hastivarman", *EI,* Vol. XXIII (Delhi), pp. 62-67.

———, 1935-36. "Srungavarapukota Plates of Anantavarman, King of Kalinga", *EI,* Vol. XXIII (Delhi), pp. 56-62.

———, 1936-37. "The Sailodbhava Dynasty", *JAHRS,* Vol. X, Pt. 1 (Rajahmundry), pp. 1-15.

———, 1945. "Midnapore Plates of Subhakirtti", *JASB* (Letters), Vol. XI (Calcutta), pp. 9 ff.

———, 1945. "Midnapore Copper Plates of Somadatta", *JASB* (Letters), Vol. XI (Calcutta), pp. 3-8.

Mirashi, V.V., 1924. "Gold Coils of the Three Kings of the Nala Dynasty", *JNSI,* Vol. I (Calcutta), pp. 29-35.

———, 1942. "Rajim Stone Inscription of the Nala King Vilasatunga", *EI,* Vol. XXVI (Delhi), pp. 49-58.

Misra-Vinayak, 1931. "Sailodbhava Rulers of Kongoda", *IHQ,* Vol. VII, Nos. 3, 4 (Calcutta), pp. 665-68.

———, 1936. "Ganjam Grant of Jayavarmadeva of Unmattakesari's Time", *IHQ,* Vol. XII, No. 3 (Calcutta), pp. 486-93.

Mitra, Haridas, 1935. "Balasore Copper Plate Grant of Sri-Bhanu", *IHQ,* Vol. XI, No. 4 (Calcutta), pp. 611-26.

Narasimham, M., 1935-36. "Srungavarapukota Plates of Anantavarman, King of Kalinga", *JAHRS,* Vol. VIII, Pts. 2-3 (Rajahmundry), pp. 153-60.

———, 1939-40. "Dhavalapeta Plates of Maharaja Umavarman", *JAHRS,* Vol. X, Pt. 2-3 (Rajahmundry), pp. 143-44.

Panchamukhi, R.S., 1935-36. "Tandivada Grant of Prthivimaharaja, 46th Year", *EI,* Vol. XXIII (Delhi), pp. 88-89.

———, 1940. "Kanteru Plates of Salankayana Vijayaskandavarman", *EI,* Vol. XXV (Delhi), pp. 42-47.

Pandey, H., 1919. "Grant of Dandimahadevi", *JBORS,* Vol. V, Pt. 4 (Patna), pp. 571-81.

Panigrahi, K.C., 1937-38. "Komanda Copper Plate Grant of Nettabhanja", *EI,* Vol. XXIV (Delhi), pp. 172-75.

———, 1948. "Stone Inscriptions from the Temples of Parasuramesvara and Satrughnesvara", *JASB* (Letters), Vol. XV (Calcutta), pp. 109-18.

Pargiter, F.E., 1910. "Three Copper Plate Grants from East Bengal", *IA,* Vol. XXXIX (Bombay, July), pp. 203-15.

Rajaguru, S.N. and Gopavandhu Vidyabhusan, 1933. "Tekkali Copper Plate Grant of Madhyamaraja III", *Praci*, Vol. III, Pt. 2 (Cuttack), pp. 79 ff.

Rajaguru, S.N., 1925-26. "Phulasara Plates of Kirttirajadeva", *JAHRS*, Vol. III, Pt. 1 (Rajahmundry), pp. 30-36.

———, 1927-28. "The Santha Bomvali Copper Plate Grant of Nandavarman", *JAHRS*, Vol. II, Pt. 3-4 (Rajahmundry), pp. 185-89.

———, 1928. "The Korashanda Copper Plate Grant of Visakhavarman", *JBORS*, Vol. XIV, Pt. 2 (Patna), pp. 282-84.

———, 1929-30. "Dharakota Copper Plate Grant of the Kara King Subhakaradeva of Orissa", *JAHRS*, Vol. IV, Pts. 3-4 (Rajahmundry), pp. 189-94.

———, 1930. "Puri Copper Plate Grant of Dharmaraja (Samvat 512 or 590 A.D.)", *JBORS*, Vol..XVI, Pt. 2 (Patna), pp. 176-85.

———, 1947. "Terasinga Plates of Tustikara", *JKHRS*, Vol. II, Nos. 2-3 (Bolangir), pp. 107 ff.

———, 1947-48. "Banpur Grant of Madhyamaraja", *JKHRS*, Vol. II, No. 1 (Bolangir), pp. 59-60.

———, 1947-48. "Chandesvar Plates of Dharmaraja", *JKHRS*, Vol. II, No. 1 (Bolangir), pp. 65 ff.

———, 1950. "Kanas Plates of Sri-Lokavigraha", *JKHRS*, Vol. III, Nos. 1-3 (Bolangir), pp. 261-66.

———, 1952. "Sumandala Plates of Dharmaraja of the Time of Prthivivigraha of the Gupta Samvat 250", *OHRJ*, Vol. I, No. 1 (Cuttack), pp. 66-69.

———, 1953-54. "Two Copper Plate Grants of Madhavavarman (Sri Sainya-bhita)", *OHRJ*, Vol. II, Nos. 3-4 (Bhubaneswar), pp. 6-24, 179 ff.

———, 1953-54. "Olasing Plate of Bhanudatta", *OHRJ*, Vol. II, No. 1 (Bhubaneswar), pp. 31-46.

———, 1957. "Pandiapathar Copper Plate Inscription of Maharaja-dhiraja Bhimasena of Nala Dynasty", *OHRJ*, Vol. VI, Nos. 2-3 (Bhubaneswar), pp. 97-102.

———, 1958. "Two Grants from Ganjam", *OHRJ*, Vol. VII, No. 2 (Bhubaneswar), pp. 83-90.

———, 1963. "Jayarampur Copper Plate Inscription of the Time of Gopacandra", *OHRJ*, Vol. XI, No. 4 (Bhubaneswar), pp. 206-33.

———, 1964. "Erbang Plate of Sambhuyasas, Samvat 235", *OHRJ*, Vol. XII, No. 3 (Bhubaneswar), pp. 113-22.

Ramachandran, T.N., 1948-49. "Inscriptions from Sitabhinji, Keonjhar District, Orissa", *JAHRS*, Vol. XIX, Pt. 3-4 (Rajahmundry), pp. 191-202.

Ramdas, G., 1931-32. "Koroshanda Copper Plate of Visakhavarman", *EI*, Vol. XXI, Pt. 1 (Calcutta), pp. 23-25.

———, 1932. Chicacole Plates of Anantavarman's Son Madhukamarnavadeva, dated 526 Ganga Era", *JBORS*, Vol. XVIII, Pt. 3 (Patna), pp. 272-75.

———, 1943. "Kesaribeda Plates of Nala Arthapati-Bhattaraka", *JBORS*,

Vol. XXXIV (Patna), pp. 33-42.

Rao, C. Narayana and Rao, R. Subba, 1933-34. "Six New Eastern Ganga Copper Plate Inscriptions", *JAHRS* , Vol.VII, Pts. 2-3 (Rajahmundry), pp. 161-94.

———, 1935-36. "Chicacole Plates of Madhukamarnava", *JAHRS,* Vol. VIII, Pts. 2-3 (Rajahmundry), pp. 168-80.

Rao G. V. Srinivasa, 1937-38. "Siripuram Plates of Anantavarman, Lord of Kalinga", *EI,* Vol. XXIV, Pt. 1 (Delhi), pp. 47-52.

Rao, R. Subba, 1926. "Peddabhegi Copper Plates of Nandavarman II", *JAHRS,* Vol. I, Pt. 2 (Rajahmundry), pp. 92-102.

———, 1929-30. "Jirjingi Plates of Indravarman", *JAHRS,* Vol. III, Pt. 1 (Rajahmundry), pp. 49-53 ff.

Sastri, H.P., 1908. "Tekkali Inscription of Madhyamaraja, the son of Petavyalloparaja", *JBORS,* Vol. VI, Pt. 2 (Patna), pp. 162-67.

Sircar, D.C., 1949-50. "Kanas Plates of Lokavigrahabhattaraka", *EI,* Vol. XXVIII (Delhi), pp. 321-31.

———, 1949-50. "Polasara Plates of Arkesvaradeva, Yugabda 4248", *EI,* Vol. XXVIII (Delhi), pp. 63-67.

———, 1949-50. "Sumandala Plates of the Time of Prthivivigrahabhattaraka", *EI,* Vol. XXVIII (Delhi), pp. 79-88 ff.

———, 1949-50. "Two Plates from Kanas (Plate of Bhanudatta)", *EI,* Vol. XXVIII (Delhi), pp. 332-34.

———, 1949-50. "Russelkonda Plates of Nettabhanja, Year 26", *EI,* Vol. XXVIII (Delhi), pp. 258-63.

———, 1949-50. "Kesaribeda Plates of Nala Arthapatibhattaraka", *EI,* Vol. XXVIII, Pt. 1 (Delhi), pp. 12-17.

———, 1949-50. "Hindol Plate of Kulastambha", *EI,* Vol. XXVIII (Delhi), pp. 107-14.

———, 1951-52. "Two Sailodbhava Grants from Banpur", *EI,* Vol. XXIX, p. 1 (Delhi), pp. 32-43.

———, 1954. "Terasinga Copper Plate Grant of Maharaja Tustikara", *EI,* Vol. XXX, (Delhi), pp. 274-78.

———, 1954. "Two Grants of the Sailodbhavas", *EI,* Vol. XXX (Delhi), pp. 264-73.

———, 1954. "Ningondi Grant of Prabhanjanavarman", *EI,* Vol. XXX (Delhi), pp. 112-18.

———, 1955-56. "Pedda-Dugam Plates of Satrudamana, Year 9", *EI,* Vol. XXXI, Pt. 2 (Delhi), pp. 89-93.

———, 1963-64. "Sitabhinji Tempera Painting Inscription", *EI,* Vol. XXXV, Pt. 2 (Delhi), pp. 47-49.

———, 1973. "Asanapat Nataraj Inscription of Satrubhanja", *EI,* Vol. XL, Pt. 3 (Delhi), pp. 121-26.

Sastri, H.P. and Sastri, B.N., 1967. "Tembure Plates of Umavarman", (in Telugu), *Bharati,* Vol. 44, Pt. 12, December, pp. 13 ff.

Subrahmanyam, R., 1954. "Andhavarman Plates of Indravarman", *EI*, Vol. XXX (Delhi), pp. 37-42.

———, 1949-50. "Andhavaram Plates of Anantasaktivarman", *EI*, Vol. XXVIII (Delhi), pp. 175-79.

———, 1955-56. "Two Grants from Andhavaram", *EI*, Vol. XXXI, Pt. 5 (Delhi), pp. 199-204.

Tripathi, K.B., 1966. "Banpur Copper Plate Grant of Somavamsi Indraratha", *JASB*, Vol. VIII, Pt. 4 (Calcutta), pp. 271-75.

———, 1973. "Angul Copper Plate Grant of Santikaradeva, Year 2", *EI*, Vol. XL, Pt. 1 (Delhi), pp. 113-17.

Tripathy, S., 1976. "Orissa Museum Plates of Narendradhavala", *OHRJ*, Vol. XXII, Nos. 3-4 (Bhubaneswar), pp. 53-57.

———, 1980. "A Note on the Asanapat Stone Inscription, *JOR*, Vol. I, No. 2, Orissa History Congress (Sambalpur University), pp. 5-10.

Venkataramayya, M., 1949-50. "Tekkali Plates of Maharaja Umavarman, Year 9", *EL*, Vol. XXVIII (Delhi), pp. 298-302.

———, 1949-50. "Madras Museum Plates of Anantasktivarman Year 28", *EI*, Vol. XXVIII (Delhi), pp. 226-35.

Vogel, J. Ph., 1929-30. "Prakrit Inscriptions from a Buddhist Site at Nagarjunikonda", *EI*, Vol. XX (Calcutta), pp. 1-37.

Cunningham, A., 1861-70, 1881-82. Archaeological Survey of India (Reports), (Calcutta), Vol. VII, p. 148; Vol. XVII, pp. 6-20.

Annual Report on Indian or South Indian Epigraphy (Originally Published as G.O. of the Public Department, Government of Madras), of 1935-1936, p. 64.

Bhandarkar's *List*—"A List of Inscriptions of Northern India in Brahmi and Its Berivativey Scripts from about 200 A.D.", by D.R. Bhandarkar Appendix to the *Epigraphia India*, Vols. XIX-XXXIII, pp. 297-365.

INDEX

Baradipada Grant of Nandarājadeva (No. 24)

First Plate

Second Plate: First Side

Second Plate: Second Side

PLATE II

Baradipada Grant of Nandarājadeva (No. 24)

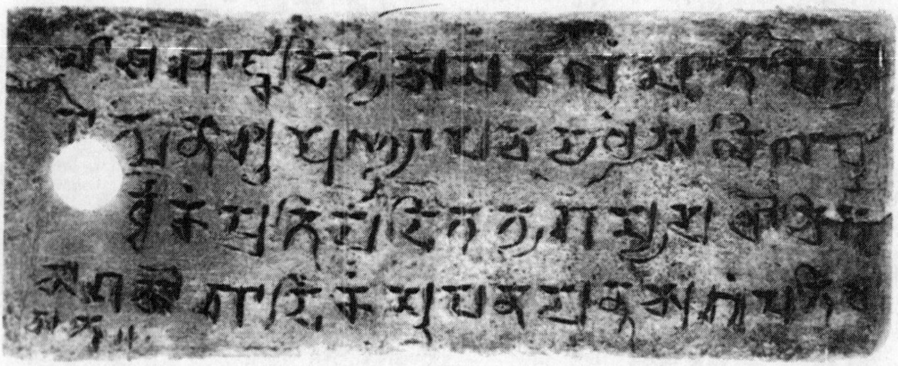

Third Plate: First Side

Third Plate: Second Side

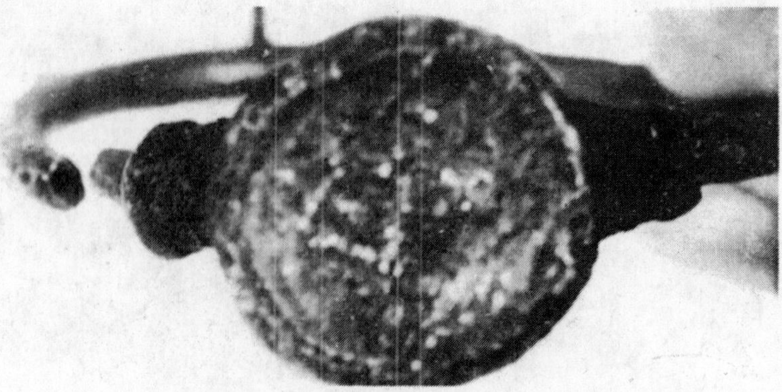

Seal of the Baradipada Grant of Nandarājadeva (No. 24)

Jayarampur Charter of the Time of Gōpachandra (No. 32)

(Obverse)

PLATE IV

Incomplete Śailōdbhava Charter (No. 60)

First Plate: First Side

Second Plate: Second Side